Reading and Writing Short Arguments

WILLIAM VESTERMAN
Rutgers University

Mayfield Publishing Company
Mountain View, California
London • Toronto

Library of Congress Cataloging-in-Publication Data

Vesterman, William
    Reading and writing short arguments / William Vesterman.
        p.   cm.
    Includes index.
    ISBN 1-55934-222-6
    1. English language—Rhetoric.   2. Persuasion (Rhetoric)
3. College readers.   I. Title.
PE1431.V47   1993
808'.0427—dc20   93–25549
                                                                      CIP

Manufactured in the United States of America
10 9 8 7 6 5 4 3 2 1

Mayfield Publishing Company
1280 Villa Street
Mountain View, CA 94041

Sponsoring editor, Thomas V. Broadbent; production editor, April
Wells-Hayes; copyeditor, Loralee Windsor; text and cover designer,
David Bullen; art director, Jeanne M. Schreiber; manufacturing
manager, Martha Branch; cover image, Gary Overacre. The text was
set in 11/12 Bembo by Thompson Type and printed on 50# Butte
des Morts by the Banta Company.

Acknowledgments and copyrights appear at the back of the book on
pages 333–335, which constitute an extension of the copyright page.

PREFACE

Reading and Writing Short Arguments is an introductory text for courses that emphasize critical thinking and argumentative writing. The book begins with an Introduction to Argument and Persuasion, followed by a collection of 64 short, lively essays by a variety of contemporary writers on controversial current issues. A Minicasebook on the Homeless and a Guide to Finding and Using Information appear at the end of the book. The selections in the minicasebook represent a variety of lengths, levels, and sources of publication, from an editorial and editorial cartoons to two professional academic articles complete with footnotes.

In the main section of the book, each of eighteen controversial issues is addressed by three readings from divergent points of view. This should discourage any belief that either analyzing the arguments of others or forming arguments of one's own is a matter of simply choosing sides between two points of view. Each reading is followed by discussion questions that invite the student to analyze the author's appeals to Logic, Character, and Emotion. In each group a major claim of one argument is analyzed in diagrammatic form according to the Toulmin method of logic. The *Instructor's Manual* that accompanies the text includes, along with other materials, the diagrams for all the readings. Each group ends with "Intertextual Questions" and "Suggestions for Writing." The goal of this main part of the book is to make the reading and writing of arguments easier by constantly encouraging the student to break down complex matters into simpler ones.

For further flexibility in instruction, the next section consists of ten topics represented by a single essay, each without any accompanying analysis or questions. This provides material with which students can practice on their own the skills of analysis and writing. This section is followed by the sections mentioned earlier—the minicasebook and library research guide—which provide material for courses that progress toward longer and more extensively researched arguments. It is hoped that all these sections taken together will support students and instructors alike in the development of argumentative skills.

Many people have helped bring this project to completion. I wish to thank the staff at Mayfield and particularly Tom Broadbent, my editor. I thank Dan Moran for extensive editorial help and Joshua Ozersky and Patti Moran for research help. Special thanks go to W. Ross Winterowd and Geoffrey R. Winterowd of the University of Southern California for allowing me to adapt the sample research paper, "The Death Penalty: For Whom the Bell Tolls," from *The Critical Reader, Thinker, and Writer.*

My thanks are extended also to the following individuals for their thoughtful review of the manuscript: Robert H. Bentley, Lansing Community College; Sue E. Cross, Mission College; Jean F. Goodine, Northern Virginia Community College; Edward McCarthy, Harrisburg Area Community College; Paul J. McVeigh, Northern Virginia Community College; Thomas A. Mozola, Macomb Community College; Joseph Nassar, Rochester Institute of Technology; Kathleen O'Shea, Monroe Community College; Teresa M. Purvis, Lansing Community College; and Richard J. Zbaracki, Iowa State University.

BRIEF CONTENTS

CONTENTS

A Minicasebook on the Homeless   *235*

Introduction to Argument
and Persuasion

MOTIVES AND METHODS OF ARGUMENT

Why Argue?

To human beings, forming opinions is as natural and necessary as breathing. Birds never have to decide what kind of nest to build, but humans decide how to build everything from a house to a society on the basis of thought and opinion. A diversity of mental and physical structures has always defined human activity.

We are not born with opinions but form them through our own mental and emotional lives and our interactions with the lives of others. At first we may receive most of our opinions unquestioningly, but very soon we begin to question even the views of our parents. The sounds of "Why?" and "Because!" echo throughout every childhood. However unsatisfactory that primitive dialogue may be (for both parties), those words present the basic structure of inquiry, and they begin to suggest some of the ways we form opinions. We want to know *why*—we want some reasons to follow the *because*—so that we can decide for ourselves whether we agree or disagree.

But our opinions are not just personal decisions. However confident we might have been of our views, and however inevitably convincing they might have seemed to us, "I wish that I had thought to say. . . !" is a common refrain when we find ourselves alone again after a dispute with other people. And merely announcing our views on a topic is seldom enough to convince anyone that we are right to think as we do. Dialogue rather than assertion is the basis of the process. If we want others to take our views seriously, let alone be persuaded by them, we have to argue our positions effectively and responsibly and find answers to reasonable objections.

We ourselves don't change our minds unless we are persuaded by responsible arguments. Yet to benefit from a dialogue, we don't need to be convinced. Though hearing other views and the arguments that support them may not change our minds, having to answer the arguments of others may clarify and strengthen our own opinions. As educated people we should never be satisfied to know what we already know, and we need all the clarity and mental strength we can get to face serious and complex issues. Clarification for ourselves and for others, rather than "winning," is a goal to which both parties in a dialogue can aspire.

Clarity and strength of opinion are necessary not only for education but also for the world of work and action. Thinking critically about problems and explaining suggested solutions are activities that play a large part in any business or profession. Even in a field as concerned with physical facts as engineering, for example, those who succeed are those who are able to explain to their superiors the importance of their work and to argue in support of the ideas they propose. The same skills are required at every level of government, from the smallest local committee to the largest national legislature. Public opinion ultimately controls democratic government, and effectively argued views ultimately control public opinion.

What We Don't Argue About

Argument is a term often incorrectly applied to quarrels, in which mere assertion and name calling replace the rational presentation of opinion and the responsible meeting of opposing viewpoints. Quarrels can take place over any issue, but responsible and effective argument is impossible in certain areas:

- We can't argue about *facts*. For example, that the American Revolution occurred is beyond dispute; we are no longer ruled by Great Britain. While it is of course possible to argue about the significance of facts or the probability that an assertion actually is a fact, verified matters are not matters of opinion.
- We can't argue about the *impossible*. For example, that men should be responsible for bearing children is not an arguable position.
- We can't argue about *preferences*. Preferences resemble opinions, but they are neither formed nor changed by logic. For example, that rap music is better than rock music, that baseball is more graceful than ballet, and that long hair is ugly on men are all matters of preference and not matters of rational debate.
- We can't argue about *beliefs* that lie beyond rational or empirical proof, such as religious faith.

What We Do Argue About

We argue about *opinions* because arguing is the process by which opinions are formed. For this reason, opinion is not the end of rational discussion but the beginning of a dialogue with others and with yourself. In fact, it is safe to say that the process of learning to argue in responsible and effective ways will expand, modify, and strengthen many of the opinions you have now.

Why Analyze the Arguments of Others?

Arguing is an activity requiring skill, and as in most activities, skill is acquired by imitation as well as by instruction. As you read the essays in this book, you will be invited by the discussion questions following them to analyze how and why the writers' arguments work. Having done this, you should be able to imitate their methods to make your own arguments more effective. For simply having opinions is not enough. You must also decide how to organize and express them and how to counter your opponent's objections. The discussion questions will help you master this task by encouraging a dialogue between you and authors of short essays like those you will be asked to write.

The essays here have been chosen because they address a variety of current topics that you can discuss, preliminarily at least, without further research. Some of the essays in this book provide instances of what to *avoid* as an effective writer of arguments. These flawed essays may be just as useful as those better argued in stimulating the growth of your argumentative skills.

Argument and Persuasion

Since arguments offer reasons for taking a position on an issue, argument is often distinguished from persuasion, since we may be persuaded by means other than evidence or logic. These other means of persuasion are generally divided into (a) matters of *character*—the trustworthiness we may grant to the reputation, ethics, or clarity and strength of mind of the writer or speaker—and (b) matters of *feeling*—the emotional agreement we may come to feel with the speaker or writer. In ancient Greece, where these distinctions were first proposed, the appeal of the moral character of the arguer, or speaker, was called *ethos,* while *logos* referred to the powers of logic or reason in the argument, and *pathos* referred to the ways emotion persuaded the audience to agree. The Greeks called the study of persuasive argument *rhetoric.* The following diagram, called the Rhetorical Triangle, may clarify the interaction of the three means of persuasion. To each point of the triangle have been added the terms of the Toulmin theory of logic to which you will shortly be introduced.

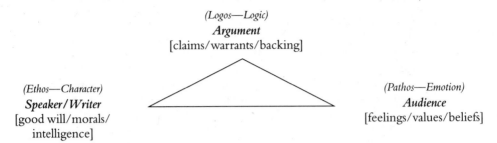

(Logos—Logic)
Argument
[claims/warrants/backing]

(Ethos—Character)
Speaker/Writer
[good will/morals/
intelligence]

(Pathos—Emotion)
Audience
[feelings/values/beliefs]

Argument is the first aspect of the rhetorical triangle that we will discuss. *Claims, warrants,* and *backing* are terms the Toulmin system uses to talk about this aspect of rhetoric.

THE WRITER AND LOGIC: APPEALS TO REASON

Logical is a word people often use informally to mean "reasonable." But the word *logic* also refers to formal systems of reasoning that depend on definite rules to determine the truth or falsity of an argument. In the West, formal logical theory began with the syllogism of Aristotle (see p. 7), and modern logicians have created various symbolic systems and techniques to meet needs for rigorous proof like those of mathematics. In ordinary verbal arguments, however, such strict proof is made extremely difficult not only by the complexity of life but also by the inherent ambiguities of language.

The Toulmin System of Logic

The feeling that logical theory was becoming too far removed from verbal arguments as they really took place among ordinary people caused British philosopher Stephen Toulmin to propose a new system of logic. Toulmin's method aimed not at the absolute truth of mathematical operations but at the kind of truth produced by argument within the legal system of English-speaking countries. In such legal argument a preponderance of evidence suggests a conclusion to a jury, and guilt needs to be proved, not beyond all conceivable doubt, but beyond a reasonable doubt. Legal argument, therefore, is close to the kind of argument used elsewhere in life. It depends for its persuasiveness on convincing an audience of the general strength of a case rather than on the rigorous but narrow standards of absolute proof used in mathematics or other formally constructed logical systems.

Toulmin's Terms

Let us look at Toulmin's names for the different parts of a logical argument, before analyzing some examples to see how the parts go together. Toulmin breaks the structure of an argument down into six parts:

- **Claim:** what you believe your whole argument proves.
- **Data:** what prompts you to make that claim, that is, the facts that lead you to believe your claim is true.
- **Qualifier:** the part of the argument that measures the strength or force of the claim. For example, is the claim *always* true? true *in the United States*? true *in modern times*?
- **Warrant:** an assumption that you expect your audience will share. The warrant supports the claim by connecting it to the data.
- **Backing:** any facts that give substance to the warrant. Not all arguments make use of explicit backing.
- **Rebuttal:** the part of an argument that allows for exceptions without having to give up the claim as generally true. The rebuttal does not so much refute your point as anticipate and answer attempts by someone else to refute it. For example, you could claim that most geese fly south for the winter, while admitting that a few are still found in the north. The very fact that *few* are found helps to prove your general point that *most* migrate.

An Example of the Toulmin System

Let us put the terms to work and illustrate them by analyzing an example Toulmin himself uses. Suppose, he suggests, you find yourself forced to argue something you thought was fairly obvious. You claim in the course of conversation that a man mentioned in the newspaper, Sven Petersen, is probably not a Roman Catholic. In a friendly dialogue, someone doubts your claim, asking, "What makes you say that?" You reply, "I think Sven Petersen is almost certainly not a Roman Catholic, because he's Swedish and very few Swedes are Catholics." Sorted out, the elements of this simple argument are:

- **Data:** Petersen is a Swede.
- **Claim:** Sven Petersen is not a Roman Catholic.
- **Qualifier:** "almost certainly."
- **Warrant:** A Swede can generally be taken not to be a Roman Catholic.
- **Backing:** The proportion of Catholics in Sweden is very low. (If you researched the religious proportions of Sweden, you might find something like the following to use as backing: "According to Whittaker's Almanac, less than 2% of Swedes are Roman Catholic.")
- **Rebuttal:** unless Petersen is one of the 2%.

The Toulmin Diagram

Shown in diagrammatic form the structure of the argument may be clearer:

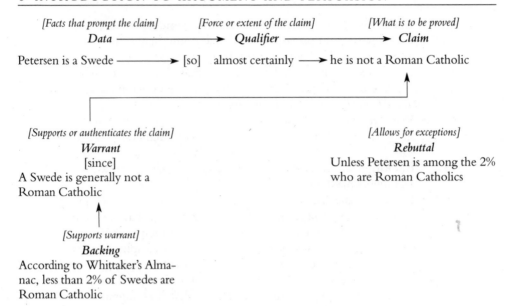

[Facts that prompt the claim]   *[Force or extent of the claim]*   *[What is to be proved]*

Data ⟶ **Qualifier** ⟶ **Claim**

Petersen is a Swede ⟶ [so] almost certainly ⟶ he is not a Roman Catholic

[Supports or authenticates the claim]   *[Allows for exceptions]*

Warrant   **Rebuttal**

[since]   Unless Petersen is among the 2%

A Swede is generally not a   who are Roman Catholics

Roman Catholic

[Supports warrant]

Backing

According to Whittaker's Almanac, less than 2% of Swedes are
Roman Catholic

Of course not all arguments are so clear-cut. And most writers argue for several things in the course of a single essay. Further, one or more of the elements of an argument may be implicit or lacking altogether. For example, in analyzing an argument you may be unable to find the backing for one claim because the author took for granted that the warrant was so obvious as not to need further evidence. And in the following passage, the qualifier is not explicitly stated, though it seems to have the force of something like "always."

The passage that follows is a single paragraph of "Government Is the Problem" by Walter E. Williams, an essay that appears in full later in this book (p. 213). In the course of arguing the main point suggested by his title, Williams devotes many single paragraphs to particular examples of what he sees as the general governmental "problem." Here is paragraph 6:

> Government control, such as the attempt to establish an official language, frequently leads to conflict, including wars and civil unrest, as we've seen in Quebec, Belgium, South Africa, Nigeria and other places. As our government creates bilingual legislation, we are seeing language become a focal point for conflict such as the ugly, racist-tainted "English Only" political campaigns in several states. The best state of affairs is to have no language laws at all.

Analyzed with the Toulmin system, here is what Williams's argument looks like:

- **Data:** As our government creates bilingual legislation, we are seeing language become a focal point for conflict such as the ugly racist-tainted "English only" political campaigns in several states.
- **Claim:** The best state of affairs is to have no language laws at all.
- **Qualifier:** Always [implied].
- **Warrant:** [since] Government control, such as the attempt to establish an official language . . . leads to conflict.
- **Backing:** as we have seen in Quebec, Belgium, South Africa, Nigeria and other places.
- **Rebuttal:** frequently.

Diagramed, the argument looks like this:

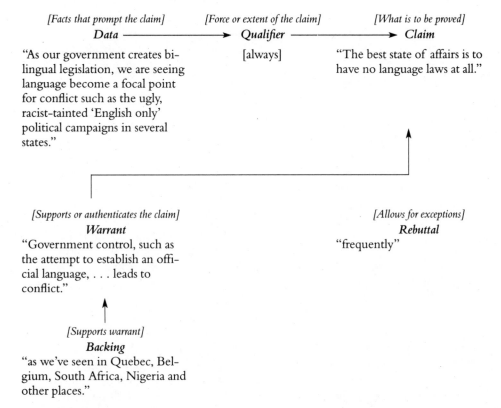

[Facts that prompt the claim] Data	*[Force or extent of the claim]* Qualifier	*[What is to be proved]* Claim
"As our government creates bilingual legislation, we are seeing language become a focal point for conflict such as the ugly, racist-tainted 'English only' political campaigns in several states."	[always]	"The best state of affairs is to have no language laws at all."

[Supports or authenticates the claim]
Warrant
"Government control, such as the attempt to establish an official language, . . . leads to conflict."

[Allows for exceptions]
Rebuttal
"frequently"

[Supports warrant]
Backing
"as we've seen in Quebec, Belgium, South Africa, Nigeria and other places."

Aristotle's Syllogism

Let us illustrate Toulmin's system further by briefly comparing its methods with the ways in which the classical syllogism invented by Aristotle might analyze the same argument. A syllogism is made up of three parts:

- **Major premise:** Conflict is bad.
- **Minor premise:** Government language laws create conflict.
- **Conclusion:** Therefore government language laws are bad.

Syllogistic reasoning assumes that if both premises are accepted as true, the conclusion must also be accepted as true. That is, if an entire class of facts is true, and if the case in question is a member of that class, the case in question must also be accepted as true, since what is true of a class must also be true of the members of that class.

You may notice that Williams's paragraph does not look like a syllogism and that the words used in the sample syllogism are not exactly his words. In fact, Aristotle says that most syllogisms are embedded in or implied by real-life arguments. He calls the implied syllogisms "enthymemes" (EN-thuh-meems). Teasing out the syllogisms from the enthymemes of a given argument is a skill that users of classical logic must acquire, just as arranging the writer's language and its implications into Toulmin's categories can often be a tricky matter at first and always subject to difference of opinion on details.

Inductive and Deductive Reasoning

Whether analyzed by the Toulmin system or by Aristotelian logic, Williams's specific argument within the sample paragraph is an example of *deductive* reasoning. He deduces his conclusion about a specific problem from general premises. That is, his argument moves from a general proposition (conflict is bad) to a particular instance (government control of language is bad).

On the other hand, as you will see, Williams's essay as a whole is an example of *inductive* reasoning—the kind that scientists employ. Inductive arguments reason from particulars (government control of language is bad) to the general (government control is always bad). Williams gives example after example of the problems that he considers are caused by governmental interference; he expects us then to agree that government control makes a general "problem," one extending well beyond the examples he cites to all or most examples.

Inductive reasoning does not claim the strengths of absolute proof but seeks to establish a high degree of *probability* for the general truths it infers from the observation of particular facts. For instance, scientists have not examined every molecule of water to see whether it is composed of hydrogen and oxygen, but since all the water molecules that *have* been examined show the same results, they conclude that all other water molecules would too.

Kinds of Arguments

Like Williams in "Government Is the Problem," many writers employ both the inductive and the deductive methods of reasoning at different times in the same essay. And whether analyzing arguments or forming them yourself, you will find that the arguments in an essay also tend to fall into some different general categories. Because it often happens that several of the categories will appear within a given essay, it will pay you both as a reader and as a writer to understand the categories.

ARGUMENTS ABOUT THE NATURE OF SOMETHING: IS IT X? Arguments about the nature of something are based on definition. For example, in the section of this book called "Hate Speech and Civil Rights," all of the arguments include the question of just how "free speech" should be defined.

Guidelines Definition usually plays a subordinate part in a larger argument, but it is important to develop a sense of when you need to define your terms and when you can take them for granted. In general you should always define terms that are new to you, ones you suspect will be new to your audience, ones you are conscious of using in a special sense, or ones you suspect an opponent will use to question your case. Imagining your opponent's potential questions in a fair-minded way will serve you well in this as well as other areas of argumentative discourse. In defining your own important terms, there are several reliable methods:

- *Dictionary definitions.* The most common (and perhaps the most overused) technique is simply to repeat what a dictionary says: for example, "According to *Webster's Third International Dictionary,* 'hate' is defined as. . . ."
- *Stipulative definitions.* A writer can simply state the particular sense in which he or she will be using a word. For example, in the section on "Strikers and Scabs" (p. 133), Jack London says that "a scab is [a laborer] who gives more value for the same price than another."
- *Definition by synonym.* You can define a word by means of synonyms. But choose carefully. *Home* is used by real estate agents as a synonym for *house,* but a poet tells us that: "It takes a heap of livin'/ To make a house a home."
- *Definitions by image or verbal picture.* For example, in one of the essays in the section "Animal Testing," medical researcher Ron Karpati attempts to show what he understands *cruelty* to mean by describing the suffering of children he has known as patients. After doing so, he argues that such cruelty might be avoided by medical advances based on a lesser degree of suffering undergone by animals in controlled experiments.
- *Definition by extended description.* The poet Langston Hughes in his essay "That Word 'Black'" (p. 165) gives a long list of the kinds

of things other than race that are expressed by the word *black*. Hughes extensively describes the many implications of the word to argue that people use the word *black* to imply more than color.

• *Operational definition*. This is a formal kind of definition designed to make clear distinctions about terms based on actions that define what they mean. For example, Susan Brownmiller in "Let's Put Pornography Back in the Closet" (p. 103) reminds her audience of a Supreme Court ruling defining obscenity: "The materials are obscene if they depict patently offensive, hard-core sexual conduct; lack serious scientific, literary, artistic or political value; and appeal to the prurient interest of an average person—as measured by contemporary community standards."

ARGUMENTS OF CAUSE AND EFFECT—HOW DID X COME TO BE? If arguments of definition generally respond to the issue of "what," arguments of cause and effect seek to answer the questions "how?" and "why?" Cause and effect can organize your argument in either direction:

• *From cause to effect*. For example, in "Arms and the Woman" (p. 65), Lou Marano argues that several causes would work together to weaken the military effectiveness of an army containing women in combat roles.

• *From effect to cause*. For example, in "Pink and Brown People" (p. 167), Thomas Sowell argues that the facts of ghetto life are not caused simply by racism, as is often claimed. Sowell argues that violence and poverty have always existed in American "ghettos," even though such areas were inhabited by whites for most of American history; hence racism could not be the unique cause of the social and economic problems of many present inhabitants of poor areas.

• *Antecedent and consequence*. This relation is useful in analyzing situations that may be deceptively similar to those involving cause and effect. Turning 18 does not cause you to become a voter: Acquisition of the right to vote is a consequence of that event but is not caused by it.

Guidelines Cause and effect reasoning is as tricky as it is important in forming effective and responsible arguments. Keep these general principles in mind:

• *An effect always follows a cause*. For example, thunder follows lightning, so the cause and effect relation must be that of "lightning-thunder" and never the other way round.

- *For repeated effects, the most likely cause is the common factor.* For example, if several children attending the same school become ill while their friends from other schools remain healthy, their sickness has most likely been contracted at their school.
- *If the effect increases and decreases, you must find a cause that acts similarly.* If violent crime increases and decreases proportionally with the size of the male population 15–25 years old, a good argument can be made that connects characteristics of young males to some causes of violent crime.

ARGUMENTS OF EVALUATION—IS X BETTER OR WORSE THAN Y? Many larger arguments contain issues of evaluation that present special difficulties. Our senses of value go so deep that we tend to treat them as self-evident warrants. Yet the well-known saying, "Everyone is entitled to his or her own opinion" need not end the discussion of values.

In the first place, differences of opinion are seldom so widespread that there is not a great deal of common ground. For example, most people come up with similar lists of the leading qualities that define good writing, and "clarity" is usually first on the list. In the second place, disagreements about values are often based on a lack of understanding about what the argument is about. Being clear on your own and others' bases of judgment and on what is being judged are basic requirements of discussion. In "On Reading Trash" (p. 179), for example, Bob Swift concedes the differences of quality in literature but argues that reading "bad" books is good for children because it leads to a love of reading that will later lead to a love of "classics."

Guidelines Some general philosophical principles are often evoked directly or indirectly as standards for judging value.

- The German philosopher Kant held in his "categorical imperative" that no human being should be used merely as a means to the ends of another.
- The British philosopher Bentham held that the greatest good for the greatest number should be the principle on which to judge actions.

Of course, more particular bases for judgment exist, and you should be aware of distinctions among them.

- Naive egoism, for example—what's good for me is obviously good—is a poor basis for argument.
- In judging that something is bad, you should make clear the basis of your negative judgment. For example, is what you condemn

bad because it is a sin, a wrong, or a crime—or is it some combination of these different categories? In "The Freedom to Destroy Yourself" (p. 185), Walter E. Williams argues that drug use may be a wrong for the individual taking drugs but making it a crime leads to more wrongs inflicted on the general public.

ARGUMENTS OF POLICY—SHOULD WE OR SHOULDN'T WE DO X? Arguments of policy are very common and are one of the main modes of argument in almost all the selections in this book. As you will see, this kind of argument often makes use of the other kinds we have been reviewing, but you should be aware of some common checkpoints that will give additional help.

Guidelines Since arguments of policy generally respond to a "problem," your analysis in this regard needs to be thorough.

- Make sure you clearly designate the problem that the policy you recommend or reject addresses.
- Spell out the consequences that will ensue if the problem is not solved and any reasons that make the need for a solution especially pressing.
- Propose the solution and make specific recommendations of the procedures that will lead to the solution while explaining how they will do so.
- Consider opposing arguments and make sure you answer them.
- Support your proposal with solid backing and evidence, but don't neglect the moral and emotional supports for your policy and for the policies you reject.

Counterarguments

A part of most arguments is taken up not with advancing the reasons for your own views but with answering the reasoning of your opponents. In general you should seek to test opposing views on the same bases you test your own; the series of policy argument guidelines just given will be helpful in this regard as well.

Some Common Forms of Fallacious Reasoning

In the course of analyzing both your own arguments and those of others, you should be aware of some common errors of reasoning. You should be sure both to avoid these errors yourself and to point them out in the arguments of others when you make your counterarguments. It is important to note that fallacious reasoning does not necessarily make the claim wrong. That is a question you must decide by examining the whole issue for yourself.

FAULTY GENERALIZATION The error of faulty generalization comes from treating all members of a class or category as if they were defined by criteria that apply only to some members. For example, in "What We Really Know About the Homeless" (p. 261), Randall K. Filer complains of a faulty generalization in other writers on the subject who lump together homeless families and homeless individuals and fail to note the very important distinctions between these two subgroups.

BEGGING THE QUESTION Users of the fallacy of begging the question try to take for granted the issues that are to be proved. They often use words and phrases like "obviously," "of course," and "simply" to preface unproved assertions. For example, in "Arms and the Woman" (p. 65), Lou Marano complains that proponents of combat roles for women are begging the question when they claim that women are capable of combat. The real issue, Morano claims, is whether women are *as* capable as men of acting as soldiers, and he attempts to prove that they are not.

FAULTY ANALOGY Comparing one issue to another is an effective and indispensable technique of argument, but an analogy is always open to question, and you should be sure that your comparisons are as solid as possible. In "The Hand That Rocks the Helm" (p. 155), Richard Mitchell argues that proponents of "nonsexist language" are guilty of false analogy when they imply that some strictly human powers are shared by language itself. Mitchell argues that language is not at all like people, who alone have the power to act, feel, or insult.

POST HOC ERGO PROPTER HOC The Latin phrase *post hoc ergo propter hoc* means roughly "after this, therefore because of this." The fallacy is a mainstay of superstitious reasoning that claims causal connection for events that merely succeed one another in time—seeing a black cat and experiencing misfortune, for example. But the issues are not always so clear-cut even to those who believe in science. In "What Is the Truth About Global Warming?" (p. 215), Robert James Bidinotto claims that the relation between a recent series of warm years and a recent increase in atmospheric pollution has not yet been established as one of cause and effect by scientific standards, though many speak as if it has been.

ARGUMENT *AD HOMINEM* The Latin *ad hominem* means "to the man," and the fallacy involves attacking someone personally as a way of attacking that person's views. For example, in "Free Speech? Yes. Drunkenness? No." (p. 37), Vartan Gregorian complains that: "As a historian I am dismayed that only one of those who have written so 'authoritatively' about my own views has bothered to contact me." Beware of attacking your opponents' morals or feelings when it is their stated opinions that are at issue.

ARGUMENT *AD POPULUM* An attempt to appeal "to the people" and their presumed common values and emotions may be another diversionary tactic designed to advance or oppose arguments unfairly. This tactic often uses what are called "God-words" (*pro-, help, family*, etc.) and "Devil-words" (*anti-, greed, mean-spirited*, etc.). In "Offering Euthanasia Can Be an Act of Love" (p. 115), Derek Humphrey implies that opponents who compare mercy killing to Nazi exterminations are guilty of using both a faulty analogy and an argument *ad populum.*

RED HERRING The figure of speech that describes this fallacy comes from the fact that a red herring has a strong odor and can be dragged across the scent trail left by humans or animals to confuse persuing dogs. In "Free Speech? Yes. Drunkenness? No." (p. 37), Vartan Gregorian implies that the issue of free speech has been used as a red herring in the debates at Brown over a disciplinary case that, according to Gregorian, centered on drunkenness and loutish behavior rather than on political dissent or free speech.

EQUIVOCATION To equivocate is to use terms in differing senses in an attempt to deceive. In "Biting the Bullets" (p. 198), Gerald Nachman makes fun of the slogan "Guns don't kill—people do." He points out the equivocation by pretending to agree and then arguing that bullets should be banned, since bullets are what *really* kill.

PROVING A NEGATIVE Arguments often take something like the following form: "If we do as you propose, what guarantees do we have that something awful will not occur as a result at some time in the future?" Negative propositions cannot be proved to an absolute degree because we can never know the future, or anything else, to an absolute degree. Recall Toulmin's example and remember that our system of logic is designed to prove only a preponderance of probability. One can argue the highly likely proposition that Sven Petersen is not a Roman Catholic without having to prove that it is impossible for him to be a member of that faith.

The foregoing examples of fallacious reasoning do not exhaust the category of logical fallacies, just as the brief introduction to logic itself is designed only to get you started. The next section looks beyond logic at other methods of presenting your views.

PERSUASION BY OTHER THAN LOGICAL MEANS

Let's look again at the Rhetorical Triangle to emphasize once more that, as important as logic is to human beings, reason is not the only attribute of human nature, and it is therefore not the only means by which we express or respond to opinions.

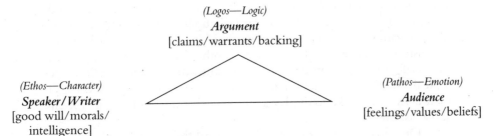

(Logos—Logic)
Argument
[claims/warrants/backing]

(Ethos—Character)
Speaker/Writer
[good will/morals/
intelligence]

(Pathos—Emotion)
Audience
[feelings/values/beliefs]

Character: The Writer's Personal Persuasion

As the diagram suggests, the strength of effective argumentation relies not only on reason but also on the credibility of the reasoner, and that credibility needs to be established with an audience. Establishing credentials is the function of the appeal to the writer's general character and personality. This "ethical appeal" acts with the appeals to logic and emotion to convince the reader that the writer's arguments are persuasive.

Classical rhetoric holds that writers and speakers should give their audiences an overall impression of a good character, including high intelligence, high moral standards, and an attitude of general good will. The audience gains its knowledge of these inward and spiritual virtues from the outward and visible signs of the writer's reputation and style and the format of the essay. Each of these elements in turn may make its ethical appeal by several means.

Reputation Intelligence and expertise can be shown through public credentials, which may strongly influence our responses one way or another. Most of the writers whose essays are included in this book are briefly identified in the "Annotated Table of Contents," and you might try the following experiments to test the force of the ethical appeal. Open the book at any point and read an essay without referring to its author's description in the table of contents. Then read the brief biographical identification and rethink your response. As another experiment, simply remind yourself of the attitudes that new acquaintances seem to take toward you when you explain what your college major is or might be!

Style Even without elaborate public reputations, another expression of character is available to all writers through their writing styles.

Carefully formed sentences and paragraphs argue intelligence in general, but you must also adapt your tone of voice and manner of presentation to the occasion at hand. For example, consider how you automatically change your presentation of the same anecdote when recounting it to your grandmother and your close friends.

Adopting an appropriate style expresses not only your relation to your audience but also your respect and consideration for its time and attention. For example, how do you feel about a fellow student's argument, regardless of its rationale, when that speaker adopts a belligerent or blustering manner in class? To take another example: Public speakers are usually invited because they are presumed to know more about the topic in question than the audience they address, but many speakers begin their talks with a joke to display a character that does not consider itself above its listeners.

One final example of the ethical appeal through style can be seen in the Declaration of Independence. Signing that document meant death to its signers if the revolution failed; yet it ends with the pledge of "our lives, our fortunes, and our sacred honor." By putting "lives" in the least important position in the list and "honor" in the climactic place, the signers affirmed a hierarchy of values that shows high ethical standards as well as personal courage.

Your own stylistic choices should aim at establishing not only your intelligence but also your good faith, rationality, fair-mindedness, and benevolence. Without sounding like a know-it-all or a show-off, you should try both to connect your personal views to wider categories of public importance and to refer to publicly acknowledged authorities who agree with you. But you can achieve all the goals of the ethical appeal most easily if you try to write in a natural style rather than the artificial grandiosity often associated with "English papers." For example, few students have ever spoken the word *thus,* though many have written it.

Format The format and mechanical correctness of writing is also taken to express the character of its author. Neatness counts! And so does accuracy. Remember how widely ridiculed Vice President Quayle was when he misspelled *potato.* If your essay is mechanically sloppy, your grammar careless, and your spelling poor, your audience will respond to those elements, whatever the strength of your reasoning might be.

GUIDELINES In checking your efforts to establish the impression of a character that includes intelligence and common sense, ask yourself:

- Have I used arguments that I myself believe? Have I qualified or modified them for my audience as I would for myself?

- Have I overstated the case or used inappropriate language or clichés?
- Have I allowed for doubts and uncertainties and acknowledged the good faith of other viewpoints?
- In trying to establish good character and good will, have I made my own beliefs clear?
- Have I connected my views to other authorities and larger contexts?
- Have I shown consideration and respect for my audience?
- Have I reviewed any potential points of disagreement?
- Have I tried to show off?
- Have I avoided name-calling?
- Have I shown that I assume my audience's sincerity and common sense?
- Have I defined questionable terms and distinguished between my facts and the opinions they are to support?

Emotion: The Writer and Persuasive Feelings

In expressing their views, people often use the phrase "I feel that" as equivalent to "I think that"—and while thought and emotion may be separated for purposes of discussion, they are closely intertwined in an audience's response to your views. In the first place, while it may hardly need saying that emotions are not subject to logic, they do have a rationale of their own. As Pascal says, "the heart has its reasons that reason knows not of." Here are some examples of the emotional appeal at work:

- When the reader of "Killing Our Future" (p. 193) knows that Sarah Brady's husband was paralyzed and mentally impaired by gunshots in an assassination attempt on President Reagan, the knowledge charges her arguments for gun control with a personal force from the reader's sympathy.
- Very early in the modern debate on abortion, the sides ceased to describe themselves as *antiabortion* or *antiregulation,* and began to use *prolife* and *prochoice* instead. The change was an acknowledgment of the greater force of positive terms in such an emotion-filled debate.
- Freedom is a concept commonly applauded, while hatred is an attitude commonly disapproved, so *free speech* and *hate speech* are often used by differing sides to describe the same phenomenon.

Emotions need not be so extreme or dramatically founded as some of the preceding examples to play an effective part in argumentative writing; many emotional appeals are more subtle. For example, absolute terms of assertion like "certainly" and "without a doubt" can evoke a mild annoyance in your readers that might lead them to hunt for minor exceptions to your argument. By avoiding them you may keep attention focused on the general strength of your case.

Avoiding negatively emotive words is only one side of a style formed to appeal to an audience's emotions. Figurative language is loaded with implied emotional appeals that can work positively—even if a term is negative in itself. For example, in her title "Notes from a Free Speech Junkie" (p. 107), Susan Jacoby uses mild self-mockery and deliberate exaggeration of *Junkie* to elicit audience approval for her modesty and tolerance for her frank inflexibility.

In checking your emotional appeals, remember that emotions play a very strong part in the process of persuasion and that logical reasoning alone is seldom enough to stir an audience to action or deep conviction. As a reader of your own and others' arguments, try to sort out the emotional appeals from the logical reasoning. As a writer, remember that you cannot command the emotions of others. Let the connotations of the words you choose and the metaphors, images, and description you employ speak for themselves.

GUIDELINES One part of the discussion questions following each essay in this book examines the many ways in which the emotional appeal operates in persuasive writing. The idea is to gain as many effective techniques for your own writing as you can by carefully observing the techniques of professional writers. For general purposes, keep in mind a simple checklist:

- Ask yourself: "Have I given examples that might prompt positive or negative emotions such as pride or indignation?"
- Use images, figures of speech, and concrete examples to elicit the emotions in your audience. Avoid abstract words or direct assertions that *tell* your audience directly how to feel, such as "Every right-thinking person will be appalled at this state of affairs." *Show* your readers that the state of affairs in question is appalling and let them do the feeling for themselves. For example, in "The Trials of Animals" (p. 81), Cleveland Amory tells us of laboratory monkeys that "first nerves in their limbs were removed and then stimuli—including electric shocks and flames—were applied to see if they could still use their appendages." He doesn't need to tell us this is horrifying; we are horrified.
- Ask yourself: "Have I taken care not to insult my audience's values and assumptions?"
- Ask yourself: "Have I defined my position on the issues in a way that will appeal to my audience's general sense of fairness and justice?"

READING AND WRITING ARGUMENTATIVE ESSAYS

This introduction and the discussion questions that follow each essay are designed to foster your skills as both reader and writer. These skills are mutually supportive: By becoming a better reader of arguments made by others, you will learn how to form better arguments of your own. At the same time, the critical thinking you do in composing your own arguments will stimulate your analytical abilities as a reader. The discussion questions will invite you to write at least three kinds of essays prompted by your reading: (1) Essays in which you critique the various appeals made by different writers on the same topic; (2) topical essays that you write without needing more information than the selections provide or you already know; and (3) essays that you write using information from outside sources such as the library. For any of these writing tasks, learning to be a better reader of arguments is a sensible first step.

Reading Arguments

While the discussion questions will provide you with particular approaches to each topic, some general advice for you as a reader of arguments is in order here. First of all, drop that highlighter, pick up a pencil, and open your dictionary! The arguments in this book are short enough to be read several times, and taking notes in the margin will be much more effective than reminding yourself to reread what you will reread anyway.

In your first reading, mark the words you don't know or are unsure of while you proceed rapidly through the essay. Next use your dictionary to make sure you understand the particular ways in which the writer uses his or her terms. Get in the habit of noting definitions in the margin, and make other notes there in your own words.

Then read the essay carefully, several times if necessary, while making more elaborate notes. For example, translating a writer's arguments into summaries is worth a dozen rereadings, because you are reading the material actively. As an active reader, you will form, modify, and strengthen your own opinions on the topic as you participate in a mental dialogue with the writer.

Some other ways of improving your reading skills include what is sometimes called *prereading*—making notes (mental or written ones) on your own view of a given topic before reading the essays on that issue. This exercise will give you a firm basis for response and help you see more clearly how writers present and back up their positions. You can even prepare for prereading. Try keeping an idea log or journal as you read to note points of view or effective techniques. When you begin to write, you will have practice and material to depend on, and if you know your topic in advance, reading any other essay will suggest ways of meeting your particular task.

You may also try the technique of rereading an essay from a point of view opposite to yours. This should sharpen your sense of how firmly argued views include attention to answering opponents. Attending to all the differing points of view in each of the topical units of the book will give you useful practice in gaining this skill.

To sum up: Learning to be an active and effective reader in the ways suggested here is part of the initial process of learning to be an active and effective *writer* of your own arguments.

Reading with the Help of Discussion Questions

The discussion questions for each essay are designed to help you become a more active reader by prompting you to pay attention to the ways in which the essayist appeals to logic, character, and emotion in the course of arguing a case. All the questions fall into some general modes of inquiry that can be employed by you as a reader of any argument, while the questions for a given case attempt to lead you to more particular answers.

In general the questions on logic will ask you to focus on the following:

- What are the data that prompt the claim?
- What are the warrants for making the claim, and what backing is offered for the warrants involved?
- What provision is made for rebuttals or qualifiers?
- Has a writer used appropriate analogies and made needed definitions?

Questions on character include:

- How does the writer attempt to establish his or her general competence for dealing with the issue?
- How do particular uses of language work to establish an impression of good character?
- What are the values, assumptions, and beliefs that underlie the writer's position?

Some general questions on emotion are:

- To what emotions in the audience does the writer appeal?
- What particular uses of language invite or evoke emotional responses and how do they do so?

Finally, questions at the end of each section will lead you to compare the approaches of different writers to the same topic.

- Where, how, and why do the writers agree and disagree?
- What are the values, assumptions, and beliefs that distinguish the positions taken?
- Does each writer imagine the same general audience?

Writing Arguments

Asking questions is the basis for writing as it is for reading. Beginning the process of writing with questions rather than conclusions can also help you solve the problem of starting a writing task. Trying to state your views first may seem like a sensible way to start writing, but it assumes that you already know everything you need to know, and that is seldom true. Even though your convictions on a topic are strongly felt, you may still end up staring at an otherwise blank page that looks like this:

I. Introduction
    a.

Such pages tend to remain blank. So don't try to express exactly what you think and feel about a topic until you have explored it fully by going through some other stages of the writing process.

The Writing Process: An Overview

You should think of writing as an activity that clarifies issues for yourself as well as for your audience. For most writers, that activity takes time. Remember, clear, well-organized thoughts do not flow out of a writer's mind onto paper as quickly and easily as they flow from the page into the reader's mind.

Many students think that they have "a lot of trouble with writing" because they have false expectations about the writing process: how easy it should be and how long it should take, for example. They believe in the myths about those legendary people for whom writing is a snap and conclude that it should be a snap for everyone. But most people find that they have to go through many stages to get to the final draft of a clear, well-organized, and complete essay. Not everything can be or need be said at once. If you divide up the many tasks involved in completing your essay, you won't have to think about everything at once, and no one stage will seem overwhelming.

In going through some or all of the exercises this section of the book suggests, you will find yourself making use of strategies that have proven successful for millions of beginning writers like yourself. You will find your ideas about your topic becoming more various in content and more forceful in expression. By examining the logic of your argument, you will discover weak points in your reasoning and be able to attend to them before your opponents do. You will discover in many instances how to use qualifiers to keep from stating your case in general or categorical terms that may unnecessarily irritate your reader.

By using the writing process to discover and explore your convictions, you will be doing a service not only to your reader but also to yourself as an educated person. Too often students turn in an unconvincing version of an essay that could have been made into an excellent one if its writer had taken it through a few more stages. Most of the errors teachers note in the margins of student essays could have been discovered and handled by the students themselves, alone or with some help from fellow students or collegiate resource centers. Similarly, matters of poor organization, such as rambling points and confused or missing transitions, are perfectly natural features of a good rough draft but unacceptable in a final draft. Any essay must crawl before it stands up to run. The point is not to turn in the earlier stages of what could eventually be a fine essay, but to go back through the processes that will make your work suitable for public display.

Perhaps the first thing to remember is to start the writing process early enough to go through—or back through—the stages that prove useful or necessary. Some writers will need more time than others on early stages like note taking or the generation of ideas; others will need more time for later stages like revision to tighten and tune the draft. For most essays you should try to have a first draft done at least a week before the due date. Such a schedule will allow you time for extensive revision, even if some of the earlier processes turn out to have taken up more time than you expected when you made your original plan. Remember that *revision* means "seeing again," and since that is what you are asking your audience to do when you address an issue with an argumentative essay, it is only fair that you be willing to look over your own work as many times as necessary. This means not only cleaning up difficulties in mechanical matters like spelling and punctuation but also revising your ideas as you discover more exactly what they entail through the process of putting them in writing.

Stages of the Writing Process

No two people go through exactly the same stages of the writing process, and a given individual may make more or less use of different stages in writing different essays. Your own sense of your strengths and weaknesses will determine how much attention you need to pay to any of the following stages or how often you need to pay conscious attention to the techniques employed in them. If you use them consciously, you may also find that you tend to skip forward to later stages or go back to earlier ones. Don't worry: Use the process the way it works best for you.

FIRST STAGE: GETTING STARTED For writers of argumentative essays, the beginning of the writing process is usually the discovery of an issue or a problem on which people disagree. You may already have taken sides, or you may think only that you can contribute something to the debate that will clarify the issue or help solve the problem. Sometimes your point of view is already decided at this stage; sometimes it gets its focus later in the process.

Expressive Writing Expressive writing is talking to yourself on paper. It is useful to keep an idea log or journal as thoughts occur to you. If you have never done this sort of writing before, you will be pleasantly surprised at how much it clarifies your thinking. You needn't make entries every day as you would in an ordinary journal but only when thoughts strike you for advancing a possible argument through appeals to character, emotion, or logic. Short entries of a sentence or two will add up to a comforting collection of things to work with as you begin an assignment.

You might do well to keep individual sections of your idea log under some headings commonly found useful for generating an inventory of issues:

- My friends and I tend to argue about . . .
- I think it's wrong that . . .
- I wish people could understand that they should . . .
- X believes . . . ; but I believe . . .
- Our college should definitely do something about . . .
- There ought to be a law that . . .

SECOND STAGE: EXPLORATION AND REHEARSAL This is the stage where you begin to assemble pertinent information on a given topic by recalling and jotting down your own experiences and views or by reading, interviewing, or undertaking other forms of research. At this stage you try to understand not only your own views but also the facts, values, assumptions, and beliefs about life that underlie all sides of the debate. This is the stage for prewriting and note taking or even for a rapidly written set of paragraphs on key points. Getting at least some of your thoughts down on paper, even though they may be revised later, makes you feel you are on your way.

Talking Try talking about ideas with a friend or a small group of classmates. Learning how others think will help turn your sense of an issue from a generalized subject into a collection of more particular views for and against various aspects of the issue. Often you'll find that what you thought could be taken for granted is hotly disputed by others and needs careful explanation on your part. Listen to any objections and try to get a feel for arguments that make sense to your friends on all sides of the issue. Generating ideas and gaining multiple perspectives like this is an especially good way to begin your writing, because it automatically maintains a clear sense of the argumentative essay not as a sermon but as a dialogue between the reader and the writer.

Notes In taking notes on what you read and discuss, get used to putting things under headings like *since* and *because* to form the habit of seeing facts in the explanatory or argumentative patterns you will need in your essay's drafts. The discussion questions and writing assignments will encourage you to get into the questioning habit, but here is some general advice to begin with. Don't worry about where to begin with your notes. You needn't worry at first about organizing your perceptions and thoughts by claim, warrant, and data. Begin anywhere, and one thing will lead to another as you generate material that can be more fully organized or reorganized at a later stage. Use the following checklist for generating notes, along with any other questions a particular subject might suggest:

- Is there really a problem here?
- Would the proposed solution really solve it? Could the problem be solved more simply without disturbing related matters?
- Is the proposed solution really practical? Would there be any unforeseen consequences?

Once you have some preliminary notes, use the categories of logic for expanding and organizing your material. Get into the habit of sorting out the various claims, warrants, and data in the arguments you read so that you can more readily sort out the notes for your own essays. Like all skills, this analytic sorting may seem awkward at first, and there will be many instances when the proper category for a point is a debatable matter. Whether a statement should be seen as a claim or a warrant, for example, may depend on your point of view.

THIRD STAGE: WRITING A DISCOVERY DRAFT If you have already begun some writing beyond notes, this stage will blend into the second stage. Discovery drafts are often messy and disorganized. They might seem chaotic to an outside reader, but this draft is meant only for you. Your efforts here should shift from gathering facts and views to putting them together. In writing this draft you will discover connections among your ideas, and rereading the draft when you're done will help you see how to reorganize what you have. Rearranging your points in a more effective order is much easier once you have expressed them in sentences and paragraphs, no matter how tentative.

Brainstorming To generate ideas and connections among them, you might try a technique sometimes called speed writing, brainstorming, or free writing. That is, write down sentences as fast as you can without worrying about whether they connect with one another. Keep going for 10 or 15 minutes, even if after the first few minutes you run out of your initial set of ideas. You will soon find that you are writing your way into a problem and discovering new views while you express some you already have.

FOURTH STAGE: REVISION OR "SEEING AGAIN" Discovery drafts may have prompted you to go back to even earlier stages for further information or to rethink some aspect of the problem at hand. Revision is the stage for rethinking, and you may do several rewrites of your discovery draft until you are satisfied that you have made all your points, however roughly and awkwardly, and have placed these points in the order that seems most effective. As your argument becomes clearer in your own mind, you will begin to imagine your readers' reactions and will look into issues like unity, coherence, and "flow" more carefully. Try to imagine your essay as a conversation rather than a lecture, and you will write more naturally, fluently, and effectively.

Try imagining a classmate who may not agree with you but is well disposed and reasonable. Keeping such an audience clearly in mind will help you decide how much to define or explain and how much to take for granted. These questions are much harder to answer if you imagine yourself high on a podium talking down to a silent, respectful, and completely receptive public. Imagine your classmate as at first agreeable and then dubious, so that you will be better able not only to make your own points but also to meet any counterarguments. Imagine this classmate in class or in some other formal setting for your dialogue rather than in a place like the snackbar. This will help you avoid needless facetiousness or gratuitous remarks, two of the vices opposite but equal to the pomposity that can control your tone of voice when sermonizing from on high. Finally, don't be afraid to revise as many times as necessary, but concentrate on important points and leave the matters of detail to the next stage.

Revision Guidelines

- Keep your vocabulary at the natural level of educated readers and writers. Avoid unnecessary specialized words, and imagine your classmate's response when weighing different choices.

- Make sure you have used examples to explain your general or abstract assertions.
- Avoid a belligerent or bossy tone of voice.
- As a rule avoid short paragraphs of one or two sentences. They may seem snappy in a journalistic text, but they suggest superficial or undeveloped thought in serious argument.
- Avoid repeating a point too often. Repetition makes you seem to underestimate your audience's abilities or attention.

FIFTH STAGE: EDITING This is where you polish your draft until it shines like an essay. Carefully go over details of grammar and punctuation, and try to tighten up the structure of each sentence to make it as clear and forceful as possible. Avoid using too many sentences of the same form and length. Learn to combine some of your short sentences, and don't begin every sentence with *The*. Variety in sentence structure and length creates flow and pacing in your essay, and a variety of sentence openers will provide opportunities for connection and transition and keep your style from seeming plodding and dull. You can learn different ways to begin a sentence by observing how the professional writers represented here use their sentence openers to make transitions and signal their patterns of reasoning.

Finally, remember that while all these dos and don'ts add up to good general advice, you will learn most about writing by actually writing and by critically reading other writers. When you find yourself admiring any aspect of a writer's method, analyze it and make it part of your own armory of stylistic resources.

Ready to Go

You are now ready to turn the theory you have learned in this Introduction to practical advantage by analyzing the argumentative essays in the rest of the book and writing essays yourself. You may of course come back to this Introduction during the course of your studies to refresh your theoretical knowledge. You will understand better how to take advantage of its advice when you have engaged some of the problems of argument and persuasion yourself.

Current Controversies from Three Points of View

DON'T EVEN BEGIN TO SACRIFICE FREE SPEECH

Joe Patrick Bean

The First Amendment, the late Texas humorist and civil libertarian   1
John Henry Faulk believed, "will guarantee in perpetuity the right and
protect the right of people to voice those opinions we loathe and despise,
to protect them with the same force it does those we cherish and live by."

Faulk's words should echo throughout United States colleges and   2
universities, where intellectual freedom and the unimpeded exchange of
ideas and opinions are absolutely essential. Sadly, however, this is not true
at many schools.

In their understandable desire to discourage verbal harassment and   3
cruelty, many schools have implemented broadly worded "hate speech"
bans that severely limit on-campus freedom of expression and undermine
the First Amendment.

The University of Michigan, for example, in 1988 banned any   4
form of expression "that stigmatizes or victimizes an individual on the
basis of race, ethnicity, religion, sex, sexual orientation, greed, national
origin, ancestry, age, marital status, handicap or Vietnam-era veteran
status."

Violators were subject to being reprimanded, ordered to perform   5
community service, suspended or expelled.

In the 1989 case of Doe v. University of Michigan, US District   6
Judge Avern Cohn overturned the school's speech code. "It is firmly
settled that under our Constitution the public expression of ideas may
not be prohibited merely because the ideas are themselves offensive to
some of their hearers," he explained.

"These principles acquire a special significance in the university   7
setting, where the free and unfettered interplay of competing views is
essential."

The Doe suit was made possible under the terms of existing federal   8
civil rights measures that authorize students and professors at *public* colleges and universities to sue when their on-campus First Amendment
rights are violated. Many more such cases will appear on federal court
dockets as more speech codes are implemented and enforced.

But this same protection does not apply to *private* institutions of   9
higher education. US Rep. Henry J. Hyde, (R) of Illinois, believes it
should, as does the American Civil Liberties Union.

Hyde recently introduced the Collegiate Speech Protection Act of   10
1991, which will amend the US Civil Rights Act of 1964 to extend free-
speech safeguards to private colleges and universities. The ACLU has
endorsed this measure.

The proposal says that these schools "shall not make or enforce any   11
rule subjecting any student to disciplinary sanctions solely on the basis of
conduct that is speech or other communication protected from governmental restriction by the first article of amendment to the Constitution
of the United States."

Hyde's measure protects words, not actions. Disruptive conduct is   12
not tolerated. "This is not carte blanche for campus chaos," he says. Nor
are obscenity, fighting words, and libel permitted.

But sacrificing legitimate freedom of expression must never be the   13
price exacted to attend or teach at any school. Every form of speech the
First Amendment protects on every street corner in the US must also be
protected.

John Henry Faulk had to fight a six-year legal battle to reclaim his   14
right to speak freely after McCarthy-era blacklisters libeled him by accusing him of being a Communist sympathizer, which cost him his job at
WCBS, the Columbia Broadcasting System's flagship radio station in
New York City.

He won that landmark libel suit three decades ago because, as he   15
said, the First Amendment "puts every American citizen, whatever color,
whatever walk of life, on precisely the same footing."

Even if they likewise have to go to court to prove that it does,   16
Faulk's faith in the First Amendment must also encompass students and
professors at private colleges and universities. By providing the legal authority for them to sue, Hyde's bill will ensure it does.

Questions for Analysis

Logic

1. Bean organizes his essay by beginning and ending with the example of John Henry Faulk. What advantages do you think the author gains by this organization of his argument? Disadvantages?
2. Explain what you see as Bean's implicit reasoning in his claim that more federal lawsuits will result from "hate speech" codes.
3. How does Bean take into account the reasoning of his opponents in the essay, those in favor of "hate speech" codes?

Character

1. Characterize the tone of voice that you think Bean generally employs in his essay. Point to some specific uses of language that create that tone. What elements of character does the tone of voice employed seem designed to establish?
2. What efforts does Bean make to link his views to those of acknowledged authorities represented by people, institutions, or laws? Point to some examples.
3. Throughout the essay, what characteristics does Bean seek to establish in the figure of John Henry Faulk? How does Bean's characterization of Faulk attempt to establish Bean's own character as one that includes fairness and broad-mindedness?

Emotion

1. What emotions are respectively evoked by the phrases "free speech" and "hate speech"? Briefly explain the values and assumptions on which an audience seems expected to respond when those phrases are used by a writer.
2. To what other emotions in his audience does Bean most generally appeal? Explain one way in which he makes his general appeal.
3. What emotions in his audience does Bean seem to seek to forestall in paragraph 12? Explain his motive and his effort.

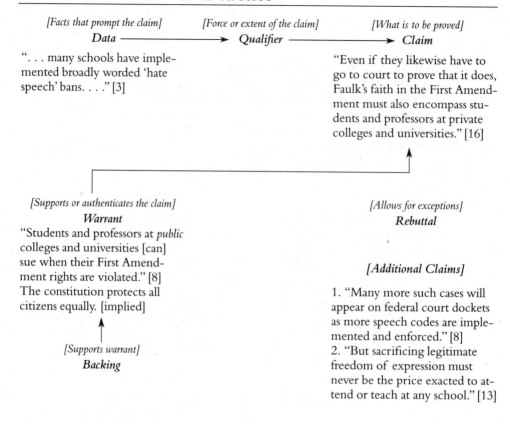

[Facts that prompt the claim]
Data ⟶

"... many schools have implemented broadly worded 'hate speech' bans. ..." [3]

[Force or extent of the claim]
Qualifier ⟶

[What is to be proved]
Claim

"Even if they likewise have to go to court to prove that it does, Faulk's faith in the First Amendment must also encompass students and professors at private colleges and universities." [16]

[Supports or authenticates the claim]
Warrant

"Students and professors at *public* colleges and universities [can] sue when their First Amendment rights are violated." [8] The constitution protects all citizens equally. [implied]

[Supports warrant]
Backing

[Allows for exceptions]
Rebuttal

[Additional Claims]

1. "Many more such cases will appear on federal court dockets as more speech codes are implemented and enforced." [8]
2. "But sacrificing legitimate freedom of expression must never be the price exacted to attend or teach at any school." [13]

FREEDOM OF HATE SPEECH

Richard Perry and Patricia Williams

Until well after the Second World War, American institutions of higher education were bastions of a sort of cheery and thoughtlessly jingoistic nativism (isn't this some part of what we've always meant when we spoke of "that old college spirit"?). Except for the historically black and women's colleges and a couple of schools serving immigrant populations (such as the City College of New York), the vast majority of the student bodies of America's hundreds of colleges were overwhelmingly U.S.-born, male, Christian, and of Northern European descent, and their faculties were even more so. The structure of the core liberal arts curriculum suggested that the university understood itself as an umpire of timeless values, high above the rough and tumble of mere politics, standing at the summit of Western civilization, which from this vantage point could be seen to have risen in an unbroken crescendo from Plato to NATO.

However, the assumptions that made the university an arbiter of "universal values" have been questioned, as multinational business and research institutions have evolved into ever more global and ethnically diverse enterprises. On the home front, meanwhile, the hard-won material gains of women and ethnic minorities have produced halting progress toward the goal of making American universities truly representative of the country's population as a whole. Responding to these historical developments, many have sought to make the core curriculum a more effective preparation for the diverse, multicultural environments of both the contemporary United States and the world. There have also been efforts to make the campus itself a more hospitable place for its newly heterogeneous population, most notably amendments to the campus conduct rules intended to discourage harassment on the basis of race, religion, ethnicity, gender, and sexual orientation.

These reform efforts have been met with a virulent backlash. This backlash has recently been fueled by a series of often scurrilous stories in the most visible national magazines and by fervent denunciations from the Left, Right, and center of political debate.

This confusion stems largely from the dishonest manner in which the debates have been reported. Most accounts of this campus dispute have been characterized by repeated distortions of fact and a profound bad faith with history. First, it is preposterous to claim, as many opponents of multiculturalism have, that these debates are about some supposed new infringement of the First Amendment rights of American citizens. No position seriously advocated by multiculturalists would have the slightest effect upon our right as Americans to be nativist, racist, anti-Semitic, sexist, homophobic, or just as narrowly monocultural-as-we-wanna-be in our personal lives. So too it remains entirely possible to stand in the public arena and call one another any of the whole litany of terms with which we as Americans have learned throughout our history to abuse one another. One might instructively compare this situation with the new Canadian constitution, which specifically limits the protection of certain kinds of hate speech, without much evidence that this provision has started Canada down that slippery slope toward being a Stalinist police state.

Nor do the multiculturalist reforms pose any institutional threat to the many securely tenured professors on the most prestigious faculties who teach doctrines (such as sociobiology and kindred theories on the margins of intellectual respectability) that are patently demeaning to members of the most long-abused groups. And the debate over multi-culturalism scarcely disturbs the work of eminent scholars who regularly contrive to put a revisionist happy face upon the history of slavery, the Czarist pogroms, the Nazi genocides, the colonial subjugation of indigenous peoples, or the oppression of women.

What has *never* been true is that one member of an institution has an unrestrained legal right to harass another member and remain in the good graces of the institution. 6

Yet the recent barrage of media coverage would have us believe that some *novel* restriction is being imposed in multiculturalist speech and behavior codes. This misinformation has been conveyed by those who are apparently unable to distinguish between a liberty interest on the one hand and, on the other, a quite specific interest in being able to spout racist, sexist, and homophobic epithets completely unchallenged—without, in other words, the terrible inconvenience of feeling bad about it. 7

There is a sharp paradox at the heart of all this, a contradiction whose effective message is: "I have the right to express as much hatred as I want, so you shut up about it." It may be appropriate to defend the First Amendment rights of students who, for example, openly advocate Nazi policies. However, there has been a good deal of unacknowledged power-brokering that has informed the refusal even to think about the effect of relentless racist propagandizing on educational institutions in particular. Now those who even criticize this selective invocation of the First Amendment on the behalf of one social group over another are themselves called Nazis. 8

This fundamental paradox has bred a host of others. Conservatives such as George Will hurriedly discard their hallowed distinction between the public and private spheres when expediency beckons. Not long ago right-wingers were asserting that the evangelical Bob Jones University should be allowed to practice segregation and still be given a tax exemption—because it was a *private* institution. Where were these free-speech patriots in 1986 when Captain Goldman, a U.S. Air Force officer and an Orthodox Jew, was denied by the Reagan Supreme Court the right to wear a yarmulke at his desk job? And where are they now, when the new Supreme Court of our new world order has just asserted that the government *can* control speech between doctor and patient—heretofore one of the most sacred of privacy privileges—when the clinic receives federal funds and the topic of conversation is reproductive choice? 9

These ironies of free-speech opportunism have been accompanied by a breathtaking effort to rewrite our history. The multiculturalist reforms on campus have been characterized as being at odds with the two moral touchstones of recent political memory: the World War II-era 10 fight against Nazi theory of Aryan supremacy and the American anti-slavery and civil rights movements. Both of these struggles were in fact fought over—among other things—the sort of contested social meanings that can be traced directly to the present university discussions. The new interpretation of these two contests, however, rewrites them as triumphs of the inevitable, forward-marching progress of modern liberal individualism. Commentators from George Will to Shelby Steele have consistently depicted Martin Luther King, Jr., for example, as having pursued the higher moral ground of individual achievement rather than the validation of African-American collective social identity—as though these notions were inherently in opposition to one another. We are to imagine, for example, that the brave people who faced fire hoses and police dogs and who sat-in at lunch counters in the 1950s and 1960s were after nothing more than, say, the market freedom of an individual black American to eat a grilled cheese sandwich in the company of raving bigots. Conservative opponents of multiculturalism would have us forget about the other part of that struggle: the fight to expand the social space of all blacks and to re-articulate the political semantics of the collective identity of the descendants of slaves.

Another striking paradox is the way that much of this backlash proceeds *11* in the name of democratic values, while mounting a sustained assault precisely on the democratic process of academic self-governance. The academic Right devotes itself to attacks on changes in curricula and conduct codes that have been adopted only after lengthy deliberation and votes by the faculty senates (such as in the Stanford Western civilization reforms or the Berkeley ethnic studies requirement), administrative committees, or student bodies. More curiously still, these assaults are typically said to be conducted in defense of something like "a free marketplace of ideas." Yet the recent multiculturalist changes might accurately be viewed as shifts in an intellectual marketplace where several positions have been rising in value, while another, older position, adamantly refusing to innovate, has been steadily losing its market share. There is a certain irony, therefore, in the spectacle of William Bennett and company engaged in a kind of status brokerage, trading on their appointed positions of authority for advantage they cannot gain via democratic votes in faculty senates or in the governing bodies of professional organizations.

Such distortions of the debate have worked to obscure what could *12* be a genuine opportunity. The market idea, considered not simply as the nineteenth-century social-Darwinist mechanism whereby big fish eat little fish for the greater good, might serve as a multidimensional matrix for the representation of certain types of social information. If, for example, we could ever get to the point where we can honestly speak of having achieved a level playing field in the marketplace of ideas (for this is precisely what is at stake in the present debates), then we might begin to understand the market as one means of representing multicentered networks of social interaction. Just as the American monetary system went off the gold standard in 1934, it is now time to get off the traditional *rational man* standard (the straight, white, male, Christian, English-speaking, middle-class individualist) as the universal measure of humanity. It is time to initiate a *perestroika* of personhood—to make a world in which all of us, in our multiple, overlapping, individual and collective identities can come to terms.

Questions for Analysis

Logic
1. Does the claim established in paragraph 5 seem to you the main claim of the essay? Why or why not? Explain the data and warrant of the claim.
2. The authors frequently point to what they see as paradoxes in the views of their opponents. Pick an example and show (a) the logic of the opponent as viewed by the authors and (b) the fallacy of that logic from the authors' point of view.
3. Explain in your own words the authors' views on the issue of Nazis as they see it.

Character
1. In what ways do the authors seek to establish their collective character as one that includes courage? Point to some examples.
2. Name a few aspects of character, other than courage, that the authors seek to establish in the essay. Pick one of these aspects and show how specific uses of language work to achieve it.
3. Where and how do the authors seek to connect their views to those of publicly acknowledged authorities, whether people, institutions, or laws?

Emotion
1. What specific emotions do the authors express in paragraph 1? Are these emotions representative of those they express in the essay as a whole? Find some examples to demonstrate your conclusion.
2. What emotions do the authors seek to evoke in the readers of paragraph 1? What part does the ironic manner seem to play in this appeal? Are readers invited to have similar emotional responses elsewhere in the essay? Give some examples to support your conclusion.
3. Locate instances beyond paragraph 1 in which the authors display a more intense emotion than they do there. What specific uses of language determine the intensity of the emotions at that point?

FREE SPEECH? YES.
DRUNKENNESS? NO.

Vartan Gregorian

During the last several decades, our nation's colleges and universities 1
have worked assiduously to develop America's potential talent and to
reach out and educate the young without regard to religion, race or
gender. Today's campuses are much different from those of the 1950s.
Students who represent the broad spectrum of our nation now expect to
be welcomed and supported, not merely accommodated or tolerated.

This is not a superficial change, nor has the process been an easy 2
one. We are still striving to build communities where students can devote
themselves to knowledge and personal growth without having to defend
their racial or ethnic background or plead that their personal dignity or
right to privacy be respected.

Today the leaders of American higher education are expected to 3
set high academic standards and codes of conduct that reflect our universities' expectations and the rights and responsibilities of our students.
Presidents of our universities are urged to protect the privacy of students,
to fight against drug and alcohol abuse, sexual and racial harassment and
to guarantee their physical safety. In addition, as educators they are supposed to speak out against intolerance of any kind. Our universities are
asked to accomplish all the above objectives while safeguarding the principles of academic freedom, which are their hallmark.

Now come the tests. How does the public respond when our uni- 4
versities take appropriate action against harassment and intimidation?

Last year aggrieved students at Brown brought charges of harass- 5
ment, intimidation and invasion of privacy against a fellow student. The
University Disciplinary Council, composed of faculty, students and
deans, found the student in question guilty of violating three major provisions of Brown University's 10-year-old code of conduct: disruptive
behavior, harassment and drunkenness.

I upheld that expulsion on appeal. Because the university's discipli- 6
nary rulings are held in confidence, there was no public release of information. Press accounts, however, described the incident as one of loud
drunkenness, of shouting anti-Semitic, anti-black, anti-homosexual obscenities at students in their dormitory rooms, of students driven from
their rooms at 2 a.m. by disruption, of a confrontation during which the
intoxicated student was physically restrained. It has even been noted that
this was the second time the student had been found guilty of similar
charges, the first incident having resulted in probation and counseling.

What has astonished me is how some members of the press have   7
interpreted their own reports. Bouts of drunkenness and disruption have
been excused as "sophomoric behavior," threats of physical violence and
disruptive behavior have been rationalized or dismissed if no actual blows
were struck, and the 2 a.m abuse of fellow students in their dormitory
rooms, through anti-Semitic, anti-black and anti-homosexual baiting, has
been relabeled an exercise of "free speech." Obscenities have been trans-
formed into "unpopular views."

Other voices operating on third-hand information have criticized   8
the university for expelling a student under a so-called "hate speech"
rule—the first such expulsion in the country, they say. It is not; and this
is not a "free speech" issue. It does not seem to matter to them that Brown
has no rule against "hate speech." Like a radioactive material, this canard
about "hate speech" has a half-life; its contamination remains for a very
long time.

It is ironic that those who have attempted to reconstruct this case as   9
an infringement of "free speech" and defend without qualms the right
of any student to shout racist or ethnic slanders at any hour, at any person,
in any setting are unable or unwilling to publish the obscenities involved
in this case for fear of offending their readers.

And a minor point: As a historian I am dismayed that only one of   10
those who have written so "authoritatively" about my own views has
bothered to contact me.

The day when drunkenness was romanticized, when racial or sexual   11
harassment could be winked at, condoned or considered merely in poor
taste has long passed. In the nation's workplaces, a considerable corpus of
federal and state law protects the rights and the dignity of employees.

The American Civil Liberties Union, which has opposed campus   12
regulations that may "interfere with the freedom of professors, students
and administrators to teach, learn, discuss and debate, or to express ideas,
opinions or feelings in the classroom, public or private discourse," stated
recently that colleges and universities are not prohibited from enacting
"disciplinary codes aimed at restraining acts of harassment, intimidation
and invasion of privacy. The fact that words may be used in connection
with otherwise actionable conduct does not immunize such conduct
from appropriate regulation."

Brown, the nation's seventh oldest college, was the only colonial   13
college that did not exact a religious test for admission. Our tradition of
openness, tolerance and intellectual freedom has extended over the two
centuries since then and is vigorously sustained today. The exchange of
ideas, public discourse and debate nurture in each succeeding generation
a respect for the right of all individuals to form, espouse and defend their
beliefs and thoughts. Imposed orthodoxies of all sorts, including that

which is called "politically correct" speech, are anathema to our enterprise. So is the great silence between races, genders and ideologies. We must know what each other thinks.

However, as the First Amendment lawyer Floyd Abrams pointed   14
out at Brown during a recent conference on free expression, there is a difference between unpopular ideas expressed in a public context and epithets delivered in the context of harassing, intimidating or demeaning behavior. At Brown, we expect our students to know the difference. For 10 years, Brown freshmen have received the university's "Tenets of Community Behavior" and have acknowledged in writing their understanding that the university will hold them to that standard of behavior. Indeed, the underlying principle of the "Tenets" is that "a socially responsible community provides a structure within which individual freedoms may flourish, but not so self-indulgently that they threaten the rights or freedoms of other individuals or groups." Intellectual independence and social responsibility are not mutually exclusive.

Today our nation's best campuses can be neither bastions of privi-   15
lege nor enclaves of trendiness catering to the whims of clamorous and transitory groups. Our universities have been, are and must remain open intellectual communities. They also have an obligation to protect the safety and dignity of our students and their right to learn without intimidation or fear.

Questions for Analysis

Logic
1. How does the organization of Gregorian's essay reflect the dual nature of the tasks he sees as necessary for him to achieve as a university president?
2. The student in question was found guilty of three offenses. In what ways do Gregorian's arguments link them? In what ways are they treated separately?
3. What is the basis of reasoning involved in the author's quarrel with the press as opposed to his views of the incident covered by the press?

Character
1. How would you characterize the tone of voice created by the author's style? What elements of character does that tone seem to you to express?
2. In what ways is your sense of the author's character created by his allusions to the history of universities in general and of Brown in particular with regard to toleration of opinion?
3. What aspects of the author's character seem to you to be expressed by the ways in which he meets opposing points of view in the essay?

Emotion
1. Where and how does the author appeal to the reader's emotions when the essay treats the subject of the student who was disciplined?
2. Where and how does the author appeal to the reader's emotions when the essay treats the subject of the students who brought the charges?
3. Where and how does the author appeal to the reader's emotions when the essay treats the subject of the press?

EXERCISES: HATE SPEECH
AND CIVIL RIGHTS

Intertextual Questions
1. Freedom of speech is notably absent under totalitarian governments. Compare the ways in which Perry and Williams treat the subject of Nazis with those in which Bean treats his Communist theme. What techniques does Gregorian use when alluding to the religious tests of colonial colleges?
2. Each of the essays evokes the First Amendment. In what different and similar ways do the essays do so? Pick specific passages for comparison and contrast.
3. Which of the other essays do you think President Gregorian would find most compatible with his own views? Ask yourself the same question with regard to the other authors and explain your reasoning in each case.

Suggestions for Writing
1. Hate speech and freedom of speech are emotion-laden topics. Write an essay in which you compare some of the ways in which the authors of these essays employ emotional appeals on these topics.
2. In a campus or local newspaper, find an opinion piece that you consider in some way offensive to your own values and assumptions about life. Write an essay in which you argue that the writing in question does or does not violate your own sense of the proper limits of speech.
3. Which of the three essays best expresses your own views of the proper limits of speech? Write an essay in which you explain why its arguments seem most convincing to you.

Comparable Worth and Pay Equity for Women

QUIET PROGRESS TOWARD PAY EQUITY

Ruth Walker

Whatever happened to comparable worth? The doctrine of com-   *1*
parable worth, or to put it more fully, the doctrine of equal pay for work
of comparable worth, was touted a few years back as the major women's
issue of the 1980s. It hasn't turned out quite that way, but it's not a dead
issue, either.

The idea behind comparable worth, or pay equity, is that some jobs   *2*
are paid less than they deserve because they are performed mostly by
women. If these jobs were fairly evaluated according to their skills, responsibility, and educational requirements, the theory goes, we would see
wholesale upgrading of women's earnings. Teachers and nurses would be
paid at least as well as school janitors and truck drivers.

Earlier this month, in the largest comparable worth lawsuit in the   *3*
United States, a federal judge ruled that State of California had not
deliberately underpaid its female employees. The California ruling came
a few days after dismissal of a pay-equity suit by the United Auto Workers in Michigan.

But such reversals notwithstanding, there remains an active move-   *4*
ment toward pay equity. The National Committee on Pay Equity reports
that some $450 million has been allocated over the past eight years for
the upgrading of women's pay.

And more unions are putting pay equity on their collective-   *5*
bargaining agenda. Many would say that that's where the matter belongs.
Obviously, unions and employers are free to bargain on whatever they
please.

41

It's hard to avoid noticing, however, that many advocates of this   6
approach are generally opposed to unions; one suspects that they favor
it because they think it won't work.

Some legal and semantic fog surrounds the whole issue. If "Com-   7
parable Worth" were a would-be actress, and I were her agent, I'd insist
she change her name to something that looks better up in lights.

Comparable worth differs from equal pay for equal work. The   8
Equal Pay Act requires that a man and woman side by side on an assembly
line, for instance, doing the same task with the same skill and experience
be paid the same. (Don't laugh; it was progress at the time.)

But many advocates find a legal basis for comparable worth in Title   9
VII of the Civil Rights Act. In this view, compensating "women's work"
at lower rates because it's done by women amounts to sex discrimination
in employment, which Title VII forbids. The classic argument against
pay equity, by whatever name, is that it disrupts market forces. If salaries
for certain jobs are held down to pay more for other jobs, then shortages
will develop; employers won't be able to fill positions. But what makes
anyone think we don't have shortages of teachers and nurses?

We need to be careful to distinguish economic value from inherent   10
worth. Employers who insist they can't offer more aren't necessarily being
stingy, and would-be employees who say they can't work for less aren't
just greedy.

But unquestionably, one of the attitudes that market forces reflect   11
is that it's acceptable to pay women less than men. Many have heard that
American women earn 59 cents for every dollar men earn. The ratio has
improved in recent years, by some estimates, and can be expected to
improve further. But that three-fifths proportion has had a longevity that
is almost eerie. The Bible records the Lord telling Moses that the "esti-
mation" of a male of working age "shall be fifty shekels of silver" and
that of the female thirty shekels—see Lev. 27:1–4.

More recently, the Wall Street Journal reported that an executive   12
compensation survey found that "women at the vice-presidential level
and above earn 42 percent less than male counterparts"—in other words,
58 cents on the dollar.

Overwhelmingly, women are in the job market for the same reason   13
as men, namely to support themselves and their families. The arguments
that the 60 percent ratio is justified by women's different career patterns
hold less water every year.

Questions for Analysis

Logic
1. In what ways does Walker use statistics to bolster her argument? Pick
   a specific example and explain its operation.

2. In paragraph 10, the author says, "We need to be careful to distinguish economic value from inherent worth." In what ways does she or does she not distinguish these issues in the essay?
3. In what sense or senses does Walker use the term *acceptable* in paragraph 11? To whom or to what does she imply that the facts about women's pay are acceptable? To whom or to what does she imply that the facts about women's pay are not acceptable? Explain the implied reasoning that centers on this term.

Character
1. What effect on your sense of the author's character is created by knowing that the author is assistant managing editor of *The Christian Science Monitor?*
2. What sense of the author's character is created by the careful definition of the key term of her essay in paragraphs 1 and 2?
3. How and where does the author present views that balance or oppose her own?

Emotion
1. How would you rate the emotional temperature of the last sentence in paragraph 1? High? Moderate? Low? Do you find the sentence represents the level of emotion in the argument as a whole? Explain.
2. In paragraph 7, what do you think the author finds lacking in the emotional appeal of the phrase "comparable worth"?
3. What emotions are appealed to by the rhetorical question at the end of paragraph 9?

LET THE MARKETPLACE DECIDE PAY

James J. Kilpatrick

Proponents of that bizarre movement known as "comparable 1 worth" were whooping it up last week. The City Council of Los Angeles had voted 12-1 for a union contract that reportedly was intended to equate secretaries with garage attendants and librarians with gardeners. Unless I am misinformed, there is much less here than meets the eye.

These days, to speak or write of "comparable worth" is to evoke 2 the solemn foolishness witnessed in the state of Washington. There the state engaged in an elaborate evaluation of its mostly male and mostly female job classifications. A five-member committee adopted a plan of numerical values. Points were awarded according to the committee's judgment of (1) the knowledge and skill required for a given job; (2) the mental demands of the job; (3) the workers' accountability on the job; and (4) the working conditions—such as cold, wind, dust, fumes and dirt—on the job. When the scores were tallied, it appeared that the jobs of laundry worker and delivery truck driver, for example, were jobs of "comparable worth," and a federal judge late in 1983 decreed that the jobs must be equally paid.

The Los Angeles case was nothing like that. There the city government met with negotiators for the American Federation of State, County and Municipal Employees representing about 3,950 of the city's 26,800 workers. As it happens, the union's collective bargaining unit is made up of members in jobs that historically have been "women's jobs," e.g., secretaries and librarians.

For six months the negotiators went at it. The union argued eloquently that these "women's jobs" were irrationally underpaid. No portentous study of "comparable worth" ever was made; no conjectural values ever were quantified. The union won its point. The city agreed to raise the entrance salaries of these AFSCME members over a three-year period from an average of $1,310 a month to an average of $1,492 a month. At that point in 1988 the new librarian and the new gardener will start at the same rate of pay, but this is by accident, not by design.

Nothing in the Los Angeles process should set off cries of alarm among those of us who regard the Washington state process as essentially loony. The voluntary agreement reached in Los Angeles was the product of old-fashioned arm's-length bargaining; the underlying premise was not comparable worth, but simple equity. By contrast, Washington let itself be transfixed by arbitrary numbers, and U.S. District Judge Jack E. Tanner swallowed the numbers whole. Unless his decree is reversed, it will cost state taxpayers an estimated $1 billion to equalize the washers and the drivers.

Charles W. Baird, professor of economics at California State University in Hayward, believes Tanner's opinion may well be overturned on appeal. Writing in *Government Union Review,* Baird contends that the subjective judgments of the Washington committee are unimpressive as hard evidence of unlawful discrimination on account of sex. The comparative job scores, he says, are necessarily arbitrary. A different set of consultants, applying 45 factors instead of four, found no pay disparities between jobs of comparable worth on the Washington payroll.

Regardless of the outcome in Washington, "comparable worth" has become the latest rallying cry for women's groups. Thus far the concept appears to have been adopted by only a handful of state and local governments, but suits by women state employees, echoing the Washington allegations, are pending in Illinois, Michigan, Hawaii and California. In Minnesota, the Legislature has ordered local governments to see that traditionally women's jobs are better paid by 1986.

To the extent that these pay scales voluntarily are adjusted, only   *8* the most rabid male chauvinist could object. What Los Angeles wants to pay a librarian is the business of Los Angeles. The women may be discomfited when they find bookish males competing for their jobs, but that's another story. What Baird deplores is the prospect of substituting the decrees of seers and diviners for the function of the marketplace in fixing the value of labor. It is only a matter of time before some nitwitted member of Congress proposes to write such wage boards into the 1963 Equal Pay Act. When that day comes, let us pray for a resounding vote of "no."

Questions for Analysis

Logic
1. Explain in your own words the author's account of the reasoning behind the collective bargaining method of arriving at wages.
2. Explain in your own words the author's account of the reasoning behind the state of Washington's method for setting wages.
3. What seems to be the implied reasoning behind Kilpatrick's argument about librarian's wages in the final paragraph?

Character
1. Where and how does Kilpatrick appeal to his audience to see him as clear-headed?
2. Where and how does Kilpatrick appeal to his audience to see him as fair-minded?
3. How does the author connect his views to those of publicly acknowledged authorities?

Emotion
1. What emotions are appealed to by the author's use of the words "bizarre" [1], "loony" [5], and "nitwitted" [8] to characterize his opposition?
2. In what tone of voice do you hear the author's use of the words "solemn" [2] and "portentous" [4]? To what emotions in his audience does that tone seem to appeal?
3. To what emotions does the phrase "swallowed the numbers whole" appeal? Explain.

WHY WOMEN ARE PAID LESS THAN MEN

Lester C. Thurow

In the 40 years from 1939 to 1979 white women who work full time have with monotonous regularity made slightly less than 60 percent as much as white men. Why? 1

Over the same time period, minorities have made substantial progress in catching up with whites, with minority women making even more progress than minority men. Black men now earn 72 percent as much as white men (up 16 percentage points since the mid-1950s) but black women earn 92 percent as much as white women. Hispanic men make 71 percent of what their white counterparts do, but Hispanic women make 82 percent as much as white women. As a result of their faster progress, fully employed black women make 75 percent as much as fully employed black men while Hispanic women earn 68 percent as much as Hispanic men. 2

This faster progress may, however, end when minority women finally catch up with white women. In the bible of the New Right, George Gilder's *Wealth and Poverty,* the 60 percent is just one of Mother Nature's constants like the speed of light or the force of gravity. Men are programmed to provide for their families economically while women are programmed to take care of their families emotionally and physically. As a result men put more effort into their jobs than women. The net result is a difference in work intensity that leads to that 40 percent gap in earnings. But there is no discrimination against women—only the biological facts of life. 3

The problem with this assertion is just that. It is an assertion with no evidence for it other than the fact that white women have made 60 percent as much as men for a long period of time. 4

"Discrimination against women" is an easy answer but it also has its problems as an adequate explanation. Why is discrimination against women not declining under the same social forces that are leading to a lessening of discrimination against minorities? In recent years women have made more use of the enforcement provisions of the Equal Employment Opportunities Commission and the courts than minorities. Why do the laws that prohibit discrimination against women and minorities work for minorities but not for women? 5

When men discriminate against women, they run into a problem. To discriminate against women is to discriminate against your own wife and to lower your own family income. To prevent women from working is to force men to work more. 6

When whites discriminate against blacks, they can at least think that   7
they are raising their own incomes. When men discriminate against
women they have to know that they are lowering their own family income and increasing their own work effort.

While discrimination undoubtedly explains part of the male-female   8
earnings differential, one has to believe that men are monumentally stupid or irrational to explain all of the earnings gap in terms of discrimination. There must be something else going on.

Back in 1939 it was possible to attribute the earnings gap to large   9
differences in educational attainments. But the educational gap between
men and women has been eliminated since World War II. It is no longer
possible to use education as an explanation for the lower earnings of
women. Some observers have argued that women earn less money since
they are less reliable workers who are more apt to leave the labor force.
But it is difficult to maintain this position since women are less apt to quit
one job to take another and as a result they tend to work as long, or
longer, for any one employer. From any employer's perspective they are
more reliable, not less reliable, than men.

Part of the answer is visible if you look at the lifetime earnings   10
profile of men. Suppose that you were asked to predict which men in a
group of 25-year-olds would become economically successful. At age 25
it is difficult to tell who will be economically successful and your predictions are apt to be highly inaccurate. But suppose that you were asked to
predict which men in a group of 35-year-olds would become economically successful. If you are successful at age 35, you are very likely to
remain successful for the rest of your life. If you have not become economically successful by age 35, you are very unlikely to do so later.

The decade between 25 and 35 is when men either succeed or fail.   11
It is the decade when lawyers become partners in the good firms, when
business managers make it onto the "fast track," when academics get
tenure at good universities, and when blue collar workers find the job
opportunities that will lead to training opportunities and the skills that
will generate high earnings. If there is any one decade when it pays to
work hard and to be consistently in the labor force, it is the decade
between 25 and 35. For those who succeed, earnings will rise rapidly.
For those who fail, earnings will remain flat for the rest of their lives.

But the decade between 25 and 35 is precisely the decade when   12
women are most apt to leave the labor force or become part-time workers
to have children. When they do, the current system of promotion and
skill acquisition will extract an enormous lifetime price.

This leaves essentially two avenues for equalizing male and female   13
earnings. Families where women who wish to have successful careers,
compete with men, and achieve the same earnings should alter their
family plans and have their children either before 25 or after 35. Or

society can attempt to alter the existing promotion and skill acquisition system so that there is a longer time period in which both men and women can attempt to successfully enter the labor force. Without some combination of these two factors, a substantial fraction of the male-female earnings differentials are apt to persist for the next 40 years, even if discrimination against women is eliminated.

Questions for Analysis

Logic
1. What factors in the author's organization of his essay contribute to your sense of its rationality?
2. What part does history play in Thurow's reasoning to establish his claim?
3. What does Thurow see as lacking in the historical reasoning of his opponents?

Character
1. What sense of the author's character is created by knowing that he is the former dean of MIT's Sloan School of Management?
2. Where and how does the author appeal to his audience to see him as fair-minded?
3. Where and how does the author appeal to his audience to see him as reasonable and intelligent?

Emotion
1. How would you rate the emotional temperature of the argument as a whole? High? Moderate? Low? Point to some examples of style that confirm your view.
2. What emotions does the author generally seem to invite in his audience as a response to the explanations that he finds unsatisfactory? Explain.
3. With what tone of voice does the author describe the particular conclusions of George Gilder in paragraph 3? To what emotions in his audience does the tone appeal?

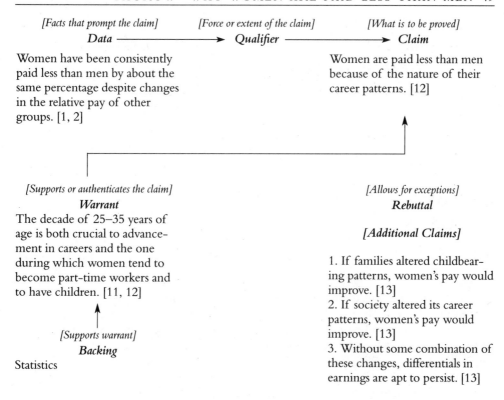

[Facts that prompt the claim]
Data ──────────→

[Force or extent of the claim]
Qualifier ──────────→

[What is to be proved]
Claim

Women have been consistently paid less than men by about the same percentage despite changes in the relative pay of other groups. [1, 2]

Women are paid less than men because of the nature of their career patterns. [12]

[Supports or authenticates the claim]
Warrant
The decade of 25–35 years of age is both crucial to advancement in careers and the one during which women tend to become part-time workers and to have children. [11, 12]

[Supports warrant]
Backing
Statistics

[Allows for exceptions]
Rebuttal

[Additional Claims]

1. If families altered childbearing patterns, women's pay would improve. [13]
2. If society altered its career patterns, women's pay would improve. [13]
3. Without some combination of these changes, differentials in earnings are apt to persist. [13]

EXERCISES: COMPARABLE WORTH AND PAY EQUITY FOR WOMEN

Intertextual Questions
1. Compare Walker's account of market forces with Kilpatrick's.
2. Compare Walker's view of career patterns with Thurow's.
3. Where and how might Kilpatrick and Thurow agree and disagree?

Suggestions for Writing
1. Pick the argument that you find least convincing and write an essay explaining why you find it so.
2. Write a letter as if from one of the authors to another that comments on the strengths and weaknesses of the third author's arguments.
3. Write an essay arguing your own views on comparable worth.

Should Rock Be Censored?

CURBING THE SEXPLOITATION INDUSTRY

Tipper Gore

I can't even count the times in the last three years, since I began to *1*
express my concern about violence and sexuality in rock music, that I
have been called a prude, a censor, a music hater, even a book burner. So
let me be perfectly clear: I detest censorship. I'm not advocating censorship but rather a candid and vigorous debate about the dangers posed for
our children by what I call the "exploitation industry."

We don't need to put a childproof cap on the world, but we do *2*
need to remind the nation that children live in it, too, and deserve respect
and sensitive treatment.

When I launched this campaign in 1985 (long before my husband *3*
dreamed of running for president), I went to the source of the problem,
sharing my concerns and proposals with the entertainment industry.
Many producers were sympathetic. Some cooperated with my efforts.
But others have been overtly hostile, accusing me of censorship and
suggesting, unfairly, that my motives are political.

This resistance and hostility has convinced me of the need for a *4*
two-pronged campaign, with equal effort from the entertainment industry and concerned parents. Entertainment producers must take the first
step, by labeling sexually explicit material.

But the industry cannot be expected to solve the problem on its *5*
own. Parents should encourage producers to cooperate and praise them
when they do. Producers need to know that parents are aware of the
issue and are reading their advisory labels. Above all, they need to know
that somebody out there cares, that the community at large is not apathetic about the deep and lasting damage being done to our children.

What's at issue is not the occasional sexy rock lyric. What trou- *6*
bles—indeed, outrages—me is far more vicious: a celebration of the

most gruesome violence, coupled with the explicit message that sado-masochism is the essence of sex.

We're surrounded by examples—in rock lyrics, on television, at the movies and in rental videos. One major TV network recently aired a preview of a soap opera rape scene during a morning game show. *7*

The newest craze in horror movies is something called the "teen slasher" film, and it typically depicts the killing, torture and sexual muti-lation of women in sickening detail. Several rock groups now simulate sexual torture and murder during live performances. Others titillate youthful audiences with strippers confined in cages on stage and with half-naked dancers, who often act out sex with band members. Sexual brutality has become the common currency of America's youth culture and with it the pervasive degradation of women. *8*

Why is this graphic violence dangerous? It's especially damaging for young children because they lack the moral judgment of adults. Many children are only dimly aware of the consequences of their actions, and, as parents know, they are excellent mimics. They often imitate violence they see on TV, without necessarily understanding what they are doing or what the consequences might be. *9*

One 5-year-old boy from Boston recently got up from watching a teen slasher film and stabbed a 2-year-old girl with a butcher knife. He didn't mean to kill her (and luckily he did not). He was just imitating the man in the video. *10*

Nor does the danger end as children grow older. National health officials tell us that children younger than teen-agers are apt to react to excessive violence with suicide, satanism, drug and alcohol abuse. Even grown-ups are not immune. One series of studies by researchers at the University of Wisconsin found that men exposed to films in which women are beaten, butchered, maimed and raped were significantly de-sensitized to the violence. Not only did they express less sympathy for the victims, they even approved of lesser penalties in hypothetical rape trials. *11*

Sado-masochistic pornography is a kind of poison. Like most poi-sons, it probably cannot be totally eliminated, but it certainly could be labeled for what it is and be kept away from those who are most vulnerable. *12*

The largest record companies have agreed to this—in principle at least. In November 1985, the Recording Industry Association of Amer-ica adopted my proposal to alert parents by having producers either put warning labels on records with explicitly sexual lyrics or display the lyrics on the outside of the record jackets. Since then, some companies have complied in good faith, although others have not complied at all. *13*

This is where we parents must step in. We must let the industry know we're angry. We must press for uniform voluntary compliance with labeling guidelines. And we must take an active interest at home in what *14*

our children are watching and listening to. After all, we can hardly expect
that the labels or printed lyrics alone will discourage young consumers.

Some parents may want to write to the record companies. Others   *15*
can give their support to groups like the Parent Teacher Association,
which have endorsed the labeling idea. All of us can use our purchasing
power. We have more power than we think, and we must use it. For the
sake of our children, we simply can't afford to slip back into apathy.

My concern for the health and welfare of children has nothing to   *16*
do with politics: It is addressed to conservatives and liberals alike. Some
civil libertarians believe it is wrong even to raise these questions—just as
some conservatives believe that the government should police popular
American culture. I reject both these views. I have no desire to restrain
artists or cast a "chill" over popular culture. But I believe parents have
First Amendment rights, too.

The fate of the family, the dignity of women, the mental health of   *17*
children—these concerns belong to everyone. We must protect our children with choice, not censorship. Let's start working in our communities
to forge a moral consensus for the 1990s. Children need our help, and we
must summon the courage to examine the culture that shapes their lives.

Questions for Analysis

Logic
1. Explain some of the ways in which you think the organization of
   Gore's essay does or does not support her argument.
2. According to Gore, what is the reasoning of those who oppose her
   efforts "with hostility"? How does she attempt to refute the arguments
   of her opponents through an appeal to reason?
3. Gore says that her concern has nothing to do with politics. Explain
   how she attempts to prove this claim through an appeal to reason.

Character
1. In her argument Gore sometimes uses *I* and sometimes *we*. Describe
   the identities implied in each case that give substance to the appeal by
   character of her essay. For example, how does her having begun her
   campaign before her husband entered presidential politics affect your
   sense of her character in this essay?
2. In paragraph 1 Gore says that her character has been called that of "a
   prude, a censor, a music hater, even a book burner." Pick one label
   and show how Gore works to refute the charge by creating a sense of
   her character in the essay.
3. In paragraph 15 Gore decries "apathy" in the face of the issue. Describe some ways in which she creates a sense of her own character as
   one that is not apathetic.

Emotion

1. In paragraph 2 Gore speaks of a "childproof cap" and in paragraph 12 of "poison." Compare the ways in which these related metaphors create different emotional appeals.
2. Describe some of the ways in which Gore uses language to create an appeal to emotion in her description of "teen slasher" films beginning in paragraph 8.
3. Gore speaks of "outrage" in paragraph 6 and of "anger" in paragraph 14. What might Gore reply to someone who thought she did not *sound* outraged or angry in her essay?

ROMANTIC ROT

Charlene Choy

Oliver Wendell Holmes drew a sensible line as a limit for free speech when he said that the U.S. Constitution did not protect the right falsely to shout "Fire" in a crowded theater. Yet every day the crowded theaters of immature emotions within our nation's children are perversely panicked by the young fools who perform within the music business and the old knaves who own it. Neither party cares about freedom in any form or about anything but fame and money—they raise the issues of "free speech" and "artistic censorship" in complete bad faith.

The performers—Kiss and W.A.S.P. are two pioneering examples—all want to be as famous as The Beatles but find themselves not nearly as good as poets or musicians. Lacking these talents does not, of course, make them stupid. With the knowledge all Romantic artists inherit as birthright from their spiritual ancestor, Jean Jacques Rousseau, they know that "If I can't be better than everyone else at least I can be different!" Romantic artists want especially to be different from the hated "Society" of whose history, real constitution, and precarious existence they know next to nothing. But they do know the difference between what ordinary people consider right and wrong, and so it is here they focus their ambitions to be different by making wrong into right within the crude fantasies of what are still called lyrics.

Suicide, sadism, incest, bestiality—you name it and they'll scream about it to musical accompaniment. Violence (safely offered from the locked recording studio) to "Society's" representatives like parents and the police also makes a common and easy pose of difference through rebellion—though the rebels will run to the protection of Society's legal system when even the mildest of verbal attacks are made on them. Of course, far from rebelling, what they actually want is to get the ear of those who really represent the materialism and exploitation that the performers pretend to hate in "Society"—I am talking about the owners of the multibillion-dollar music business.

These are the people who don't care whether they exploit the saccharine sweetness of Minnie Mouse and her shy affection for Mickey or the raunchiest refrain of Prince's "Darling Nikki" and her masturbatory salute to him. The only difference the profiteers care about is the difference in their profits from last quarter's—and that difference had better be defined as an increase.

Meanwhile, teens and preteens are robbed of the tender pleasures of traditional reveries about true romance—robbed by the brutalities that have replaced the "Moon/June/Croon" lyrics of a hundred years ago. New groups must make their "difference" apparent by being even more revolting. Radio stations and record companies want to thrive by becoming as "different" as the FCC will let them. Thank God the FCC is finally beginning to act like adults and has gone after the arch-romantic Howard Stern. They should enforce the same standards of decency in the national media that parents would enforce on the entertainment they allow to enter their homes—if the electronic age would let any private person do that with any consistency. Since the FCC is responsible for the airwaves, it is up to them to be responsible to the parents. Free speech is in no conceivable trouble in our country—it's the freedom not to have to listen that we need to worry about.

Questions for Analysis

Logic
1. Choy might generally agree with Gore's arguments in the previous essay, but she seems to want to go even further. What seems to be her implicit reasoning for wanting to do so?
2. Choy does not explicitly define *Romanticism*. What methods of definition does she employ concerning this key term in her essay?
3. What does Choy find lacking in the reasoning of the performers and owners she opposes?

Character
1. How would you best describe the tone of voice Choy uses in her essay to express her attitude toward what she opposes? Outrage? Contempt? Shock? Pick a representative moment in the essay and describe its tone of voice more fully.
2. What tone does Choy employ in urging her audience to agree with her call for action? Again pick an example and describe its effects.
3. Where and how does Choy make implicit claims for her own expertise on the subject of music in particular and art in general?

Emotion
1. To what emotions in her audience does Choy appeal by the topics she uses to exemplify the lyrics she opposes?
2. To what emotions does Choy appeal by lumping suicide with other subjects of rock lyrics?
3. To what emotions does she appeal in her use of financial issues?

RAISED ON ROCK-AND-ROLL

Anna Quindlen

Mister Ed is back on television, indicating that, as most middle-of-the-road antique shops suggest, Americans cannot discriminate between things worth saving and things that simply exist. *The Donna Reed Show* is on, too, and *My Three Sons,* and those dopey folks from *Gilligan's Island.* There's *Leave It to Beaver* and *The Beverly Hillbillies* and even *Lassie,* whose plaintive theme song leaves my husband all mushy around the edges.

Social historians say these images, and those of Howdy Doody and Pinky Lee and Lamb Chop and Annette have forever shaped my consciousness. But I have memories far stronger than that. I remember sitting cross-legged in front of the tube, one of the console sets with the ersatz lamé netting over the speakers, but I was not watching puppets or pratfalls. I was born in Philadelphia, a city where if you can't dance you might as well stay home, and I was raised on rock-and-roll. My earliest television memory is of *American Bandstand,* and the central question of my childhood was: Can you dance to it?

When I was fifteen and a wild devotee of Mitch Ryder and the Detroit Wheels, it sometimes crossed my mind that when I was thirty-four years old, decrepit, wrinkled as a prune and near death, I would have moved on to some nameless kind of dreadful show music, something akin to Muzak. I did not think about the fact that my parents were still listening to the music that had been popular when they were kids; I only thought that they played "Pennsylvania 6-5000" to torment me and keep my friends away from the house.

But I know now that I'm never going to stop loving rock-and-roll, all kinds of rock-and-roll: the Beatles, the Rolling Stones, Hall and Oates, Talking Heads, the Doors, the Supremes, Tina Turner, Elvis Costello, Elvis Presley. I even like really bad rock-and-roll, although I guess that's where my age shows; I don't have the tolerance for Bon Jovi that I once had for the Raspberries.

We have friends who, when their son was a baby, used to put a   5
record on and say, "Drop your butt, Phillip." And Phillip did. That's what
I love: drop-your-butt music. It's one of the few things left in my life that
makes me feel good without even thinking about it. I can walk into any
bookstore and find dozens of books about motherhood and love and
human relations and so many other things that we once did through a
combination of intuition and emotion. I even heard recently that some
school is giving a course on kissing, which makes me wonder if I'm
missing something. But rock-and-roll flows through my veins, not my
brain. There's nothing else that feels the same to me as, say, the faint
sound of the opening dum-doo-doo-doo-doo-doo of "My Girl" coming from a radio on a summer day. I feel the way I felt when I first heard
it. I feel good, as James Brown says.

There are lots of people who don't feel this way about rock-and-   6
roll. Some of them don't understand it, like the Senate wives who said
that records should have rating stickers on them so that you would know
whether the lyrics were dirty. The kids who hang out at Mr. Big's sub
shop in my neighborhood thought this would make record shopping a
lot easier, because you could choose albums by how bad the rating was.
Most of the people who love rock-and-roll just thought the labeling idea
was dumb. Lyrics, after all, are not the point of rock-and-roll, despite
how beautifully people like Bruce Springsteen and Joni Mitchell write.
Lyrics are the point only in the case of "Louie, Louie"; the words have
never been deciphered, but it is widely understood that they are about
sex. That's understandable, because rock-and-roll is a lot like sex: If you
talk seriously about it, it takes a lot of the feeling away—and feeling is
the point.

Some people over-analyze rock-and-roll, just as they over-analyze   7
everything else. They say things like "Bruce Springsteen is the poet lau-
reate of the American dream gone sour," when all I need to know about
Bruce Springsteen is that the saxophone bridge on "Jungleland" makes
the back of my neck feel exactly the same way I felt the first time a boy
kissed me, only over and over and over again. People write about Prince's
"psychedelic masturbatory fantasies," but when I think about Prince, I
don't really think, I just feel—feel the moment when, driving to the
beach, I first heard "Kiss" on the radio and started bopping up and down
in my seat like a seventeen-year-old on a day trip.

I've got precious few things in my life anymore that just make me   8
feel, that make me jump up and dance, that make me forget the schedule
and the job and the mortgage payments and just let me thrash around
inside my skin. I've got precious few things I haven't studied and considered and reconsidered and studied some more. I don't know a chord
change from a snare drum, but I know what I like, and I like feeling this

way sometimes. I love rock-and-roll because in a time of talk, talk, talk, it's about action.

Here's a test: Get hold of a two-year-old, a person who has never 9 read a single word about how heavy-metal musicians should be put in jail or about Tina Turner's "throaty alto range." Put "I Heard It Through the Grapevine" on the stereo. Stand the two-year-old in front of the stereo. The two-year-old will begin to dance. The two-year-old will drop his butt. Enough said.

Questions for Analysis

Logic
1. Is the rebuttal as diagramed intended seriously by Quindlen or only as a joke? Explain.
2. How does Quindlen implicitly meet the charge that some lyrics are obscene?
3. Do you think Quindlen effectively uses logic to deny the importance of logic in the case of her subject? Exemplify and explain.

Character
1. What appeal through character does Quindlen make by means of the anecdotes of her childhood in the beginning of the essay?
2. Given that her argument is based on emotion, does Quindlen employ any techniques to establish that intelligence and thought are also parts of her character? Explain.
3. What efforts does Quindlen make to establish a personality that seems sympathetic to other generations and experiences than her own?

Emotion
1. What emotions in her audience does Quindlen appeal to with the account of her youthful imagination of her life in her thirties?
2. What images does Quindlen create to express her own emotions on listening to rock? How does she suggest that these are widely shared?
3. What emotions does the author invite her reader to feel about people who analyze lyrics? How does she invite these feelings?

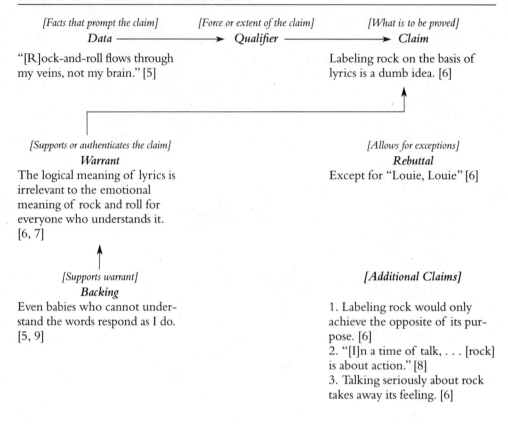

[Facts that prompt the claim]
Data ————————→

"[R]ock-and-roll flows through
my veins, not my brain." [5]

[Force or extent of the claim]
Qualifier ————————→

[What is to be proved]
Claim

Labeling rock on the basis of
lyrics is a dumb idea. [6]

[Supports or authenticates the claim]
Warrant
The logical meaning of lyrics is
irrelevant to the emotional
meaning of rock and roll for
everyone who understands it.
[6, 7]

[Allows for exceptions]
Rebuttal
Except for "Louie, Louie" [6]

[Supports warrant]
Backing
Even babies who cannot understand the words respond as I do.
[5, 9]

[Additional Claims]

1. Labeling rock would only
achieve the opposite of its purpose. [6]
2. "[I]n a time of talk, . . . [rock]
is about action." [8]
3. Talking seriously about rock
takes away its feeling. [6]

EXERCISES: SHOULD ROCK BE CENSORED?

Intertextual Questions
1. What issues do Gore, Choy, and Quindlen agree on? On what do they
   disagree? Make two lists.
2. What is the difference between the kind of good that Choy allows
   can come from rock and the kind that Quindlen claims?
3. In what differing ways does each writer attempt to express a sense of
   her characters that implies a serious concern with the topic at hand?

Suggestions for Writing
1. Write a letter from Gore or Choy to Quindlen that attempts to refute
   the latter's views.
2. Do the same in a letter from Quindlen to Choy or Mann.
3. Write an essay that argues for your own point of view on the issue of
   rock censorship, being sure to take into account in some way (if only
   to refute them) the arguments of the writers here.

MOST OPPOSE WOMEN IN COMBAT

Suzanne Fields

A famous Bill Mauldin cartoon from World War II puts Willie and   *1*
Joe in their familiar foxhole, muddy, stinking, wet, cold and filthy. Willie
turns to Joe and asks poignantly: "Why weren't you born a beautiful girl?"

It isn't hilarious, but it's funny. Or it was way back then, reflecting   *2*
the fundamental yearnings of men at war. But today this cartoon is not
only sexist, but scary. Willie might get his wish.

The President's Commission on the Assignment of Women in the   *3*
Armed Forces recommended against women entering combat on land
and in the air, but they recommended that female sailors serve on certain
combat ships, such as aircraft carriers and destroyers.

The fight over whether women should be allowed to enter military   *4*
combat is about to move toward resolution.

Both President George Bush and President-elect Bill Clinton have   *5*
said they would not express their own views until they see the report, but
pressure on Congress to overrule the commission will be fierce.

The commission vote was close, 8 to 7 opposing women flying   *6*
combat planes, a prohibition that Congress repealed only last year. The
votes against women in ground combat was by a larger margin. But the
logic of the majority is irrefutable. Women in combat would interfere
with male "bonding," undercut military readiness and cause sexual confusion on the battlefield, making men vulnerable to the ancient male
instinct to protect women in danger.

The commission heard testimony from prisoners of war that   *7*
women taken prisoner could expect to be routinely abused and tortured
in a way that a man would not, and that such torture would be used to
break men who were forced to witness it. (The military now tries to
"desensitize" men to female suffering.)

"The idea that we would position women in the arena of being   *8*
subjected to violence, death, depravity as prisoners is one I won't sign up

to," said retired Army Gen. Maxwell Thurman, who commanded the U.S. assault on Panama and who was one of the eight commissioners voting against women as combat aviators.

A Roper poll of 4,500 American fighting men found that 57 per- 9 cent oppose women in combat. These men cited the many cases of sexual fun and games between male and female troops in Operation Desert Storm. (Surprise. Surprise.)

Women are held to different (i.e., lower) physical standards in train- 10 ing and they aren't expected to do the same heavy lifting as men, because they can't. Women lack the upper body strength.

Fighter pilots, soldiers and Marines who don't want women in 11 combat deserve to be listened to closely because their lives will be the ones most affected by the change. The commission concluded that even the most physically fit women rarely exceed the physical fitness of merely average men. (At West Point running groups are often determined by sex, so that women can run in slower units and not be outpaced or embarrassed by faster men.)

While combat readiness is the major issue, the social and psycholog- 12 ical consequences—the cultural consequences—of women in combat are equally important.

Do we want to teach women to kill? Do we want to teach the 13 mothers of our children to kill? Do we want to take mothers away from their children to kill? Do we want to desensitize our male soldiers to female suffering? Do wives back home want women in their husband's foxhole?

"I've seen men freeze, cry and go mad at the sight of war," one 14 Marine combat veteran of Vietnam tells me. "Only women who have never seen its horror would ask to be entitled to kill. Why on earth do they want to?"

Why on earth? 15

Questions for Analysis

Logic
1. In what ways does Fields use the cartoon she describes in the begin-ning to support her reasoning at different points in the essay?
2. How does the placement of Fields's rhetorical questions affect the strength of her argument? Suppose that the questions of paragraph 13 had begun the essay. In your opinion would that different organization make the essay stronger or weaker? Explain.
3. Fields addresses both "cultural" and combat issues. In what ways does her anecdote in paragraph 14 seek to support her reasoning in both cases?

Character
1. Fields begins with a joke. In what ways does she work to create a sense of her character as one who takes the issues of the essay seriously?
2. In what ways does Fields attempt to connect her views to those of publicly acknowledged authorities?
3. When authorities disagree with her (e.g., the minority vote in paragraph 6), how does Fields's argument implicitly work to refute their views?

Emotion
1. What emotions does Fields appeal to with regard to male soldiers in combat? Pick an example and explain how the emotional appeal operates.
2. What emotions does Fields appeal to with regard to women soldiers in combat? Pick an example and explain how the emotional appeal operates.
3. How would you describe the emotions Fields herself expresses at the end of her essay? Horror? Exasperation? Disdain? Explain the mixture of emotions and how they are created.

AN OFFICER AND A FEMINIST

James M. Dubik

I'm a member of a last bastion of male chauvinism. I'm an infantry   1
officer, and there are no women in the infantry. I'm a Ranger and no women go to Ranger School. I'm a member of America's special-operation forces—and there, although women are involved in intelligence, planning and clerical work, only men can be operators, or "shooters." Women can become paratroopers and jump out of airplanes alongside me—yet not many do. All this is as it should be, according to what I learned while growing up.

Not many women I knew in high school and college in the 60s and   2
early 70s pushed themselves to their physical or mental limits or had serious career dreams of their own. If they did, few talked about them. So I concluded they were exceptions to the rule. Then two things happened. First, I was assigned to West Point, where I became a philosophy instructor. Second, my two daughters grew up.

I arrived at the Academy with a master's degree from Johns Hopkins   3
University in Baltimore and a graduation certificate from the U.S. Army

Command and General Staff College at Fort Leavenworth. I was ready to teach, but instead, I was the one who got an education.

The women cadets, in the classroom and out, did not fit my stereo- 4 type of female behavior. They took themselves and their futures seriously. They persevered in a very competitive environment. Often they took charge and seized control of a situation. They gave orders; they were punctual and organized. They played sports hard. They survived, even thrived, under real pressure. During field exercises, women cadets were calm and unemotional even when they were dirty, cold, wet, tired and hungry. They didn't fold or give up.

Most important, such conduct seemed natural to them. From my 5 perspective all this was extraordinary; to them it was ordinary. While I had read a good bit of "feminist literature" and, intellectually, accepted many of the arguments against stereotyping, this was the first time my real-life experience supported such ideas. And seeing is believing.

Enter two daughters: Kerith, 12; Katie, 10. 6

Kerith and Katie read a lot, and they write, too—poems, stories, 7 paragraphs and answers to "thought questions" in school. In what they read and in what they write, I can see their adventurousness, their inquisitiveness and their ambition. They discover clues and solve mysteries. They take risks, brave dangers, fight villains—and prevail. Their schoolwork reveals their pride in themselves. Their taste for reading is boundless; they're interested in everything. "Why?" is forever on their lips. Their eyes are set on personal goals that they, as individuals, aspire to achieve: Olympic gold, owning their own business, public office.

Both play sports. I've witnessed a wholesome, aggressive, competi- 8 tive spirit born in Kerith. She played her first basketball season last year, and when she started, she was too polite to bump anyone, too nice to steal anything, especially if some other girl already had the ball. By the end of the season, however, Kerith was taking bumps and dishing them out. She plays softball with the intensity of a Baltimore Oriole. She rides and jumps her horse in competitive shows. Now she "can't imagine" not playing a sport, especially one that didn't have a little rough play and risk.

In Katie's face, I've seen Olympic intensity as she passed a runner in 9 the last 50 yards of a mile relay. Gasping for air, knees shaking, lungs bursting, she dipped into her well of courage and "gutted out" a final kick. Her comment after the race: "I kept thinking I was Mary Decker beating the Russians." For the first time she experienced the thrill of pushing herself to the limit. She rides and jumps, too. And her basketball team was a tournament champion. The joy and excitement and pride that shone in the eyes of each member of the team was equal to that in any NCAA winner's locker room. To each sport Katie brings her dedication to doing her best, her drive to excel and her desire to win.

Both girls are learning lessons that, when my wife and I were their age, were encouraged only in boys. Fame, aggressiveness, achievement, self-confidence—these were territories into which very few women (the exception, not the rule) dared enter. Kerith and Katie, most of their friends, many of their generation and the generations to come are redefining the social game. Their lives contradict the stereotypes with which I grew up. Many of the characteristics I thought were "male" are, in fact, "human." Given a chance, anyone can, and will, acquire them. *10*

My daughters and the girls of their generation are lucky. They receive a lot of institutional support not available to women of past generations: from women executives, women athletes, women authors, women politicians, women adventurers, women Olympians. Old categories, old stereotypes and old territories don't fit the current generation of young women; and they won't fit the next generation, either. As Kerith said, "I can't even imagine not being allowed to do something or be something just because I am a girl." *11*

All this does not negate what I knew to be true during my own high-school and college years. But what I've learned from both the women cadets at West Point and from my daughters supports a different conclusion about today's women and the women of tomorrow from the beliefs I was raised with. Ultimately we will be compelled to align our social and political institutions with what is already becoming a fact of American life. Or more precisely, whenever biological difference is used to segregate a person from an area of human endeavor, we will be required to demonstrate that biological difference is relevant to the issue at hand. *12*

Questions for Analysis

Logic
1. Explain some of the ways in which Dubik uses the theme of "past and present" to organize the reasoning of his argument.
2. Is there any necessary logical contradiction between the first sentence of paragraph 12 and the rest of Dubik's essay? Explain.
3. Is there any necessary logical contradiction between the "institutions" imagined in paragraph 11 and those imagined in paragraph 12?

Character
1. In the first paragraph, what sense of Dubik's character is created by the ways in which his credentials interact with his title?
2. How do the nonmilitary credentials of paragraph 3 affect your sense of Dubik's character?
3. What aspect of character is suggested by the tone of voice Dubik partly creates by beginning the vast majority of his sentences with

their subject? Compare a representative paragraph to paragraph 5 where Dubik's sentence openers are more varied. Do you hear a different tone of voice there?

Emotion
1. What are the different emotional appeals of the two synonyms *operators* and *shooters* in paragraph 1?
2. When he observed the women cadets during field exercises [paragraph 4] what emotions do you imagine Dubik felt? What emotions does he invite you to feel, and how would those emotions help in his effort to persuade?
3. In paragraph 9, what emotions do you imagine Dubik feels? Which of them does he invite you to feel, and how is his argument advanced by such an appeal?

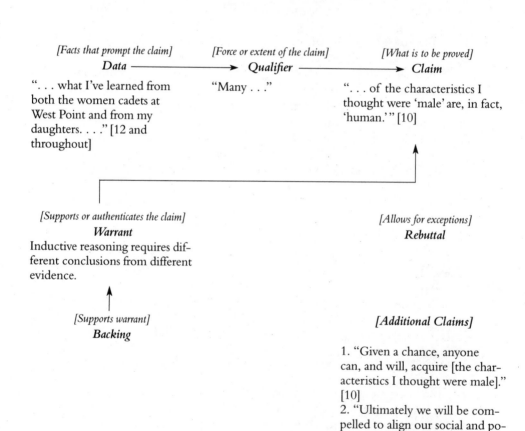

ARMS AND THE WOMAN
Would a Sexually Mixed U.S. Army Lose Its Wars?

Lou Marano

In the weeks since American women soldiers fought alongside men   *1*
in Panama, a consensus has begun to emerge that women should be
allowed to serve in combat units if they want to. A recent New York
Times/CBS News poll says that seven out of 10 Americans now hold
this view.

I respect and admire women who want to serve, but I believe an   *2*
expanded role for women in the U.S. armed forces is a demonstrably
bad idea.

Mine is an unusual perspective. I am a Vietnam veteran, a social   *3*
scientist and a journalist who has done some reporting on the military. In
1967 and 1968 I was a junior officer in a Seabee battalion that provided
construction support to the 3rd Marine Division near the demilitarized
zone separating the two Vietnams. Until 1984, I was an anthropology
professor who tried to teach his students to understand why cultures
develop the way they do, and that history is not just the story of one
damn thing after another.

The simple truth is this: However well one woman (or 1,000   *4*
women) may have performed in a firefight in Panama, it does not change
the fact that men—as a group—fight better than women. This fact is as
unremarkable (and as unsexist) as saying that young men usually make
better soldiers than do men who are no longer young. All other things
being equal, an army whose average age is 26 will beat an army whose
average age is 46. All other things being equal, an army of men will beat
an army of women. All other things being equal, a society that puts
women in the field at the expense of fielding a like number of men will
lose its wars.

Of course, all other things are never equal. This is why the United   *5*
States can probably get away for a long time with its policy of using an
increasing number of women volunteers to make up for the men who
fail to enlist or for Congress's failure to conscript them. Diminishing East-
West tensions make a major war seem less likely. Defense cuts, including
cuts in personnel, appear inevitable. Since our forces will be smaller anyway, why not let motivated women do as much of the job as they can
handle? Isn't it unfair to exclude military women from the most career-
enhancing assignments?

Different things are at stake in the short and long terms. I taught   *6*
my anthropology students that taboos (such as the incest taboo) evolve

when the benefits of a contemplated action are immediate and obvious but the costs are veiled and postponed. For untold millennia, every society of which I am aware has had a taboo against sending women to fight while able-bodied men were still available. Now we are on the verge of violating this taboo. Before we embrace the violation as our national policy, we should try to consider the consequences.

The short-term benefits are clear. Americans prize autonomy of the individual. That's what we fought for in past wars, isn't it? Women now make up almost 11 percent of the armed forces. Why exclude them from combat only to replace them with men less eager? The United States may be entering an era of brushfire wars and relatively small regional conflicts that present no immediate threat to the survival of the nation. America is still a vast, rich country that will continue to hold a huge advantage in resources, population and technology over any probable combination of enemies. Under these circumstances an expanded military role for women could cause serious problems, perhaps even defeat, but would not result in the conquest of the United States by foreign powers. 7

The long-term costs are hidden but deadly. One way to think about these costs is to consider the "law of the minimum," propounded by Justus von Liebig, a 19th-century German chemist and a pioneer in agricultural research. He discovered that plant growth is limited if one necessary factor is unavailable—even if all the other factors are available in abundance. Applied to human societies, Liebig's "law of the minimum" suggests that survival is not geared to coping with good conditions, or even to average conditions, but to an ability to get through the worst crises. 8

Militarily, that worst crisis is total war, which has come to the world twice in this century. Both times America got off easy in the expenditures of one necessary factor—manpower. 9

Unlike Europe, the United States never fully mobilized its population for military service. Even during World War II, we didn't push up against Liebig's law of the minimum. On Sept. 20, 1943, Gen. George C. Marshall testified before the Senate against a bill that would have deferred from the draft men who were fathers before Pearl Harbor. Similar bills would have been laughed out of the legislatures of the European powers. 10

Take a look at photographs of soldiers in the European armies of both world wars. You will see faces of many older men, many of them fathers. Still, they did not draft women. And with the exception of the Soviet Union, which ran out of men in World War II, they didn't push women toward combat. There are two good reasons for this: Men generally fight better than women, and men generally fight better when women aren't around. 11

A misunderstanding of the Israeli example clouds the issue. Contrary to popular belief, Israel does not conscript women to fight—and certainly not so that able-bodied men can be excused from military service—but to free men to fight in combat units. Israelis I've talked to think that the U.S. trend of pushing women toward combat to take the place of men who stay home is folly.

It is often said that modern technology has erased the physical advantage men have brought to war. This is fantasy. It is not even true in support units. I recall several occasions in Vietnam when I grew faint after manhandling (good word, that) ammunition crates or sandbags for hours in the blinding heat. The point is not that some women could have done better; it is that most women could not have done as well.

It is also said that sexual distraction in military life is an issue only for relics like me, and that today's more enlightened generation of young men develop nothing but brotherly affection for their female "buddies." Not only does this go against all experience and common sense, but I found it to be false when reporting on U.S. forces deployed to the mountains of Honduras in 1988. While frustration, heartbreak and jealousy did not seem to be problems for the Army reservists and National Guard members who came into the camp and returned to the United States after a few weeks, they certainly were present among the sexually mixed camp cadre, who had to live with each other for almost a year. Human nature doesn't change, and we are asking for trouble by pretending it has.

It was drilled into my head when I was on active duty that the mission came first and the welfare of the people I led came second. Aren't those who demand equal opportunity for women in combat violating that most basic principle of military leadership? What's good for individual careers isn't necessarily good for the country. The mission of the armed forces is to win wars, not under the best conditions or average conditions but with a margin for error under worse conditions than can be imagined. In a crisis, the country that puts women in the field at the expense of men will lose. Meeting such a crisis successfully is never easy, and it may become impossible if our culture changes to the point where American men are no longer embarrassed to have women do their fighting for them.

During just a few months in 1914, the small, professional British army, which had sustained the world's largest empire for a century, was all but swept away by the tides of continental war. The same thing could happen to us, if not in one year or 10, then in 100. Under those conditions, the issue will no longer be who has the right to fight, but who can be compelled to fight. The British responded by sending pretty girls into the streets, where they would pass out a white feather—a symbol of cowardice—to any young man they saw who was not in uniform. In his book "The Myth of the Monstrous Male," John Gordon recounts the story of a society lady meeting an Edwardian dandy during World War I and demanding to know why he wasn't with the boys fighting in France. "Madame," he is reported to have replied, "I am the civilization which they are dying to defend."

What will happen to us when men like that are not the outrageous and memorable exception but the accepted norm, and half of those dying to defend them are women?   *17*

Questions for Analysis

Logic

1. Explain the part in his argument played by Marano's admission that small-scale wars could be lost without disaster to the nation [7]. Does it diminish the force of his main claim? Enhance it?
2. Explain in your own words "Liebig's law of the minimum." Do you agree that its logic applies to human affairs? Explain.
3. How does the anecdote of exhaustion in paragraph 13 attempt to refute the logic of Marano's imagined opponents?

Character

1. Does anything in the essay contradict Marano's statement in paragraph 2 that "I respect and admire women who want to serve"? Explain.
2. How do the various credentials listed in paragraph 3 contribute to our sense of Marano's expertise on the issue?
3. How would you characterize the tone of voice in which Marano argues? How does it compare with Dubik's? With Fields's?

Emotion

1. What emotions does Marano appeal to in paragraph 15 and how might they advance his argument?
2. What emotions does Marano appeal to by using the anecdote with which he ends the essay, and how might they advance his argument?
3. What emotions does Marano see as being mobilized by his opponents, and how does he attempt to answer their emotional appeal?

EXERCISES: WOMEN IN COMBAT

Intertextual Questions

1. Explain some ways in which Fields agrees and disagrees with the other authors. For example, what do you think she might reply to Dubik's contention about what is becoming "a fact" of American life in his paragraph 12?

2. List the points concerning women in combat that Dubik and Marano agree on. What do these points have in common with one another? Are they all, for example, concerned with justice or fairness?
3. With which author's ideas and assumptions about "human nature" do you most agree? Explain.

Suggestions for Writing
1. Write a letter as though from Fields or Marano to Dubik's daughters in which you make clear both admiration for and disagreement with their views.
2. Write an essay that analyzes and exemplifies the contrasting views of human nature held by any two authors in the unit. Be sure to analyze their appeals to logic, character, and emotion in this regard.
3. Write an essay in which you argue for your own position on the issue of women in combat, being sure to answer any of the views expressed in the unit that oppose your own.

Is It Right to Identify AIDS Victims?

ON AIDS AND MORAL DUTY

Willard Gaylin

Potential AIDS victims who refuse to be tested for the disease and 1 then defend their right to remain ignorant about whether they carry the virus are entitled to that right. But ignorance cannot be used to rationalize irresponsibility. Nowhere in their argument is there concern about how such ignorance might endanger public health by exposing others to the virus.

All disease is an outrage, and disease that affects the young and 2 healthy seems particularly outrageous. When a disease selectively attacks the socially disadvantaged, such as homosexuals and drug abusers, it seems an injustice beyond rationalization. Such is the case with acquired immune deficiency syndrome.

Decent people are offended by this unfairness and in the name of 3 benevolence have been driven to do morally irresponsible things such as denying the unpleasant facts of the disease, out of compassion for the victims. We cannot fudge the facts to comfort the afflicted when such obfuscation compounds the tragedy.

Some crucial facts: AIDS is a communicable disease. The per- 4 centage of those infected with the AIDS virus who will eventually contract the disease is unknown, but that percentage rises with each new estimate. The disease so far has been 100 percent fatal. The latency period between the time the virus is acquired and the disease develops is also unknown.

We now have tests for the presence of the virus that are as efficient 5 and reliable as almost any diagnostic test in medicine. An individual who tests positive can be presumed with near-certainty to carry the virus, whether he has the disease or not.

To state that the test for AIDS is "ambiguous," as a clergyman re- 6 cently said in public, is a misstatement and an immoral act. To state that the test does not directly indicate the presence of the virus is a half-truth

70

that misleads and an immoral act. The test correlates so consistently with the presence of the virus in bacteria cultures as to be considered 100 percent certain by experts.

Everyone who tests positive must understand that he is a potential *7* vector for the AIDS virus and has a moral duty and responsibility to protect others from contamination. We need not force everyone in high-risk populations to take the test. There is no treatment for the disease. Therefore, to insist on testing serves no therapeutic purpose.

Certainly there are those who would prefer ambiguity to certitude. *8* However, a person who is at risk and refuses to have himself tested must behave as though he had been tested and found positive. To do otherwise is cowardice compounding hypocrisy with wrongdoing.

Surely an individual has a right to spare himself the agony of *9* knowledge if he prefers wishful thinking to certitude. He must not use his desire for hope as an excuse for denial.

We have a duty to protect the innocent and the unborn. Voluntary *10* premarital testing for AIDS is a protection for both partners and for the uncontaminated and unborn children. We know that AIDS is transmissible from male to female, from female to male, from parent to conceived child. We are dealing not just with the protection of the innocent but with an essential step to contain the spread of an epidemic as tragic and as horrible as any that has befallen modern man. We must do everything in our power to keep this still untreatable disease from becoming pandemic.

It may seem unfair to burden the tragic victims with concern for *11* the welfare of others. But moral responsibility is not a luxury of the fortunate, and evil actions perpetrated in despair cannot be condoned out of pity. It is morally wrong for a healthy individual who tests positive for AIDS to be involved with anyone except under the strictest precautions now defined as safe sex.

It is morally wrong for someone in a high risk population who *12* refuses to test himself to do other than to assume that he tests positively. It is morally wrong for those who, out of sympathy for the heartbreaking victims of this epidemic, act as though well-wishing and platitudes about the ambiguities of the disease are necessary in order to comfort the victims while they contribute to enlarging the number of those victims. Moral responsibility is the burden of the sick as well as the healthy.

Questions for Analysis

Logic
1. Explain in your own words the logic of the opponents whom Gaylin argues against.

2. Explain Gaylin's logic in refutation of his opponents.
3. Gaylin seems quite certain about all the things he speaks of as moral matters. Which of these matters is, in your view, *least* supported by an appeal to reason? Explain your answer.

Character

1. Gaylin's style in his statements on moral matters relies heavily on the verb *to be* (*is, are,* etc.). What sense of his character does this aspect of his style create for you?
2. What sense of Gaylin's capacity for fair-mindedness is created for you by the ways in which he expresses his attitudes toward the individuals who are carriers of the virus? Pick an example and show how particular uses of language work in this regard.
3. What aspects of Gaylin's character are revealed by the ways in which he treats opposing arguments in the essay?

Emotion

1. In paragraph 2, what emotions in his audience are appealed to when the author says that "all disease is an outrage"?
2. What emotions in his audience are appealed to when Gaylin describes as "decent people" some of those whose "morally irresponsible" action he opposes?
3. To what emotions does the author appeal in his final paragraph when he calls moral responsibility a "burden" rather than, say, "a glorious and noble quality in human beings"?

DISCRIMINATION GOES ON

Robert H. Cohen

To the Editor:

"Dr. Joseph and AIDS Testing" (editorial, November 16) supports   *1* the call by Dr. Stephen Joseph, New York City's departing health commissioner, for tracing the sexual contacts of those who test positive for the human immunodeficiency virus, apparently in the belief that discrimination is no longer a problem.

Unfortunately, discrimination against HIV-infected people is real.   *2* Beyond press reports, I know people who have been fired from jobs, evicted from their homes, denied health insurance, or refused medical or dental care once their HIV-positive status became known. Legal protections are often ineffective because of expenses of the legal system; often the complainant dies before a case can be heard.

And while HIV infection is probably lifelong, antidiscrimination 3
ordinances may not be: Just this month, after a well-funded and professional campaign by religious zealots, voters in the town of Concord, California, repealed a city ordinance banning HIV-related discrimination. No law can prevent mindless violence; only two years ago, angry townspeople in Arcadia, Florida, firebombed the home of three HIV-infected children.

Without a federal antidiscrimination law for people with HIV, and 4
a commitment to enforcing that law, contact tracing will not be effective and will frighten away those the program is intended to reach. I know Colorado residents who traveled out of state for anonymous testing elsewhere or deferred testing until too late.

If the solution to this epidemic were as simple as testing and contact 5
tracing, life would be easier for public officials and medical experts. Under a national commitment to bar discrimination, infected people could come forward without fear and receive treatment that could not only prolong their lives but that also shows promise of reducing their infectivity and the risk to others.

—*Robert H. Cohen*

Questions for Analysis

Logic
1. In what ways, if any, does Cohen reconcile the present ineffective legal protection [2] with the effectiveness he claims for those legal protections that he recommends?
2. Explain in your own words Cohen's implied reasoning when he suggests that "infectivity" [5] would be reduced by the actions he recommends.
3. In paragraph 5, how does Cohen's reasoning distinguish between the benefits of what he proposes for public officials on the one hand and what he proposes for infected people on the other hand?

Character
1. How would you characterize the general tone of voice in which Cohen presents his argument? Outraged and sarcastic? Patient and reasonable? Describe his manner as fully as you can, and then explain how it is created through particular uses of language.
2. What sense of character does the general tone of voice in the essay create for you? How in your opinion does it help or hinder Cohen's argument?
3. In paragraph 5, what sense of Cohen's character is created for you by the way in which he distinguishes between the benefits of what he proposes for public officials on the one hand and what he proposes for infected people on the other?

Emotion

1. The subject of AIDS is obviously charged with emotion. Describe in general the ways in which you think Cohen's argument does or does not take account of this fact.
2. Find the moment in which Cohen seems to express emotion most intensely, and analyze the ways in which he does so by reference to particular uses of language.
3. What emotional appeal is created by the author's ending his essay with *others* rather than with *infected people*?

AIDS: IN PLAGUES, CIVIL RIGHTS AREN'T THE ISSUE

Richard Restak

Paradoxically, the truly humanitarian position in the face of an AIDS plague is that we not identify with the victims and instead cast our lot with what in earlier times was dubbed the "common good." *1*

More than 1 million Americans may have been infected with the AIDS virus. And the 13,000 Americans with confirmed cases of the disease, whose number is doubling every year, should be treated with the care and compassion due to anyone with a disease that is thus far incurable and invariably fatal. This shouldn't be confused, however, with a refusal to make painful, sometimes anguishing but nonetheless necessary distinctions in the interest of diminishing the likelihood that this awful disease will spread further. *2*

Plagues are not new. They have been encountered in every age and among every nationality: syphilis among the Spanish, bubonic plague among the French, tuberculosis among the Eskimos, polio in America. *3*

What is new are efforts by medically unsophisticated politicians and attorneys to dictate policy in regard to an illness that has the potential for wreaking devastation on a scale that has not been encountered on this planet in hundreds of years. *4*

Also different is the response that, in some quarters, is being suggested: Accept the AIDS victim into our schools, place little or no restrictions on employment or housing. The AIDS victims' "rights" in these areas, we are told, should take precedence over the so far incompletely determined potential for these victims to spread this dread illness. *5*

But what some are describing as "discrimination" and "segregation" has a long and not inglorious history in medicine. Quarantines have been *6* effective in beating outbreaks of scarlet fever, smallpox, and typhoid in this century. Indeed, by protecting the well from the ill we follow a long-established, sensible, and ultimately compassionate course. Throughout history, true humanitarianism traditionally has involved the compassionate but firm segregation of those afflicted with communicable diseases from the well. By carrying out such a policy, diseases have been contained.

REFUSING TO DISTINGUISH

Only sentimentalists refuse to distinguish between the victims of a scourge and those not currently afflicted. 7

Scientists still are unsure why the AIDS virus targets the white blood cells that are the one indispensable element of the body's immune system. But the threat of AIDS demands from us all a discrimination based on our instinct for survival against a peril that, if not somehow controlled, can destroy this society. This is a discrimination that recognizes that caution is in order when knowledge is incomplete, so the public interest can be protected. 8

This argument is not a counsel against good medical care or proper concern for AIDS victims. Nor is it a suggestion that we curtail any "civil right" which doesn't potentially imperil the lives of others. 9

It is a suggestion that the humanitarian response to AIDS is exactly the opposite of a humanitarian response to sexism or racism: In the presence of considerable ignorance about the causes and effects of the syndrome, the benefit of the doubt should not be given to the victim of AIDS. This is not a civil-rights issue; this is a medical issue. To take a position that the AIDS virus must be eradicated is not to make judgments on morals or life-styles. It is to say that the AIDS virus has no "civil rights." 10

At the moment, social and legal solutions to the AIDS problem are proceeding at a pace disproportionate to the knowledge experts possess concerning the illness. 11

For instance, on August 14, [1985], the Los Angeles City Council unanimously approved an ordinance making it illegal to discriminate against AIDS patients in regard to jobs, housing, and health care. 12

"We have an opportunity to set an example for the whole nation, to protect those people who suffer from AIDS against insidious discrimination," said the councilman who introduced the measure. Councilman Ernani Bernardi said the ordinance was meant to educate the public to "prevent hysteria." 13

Preventing hysteria is good, but this ordinance was passed despite doctors' not having yet made up their minds about the degree of contact required for the disease to be spread from one person to another. 14

Consider, for example, the varied and patently contradictory mea- 15
sures put into effect across the country in response to the recent discovery
that the AIDS virus can be isolated from a victim's tears.

CONTRADICTORY MEASURES

At Boston University, when an AIDS patient is examined, "We are 16
not using the applanation tonometer [a device that tests for glaucoma]
because we don't feel we can adequately sterilize it," said the chairman of
the department of ophthalmology.

The Massachusetts Eye and Ear Infirmary specialists plan to "review 17
our technique." Translation: We're not sure yet what we're going to do.

At San Francisco General Hospital, the chief of the eye service 18
routinely sterilizes his optic instruments with merthiolate which "as far
as I know" kills the AIDS virus.

At this point live AIDS virus has been isolated from blood, semen, 19
serum, saliva, urine, and now tears. If the virus exists in these fluids, the
better part of wisdom dictates that we assume the possibility that it can
also be transmitted by these routes.

It seems reasonable, therefore, that AIDS victims should not donate 20
blood or blood products, should not contribute to semen banks, should
not donate tissues or organs to organ banks, should not work as dental or
medical technicians, and should probably not be employed as food
handlers.

While the Los Angeles ordinance exempts blood banks and sperm 21
banks, it's prepared to exert the full power of the law against noncon-
formists who exclude AIDS sufferers from employment in restaurants,
hotels, barber shops, and dental offices.

According to the new law, then, a person afflicted with AIDS may, 22
if properly trained, work as a dental hygienist. He may clean your teeth.
He may even clean your teeth if he has a paper cut on one of his fingers.
This despite the fact that the AIDS virus can be transmitted from bloodstream to bloodstream.

AIDS IN THE SCHOOLS

The battle lines forming over the admission of AIDS victims in the 23
schools are similarly disturbing. "This is the test case for the nation," says
attorney Charles Vaughn, who represents thirteen-year-old AIDS victim
Ryan White, who has been refused admission to his local school in Ko-
komo, Indiana. "What happens here will set the trends across the country." (In America there are about 180 children, not all of school age,
diagnosed as having AIDS.)

To those like Vaughn who see this issue in civil liberties terms, the   24
plight of Ryan White represents simply another instance of discrimination that should be opposed with all the vigor that has marked past efforts
against racism and sexism. In support of their position, they point to the
recent directive of the Centers for Disease Control that AIDS cases be
evaluated on an individual basis to determine whether a child should be
admitted to school.

NOT CONTAGIOUS?

Spokesmen from the CDC and other AIDS authorities, including   25
Dr. Arye Rubenstein, who treats the largest group of children with
AIDS, may be correct in stating that there is "overwhelming evidence
that AIDS is not a highly contagious disease." However, in a combined
interview, they gave the following responses to the interviewer's questions:

Q: Suppose my child got into a fight with an AIDS victim and both   26
began to bleed?

A: That kind of fight with a possible exchange of body fluids   27
would arouse some concern about transmission of the virus.

Q: What if my child is in a classroom with an AIDS victim who   28
threw up or had diarrhea?

A: Such events would be a matter of concern. In its guidelines, the   29
CDC said that AIDS victims who cannot control body secretions should
be kept out of ordinary classrooms.

Q: Suppose a child with AIDS bit my child?   30
A: Again, a bite would arouse concern.   31

Any grade-school teacher can attest that "body-fluid contamina-   32
tion" in the form of scratching, throwing up, diarrhea, biting, and spitting are everyday fare in a schoolroom. That's why infectious diseases like
the flu spread through schools like flash fires.

It is difficult to imagine how the CDC or anyone else is going to   33
make individual determinations under such circumstances.

"I'd rather err on the side of caution," says New York Mayor   34
Edward Koch about admitting AIDS-afflicted children to schools. In this
sentiment, he echoes the concerns of parents everywhere: What if future
research shows AIDS can be caught in other ways? Isn't it more sensible
to forgo premature steps against "discrimination" and await scientific
developments?

AIDS IS NOT ABOUT CIVIL RIGHTS

AIDS is not about civil rights, political power, or "alternative life-   35
styles." It's a disease, a true plague which, in the words of infectious
disease expert Dr. John Seale, writing in the August [1985] issue of

Britain's *Journal of the Royal Society of Medicine,* is already capable of producing "a lethal pandemic throughout the crowded cities and villages of the Third World of a magnitude unparalleled in human history." This disease is only partially understood, is currently untreatable, and is invariably fatal. For these reasons alone, caution would seem in order when it comes to exposing the public to those suffering from this illness.

But in addition, the incubation period is sufficiently lengthy to cast   36
doubt on any proclamations, no matter how seemingly authoritative, in regard to the transmissibility of the illness: "The virus may be transmitted from an infected person many years before the onset of clinical manifestations," according to Dr. George D. Lundberg, editor-in-chief of the *Journal of the American Medical Association.* "Latency of many years may occur between transmission, infection, and clinically manifest disease."

Indeed, truly authoritative statements regarding AIDS cannot cur-   37
rently be made. "The eventual mortality following infection with a lentivirus such as the AIDS virus cannot be ascertained by direct observation till those recently infected have been followed well into the twenty-first century," according to Dr. Seale.

Given these grim realities, lawyers and legislators should ponder   38
long and hard whether or not they wish, by means of legal maneuvering, to inadvertently create situations—child AIDS victims in the schools, adult AIDS victims working in medical, dental offices, and other health-care facilities—in which those afflicted are in a position to pass this virus on to the general public.

Obviously, the most pressing issue at this point is to arrive at an   39
understanding of all of the ways the AIDS virus spreads. But until we do that, political posturing, sloganeering, hollow reassurances, and the inappropriate application of legal remedies to a medical problem can only make matters worse and potentially imperil the health of us all.

Questions for Analysis

Logic

1. Explain the author's implied reasoning in support of his use of the word *paradoxically* at the beginning of his essay.
2. What support for the logic of his argument does the author seem to seek by his historical attention, beginning in paragraph 3, to diseases other than AIDS?
3. Explain the author's reasoning in paragraph 24 and following, where he attempts to refute some opposing views.

Character

1. The author is a neurologist who has studied the effects of AIDS on the brain. What qualities of character in the author are created for you by his not referring to his own medical expertise within the essay?

2. What qualities of character in the author are created for you when he translates the phrase of medical testimony "review our technique" as "we're not sure yet what we're going to do."

3. In what ways does the author seek to establish a sense of his character that includes compassion and fair-mindedness toward victims of AIDS?

Emotion

1. What emotions does the author seem to express *himself* by the use of the phrase "medically unsophisticated" in paragraph 4? What emotions are appealed to in his audience with this phrase?

2. Explain the particular emotional appeal created in paragraph 22. What uses of language operate to create it? How, for example, does the word *your* work in this regard?

3. What is the emotional appeal created by the allusion to the twenty-first century in paragraph 37? Explain what this particular appeal adds to the general argument at this point.

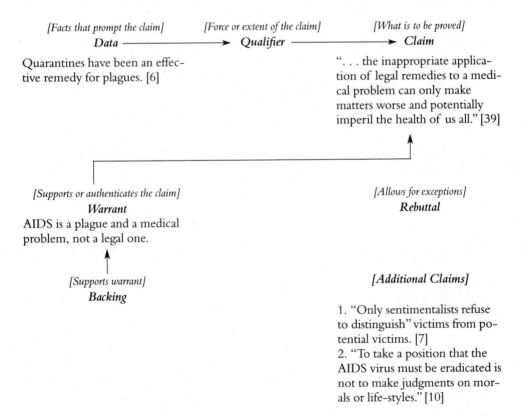

[Facts that prompt the claim]
Data ⟶

[Force or extent of the claim]
Qualifier ⟶

[What is to be proved]
Claim

Quarantines have been an effective remedy for plagues. [6]

". . . the inappropriate application of legal remedies to a medical problem can only make matters worse and potentially imperil the health of us all." [39]

[Supports or authenticates the claim]
Warrant
AIDS is a plague and a medical problem, not a legal one.

[Allows for exceptions]
Rebuttal

[Supports warrant]
Backing

[Additional Claims]

1. "Only sentimentalists refuse to distinguish" victims from potential victims. [7]
2. "To take a position that the AIDS virus must be eradicated is not to make judgments on morals or life-styles." [10]

EXERCISES: IS IT RIGHT TO IDENTIFY AIDS VICTIMS?

Intertextual Questions

1. On what issues do all the authors seem to agree? On which issues does any one author seem to agree with another? Make some lists.
2. In what ways do the others address the moral issues that Gaylin raises without insisting on their moral nature? In what ways do the other authors use the terms *moral* and *morality*? In what ways do all the authors seek to establish that they are not morally prejudiced against homosexuality?
3. Decide as objectively as possible without regard to your personal views which of the authors makes the best appeal to reason? Which to character? Which to emotion?

Suggestions for Writing

1. Write an essay that expresses your own views on the issue of publicly identifying carriers of the HIV virus. Be sure to take account of the arguments presented in the section, whether you refute them or use them in support of your own.
2. Write a letter as if from Cohen to one of the other authors in which you attempt to imagine his responses to the arguments made.
3. Write an essay in which you attempt to assign proper places to the moral, medical, and legal aspects of attempts to battle AIDS.

THE TRIALS OF ANIMALS

Cleveland Amory

Ask an experimenter about the animals in his laboratory. Nine times   1
out of ten he will tell you that they are well cared for and that he abides
by the Animal Welfare Act passed by Congress in 1966.

What he will not say is that both he and his colleagues fought the   2
act and the amendments to it every step of the way; that, under the act,
his laboratory is inspected at most (if at all) once a year; that when his
animals are under experimentation, the act doesn't apply. Nor will he say
that many laboratories ignore the act's most important amendment,
passed in 1986, which mandates that at least one member of the public
vote on the laboratory's animal-care committee.

Your experimenter is not a scofflaw. Having been for so long sole   3
judge and jury of what he does, he believes that he is above the law. A
prime example is that of the monkeys in Silver Spring, Maryland.

The monkeys were used in experiments in which, first, nerves in   4
their limbs were removed and then stimuli—including electrical shocks
and flames—were applied to see if they could still use their appendages.

Dr. Edward Taub, who ran the laboratory, was eventually tried and   5
found guilty, not of cruelty to animals but of maintaining a filthy lab.
Maryland is one of many states that exempts federally funded experiments from cruelty charges.

Dr. Taub is today a free man. His monkeys, however, are not. They   6
are still in a laboratory under the jurisdiction of the National Institutes
of Health, which first funded these cruel experiments. Three hundred
members of Congress have asked the NIH to release the monkeys; the
NIH says it does not want them; two animal sanctuaries have offered to
take them. Why can't they live what remains of their lives receiving the
first evidence of human kindness they have ever known?

In the overcrowded field of cat experimentation, researchers at   7
Louisiana State University, under an eight-year, $2 million Department

of Defense contract, put cats in vises, remove part of their skulls, and then shoot them in the head.

More than two hundred doctors and Senator Daniel Inouye, chair- 8 man of the Defense Appropriations Subcommittee, have protested this cruelty. The experimenters say that their purpose is to find a way to return brain-wounded soldiers to active duty.

"Basic training for an Army infantryman costs $9,000," one exper- 9 imenter argued. "If our research allows only 170 additional men to re- turn to active duty . . . it will have paid for itself." But Dr. Donald Doll of Truman Veterans Hospital in Columbia, Missouri, said of these ex- periments: "I can find nothing which supports applying any of this data to humans."

At the University of Oregon, under a seventeen-year, $1.5 million 10 grant, psychologists surgically rotated the eyes of kittens, implanted elec- trodes in their brains, and forced them to jump onto a block in a pan of water to test their equilibrium. These experiments resulted in a famous laboratory break-in in 1986, and the subsequent trial and conviction of one of the animals' liberators.

During the trial, experimenters were unable to cite a single case in 11 which their research had benefited humans. Additional testimony re- vealed instances of cats being inadequately anesthetized while having their eye muscles cut, untrained and unlicensed personnel performing the surgery, and mother cats suffering such stress that they ate their babies.

The trial judge, Edwin Allen, stated that the testimony was "dis- 12 turbing to me as a citizen of this state and as a graduate of the University of Oregon. It would be highly appropriate to have these facilities opened to the public."

It would, indeed—and a judge is just what is needed. A judge first, 13 then a jury. The experimenters have been both long enough.

Questions for Analysis

Logic
1. Is there anything puzzling to you about the logic of paragraph 6? Give an example of some facts or reasons that could be added to the para- graph to help clear up any problems or sharpen the reasoning there.
2. Two acknowledged experts testify in paragraph 9. In what ways does Amory work here and in the surrounding paragraphs to influence your view of the testimonies?
3. Throughout the essay Amory supports public scrutiny, and his own essay may be seen as a means toward allowing that scrutiny. Explain in your own words Amory's apparent reasoning on the benefits of greater public scrutiny.

Character

1. What qualities of character does the beginning of the essay seek to establish in its author? How do the implications about the element of character in his opponents' arguments contribute here to your sense of Amory's own character?
2. Some of the people who figure in the essay are named and some are not. What differences of effect does Amory's choice in naming create for your sense of the characters involved?
3. Amory uses selected and edited quotations in his essay. In what differing ways do the differences among the quotations contribute to your senses of their speakers? How for example does the emphasis on costs in the content of paragraph 9 affect your sense of the speaker?

Emotion

1. After you have read the essay, what two senses does the word *trials* in the essay's title come to have for you? Briefly describe the emotional appeal made in the essay by each sense of the word.
2. Two legal trials resulting in convictions are described in the course of the essay [5–6; 10]. What emotional appeals does Amory make in each case?
3. How would you describe the general tone of voice that Amory uses in the essay? Formal and scholarly? Breezy and amused? Controlled outrage? Point to some examples and show how particular uses of language create the tone you hear.

A SCIENTIST: "I AM THE ENEMY"

Ron Karpati

I am the enemy! One of those vilified, inhumane physician-scientists involved in animal research. How strange, for I have never thought of myself as an evil person. I became a pediatrician because of my love for children and my desire to keep them healthy. During medical school and residency, however, I saw many children die of leukemia, prematurity and traumatic injury—circumstances against which medicine has made tremendous progress, but still has far to go. More important, I also saw children, alive and healthy, thanks to advances in medical science such as infant respirators, potent antibiotics, new surgical techniques and the entire field of organ transplantation. My desire to tip the scales in favor of the healthy, happy children drew me to medical research.

My accusers claim that I inflict torture on animals for the sole   2
purpose of career advancement. My experiments supposedly have no
relevance to medicine and are easily replaced by computer simulation.
Meanwhile, an apathetic public barely watches, convinced that the issue
has no significance, and publicity-conscious politicians increasingly give
way to the demands of the activists.

We in medical research have also been unconscionably apathetic.   3
We have allowed the most extreme animal-rights protesters to seize the
initiative and frame the issue as one of "animal fraud." We have been
complacent in our belief that a knowledgeable public would sense the
importance of animal research to the public health. Perhaps we have been
mistaken in not responding to the emotional tone of the argument created by those sad posters of animals by waving equally sad posters of
children dying of leukemia or cystic fibrosis.

Much is made of the pain inflicted on these animals in the name of   4
medical science. The animal-rights activists contend that this is evidence
of our malevolent and sadistic nature. A more reasonable argument, however, can be advanced in our defense. Life is often cruel, both to animals
and human beings. Teenagers get thrown from the back of a pickup truck
and suffer severe head injuries. Toddlers, barely able to walk, find themselves at the bottom of a swimming pool while a parent checks the mail.
Physicians hoping to alleviate the pain and suffering these tragedies cause
have but three choices: create an animal model of the injury or disease
and use that model to understand the process and test new therapies;
experiment on human beings—some experiments will succeed, most
will fail—or finally, leave medical knowledge static, hoping that acciden-
tal discoveries will lead us to the advances.

Some animal-rights activists would suggest a fourth choice, claim-   5
ing that computer models can simulate animal experiments, thus making
the actual experiments unnecessary. Computers can simulate, reasonably
well, the effects of well-understood principles on complex systems, as in
the application of the laws of physics to airplane and automobile design.
However, when the principles themselves are in question, as is the case
with the complex biological systems under study, computer modeling
alone is of little value.

One of the terrifying effects of the effort to restrict the use of   6
animals in medical research is that the impact will not be felt for years and
decades: drugs that might have been discovered will not be; surgical
techniques that might have been developed will not be, and fundamental
biological processes that might have been understood will remain mysteries. There is the danger that politically expedient solutions will be
found to placate a vocal minority, while the consequences of those decisions will not be apparent until long after the decisions are made and
the decision making forgotten.

Fortunately, most of us enjoy good health, and the trauma of 7 watching one's child die has become a rare experience. Yet our good fortune should not make us unappreciative of the health we enjoy or the advances that make it possible. Vaccines, antibiotics, insulin and drugs to treat heart disease, hypertension and stroke are all based on animal research. Most complex surgical procedures, such as coronary-artery bypass and organ transplantation, are initially developed in animals. Presently undergoing animal studies are techniques to insert genes in humans in order to replace the defective ones found to be the cause of so much disease. These studies will effectively end if animal research is severely restricted.

In America today, death has become an event isolated from our 8 daily existence—out of the sight and thoughts of most of us. As a doctor who has watched many children die, and their parents grieve, I am particularly angered by people capable of so much compassion for a dog or a cat, but with seemingly so little for a dying human being. These people seem so insulated from the reality of human life and death and what it means.

Make no mistake, however: I am not advocating the needlessly cruel 9 treatment of animals. To the extent that the animal–rights movement has made us more aware of the needs of these animals, and made us search harder for suitable alternatives, they have made a significant contribution. But if the more radical members of this movement are successful in limiting further research, their efforts will bring about a tragedy that will cost many lives. The real question is whether an apathetic majority can be aroused to protect its future against a vocal, but misdirected, minority.

Questions for Analysis

Logic
1. How does the metaphor of "scales" in paragraph 1 represent the reasoning as a whole in Karpati's support for animal experimentation?
2. In paragraphs 4 and 5 Karpati lists the choices he sees as available on the issue of experiment and medical advance. In your own words explain the implied logic of the support these paragraphs create for his own choice.
3. In what ways during the essay does the author acknowledge and concede well-made points of argument to his opponents?

Character
1. How does the essay as a whole work to refute the self-styled negative characterization of Karpati's first two sentences?
2. How does Karpati establish a sense of character that includes compassion? Does his compassion extend to the point of view that his essay opposes? Explain.

3. Karpati attributes apathy on the issue of experimentation to the general public. Does he seem to include his readers in that characterization? Explain. How does he work to overcome apathy in the essay?

Emotion
1. Karpati is a pediatrician, and his examples focus on children. Explain the operation of the emotional appeal created by that focus.
2. In paragraph 4 Karpati examines some emotional appeals of his opponents and makes some emotional appeals of his own. Explain why he thinks his own arguments in this regard "more reasonable."
3. What is the emotional appeal of the "computer model" discussed in paragraph 5? In what ways does Karpati seek to refute this emotional appeal?

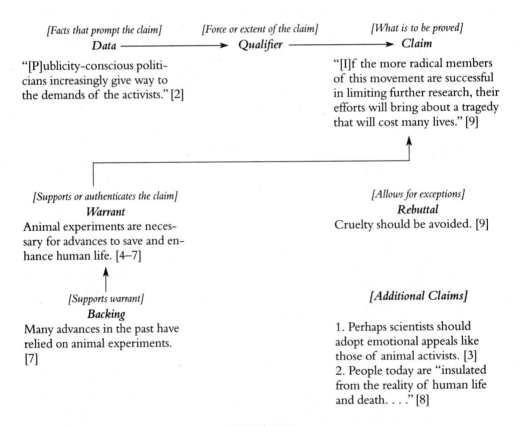

[Facts that prompt the claim]
Data ⟶

"[P]ublicity-conscious politicians increasingly give way to the demands of the activists." [2]

[Force or extent of the claim]
Qualifier ⟶

[What is to be proved]
Claim

"[I]f the more radical members of this movement are successful in limiting further research, their efforts will bring about a tragedy that will cost many lives." [9]

[Supports or authenticates the claim]
Warrant
Animal experiments are necessary for advances to save and enhance human life. [4–7]

[Supports warrant]
Backing
Many advances in the past have relied on animal experiments. [7]

[Allows for exceptions]
Rebuttal
Cruelty should be avoided. [9]

[Additional Claims]

1. Perhaps scientists should adopt emotional appeals like those of animal activists. [3]
2. People today are "insulated from the reality of human life and death. . . ." [8]

IN DEFENSE OF THE ANIMALS
Meg Greenfield

I might as well come right out with it: Contrary to some of my   *1*
most cherished prejudices, the animal-rights people have begun to get to
me. I think that in some part of what they say they are right.

I never thought it would come to this. As distinct from the old-   *2*
style animal rescue, protection, and shelter organizations, the more aggressive newcomers, with their "liberation" of laboratory animals and
periodic championship of the claims of animal well-being over human
well-being when a choice must be made, have earned a reputation in the
world I live in as fanatics and just plain kooks. And even with my own
recently (relatively) raised consciousness, there remains a good deal in
both their critique and their prescription for the virtuous life that I reject,
being not just a practicing carnivore, a wearer of shoe leather, and so
forth, but also a supporter of certain indisputably agonizing procedures
visited upon innocent animals in the furtherance of human welfare, especially experiments undertaken to improve human health.

So, viewed from the pure position, I am probably only marginally   *3*
better than the worst of my kind, if that: I don't buy the complete
"speciesist" analysis or even the fundamental language of animal "rights"
and continue to find a large part of what is done in the name of that
cause harmful and extreme. But I also think, patronizing as it must sound,
that the zealots are required early on in any movement if it is to succeed
in altering the sensibility of the leaden masses, such as me. Eventually
they get your attention. And eventually you at least feel obliged to weigh
their arguments and think about whether there may not be something
there.

It is true that this end has often been achieved—as in my case—by   *4*
means of vivid, cringe-inducing photographs, not by an appeal to reason
or values so much as by an assault on squeamishness. From the famous
1970s photo of the newly skinned baby seal to the videos of animals
being raised in the most dark, miserable, stunting environment as they
are readied for their life's sole fulfillment as frozen patties and cutlets,
these sights have had their effect. But we live in a world where the animal
protein we eat comes discreetly prebutchered and prepacked so the original beast and his slaughtering are remote from our consideration, just as
our furs come on coat hangers in salons, not on their original proprietors;
and I see nothing wrong with our having to contemplate the often unsettling reality of how we came by the animal products we make use of.
Then we can choose what we want to do.

The objection to our being confronted with these dramatic, dis- 5
turbing pictures is first that they tend to provoke a misplaced, uncritical,
and highly emotional concern for animal life at the direct expense of a
more suitable concern for human suffering. What goes into the animals'
account, the reasoning goes, necessarily comes out of ours. But I think
it is possible to remain stalwart in your view that the human claim comes
first and in your acceptance of the use of animals for human betterment
and *still* to believe that there are some human interests that should not
take precedence. For we have become far too self-indulgent, hardened,
careless, and cruel in the pain we routinely inflict upon these creatures
for the most frivolous, unworthy purposes. And I also think that the more
justifiable purposes, such as medical research, are shamelessly used as
cover for other activities that are wanton.

For instance, not all of the painful and crippling experimentation 6
that is undertaken in the lab is being conducted for the sake of medical
knowledge or other purposes related to basic human well-being and
health. Much of it is being conducted for the sake of superrefinements
in the cosmetic and other frill industries, the noble goal being to contrive
yet another fragrance or hair tint or commercially competitive variation
on all the daft, fizzy, multicolored "personal care" products for the medicine cabinet and dressing table, a firmer-holding hair spray, that sort of
thing. In other words, the conscripted, immobilized rabbits and other
terrified creatures, who have been locked in boxes from the neck down,
only their heads on view, are being sprayed in the eyes with different
burning, stinging substances for the sake of adding to our already obscene
store of luxuries and utterly superfluous vanity items.

PHONY KINSHIP

Oddly, we tend to be very sentimental about animals in their ideal- 7
ized, fictional form and largely indifferent to them in realms where our
lives actually touch. From time immemorial, humans have romantically
attributed to animals their own sensibilities—from Balaam's biblical ass
who providently could speak and who got his owner out of harm's way
right down to Lassie and the other Hollywood pups who would invariably tip off the good guys that the bad guys were up to something. So we
simulate phony cross-species kinship, pretty well drown in the cuteness
of it all—Mickey and Minnie and Porky—and ignore, if we don't actually countenance, the brutish things done in the name of Almighty Hair
Spray.

This strikes me as decadent. My problem is that it also causes me to 8
reach a position that is, on its face, philosophically vulnerable, if not
absurd—the muddled, middling, inconsistent place where finally you are

saying it's all right to kill them for some purposes, but not to hurt them gratuitously in doing it or to make them suffer horribly for one's own trivial whims.

I would feel more humiliated to have fetched up on this exposed rock, if I didn't suspect I had so much company. When you see pictures of people laboriously trying to clean the Exxon gunk off of sea otters even knowing that they will only be able to help out a very few, you see this same outlook in action. And I think it *can* be defended. For to me the biggest cop-out is the one that says that if you don't buy the whole absolutist, extreme position it is pointless and even hypocritical to concern yourself with lesser mercies and ameliorations. The pressure of the animal-protection groups has already had some impact in improving the way various creatures are treated by researchers, trainers, and food producers. There is much more in this vein to be done. We are talking about rejecting wanton, pointless cruelty here. The position may be philosophically absurd, but the outcome is the right one.

Questions for Analysis

Logic

1. In paragraph 4 Greenfield says that the ends of animal-rights activists have "often been achieved—as in my case—by means of vivid, cringe-inducing photographs, not by an appeal to reason or values so much as by an assault on squeamishness." In your view, have the nonlogical means by which Greenfield herself has been persuaded affected the logic of her argument? Explain.

2. In your view, have the nonlogical means of Greenfield's own persuasion affected the organization of her argument?

3. On what basis does Greenfield fault the "philosophical" logic of her own position? Explain in your own words with examples.

Character

1. What aspects of her character does Greenfield seek to establish in paragraph 1? Pick another moment in the essay where she also seeks to establish similar qualities and analyze the ways in which she does so.

2. In paragraph 2 Greenfield says that she rejects "a good deal" of the animal-rights activists' "prescription for the virtuous life." What elements in her own implied definition of the virtuous life does she seek to establish by this rejection?

3. What does Greenfield define in her last paragraph as "the biggest cop-out"? What elements of her own character does she seek to establish by her definition here?

Emotion

1. Greenfield says she is embarrassed by her new position on the issue. In your own words explain (a) the source of her embarrassment and (b) the ways in which she uses this embarrassment as an emotional appeal to her reader.

2. In paragraph 6 Greenfield argues against experiments for purposes other than those related to "basic human well-being and health." In your own words, analyze the ways in which she creates her emotional appeal within this paragraph.

3. In paragraph 7 Greenfield argues against human sentimentality about animals. In your own words analyze the ways in which she creates her emotional appeal in this paragraph.

EXERCISES: ANIMAL TESTING

Intertextual Questions

1. All the authors may be said to oppose "needless" cruelty. Compare the differing ways in which you understand each author to define implicitly or explicitly this key term.

2. In your view, which of the writers best counters the position of those opposed to the writer's own opinions? Explain your answer using particular examples.

3. Another writer has said: "All other animals are always cruel. Human beings are the only animals who *don't* treat animals like animals." Discuss the ways in which you think each of the three authors would respond to this statement.

Suggestions for Writing

1. In your opinion, which argument makes the most effective emotional appeal, whether or not you agree with its conclusion? Write an essay in which you analyze the strength of the essay's emotional appeal by comparing it to the emotional appeals of the other essays.

2. Another writer has said: "The sufferings of animals take place in the present, while the benefits to human beings are only imagined for the future—this is the strength of the claims to animal rights." Write an essay on animal experimentation in which you examine and discuss the theme of time as it affects differing points of view on the topic.

3. Another writer has said: "Almost all animals used in experiments are bred only for that purpose. If life is a good, they are rewarded by existence. If their lives include suffering and end in death, they are no different from other lives." Write an essay that begins with your response to this proposition and goes on to argue for your further views on animal experimentation.

Political Correctness, Multiculturalism, and the College Curriculum

RADICAL ENGLISH

George F. Will

At the University of Texas in Austin, as on campuses across the country, freshmen are hooking up their stereos and buckling down to the business of learning what they should have learned in high school—particularly English composition. Thousands of young Texans will take English 306, the only required course on composition. The simmering controversy about that course illustrates the political tensions that complicate, dilute, and sometimes defeat higher education today.

Last summer an attempt was made to give a uniform political topic and text to all sections of E306. It was decided that all sections would read *Racism and Sexism,* an anthology of writings with a pronounced left-wing slant.

The text explains that a nonwhite "may discriminate against white people or even hate them" but cannot be called "racist." The book's editor, a New Jersey sociologist, sends her students to make "class analysis of shopping malls." "They go to a boutiquey mall and a mall for the masses. I have them count how many public toilets are in each and bring back samples of the toilet paper. It makes class distinctions visible."

After some faculty members protested the subordination of instruction to political indoctrination, that text was dropped and the decision about recasting E306 was postponed until next year. But the pressure is on for political content, thinly disguised under some antiseptic course title such as "Writing about Difference—Race and Gender."

Such skirmishes in the curricula wars occur because campuses have become refuges for radicals who want universities to be as thoroughly politicized as they are. Like broken records stashed in the nation's attic in 1968, these politicized professors say:

America is oppressive, imposing subservience on various victim   6
groups. The culture is permeated with racism, sexism, heterosexism,
classism (oppression of the working class), so the first task of universities
is "consciousness-raising." This is done with "diversity education," which
often is an attempt to produce intellectual uniformity by promulgating
political orthodoxy.

Such "value clarification" aims at the moral reformation of young   7
people who are presumed to be burdened with "false consciousness"
as a result of being raised within the "hegemony" of America's "self-
perpetuating power structure."

The universities' imprimatur is implicitly bestowed on a particular   8
view of American history, a political agenda, and specific groups deemed
authoritative regarding race, sex, class, etc.

This orthodoxy is reinforced—and enforced—by codes of conduct   9
called "anti-harassment" codes, under which designated groups of victims are protected from whatever they decide offends them. To cure the
offensiveness of others, therapists and thought police are proliferating on
campuses, conducting "racial awareness seminars" and other "sensitivity
training."

These moral tutors have a professional interest in the exacerbation   10
of group tensions, to which university administrations contribute by allowing, even encouraging, the Balkanization of campus life. This is done
by encouraging group identities—black dorms, women's centers, gay
studies, etc.

The status of victim is coveted as a source of moral dignity and   11
political power, so nerves are rubbed raw by the competitive cultivation
of grievances. The more brittle campus relations become, the more aggressive moral therapy becomes, making matters worse.

The attempt to pump E306 full of politics is a manifestation of a   12
notion common on campuses: Every academic activity must have an
ameliorative dimension, reforming society and assuaging this or that
group's grievance. From that idea, it is but a short step down the slippery
slope to this idea: All education, all culture, is political, so it should be
explicitly so.

And any academic purpose is secondary to political consciousness-   13
raising. The classroom is an "arena of struggle" and teaching should be
grounded in the understanding that even teaching English composition
is a political activity.

Recently at the University of Michigan, a teacher's description of   14
a freshman composition course said that writing skills should be learned
"in connection to social and political contexts" so "all of the readings
I have selected focus on Latin America, with the emphasis on the
U.S. government's usually detrimental role in Latin American poli-

tics . . . damning commentary on the real meaning of U.S. ideology . . . responsibility for 'our' government's often brutal treatment of. . . ." And so on.

This, remember, for a course on composition. But, then, the 15 teacher is candid about sacrificing writing skills to indoctrination: "Lots of reading . . . Consequently, I will assign considerable (sic) less writing than one would normally expect . . ."

On other campuses, writing requirements are reduced to the mere 16 writing of a journal, a virtually standardless exercise in "self-expression" that "empowers" students. This is regarded as political liberation because rules of grammar and elements of style are "political" stratagems reinforcing the class structure to the disadvantage of the underclass, which has its own rich and authentic modes of expression from the streets.

So it goes on many campuses. The troubles at Texas are, as yet, 17 mild. But the trajectory is visible: down. So is the destination: political indoctrination supplanting education.

Questions for Analysis

Logic
1. Would you agree that the warrant for Will's main claim is to the effect that politics can be separated from education? If you think so, show where and how you understand him to express or imply that warrant. If you think not, explain and exemplify his warrant as you understand it.
2. Explain in your own words Will's reasoning about the "slippery slope" in paragraph 12.
3. Explain Will's reasoning in objecting to the course that required fewer writing assignments [14–15]. In your view, is his reasoning here logically compatible with his assertion that students should have learned composition in high school? Explain.

Character
1. Does Will seem to characterize the arguments of his opponents in a fair-minded way? Explain your answer by pointing to particular examples.
2. Consider Will's remarks about "the status of victim" in and around paragraph 11. In your view, does he seem to make an appeal to his audience to consider himself and his supporters "in the status of victim"? Explain your answer.
3. When, where, and how does Will use irony in the essay? Pick one example and explain the appeal to character that it expresses.

Emotion

1. Explain the emotional appeal Will implicitly makes in paragraph 3 on the subject of the textbook he mentions. Note that its author, Paula Rothenberg, replies to Will and others in the next essay.
2. How does Will use quotation marks to make emotional appeals in the essay? Pick a paragraph that uses words or phrases within quotation marks and explain how and why the author does so.
3. Explain the emotional appeal of the phrase "moral tutors" as Will uses it in paragraph 10.

CRITICS OF ATTEMPTS TO DEMOCRATIZE THE CURRICULUM ARE WAGING A CAMPAIGN TO MISREPRESENT THE WORK OF RESPONSIBLE PROFESSORS

Paula Rothenberg

I remember watching hearings of the House Un–American Activities Committee on television as a very young girl, sharing my mother's horror at the way in which Wisconsin Senator Joseph McCarthy trampled on the Bill of Rights. I knew kids whose parents were public-school teachers who had hidden books away in the cellar or destroyed them for fear of being accused wrongly of some amorphous crime and losing their jobs.

Later, I was moved to tears by Eric Bentley's dramatization of the hearings, which I heard on the radio. I have read endless accounts of that terrible time of redbaiting and blacklisting, ranging from the much-publicized stories of Lillian Hellman and Dashiell Hammett to the recent article in *The New York Times Magazine* by television producer Mark Goodson, father of a childhood friend and classmate. Each one chills my soul.

Imagine my feeling then, when I picked up the December 24 issue of *Newsweek* and found the cover story on integrating issues of race and gender into college curricula asking the question, "Is This the New Enlightenment—or the New McCarthyism?" and referring to my own book, *Racism and Sexism: An Integrated Study* (St. Martin's Press, 1988) as the "primer of politically correct thought." In fact, rather than trying to direct thought into approved channels, the book is an interdisciplinary text designed to allow students and teachers to examine the comprehensive and interconnected nature of racism, sexism, and class privilege within the United States. It employs scholarly writings from the humanities and social sciences, Supreme Court decisions and other historical documents, newspaper and magazine articles, poetry, and fiction.

But I suppose I should not have been surprised by the headline. 4 Three months earlier George Will, in a nationally syndicated column, had announced "Political Indoctrination Supplants Education in Nation's Universities," referring to me (mistakenly) as a "New Jersey sociologist" (my graduate training was in philosophy) and describing some of my work in terms so ludicrous they would have been funny were the man not so widely read or his conclusions so dangerous.

Earlier, *The New York Times,* as well as *The Chronicle,* had reported on the 5 decision at the University of Texas at Austin to use my book as the primary text in its required composition course—and the subsequent retraction of that decision in response to political pressure from inside and outside the university. Since that time, a steady stream of articles on "politically correct" thought have appeared in countless national, regional, and local publications. None of them, whether news stories or opinion pieces, makes even a pretense of presenting a fair and balanced account of the issues; each of them seems content to repeat the same set of half-truths and distortions being circulated by the National Association of Scholars, a Princeton-based organization of academics seemingly committed to curricula based on the Orwellian slogans: *War Is Peace, Freedom Is Slavery,* and *Ignorance Is Strength.*

For example, the writer of an article in *The New Republic* reduced 6 the comments I had made during a lengthy telephone interview to a single sentence that misrepresented what I had said. The article reported that I couldn't name a single book that was so racist and sexist that it should be dropped from the canon. In fact, when asked to specify such works during the interview, I had refused on the grounds that transforming the college curriculum was not about banning books. I had added that other teachers might use very effectively books that I might find objectionable. Needless to say, this comment did not appear in the article.

In response to a curriculum-reform movement that seeks to expand the 7 horizons of students' learning to include all peoples and all places, the N.A.S. and other opponents of a multicultural, gender-balanced curriculum propose the continued silencing of all but a tiny fraction of the world's population. They have so little faith in this nation's potential to realize the democratic values we have so long espoused that they mistakenly believe that identifying the racism and sexism in our past and present will weaken this nation rather than strengthen it. They have even managed to persuade some people that those who seek to decrease the violence of our language and our behavior somehow seek to limit the Bill of Rights rather than to extend its protections to all.

Recoiling in horror from those who advocate a critical reading of Shakespeare or Milton (I thought scholarship was about critical readings), they show no equivalent concern for the peoples and cultures rendered invisible by the traditional curriculum. At another time in history opponents' attempts to misrepresent so completely the goals of curriculum reform might well have attracted little serious attention; at this moment they have gained a hearing because they express the collective fears of a small but still dominant group within the academy that sees its continued power and privilege in jeopardy. What exactly is the critique of the traditional curriculum they have tried so hard to silence—and failing that—to misrepresent? How does the traditional curriculum serve their interests and perpetuate their power? 8

The traditional curriculum teaches all of us to see the world through the eyes of privileged, white, European males and to adopt their interests and perspectives as our own. It calls books by middle-class, white, male writers "literature" and honors them as timeless and universal, while treating the literature produced by everyone else as idiosyncratic and transitory. The traditional curriculum introduces the (mythical) white, middle-class, patriarchal, heterosexual family and its values and calls it "Introduction to Psychology." It teaches the values of white men of property and position and calls it "Introduction to Ethics." It reduces the true *majority* of people in this society to "women and minorities" and calls it "political science." It teaches the art produced by privileged white men in the West and calls it "art history." 9

The curriculum effectively defines this point of view as "reality" rather than as a point of view itself, and then assures us that it and it alone is "neutral" and "objective." It teaches all of us to use white male values and culture as the standard by which everyone and everything else is to be measured and found wanting. It defines "difference" as "deficiency" (deviance, pathology). By building racism, sexism, heterosexism, and class privilege into its very definition of "reality," it implies that the current distribution of wealth and power in the society, as well as the current distribution of time and space in the traditional curriculum, reflects the natural order of things. 10

In this curriculum, women of all colors, men of color, and working people are rarely if ever subjects or agents. They appear throughout history at worst as objects, at best as victims. According to this curriculum, only people of color have a race and only women have a gender, only lesbians and gays have a sexual orientation—everyone else is a human being. This curriculum values the work of killing and conquest over 11 the production and reproduction of life. It offers abstract, oppositional thinking as the paradigm for intellectual rigor.

The traditional curriculum is too narrow. It leaves out too much. Its narrow approach to defining knowledge implies that people who look different, talk differently, and embrace different cultural practices are not studied because they have nothing to teach "us."   *12*

Not content to debate curriculum reform in a straightforward and intellectually honest fashion, the opponents of such reform are mounting a nationwide campaign to smear and misrepresent the work of responsible teachers and scholars all across the country who are committed to democratizing the curriculum. After serving as "thought police" for generations, effectively silencing the voices and issues of all but a few, they now attempt to foist that label on the very forces in the university seeking to expand, rather than to contract, the discourse. The opponents of curriculum reform seek to effectively ban books like my own that, among other things, survey U.S. history by asking students to read our Constitution, Supreme Court decisions, and other public documents so that the "founding fathers" and their descendants can speak for themselves. Perhaps their fear is justified. I read the *Dred Scott* decision in ninth grade and have never been the same since.   *13*

And what of white males' scholarship and perspectives in this new and evolving curriculum? Will there be a place for them? The question is absurd, and the need to answer it reflects how far the misrepresentations have gone. The perspectives and contributions of that group are valid and valuable: there is much to be learned from them. The difficulty is not with their inclusion but with the exclusion of everyone else. The difficulty is with universalizing that experience and those interests.   *14*

Yes, *Newsweek,* there may well be a new McCarthyism. If so, it is coming directly from the irresponsible right and its fellow travelers. How ironic that those who actively attempt to dictate what books students will and will not read portray themselves as defenders of academic freedom. How ironic that those of us seeking to make the curriculum and campus climate *less* racist, *less* sexist, and *less* heterosexist are portrayed as threats to democratic freedoms rather than their champions. But in the end, war is *not* peace, slavery is *not* freedom, and no matter what the N.A.S. may believe, ignorance is *not* strength.   *15*

Questions for Analysis

Logic
1. How does Rothenberg use autobiography as an organizational device throughout the essay?

2. Explain in your own words the author's reasoning when she claims that the traditional curriculum falsely claims to represent "reality."
3. Explain in your own words the author's reasoning when she claims that a multicultural curriculum would truly represent "reality."

Character
1. Explain the sense of her character that you see Rothenberg attempting to create in the autobiographical account of the first two paragraphs.
2. Explain the sense of her character that you see Rothenberg attempting to create through her claim in paragraph 6 to have been misrepresented.
3. Where and how does Rothenberg use irony in the essay? Pick one example and explain the appeal to character it expresses.

Emotion
1. Describe the emotions that the author expresses and those that she appeals to by referring to McCarthy and Orwell in the essay.
2. How does Rothenberg use quotation marks to make emotional appeals in the essay? Pick a paragraph that uses words or phrases within quotation marks and explain how and why the author does so.
3. Explain the operation of the author's emotional appeal on the theme of "thought police" at the end of the essay.

EQUAL CULTURES—OR EQUALITY?
There's a Choice to Make between Feminism and Multiculturalism

Cathy Young

Feminism and multiculturalism have become essential articles of   1
current progressive faith. A recent report from the American Association
of University Women on eliminating gender bias in high school, for
example, also enthusiastically endorsed a multicultural curriculum. But,
like most academics, the report's authors fail to recognize that these two
tenets are often incompatible.

The central premise of the multiculturalist credo, after all, is that all   2
cultures are created equal. To judge other cultures by Western standards
is unforgivably ethnocentric. Yet, as Islamic fundamentalists remind us,
equality of the sexes is a Western value judgment. It is, moreover, a

standard by which most non-Western cultures—even allowing for a few quasi-matriarchal tribes—come up short.

Last year, the New York Times reviewed anthropologist Kenneth 3 Good's memoir of life with the Yanomamo tribe in Venezuela. Having summarized his account of the tribe's misogynist brutality—unmarried girls past puberty, widows and runaway wives are routinely gang-raped and sometimes maimed—the critic went on to quote, approvingly, Good's assertion that "violence [was] not a central theme of Yanomamo life." This angered a woman reader, who wrote to the Times denouncing "the myopia . . . where violence against women is concerned."

Yet surely there was something else at work. One can hardly imag- 4 ine a Times reviewer extending such tolerance to violence against women by *American* men. With a Stone Age Amazonian tribe, however, it is safer to be myopic than "ethnocentric," even at the price of mental contortion.

In a world civilization course I once took at a community college 5 in New Jersey, our female professor explained that while the status of women in India might seem low, they often wielded much power in the household and were revered as mothers of sons. I expressed surprise she would make excuses for an oppressive patriarchy. "Well," the professor snapped back, "there's no reason for us to be smug. We still have a lot of discrimination against women in this society too." As if female infanticide and the immolation of widows equaled the unfair denial of a promotion.

Similarly, advocates of Afrocentrism rarely say much about clitero- 6 dectomy, polygamy or the acceptance of wife-beating in much of Africa. It seems that the position of women has to be cast in the best possible light when it comes to non-Western cultures—and in the worst possible light when it comes to the West (which, even before feminism, accorded women a higher status than any other major culture).

The double standard is blatant. The only civilization that made an 7 effort to overcome its sexist traditions, the West is berated for failing to do away with them completely. But Third World cultures are treated as static; to try to protect the Yanomamo's ancestral customs from the on-slaught of Western ways is noble.

The issue is not just an academic one. America is home to millions 8 of immigrants from a diverse array of cultures. Current "politically cor-rect" thinking holds that these immigrants and their children should be encouraged to preserve their cultural identities and values; assimilation is viewed as a form of psychic violence. But what if these values include polygamy or arranged marriages of nine-year-old girls? Shall we con-done the slaying of unfaithful wives by husbands avenging their honor if that was the custom in their native countries?

If you think I am pushing the multiculturalist logic to an absurd 9 extreme, think again. The answer to the last question is: We already do.

In 1987, a Chinese immigrant named Dong Lu Chen killed his   *10*
wife, smashing her head with a claw hammer after she confessed to an
affair. At the 1989 trial, which included testimony of an anthropologist,
the defense argued that Chen's background—"the special high place
the family holds in the Chinese community" and "the shame and humiliation" of a wife's infidelity—made him lose control. Mostly on the
strength of this "cultural defense," a Brooklyn judge sentenced Chen to
five years probation on a manslaughter charge.

The sentence initially sparked protests among women's groups and   *11*
Asian activist groups alike. But the coalition fell apart because Asian
groups were fearful of undermining the notion of a cultural defense. To
bar it "would promote the idea that when people come to America, they
have to give up their way of doing things," huffed Margaret Fung, executive director of the Asian-American Legal Defense and Education Fund.

Yet is it not possible that many people come here because they are   *12*
attracted to the *American* way of doing things? This may be particularly
true of women, who often relish liberation from the patriarchal customs
back home. What a cruel mockery if, out of deference to multicultural
sensitivities, our institutions began to mimic these customs.

That was just how the Chen sentence was perceived by women   *13*
who had the most reason to take it personally: Asian-American battered
wives. After that case, according to *Newsday,* many told counselors that
the threat of taking their men to court had ceased to be a deterrent. Said
an immigration lawyer, "Their view is that maybe the courts here protect
the male the same way the system protects the male in China." The
"cultural defense" has since cropped up in several spousal homicide and
rape cases involving immigrants from other Third World countries.

One powerful symbol of Desert Storm was the contrast between   *14*
the veiled and silent women of Saudi Arabia and U.S. female soldiers
working alongside the men. It was a source of pride to most Americans,
and a reminder that at least when it comes to gender, some cultures are
clearly more equal than others.

Once this simple fact is recognized, it might bring us to ponder the   *15*
possibility that women may owe something to such uniquely Western
ideals as reverence for the individual, freedom of choice, and even technological mastery of nature—which helped ease the biological con-
straints whose weight on women has always been especially heavy. And
once we start thinking of that, who knows what heresies could be next?

Questions for Analysis

Logic
1. Do you find that Young adequately defines the key terms of her
   argument? Explain by discussing examples.

2. Explain Young's reasoning on the theme of anthropology in paragraphs 3–5.
3. Explain Young's reasoning on the theme of "the cultural defense" mentioned in paragraph 13.

Character
1. Explain the sense of character that you feel Young attempting to create in the autobiographical account of paragraph 5.
2. Explain the sense of character that you feel Young attempting to create through her use of rhetorical questions in paragraph 8.
3. Where and how does Young use irony in the essay? Pick one example and explain the appeal to character it expresses.

Emotion
1. Explain the emotional appeal created by Young's use of the phrase "double standard" in paragraph 7.
2. How does Young use quotation marks to make an emotional appeal in the essay? Pick a paragraph that uses words or phrases within quotation marks and explain how and why the author does so.
3. Explain the ways in which Young creates her appeal to emotion in discussing the "Chen sentence" beginning in paragraph 10.

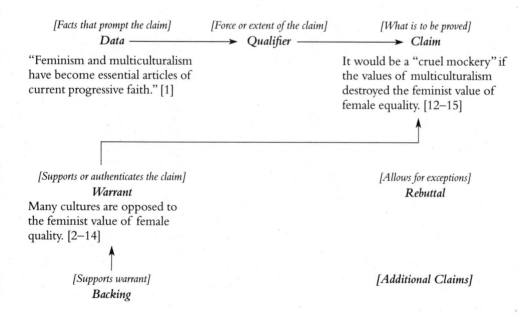

[Facts that prompt the claim]
Data ⟶

[Force or extent of the claim]
Qualifier ⟶

[What is to be proved]
Claim

"Feminism and multiculturalism have become essential articles of current progressive faith." [1]

It would be a "cruel mockery" if the values of multiculturalism destroyed the feminist value of female equality. [12–15]

[Supports or authenticates the claim]
Warrant
Many cultures are opposed to the feminist value of female quality. [2–14]

[Allows for exceptions]
Rebuttal

[Supports warrant]
Backing

[Additional Claims]

EXERCISES: POLITICAL CORRECTNESS, MULTICULTURALISM, AND THE COLLEGE CURRICULUM

Intertextual Questions

1. Do you find Will and Young to be fair in their representations of advocates of a multicultural curriculum as exemplified by Rothenberg? Explain and exemplify your answer.
2. Do you find Rothenberg to be fair in her representation of opponents of a multicultural curriculum as exemplified by Will? Explain and exemplify your answer.
3. Which author's arguments do you find most convincing overall on the issue of a multicultural curriculum? Explain and exemplify your answer.

Suggestions for Writing

1. In your view, which author most effectively employs the appeal to reason? Write an essay in which you explain your judgment through comparison and contrast.
2. In your view, which author most effectively employs the appeal to emotion? Write an essay in which you explain your judgment.
3. Write an essay that argues in favor of your own views for or against a multicultural curriculum.

Pornography

LET'S PUT PORNOGRAPHY BACK IN THE CLOSET

Susan Brownmiller

Free speech is one of the great foundations on which our democracy rests. I am old enough to remember the Hollywood Ten, the screenwriters who went to jail in the late 1940s because they refused to testify before a congressional committee about their political affiliations. They tried to use the First Amendment as a defense, but they went to jail because in those days there were few civil liberties lawyers around who cared to champion the First Amendment right to free speech, when the speech concerned the Communist Party.

The Hollywood Ten were correct in claiming the First Amendment. Its high purpose is the protection of unpopular ideas and political dissent. In the dark, cold days of the 1950s, few civil libertarians were willing to declare themselves First Amendment absolutists. But in the brighter, though frantic, days of the 1960s, the principle of protecting unpopular political speech was gradually strengthened.

It is fair to say now that the battle has largely been won. Even the American Nazi Party has found itself the beneficiary of the dedicated, tireless work of the American Civil Liberties Union. But—and please notice the quotation marks coming up—"To equate the free and robust exchange of ideas and political debate with commercial exploitation of obscene material demeans the grand conception of the First Amendment and its high purposes in the historic struggle for freedom. It is a misuse of the great guarantees of free speech and free press."

I didn't say that, although I wish I had, for I think the words are thrilling. Chief Justice Warren Burger said it in 1973, in the United States Supreme Court's majority opinion in *Miller v. California*. During the same decades that the right to political free speech was being strengthened in the courts, the nation's obscenity laws also were undergoing extensive revision.

It's amazing to recall that in 1934 the question of whether James Joyce's *Ulysses* should be banned as pornographic actually went before the Court. The battle to protect *Ulysses* as a work of literature with redeeming social value was won. In later decades, Henry Miller's *Tropic* books, *Lady Chatterley's Lover* and the *Memoirs of Fanny Hill* also were adjudged not obscene. These decisions have been important to me. As the author of *Against Our Will,* a study of the history of rape that does contain explicit sexual material, I shudder to think how my book would have fared if James Joyce, D. H. Lawrence and Henry Miller hadn't gone before me.

I am not a fan of *Chatterley* or the *Tropic* books, I should quickly mention. They are not to my literary taste, nor do I think they represent female sexuality with any degree of accuracy. But I would hardly suggest that we ban them. Such a suggestion wouldn't get very far anyway. The battle to protect these books is ancient history. Time does march on, quite methodically. What, then, is unlawfully obscene, and what does the First Amendment have to do with it?

In the Miller case of 1973 (not Henry Miller, by the way, but a porn distributor who sent unsolicited stuff through the mails), the Court came up with new guidelines that it hoped would strengthen obscenity laws by giving more power to the states. What it did in actuality was throw everything into confusion. It set up a three-part test by which materials can be adjudged obscene. The materials are obscene if they depict patently offensive, hard-core sexual conduct; lack serious scientific, literary, artistic or political value; and appeal to the prurient interest of an average person—as measured by contemporary community standards.

"Patently offensive," "prurient interest" and "hard-core" are indeed words to conjure with. "Contemporary community standards" are what we're trying to redefine. The feminist objection to pornography is not based on prurience, which the dictionary defines as lustful, itching desire. We are not opposed to sex and desire, with or without the itch, and we certainly believe that explicit sexual material has its place in literature, art, science and education. Here we part company rather swiftly with old-line conservatives who don't want sex education in the high schools, for example.

No, the feminist objection to pornography is based on our belief that pornography represents hatred of women, that pornography's intent is to humiliate, degrade and dehumanize the female body for the purpose of erotic stimulation and pleasure. We are unalterably opposed to the presentation of the female body being stripped, bound, raped, tortured, mutilated and murdered in the name of commercial entertainment and free speech.

These images, which are standard pornographic fare, have nothing   10
to do with the hallowed right of political dissent. They have everything to do with the creation of a cultural climate in which a rapist feels he is merely giving in to a normal urge and a woman is encouraged to believe that sexual masochism is healthy, liberated fun. Justice Potter Stewart once said about hard-core pornography "You know it when you see it," and that certainly used to be true. In the good old days, pornography looked awful. It was cheap and sleazy, and there was no mistaking it for art.

Nowadays, since the porn industry has become a multimillion   11
dollar business, visual technology has been employed in its service. Pornographic movies are skillfully filmed and edited, pornographic still shots using the newest tenets of good design artfully grace the covers of *Hustler, Penthouse,* and *Playboy,* and the public—and the courts—are sadly confused.

The Supreme Court neglected to define "hard-core" in the Miller   12
decision. This was a mistake. If "hard-core" refers only to explicit sexual intercourse, then that isn't good enough. When women or children or men—no matter how artfully—are shown tortured or terrorized in the service of sex, that's obscene. And "patently offensive," I would hope, to our "contemporary community standards."

Justice William O. Douglas wrote in his dissent to the Miller case   13
that no one is "compelled to look." This is hardly true. To buy a paper at the corner newsstand is to subject oneself to a forcible immersion in pornography, to be demeaned by an array of dehumanized, chopped-up parts of the female anatomy, packaged like cuts of meat at the supermarket. I happen to like my body and I work hard at the gym to keep it in good shape, but I am embarrassed for my body and for the bodies of all women when I see the fragmented parts of us, so frivolously, and so flagrantly, displayed.

Some constitutional theorists (Justice Douglas was one) have main-   14
tained that any obscenity law is a serious abridgement of free speech. Others (and Justice Earl Warren was one) have maintained that the First Amendment was never intended to protect obscenity. We live quite compatibly with a host of free-speech abridgements. There are restraints against false and misleading advertising or statements—shouting "fire" without cause in a crowded movie theater, etc.—that do not threaten, but strengthen, our societal values. Restrictions on the public display of pornography belong in this category.

The distinction between permission to publish and permission to   15
display publicly is an essential one and one which I think consonant with

First Amendment principles. Justice Burger's words which I quoted above support this without question. We are not saying "Smash the presses" or "Ban the bad ones," but simply "Get the stuff out of our sight." Let the legislatures decide—using realistic and humane contemporary community standards—what can be displayed and what cannot. The courts, after all, will be the final arbiters.

Questions for Analysis

Logic

1. In what ways does the organization of Brownmiller's essay contribute to the strength of her appeal to reason? Explain by finding an example of a section where the essay would be weakened if the material were shifted to another position.
2. Explain the author's reasoning on her willingness to condone pornography if it is not displayed.
3. What arguments of her opponents does Brownmiller specifically attempt to refute? Are there any she does not attempt to refute?

Character

1. How does Brownmiller use the anecdote of the Hollywood Ten to create a sense of her values and assumptions? What sense is thereby established of her views on civil liberties in general and the First Amendment in particular?
2. What effect does Brownmiller's insistence on the quotation marks in paragraph 3 create? What does insisting that she wishes she had said the words do for her personal views? Where else does she speak of her views as other than personal?
3. Does Brownmiller seem fair-minded? What do the references to the American Nazi Party, *Lady Chatterley's Lover,* and Henry Miller's *Tropic* books contribute to establishing this part of her character for her audience? Where else does she display a mind capable of broad and balanced views?

Emotion

1. What attitude toward her subject does the author invite by frequently shortening *pornography* to *porn?* Where and how does Brownmiller invite her reader to feel contempt for pornography? What does she invite us to feel about the artistic claims of pornography and how does she do so?
2. Where and to what effect does Brownmiller shift from *I* to *we* in the essay? What emotional appeals are made by the use of differing pronouns?
3. What differences are there in emotional temperature among the phrases of the last paragraph: "Smash the presses," "Ban the bad ones,"

and "Get the stuff out of our sight"? What emotions are expressed
by the author and tend to be evoked in us by her specific uses of language here?

———————

NOTES FROM A FREE-SPEECH JUNKIE

Susan Jacoby

It is no news that many women are defecting from the ranks of civil   *1*
libertarians on the issue of obscenity. The conviction of Larry Flynt,
publisher of *Hustler* magazine—before his metamorphosis into a born-
again Christian—was greeted with unabashed feminist approval. Harry
Reems, the unknown actor who was convicted by a Memphis jury for
conspiring to distribute the movie *Deep Throat,* has carried on his legal
battles with almost no support from women who ordinarily regard themselves as supporters of the First Amendment. Feminist writers and scholars have even discussed the possibility of making common cause against
pornography with adversaries of the women's movement—including
opponents of the equal rights amendment and "right to life" forces.

All of this is deeply disturbing to a woman writer who believes, as   *2*
I always have and still do, in an absolute interpretation of the First
Amendment. Nothing in Larry Flynt's garbage convinces me that the late
Justice Hugo L. Black was wrong in his opinion that "the federal government is without any power whatsoever under the Constitution to put any
type of burden on free speech and expression of ideas of any kind (as
distinguished from conduct)." Many women I like and respect tell me I
am wrong; I cannot remember having become involved in so many
heated discussions of a public issue since the end of the Vietnam War. A
feminist writer described my views as those of a "First Amendment
junkie."

Many feminist arguments for controls on pornography carry the   *3*
implicit conviction that porn books, magazines, and movies pose a
greater threat to women than similarly repulsive exercises of free speech
pose to other offended groups. This conviction has, of course, been
shared by everyone—regardless of race, creed, or sex—who has ever
argued in favor of abridging the First Amendment. It is the argument
used by some Jews who have withdrawn their support from the American
Civil Liberties Union because it has defended the right of American
Nazis to march through a community inhabited by survivors of Hitler's
concentration camps.

If feminists want to argue that the protection of the Constitution should not be extended to *any* particularly odious or threatening form of speech, they have a reasonable argument (although I don't agree with it). But it is ridiculous to suggest that the porn shops on 42nd Street are more disgusting to women than a march of neo-Nazis is to survivors of the extermination camps.

The arguments over pornography also blur the vital distinction between expression of ideas and conduct. When I say I believe unreservedly in the First Amendment, someone always comes back at me with the issue of "kiddie porn." But kiddie porn is not a First Amendment issue. It is an issue of the abuse of power—the power adults have over children—and not of obscenity. Parents and promoters have no more right to use their children to make porn movies than they do to send them to work in coal mines. The responsible adults should be prosecuted, just as adults who use children for back-breaking farm labor should be prosecuted.

Susan Brownmiller, in *Against Our Will: Men, Women and Rape,* has described pornography as "the undiluted essence of anti-female propaganda." I think this is a fair description of some types of pornography, especially of the brutish subspecies that equates sex with death and portrays women primarily as objects of violence.

The equation of sex and violence, personified by some glossy rock record album covers as well as by *Hustler,* has fed the illusion that censorship of pornography can be conducted on a more rational basis than other types of censorship. Are all pictures of naked women obscene? Clearly not, says a friend. A Renoir nude is art, she says, and *Hustler* is trash. "Any reasonable person" knows that.

But what about something between art and trash—something, say, along the lines of *Playboy* or *Penthouse* magazines? I asked five women for their reactions to one picture in *Penthouse* and got responses that ranged from "lovely" and "sensuous" to "revolting" and "demeaning." Feminists, like everyone else, seldom have rational reasons for their preferences in erotica. Like members of juries, they tend to disagree when confronted with something that falls short of 100 percent vulgarity.

In any case, feminists will not be the arbiters of good taste if it becomes easier to harass, prosecute, and convict people on obscenity charges. Most of the people who want to censor girlie magazines are equally opposed to open discussion of issues that are of vital concern to women: rape, abortion, menstruation, contraception, lesbianism—in fact, the entire range of sexual experience from a woman's viewpoint.

Feminist writers and editors and filmmakers have limited financial resources: Confronted by a determined prosecutor, Hugh Hefner will fare better than Susan Brownmiller. Would the Memphis jurors who convicted Harry Reems for his role in *Deep Throat* be inclined to take a more positive view of paintings of the female genitalia done by sensitive feminist artists? *Ms.* magazine has printed color reproductions of some of those art works; *Ms.* is already banned from a number of high school libraries because someone considers it threatening and/or obscene.

Feminists who want to censor what they regard as harmful pornography have essentially the same motivation as other would-be censors: They want to use the power of the state to accomplish what they have been unable to achieve in the marketplace of ideas and images. The impulse to censor places no faith in the possibilities of democratic persuasion. 11

It isn't easy to persuade certain men that they have better uses for $1.95 each month than to spend it on a copy of *Hustler*? Well, then, give the men no choice in the matter. 12

I believe there is also a connection between the impulse toward censorship on the part of people who used to consider themselves civil libertarians and a more general desire to shift responsibility from individuals to institutions. When I saw the movie *Looking for Mr. Goodbar,* I was stunned by its series of visual images equating sex and violence, coupled with what seems to me the mindless message (a distortion of the fine Judith Rossner novel) that casual sex equals death. When I came out of the movie, I was even more shocked to see parents standing in line with children between the ages of ten and fourteen. 13

I simply don't know why a parent would take a child to see such a movie, any more than I understand why people feel they can't turn off a television set their child is watching. Whenever I say that, my friends tell me I don't know how it is because I don't have children. True, but I do have parents. When I was a child, they did turn off the TV. They didn't expect the Federal Communications Commission to do their job for them. 14

I am a First Amendment junkie. You can't OD on the First Amendment, because free speech is its own best antidote. 15

Questions for Analysis

Logic

1. What does the term *Notes* in Jacoby's title imply about the organization of her argument? Do you agree with the organizational implications? Explain.
2. In what ways does Jacoby's reasoning attempt to reconcile her personal feelings and her principles? Analyze an example.
3. Which counterarguments do you think Jacoby meets most successfully? Which least? Briefly discuss the reasoning behind your judgments.

Character
1. How does Jacoby's title work to establish her character? What kind of attitude toward herself is expressed in her choice of words, particularly *Notes* and *Junkie*? What is the effect of combining these words with the formal, serious, and dignified association of the term *free speech*?
2. What about our sense of Jacoby's character is created by her mentioning "many women I like and respect" in paragraph 2? Where else in the essay is a similar sense created?
3. How does Jacoby meet a potential questioning of her credentials to talk about child pornography in the last paragraph? How does her tactic here function in the same way as other techniques elsewhere in the essay?

Emotion
1. What emotional attitude does the phrase "defecting from the ranks" in paragraph 1 invite us to take toward those whose views Jacoby opposes? What other military metaphors does the author use in the first paragraph and what are the effects of their emotional appeals?
2. What are the emotions invited in her audience by the comparison between porn shops and neo-Nazis in paragraph 4? Where else does she use strong comparisons for similar effects?
3. How does Jacoby argue for a *lack* of emotion as the proper attitude to take about erotica and pornography in paragraph 8? Where else does she use similar techniques for a similar end?

NOBODY EVER GOT RAPED BY A BOOK

Mike Royko

When I was a young crime reporter, I hung around police stations and watched the dregs drift by. 1

They included every sort of sexual adventurer. Rapists, peepers, flashers, child molesters, zoo invaders and guys who wore pink negligees. 2

Some were harmless; others were deadly. But one thing that I never saw was a dirty book sticking out of any of their pockets. 3

Nor did any of them confess to having dashed from a porno movie house to satisfy their lusts. 4

That would have been unlikely, because there was little pornography available. There were no smutty bookstores or porno movie houses. If you wanted to read something lewd, you were limited to the old eight- 5 pagers—silly little cartoon pamphlets that showed Mickey Mouse doing it to Minnie.

For a dirty movie, you had to know somebody who could get you 6 into an American Legion post where they were showing a stag film starring some skinny guy wearing black socks and a pimply woman who moved like she had just worked a double shift on an assembly line.

Yet sex crimes were a routine entry on the police blotter. Anything 7 that sex offenders do today, they were doing then.

But now we're being told by some Washington panel that pornog- 8 raphy is a major cause of sexual violence. Convenience store chains have been pressured into not selling magazines that have centerfolds. And in many states and local communities, there is a new push for more restrictive laws.

So my question is, if pornography turns people into sex fiends, why 9 did we have so much sexual violence before the stuff was available?

One group of experts say that because of pornography, there is 10 more sexual violence than there used to be.

But another group will say that's bunk, that the increase in the crime 11 statistics is simply the result of victims reporting crimes that they used to keep quiet out of embarrassment or because cops and prosecutors brushed them off.

Child abuse, for example. Incest. People used to be ashamed to go 12 to the law. Now most aren't.

So nobody has made a conclusive case that Hefner and Guccione 13 are guilty of anything more provocative than being a couple of pompous, profiteering jerks. Or that seeing an X-rated movie inspires a lout to dash into the streets and drag a woman into a gangway.

But for the sake of argument, let's conclude that pornography does 14 inspire a certain amount of violence.

If that's the case, we should be consistent in outlawing things that 15 cause violence.

Consider that in recent years, there have been more than 220 16 bombings of abortion clinics. Bombs are pretty violent devices.

And what motivates the bombers? Those who have been arrested 17 have expressed deep religious convictions. They say their beliefs justified setting off bombs.

Then there have been the extremist groups that shoot rural sheriffs, 18 talk show hosts and lawyers they suspect of being liberal. They, too, spout religious devotion.

So maybe we should begin considering the outlawing of religion 19 because it is the root cause of so much violence.

But you, as a religious person, answer that religion isn't the cause, 20 that people who set off bombs or shoot talk show hosts have a few screws loose and will always find a reason to be violent.

I agree. Just as I agree with those who say that the guy who crawls   21
through a window and rapes and murders a woman or a child didn't get
turned on by some $6 paperback he bought in Times Square.

Maybe he did it because his brain cells aren't arranged right, or he   22
was dropped on his head as a kid or he is simply evil. And there have
been people like that long before the first book was printed.

Personally, I don't like pornography. But not because I fear it will   23
turn me or someone else into a raging fiend. I dislike it because it is
tasteless, embarrassing and boring.

But that's no reason to ban it. If being tasteless or embarrassing or   24
boring was a crime, we'd have to get rid of 90 percent of the TV shows
and hit records, close down most of the franchise food joints, muzzle the
politicians and prohibit any preacher from talking more than 90 seconds.

Ah, those are some censorship movements I might like to join.   25

Questions for Analysis

Logic
1. According to the following diagram, both the warrant and the claim
   of Royko's main claim are implicit. In your view, what would be
   gained or lost in the essay if these aspects appeared explicitly?
2. Diagram the logic of Royko's claim concerning "root causes."
3. Read Royko's essay as though it began with paragraph 10 and ended
   with what are now his first nine paragraphs. What advantages might
   Royko have seen in the arrangement he chooses? Explain your answer
   using elements of the appeals to character and emotion but emphasizing the appeal to reason.

Character
1. Would you describe the voice Royko creates to speak for him in the
   essay as "tough," "sweet," or "stuffy"? Point to some particular uses of
   language, especially word choice, that create the personality of his
   style for you.
2. Royko says in paragraph 23, "Personally, I don't like pornography."
   By what means has he given you that impression long before this
   explicit statement? Give some specific examples.
3. Is Royko's last sentence ironic—does it say one thing and mean another? If you think so, say what you think the sentence means.
   Whether you think the sentence ironic or not, show how it contributes to your sense of Royko's character.

Emotion
1. What emotions are elicited by Royko's examples of old-time pornography in paragraphs 5 and 6? Explain how and why.

2. What emotions does Royko invite in his audience by phrases like "some Washington panel"[8], "One group of experts" [10], and "But another group" [11]? Find some other examples in which you think Royko generally seeks to elicit the same emotions.
3. What emotions does Royko invite by his characterizations of pornographic publishers in paragraph 13? Explain how and why.

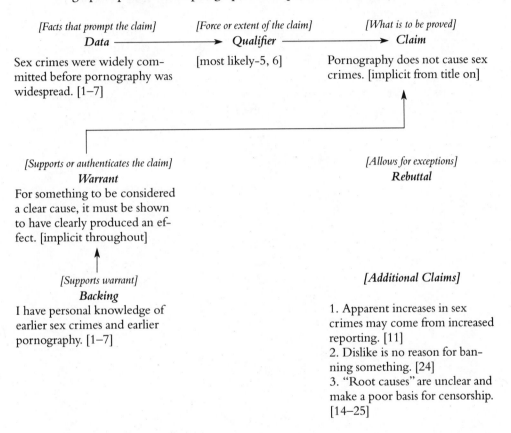

[Facts that prompt the claim]	*[Force or extent of the claim]*	*[What is to be proved]*
Data —————→	Qualifier —————→	Claim
Sex crimes were widely committed before pornography was widespread. [1–7]	[most likely–5, 6]	Pornography does not cause sex crimes. [implicit from title on]

[Supports or authenticates the claim]
Warrant
For something to be considered a clear cause, it must be shown to have clearly produced an effect. [implicit throughout]

[Allows for exceptions]
Rebuttal

[Supports warrant]
Backing
I have personal knowledge of earlier sex crimes and earlier pornography. [1–7]

[Additional Claims]

1. Apparent increases in sex crimes may come from increased reporting. [11]
2. Dislike is no reason for banning something. [24]
3. "Root causes" are unclear and make a poor basis for censorship. [14–25]

EXERCISES: PORNOGRAPHY

Intertextual Questions
1. Each of the writers expresses personal contempt for pornography. Compare the ways each writer expresses his or her contempt.
2. Each writer deals at some point with expert testimony. Compare the ways in which each does so and explain which of the writers makes best use of the technique in your judgment.

3. For most people pornography is an embarrassing subject for discussion. In your opinion, which writer handles this difficulty most effectively. Explain.

Suggestions for Writing

1. Which writer's argument do you find to be the weakest on the whole? Write an essay in which you analyze and explain your evidence for that judgment.

2. Which writer's argument do you find to be the strongest on the whole? Write an essay in which you analyze and explain your evidence for that judgment.

3. D. H. Lawrence defined pornography as something "that does dirt on sex." Write an essay taking off from this statement in which you discuss your views of pornography.

Euthanasia

OFFERING EUTHANASIA CAN BE AN ACT OF LOVE

Derek Humphrey

The American Medical Association's decision to recognize that artificial feeding is a life-support mechanism and can be disconnected from hopelessly comatose patients is a welcome, if tardy, acceptance of the inevitable.

Courts in California and New Jersey have already ruled this way, and although a Massachusetts court recently ruled in an opposite manner, this is being appealed to a higher court.

The AMA's pronouncement is all the more welcome because it comes at a time when the benefits of some of our modern medical technologies are in danger of being ignored because of the public's fear that to be on life-support machinery can create problems.

People dread having their loved ones put on such equipment if it means they are never likely to be removed if that proves later to be the more sensible course. As medical ethicist and lawyer George Annas has said, "People have rights, not technologies."

The argument by the pro-life lobby that food is a gift from God, no matter how it is introduced, and thus to deprive a comatose person of pipeline food is murder, is fallacious. A pipe is a manufactured item; the skill to introduce it into the body and maintain it there is a medical technology. Without the pipeline, the person would die. Food is common to all humans, but taking it through a pipeline is a technique carried out because the person has sustained an injury or suffers an illness which prevents normal feeding.

The pro-life lobby also harks back to Nazi excesses of the 1930s and '40s as part of its argument for continued pipeline feeding. True, Nazi Germany murdered about one hundred thousand Aryan Germans who were mentally or physically defective because it considered them "useless eaters," detracting from the purity of the German race.

But neither the views of the victims nor their relatives were ever sought: they were murdered en masse in secret fashion and untruths concocted to cover the crimes. 7

No terminally ill or comatose person was ever helped to die by the Nazis. Moreover, their barbarous killing spree took in 6 million Jews and 10 million noncombatant Russians, Slavs, and gypsies. Life was cheapened by the Nazis to an appalling degree. What connection is there between the Nazis then and the carefully considered euthanasia today of a permanently comatose person who might, as Karen Quinlan did, lie curled up for ten years without any signs of what most of us consider life? 8

Helping another to die in carefully considered circumstances is part of good medicine and also demonstrates a caring society that offers euthanasia to hopelessly sick persons as an act of love. 9

Questions for Analysis

Logic
1. Where does Humphrey suggest a definition of the "carefully considered circumstances" of his last paragraph?
2. Explain the logic of Humphrey's distinction between the Nazi murder of "useless eaters" and his own position on artificial feeding.
3. What in your view would be gained or lost for Humphrey's argument if the essay were reorganized with the last paragraph made the second paragraph?

Character
1. What does the separation of the medical and legal issues in paragraphs 1 and 2 contribute to your sense of the author's character?
2. What attempts does Humphrey make through his word choice to avoid a possible accusation of unfeeling brutality?
3. What sense of the author's character is created by the fact that almost all his sentences are declarative in their grammatical form?

Emotion
1. The phrase in paragraph 1, "acceptance of the inevitable," is one often used to describe dying. Do you think Humphrey is making a joke here about the AMA? Explain your answer.
2. To what emotions does the author appeal in his characterization of his opponents as "the pro-life lobby" in paragraphs 5 and 6?
3. To what emotions does the author appeal by using the word *helping* in reference to euthanasia?

EUTHANASIA IS NOT THE ANSWER

Matthew E. Conolly

From the moment of our conception, each of us is engaged in a   *1*
personal battle that we must fight alone, a battle whose final outcome is
never in any doubt, for, naked, and all too often alone, sooner or later we
all must die.

We do not all make life's pilgrimage on equal terms. For some the   *2*
path is strewn with roses, and after a long and healthy life, death comes
swiftly and easily, for others it is not so. The bed of roses is supplanted by
a bed of nails, with poverty, rejection, deformity, and humiliation the
only lasting companions they ever know.

I know that many people here today carry this problem of pain in   *3*
a personal way, or else it has been the lot of someone close to you.
Otherwise you would not be here. So let me say right at the outset, that
those of us who have not had to carry such a burden dare not criticize
those who have, if they should plead with us for an early end to their
dismal sojourn in this world.

HARD CASES MAKE BAD LAWS

Society in general, and the medical profession in particular, cannot   *4*
just turn away. We must do *something;* the question is—what?

The "what" we are being asked to consider today, of course, is   *5*
voluntary euthanasia. So that there be no confusion, let me make it quite
clear that to be opposed to the active taking of life, one does not have to
be determined to keep the heart beating at all costs.

I believe I speak for all responsible physicians when I say that there   *6*
clearly comes a time when death can no longer be held at bay, and when
we must sue for peace on the enemy's terms. At such a time, attending to
the patient's comfort in body, mind, and soul becomes paramount. There
is no obligation, indeed no justification, for pressing on at such a time
with so-called life-sustaining measures, be they respirators, intravenous
fluids, CPR, or whatever. I believe that there is no obligation to continue
a treatment once it has been started, if it becomes apparent that it is doing
no good. Also, withholding useless treatment and letting nature take its
course is *not* equivalent to active euthanasia. Some people have attempted
to blur this distinction by creating the term "passive euthanasia." The least
unkind thing that can be said about this term is that it is very confusing.

Today's discussion really boils down to the question—do hard and   *7*
tragic cases warrant legalization of euthanasia? There can be no doubt

that hard and tragic cases do occur. However, the very natural tendency to want to alleviate human tragedy by legislative change is fraught with hazard, and I firmly believe that every would-be lawmaker should have tattooed on his or her face, where it can be seen in the mirror each morning, the adage that HARD CASES MAKE BAD LAWS.

If we take the superficially humane step of tailoring the law to the supposed wishes of an Elizabeth Bouvia (who, incidentally, later changed her mind), we will not only bring a hornet's nest of woes about our own ears, but, at a stroke, we will deny many relatives much good that we could have salvaged from a sad situation, while at the same time giving many *more* grief and guilt to contend with. Even worse, we will have denied our patients the best that could have been offered. Worst of all, that soaring of the human spirit to heights of inspiration and courage which only adversity makes possible will be denied, and we will all, from that, grow weaker, and less able to deal with the crisis of tomorrow. 8

UNLEASHING EUTHANASIA

Let's look at these problems one by one. The first problem is that once we unleash euthanasia, once we take to ourselves the right actively to terminate a human life, we will have no means of controlling it. Adolf Hitler showed with startling clarity that once the dam is breached, the principle somewhere compromised, death in the end comes to be administered equally to all—to the unwanted fetus, to the deformed, the mentally defective, the old and the unproductive, and thence to the politically inconvenient, and finally to the ethnically unacceptable. There is no logical place to stop. 9

The founders of Hemlock no doubt mean euthanasia only for those who feel they can take no more, but if it is available for one it must be available for all. Then what about those precious people who even to the end put others before themselves? They will now have laid upon them the new and horrible thought that perhaps they ought to do away with themselves to spare their relatives more trouble or expense. What will they feel as they see their 210 days of Medicare hospice payments run out, and still they are alive. Not long ago, Governor Lamm of Colorado suggested that the old and incurable have a *duty* to get out of the way of the next generation. And can you not see where these pressures will be the greatest? It will be amongst the poor and dispossessed. Watts will have sunk in a sea of euthanasia long before the first ripple laps the shore of Brentwood. Is that what we mean to happen? Is that what we want? Is there nobility of purpose there? 10

It matters to me that my patients trust me. If they do so, it is because they believe that I will always act in their best interests. How could such trust survive if they could never be sure each time I approached the bed 11 that I had not come to administer some coup de grace when they were not in a state to define their own wishes?

Those whose relatives have committed more conventional forms of *12*
suicide are often afterwards assailed by feelings of guilt and remorse. It would be unwise to think that euthanasia would bring any less in its wake.

A BETTER WAY

Speaking as a physician, I assert that unrelieved suffering need never *13*
occur, and I want to turn to this important area. Proponents of euthanasia make much of the pain and anguish so often linked in people's minds with cancer. I would not dare to pretend that the care we offer is not sometimes abysmal, whether because of the inappropriate use of aggressive technological medicine, the niggardly use of analgesics, some irrational fear of addiction in a dying patient, or a lack of compassion.

However, for many, the process of dying is more a case of gradually *14*
loosing life's moorings and slipping away. Oftentimes the anguish of dying is felt not by the patient but by the relatives: just as real, just as much in need of compassionate support, but hardly a reason for killing the patient!

But let us consider the patients who do have severe pain, turmoil, *15*
and distress, who find their helplessness or incontinence humiliating, for it is these who most engage our sympathies. It is wrong to assert that they must make a stark choice between suicide or suffering.

There is another way. *16*

Experience with hospice care in England and the United States has *17*
shown repeatedly that in *every* case, pain and suffering can be overwhelmingly reduced. In many cases it can be abolished altogether. This care, which may (and for financial reasons perhaps must) include home care, is not easy. It demands infinite love and compassion. It must include the latest scientific knowledge of analgesic drugs, nerve blocks, antinausea medication, and so on. But it can be done, it can be done, it can be done!

LIFE IS SPECIAL

Time and again our patients have shown us that life, even a de- *18*
formed, curtailed, and, to us, who are whole, an unimaginable life, can be made noble and worth living. Look at Joni Earickson—paraplegic from the age of seventeen—now a most positive, vibrant and inspirational person who has become world famous for her triumph over adversity. Time and time again, once symptoms are relieved, patients and relatives share quality time together, when forgiveness can be sought and given—for many a time of great healing.

Man, made in the image of his Creator, is *different* from all other   19
animals. For this reason, his life is special and may not be taken at will.

We do not know why suffering is allowed, but Old and New Tes-   20
tament alike are full of reassurances that we have not been, and will not
ever be, abandoned by our God. "Yea, though I walk through the valley
of the shadow of death, I will fear no evil *for thou art with me.*"

CALL TO CHANGE DIRECTION

Our modern tragedy is that man has turned his back on God, who   21
alone can help, and has set himself up as the measure of all things. Gone
then is the absolute importance of man, gone the sanctity of his life, and
the meaning of it. Gone too the motivation for loving care which is our
responsible duty to the sick and dying. Goodbye love. Hello indifference.

With our finite minds, we cannot know fully the meaning of life,   22
but though at times the storms of doubt may rage, I stake my life on the
belief that to God we are special, that with Him, murder is unacceptable,
and suicide (whatever you call it) becomes unnecessary.

Abandon God, and yes, you can have euthanasia. But a *good* death   23
it can never be, and no subterfuge of law like that before us today can
ever make it so.

My plea to the Hemlock Society is: Give up your goal of self-   24
destruction. Instead, lend your energy, your anger, your indignation, your
influence and creativity to work with us in the building of such a system
of hospice care that death, however it come, need no longer be feared. Is
not this a nobler cause? Is not this a better way?

Questions for Analysis

Logic

1. How and where does Conolly separate the medical, legal, and religious implications of his argument? How and where are they
combined?
2. What seems to be the reasoning behind Conolly's claim that with
euthanasia "there is no logical place to stop"? [9]
3. Explain Conolly's reasoning at the end of his essay when he distinguishes between the idea of "good" and what he calls a "subterfuge
of law."

Character

1. Conolly's argument is taken from a speech he delivered to the Hemlock Society—a group that favors euthanasia. What does this fact
contribute to your sense of the author's character?

2. Conolly talks as a doctor, but what other personal attributes does he imply as defining characteristics of his identity?
3. Do you find the first sentence of paragraph 9—"Let's look at these problems one by one"—is representative of the author's style in general? Explain why or why not.

Emotion
1. What emotions does the author appeal to in the third paragraph?
2. What emotions are appealed to by the author's use of the term *unleash* in paragraph 9?
3. To what emotions in his audience does Conolly appeal by his discussion of his patients' trust in paragraph 11?

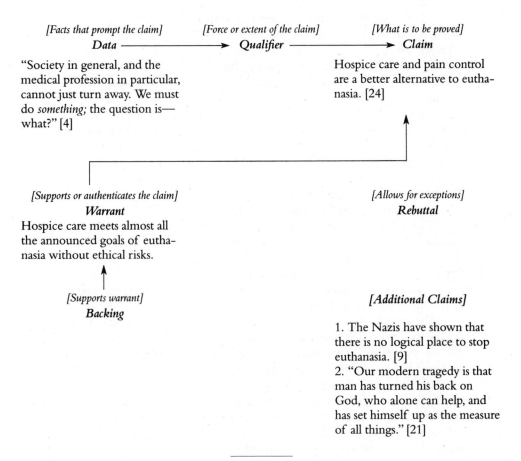

[Facts that prompt the claim] **Data**	[Force or extent of the claim] **Qualifier**	[What is to be proved] **Claim**
"Society in general, and the medical profession in particular, cannot just turn away. We must do *something;* the question is—what?" [4]		Hospice care and pain control are a better alternative to euthanasia. [24]

[Supports or authenticates the claim]
Warrant
Hospice care meets almost all the announced goals of euthanasia without ethical risks.

[Allows for exceptions]
Rebuttal

[Supports warrant]
Backing

[Additional Claims]

1. The Nazis have shown that there is no logical place to stop euthanasia. [9]
2. "Our modern tragedy is that man has turned his back on God, who alone can help, and has set himself up as the measure of all things." [21]

MUST THEY TINKER WITH THE DYING?

Nancy M. Lederman

My grandmother, Freda Weinstein, was hospitalized for more than 1
four weeks after she was hit by a little girl riding a bicycle in a New York
playground. The unwary girl knocked her over, breaking her hip. It was
a bad fracture, the surgeon said. A week later, another surgeon said my
90-year-old grandmother had a perforated ulcer, and it was immediately
repaired. Then she had internal bleeding and a heart attack.

In hospital jargon, these are "events." The older the patient, the 2
more likely a hospital stay will trigger a succession of events leading to
one final event.

My grandmother's strength was impressive. She was tied to her bed 3
to keep her from pulling out the catheter and intravenous lines that
supplied fluids, pain-killer and sedation. Despite the restraints, she pulled
out the ventilator tube that helped her breathe. Fighting the restraints,
she developed blisters on her forearms. She also had a gastro-nasal tube in
her nose.

The doctors wanted desperately to save her; that's what doctors are 4
programmed to do. To deal with the bleeding, they performed an endos-
copy, trailing another tube down her throat to her stomach. When that
didn't work, they wanted to do another. I said, enough. They wanted to
operate to stanch the bleeding, or do an angiogram, or both. Enough.
The prognosis kept changing. One doctor said, "I.C.U. psychosis." Another said, "How can you let her bleed to death?"

The odds were she would wind up where she most dreaded, in a 5
nursing home. At the least, she would need 24-hour care for a long time.
She would be "walker-dependent"—if she could walk at all. These
things, I knew, she emphatically did not want. I had her health care proxy.
I had drafted it. Although she had no living will, we discussed her wishes
many times. But we had not anticipated this.

She wasn't terminal. Once on the ventilator, she would stay there 6
as long as she needed it to breathe. Her body was fighting to live, as if
she was programmed to survive. Her mind was fighting, too. When I
squeezed her hand, she squeezed back. Hard.

If she could fully wake, what would she tell me? Would she say, Let 7
me die? In her pocketbook, I found speeches she had written, to be
delivered to her senior center. I had a "eulogy" she had prepared months
before, to be read at her funeral. It was a letter to her family and friends
telling them not to grieve: she had lived a full life.

They say our ethics have yet to catch up to our technology. Medical **8** advances are prolonging life for more and more people. Longer lives are not necessarily better ones.

They say you must have a living will or a health care proxy. Prefer- **9** ably both. Only then can you be assured that you or your chosen surrogate will be able to make critical health care decisions for you. They don't tell you what it's like to make those decisions for someone else—to play the odds with someone else's life.

My grandmother's "case" was used by the hospital ethicist on train- **10** ing rounds. Interns, nurses and physicians' assistants discussed options. One resident said he couldn't understand why I refused the angiogram, why I had signed a "do not resuscitate" order if I was continuing to permit blood transfusions.

As the doctors kept offering me interventions to save her, I began **11** looking for a way out. I wanted her off that ventilator, sooner rather than later. Once she was off, I could refuse to let her back on.

How can you let her bleed to death? How could I not? I wasn't **12** brave. But she was, and I had her proxy.

She died on Nov. 19. I wasn't there. I don't know what killed her. **13** Respiratory failure, kidney failure, heart failure—it didn't matter. No experiments, she had said. None, I promised her. I kept my promise.

Questions for Analysis

Logic
1. Lederman's essay is organized partly by chronology. Do you see any other organizing principles at work? Explain your answer.
2. A large part of the author's appeal to reason takes place in the final paragraph. What elements if any in the reasoning there also appear elsewhere in the essay?
3. In what explicit and/or implicit ways does Lederman attempt to refute the arguments of her grandmother's doctors?

Character
1. Lederman is a lawyer by profession. In what ways do you think she does or does not attempt to express that aspect of her character in the essay?
2. In what ways does the author express the intensity of her concern for her grandmother? Point to specific uses of language that work to create this aspect of the author's character as expressed in the essay.
3. In what ways does the author create a sense of her grandmother's character? How does this sense of character support Lederman's argument?

Emotion
1. Explain the ways in which the word *tinker* in the essay's title appeals to the reader's emotions. Do you find the same emotions appealed to elsewhere in the essay? Explain.
2. How would you describe the emotions expressed by the general style of the essay and the tone of voice it creates? Point to some examples in explaining your answer.
3. What emotions does the author suggest were expressed by the doctors in charge of her grandmother? How does the author suggest them? Point to some particular moments and explain the operations of the specific language involved.

EXERCISES: EUTHANASIA

Intertextual Questions
1. Compare the uses that Humphrey and Conolly make of the example of Nazi Germany in their arguments.
2. With what if anything would Humphrey and Lederman take issue in Conolly's paragraph 6? Explain your answer.
3. Compare the roles that the writers see for love in what they consider to be the proper response to suffering.

Suggestions for Writing
1. Write an essay that compares the views of all the writers on the issue of personal versus medical responsibility in euthanasia.
2. Write a letter to the author with whom you most disagree and argue for your own views while answering his or hers.
3. Write an essay that analyzes the ways in which each writer attempts to bring an appropriate dignity of style to the great issues of life and death involved.

Whose Name Is a Married Woman's Name?

TAKE THE NAME—PASS IT ON

Jennifer Ozersky

Names—and this is what some people hate about them—are given to you at birth when you are helpless. But should they stay with you forever? They represent you to the world, they're one of the biggest parts of your identity, and at first you don't even have a say in what they are. What a gyp! As a married woman, my troubles are compounded by having lost the surname I was born with—my father's name. This change comes from history in the form of social customs I had no part in forming.

Yet how much there is that comes to me from history that I had no part in forming. My mother's prematurely gray hair, my father's bulbous nose, the family tendencies toward asthma and social unease. If only there were a set of bins somewhere containing choosable noses, hair, and talents. Perhaps the genetic-design specialists of the future will provide.

But until then, these ill-assorted features are mine. They link me (even when I feel most apart from them) to my mother and my father, and they will link me to my sons and daughters, if I have any. I will also see my husband's features, which I have examined so closely on so many snore-awakened mornings, imprinted on their infant faces and mixed inextricably with my own. To give that infant a hyphenated name, an equal-time deal struck between parents' egos, would be a monstrous denial of that mixture. No, one surname is better and though the name isn't the one I was born with, it's the one I choose.

Besides, even if I don't ever have children, there isn't any map or chart on a clipboard to show where the married part of me ends and the other part begins. That kind of allocating can only be the work of egos, not of love: hyphenated names or "kept" names announce a split between, not a marriage of, two people.

Maybe this sounds too submissive. After all, if wives and husbands   5
come together, shouldn't they both give up their individual names? Well,
to look at the thing logically, I suppose you would have to say they
should. But logic doesn't make people come together in the first place,
and it doesn't rule once they have. Love does; or at least it should. In a
real and public way, I have announced that I am not one person alone
any more. I was alone for a long time, and while that time had its moments, I didn't feel complete. I traded in my ego for a family and a chance
to contribute through my children to the flow of history.

What could I have said to my husband? I'll be your wife but history   6
starts with us and I'll keep my (father's) name? Then our child will be
handed a makeshift name from both our fathers? On that reasoning, our
grandchildren will have four names and our great grandchildren eight, all
of them a tribute to "logic" and ego. The next generation would have
sixteen names, and untangling them would be enough to keep the lawyers busy until the messiah comes—if you could find a lawyer in a phone
book with columns sixteen names wide! You should take the name when
you take the husband and acknowledge past and future history by acknowledging the history of social custom.

Questions for Analysis

Logic
1. Explain in your own words the author's distinction between "individuals" and married people as far as past history is concerned.
2. Explain in your own words the author's distinction between individuals and married people as far as future history is concerned.
3. Examine the organization of the essay. Could any paragraph be placed
   in another position without changing the argument? What part do
   the transitions that begin the paragraphs play in the argument's
   organization?

Character
1. How would you describe the general tone of voice created by the
   style of the essay? Aloof? Aggressive? Chatty? Point to some examples
   and explain how particular uses of language create the tone you hear.
2. What sense of the author's character is created for you by her choosing
   apparently "negative" examples of inheritance in paragraph 2?
3. What sense of the author's character is created for you by her remarks
   about her descendants in the last paragraph?

Emotion
1. Do you think the introductory paragraph tends to increase or diminish
   the emotional intensity associated with the topic? Explain your answer
   by analyzing the emotional appeals made in paragraph 1.

2. What emotions are appealed to by the author through the phrase "equal-time deal" in paragraph 3? In answering, compare the appeal of the phrase to that made by the word *compromise*.

3. What emotions are appealed to in the audience by the example of the telephone book in the last paragraph? Do you think the joke would have been more effective if fewer or more generations had been mentioned? Explain your answer.

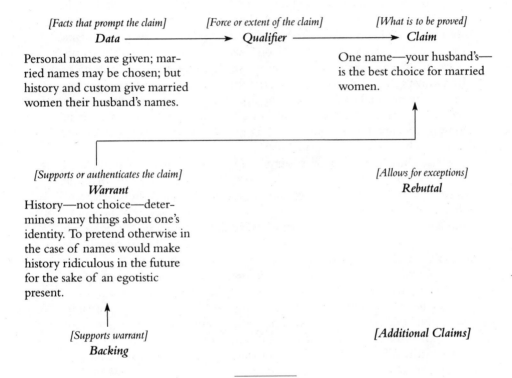

[Facts that prompt the claim]
Data ──────────→

[Force or extent of the claim]
Qualifier ──────────→

[What is to be proved]
Claim

Personal names are given; married names may be chosen; but history and custom give married women their husband's names.

One name—your husband's—is the best choice for married women.

[Supports or authenticates the claim]
Warrant
History—not choice—determines many things about one's identity. To pretend otherwise in the case of names would make history ridiculous in the future for the sake of an egotistic present.

[Allows for exceptions]
Rebuttal

[Supports warrant]
Backing

[Additional Claims]

WITH ALL POLITENESS, NO—I'LL KEEP MY OWN NAME, THANK YOU

Emma Coleman

To take one example from many: recently, my husband and I were introduced at a faculty party as "Dr. and Mrs. Tony Berruti." I protested to my host, a woman as it happened, that she of all people would know better than to call me by my husband's name. "But, Emma," she replied pacifically, "you know how conventional these other people are and I just didn't want to make a fuss."

There the matter would have rested in the "polite" silence of oppression. A woman who has known me for twenty years, known me before and after my marriage, introduces me in public as an appendage! If someone like this—an educated person with no interest in putting women down or in keeping them down—was willing to strip me of my identity for the sake of "politeness," then I knew things were worse than I thought.

We all give in to daily oppressions. Women are not the only people who are objectified, labeled or treated badly. But perhaps because there are more women in the world than any other underclass, we tend to take things we know to be wrong in our stride. I was born with a name. Admittedly, it was my father's name and not my mother's, but that objection only pushes back a legitimate grievance: an infinite historical regression of men squelching protest and women's individuality. So women have always taken their father's names. So what? I was Emma Coleman long before anyone thought of calling me Berruti. So, do I or do I not have a right to maintain my identity as a child of my parents?

My husband, after all, is supposed to be an equal, not some legal guardian who stands *in loco parentis;* if his ability to create or to form me is tantamount to my father's or mother's, I don't want to be married to him. But it isn't and I do. A little thing, you might say, but more and more people are realizing that so-called little things in society—the dropped phrases, the "polite" dismissals, the suppressed objections—are exactly the sort of grease that keeps unjust social mechanisms running "smoothly." Just let the men who consider my insistence on keeping my name be threatened with losing theirs and you'll see what I mean.

The fact is, I myself am polite and generally quite conventional in my public manners. I don't advocate wild political schemes. I just want to be known legally and socially as the same person now that I have been since birth. While it's true that emotionally and spiritually I've changed a great deal since my marriage, that doesn't mean that I am a new human being, or have become an unperson. As long as I have the individual responsibilities of an adult citizen and an independent personality, I deserve to keep my own name. Little harm may be meant by people genuflecting to custom and calling me by my husband's name; but as long as I object to it, however fussy that may seem, I have laid myself on the line by choosing my own name. Think twice before you confront me on it.

Questions for Analysis

Logic

1. Coleman's organization moves back and forth between her own ex-

perience and a more general focus on larger social issues. In what ways does she work to connect the two subjects in her essay?

2. The Latin phrase *in loco parentis* in paragraph 4 means "in the place of a parent." How does Coleman use this phrase to criticize the logic of those who oppose her views?

3. In the last paragraph the author uses the phrase "genuflecting to custom." What are the arguments against the custom implied by the metaphor of genuflecting or "bending the knee?"

Character

1. At the end of the essay, the author characterizes herself as a "polite" person. Point to an example in her essay that seems to seek to demonstrate this claim, and explain how it does or doesn't do so in your view.

2. What senses of the author's character are created for you by the ways in which she refers to her parents and her husband within her essay? For example, presumably her husband agrees with her choice, but her mother disagreed. Does Coleman implicitly praise or blame either for their views?

3. What sense of the author's character is created for you by the tone of voice in her last sentence? Do you find this tone adopted earlier at any point?

Emotion

1. What are the changing emotions the author feels about the words *politeness* and *polite*? To what emotions in her audience do these changes seem designed to appeal?

2. What emotions does the author imply she felt about her friend and host? What emotions does the author invite her reader to feel?

3. What emotional appeal seems to be made by the author's use of the word *appendage* in paragraph 2? Pick another metaphor that the author might have used here—*chattel,* for example, and compare the intensity of the emotions created by the different choices.

THE GAME OF THE NAME

Patricia Saunders-Evans

When I married, I hyphenated my name, believing at the time that 1 I fully understood the issues surrounding my action. Why, I thought, should I replace my name with my husband's? The virtue of mine was just that—it was mine—and as I understood the matter, my entering a marriage entailed nothing that would require me to relinquish it for someone else's. When asked about my decision, I enumerated the familiar feminist arguments against taking husbands' names: clearly I wasn't property; nor was I being adopted; and there was certainly nothing in my personal past so heinous as to spur me to take on an alias. On balance, I told myself there were no positive reasons simply to take my husband's name and in fact to do so suggested negative implications about my relationship to my own. By keeping my name and adding my husband's I believed I was avoiding any subscription to an ideology of marriage that privileges men over women, while at the same time making a choice that reflected my willingness to mark my new relationship to my husband as a part of my identity. I was content that I had found a solution to the problem of what to do about married names.

That was in 1987 and in the years I have lived with my new name I   2
have learned something about making choices that revises my reasoning concerning the issues that marriage and name switching raise. For one thing, I immediately discovered that while controlling my name I could not control the ways other people used it. I was, and still am, often addressed as Mrs. David Evans or Ms. Patricia Saunders. This confusion would possibly be less disconcerting to me if all the people who engaged in these acts of renaming were strangers who knew nothing of my chosen appellation, or if there weren't people who persisted in *not* choosing it for reasons of their own, even after I have pointed out their mistake.

Perhaps at this point my reader may feel that my problem is a simple   3
matter of cultural habituation that affects hyphenated names alone, and that when a sufficient number of people adopt my practice, those with hyphenated designators will regain rightful control of how they are addressed. Well, maybe; and perhaps in that future, official forms will include more space in which to record one's hyphenated name; but I submit that the problems created for me by my new name are of a different nature. For I have found that when I changed my name I was acting as though my name were my own, a part of my identity that I owned and could control as though it were an extension of my person. What I learned and now consider to be the truth about names, is that they do not belong to us as individuals; they belong to others too, and for a woman this is doubly so. Consider: had I chosen simply to keep my original name—Patricia Saunders—my marriage would none the less have effected a change in my name, because it would no longer be the family name I was given, but rather the family name I chose to keep. The two meanings are not the same, though in each case the meaning of the name is created by other people. So, when women marry, their names change even if they do not themselves actively alter them. Whatever choice you make, your name *will* change when you marry, whether you like it or not.

Questions for Analysis

Logic

1. The author's title suggests that in some ways using names is comparable to a game. List some of the various "rules" the essay seems to dramatize. For example, what are the rules for someone who wishes to offend without being accused of doing so intentionally?
2. What does the author see as the basic mistake in her earlier reasoning?
3. Explain in your own words the author's conclusion with regard to the "choice" individuals have concerning their names.

Character

1. What methods does the author use to establish a sense of sincerity in her essay? Point to some particular examples.
2. What efforts does the author make to appear fair-minded? Point to some examples.
3. "Learning" is a theme that organizes the essay. What aspects of the author's character are created by the difference between what she learns and what some of the people in her life seem to have refused to learn?

Emotion

1. What emotions toward her subject seem expressed by the author's use of the phrase "at the time" in her first sentence? What emotions in her reader seem appealed to by the phrase?
2. Think of a few phrases that would express a meaning close to "revises my reasoning" in paragraph 2; for example, "now baffles me." What are the different emotional intensities of the phrases? How is her phrase representative of her emotional "temperature" throughout the essay?
3. What emotions does the author feel toward those who refuse to use her hyphenated married name? How strongly are they expressed? Explain your answer by pointing to particular examples.

EXERCISES: WHOSE NAME IS A MARRIED WOMAN'S NAME?

Intertextual Questions

1. Which author seems most sure that her choice is the correct one? Which least sure? Explain your answers by pointing to particular examples.
2. Which argument seems most logically convincing to you? Which most emotionally convincing? Explain your answers by pointing to particular evidence in the language of the essay.

3. Which author seems most open to opposing points of view? Point to some ways in which that attitude is expressed in the writing.

Suggestions for Writing

1. None of the authors mentions a husband's views, though presumably each husband agrees with his wife's choice. Write an essay in which you describe what you think is expressed about one of the husbands by his agreement. For example, could Mr. Ozersky agree with his wife's regard for tradition *without* thinking of her as "his property"?

2. Which essay seems to you to be best argued without regard to whether you agree with its conclusion? Write an essay in which you praise the writer for her technique and performance.

3. What are your views on the topic? Write an essay in which you argue for your own view while being careful to take into account the arguments of those who might oppose it.

Strikers and Scabs

THE SCAB

Jack London

In a competitive society, where men struggle with one another for 1
food and shelter, what is more natural than that generosity, when it diminishes the food and shelter of men other than he who is generous,
should be held an accursed thing? Wise old saws to the contrary, he who
takes from a man's purse takes from his existence. To strike at a man's
food and shelter is to strike at his life; and in a society organized on a
tooth-and-nail basis, such an act, performed though it may be under the
guise of generosity, is none the less menacing and terrible.

It is for this reason that a laborer is so fiercely hostile to another 2
laborer who offers to work for less pay or longer hours. To hold his place,
(which is to live), he must offset this offer by another equally liberal,
which is equivalent to giving away somewhat from the food and shelter
he enjoys. To sell his day's work for $2, instead of $2.50, means that he,
his wife, and his children will not have so good a roof over their heads,
so warm clothes on their backs, so substantial food in their stomachs.
Meat will be bought less frequently and it will be tougher and less nutritious, stout new shoes will go less often on the children's feet, and disease
and death will be more imminent in a cheaper house and neighborhood.

Thus the generous laborer, giving more of a day's work for less 3
return (measured in terms of food and shelter), threatens the life of his
less generous brother laborer, and at the best, if he does not destroy that
life, he diminishes it. Whereupon the less generous laborer looks upon
him as an enemy, and, as men are inclined to do in a tooth-and-nail
society, he tries to kill the man who is trying to kill him.

When a striker kills with a brick the man who has taken his place, 4
he has no sense of wrong-doing. In the deepest holds of his being,
though he does not reason the impulse, he has an ethical sanction. He
feels dimly that he has justification, just as the home-defending Boer felt,
though more sharply, with each bullet he fired at the invading English.

Behind every brick thrown by a striker is the selfish will "to live" of himself, and the slightly altruistic will "to live" of his family. The family group came into the world before the State group, and society, being still on the primitive basis of tooth and nail, the will "to live" of the State is not so compelling to the striker as is the will "to live" of his family and himself.

In addition to the use of bricks, clubs, and bullets, the selfish laborer finds it necessary to express his feelings in speech. Just as the peaceful country-dweller calls the sea-rover a "pirate," and the stout burgher calls the man who breaks into his strong-box a "robber," so the selfish laborer applies the opprobrious epithet "scab" to the laborer who takes from him food and shelter by being more generous in the disposal of his labor power. The sentimental connotation of "scab" is as terrific as that of "traitor" or "Judas," and a sentimental definition would be as deep and varied as the human heart. It is far easier to arrive at what may be called a technical definition, worded in commercial terms, as, for instance, that *a scab is one who gives more value for the same price than another.* 5

The laborer who gives more time or strength or skill for the same wage than another, or equal time or strength or skill for a less wage, is a scab. This generousness on his part is hurtful to his fellow-laborers, for it compels them to an equal generousness which is not to their liking, and which gives them less of food and shelter. But a word may be said for the scab. Just as his act makes his rivals compulsorily generous, so do they, by fortune of birth and training, make compulsory his act of generousness. He does not scab because he wants to scab. No whim of the spirit, no burgeoning of the heart, leads him to give more of his labor power than they for a certain sum. 6

It is because he cannot get work on the same terms as they that he is a scab. There is less work than there are men to do work. This is patent, else the scab would not loom so large on the labor-market horizon. Because they are stronger than he, or more skilled, or more energetic, it is impossible for him to take their places at the same wage. To take their places he must give more value, must work longer hours or receive a smaller wage. He does so, and he cannot help it, for his will "to live" is driving him on as well as they are being driven on by their will "to live"; and to live he must win food and shelter, which he can do only by receiving permission to work from some man who owns a bit of land or a piece of machinery. And to receive permission from this man, he must make the transaction profitable for him. 7

Viewed in this light, the scab, who gives more labor power for a certain price than his fellows, is not so generous after all. He is no more generous with his energy than the chattel slave and the convict laborer, who, by the way, are the almost perfect scabs. They give their labor power for about the minimum possible price. But, within limits, they may loaf 8 and malinger, and, as scabs, are exceeded by the machine, which never loafs and malingers and which is the ideally perfect scab.

Questions for Analysis

Logic

1. In the context of the essay as a whole, explain the basis of London's reasoning in the first paragraph where he says that a generous person is an "accursed thing."
2. How does London distinguish between a "sentimental" and a "technical" definition in paragraph 5?
3. What advantages do you see for his argument in London's delaying the definition of his key term *scab* until the middle of the essay? For example, what would have been the effect of his having begun with that moment?

Character

1. What efforts does London make to establish his character as a reasonable and objective observer of the economic scene in general and the labor issue in particular? Give examples.
2. What efforts does London make to establish his character as one that includes benevolence and good will? Give examples.
3. What does London do to establish himself as clear-thinking and intelligent? Give examples.

Emotion

1. How does London seem to expect his audience to respond to the "generosity" of the scab at the beginning of the essay? How at the end? How does the shift support his general argument?
2. What emotions does London appeal to in paragraph 2 with his description of domestic life?
3. What emotional appeals does London make in paragraph 5 when he defines the "scab" by analogy?

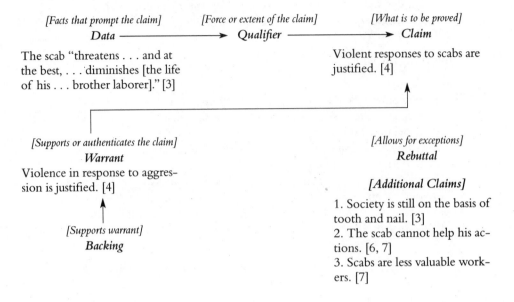

[Facts that prompt the claim]
Data —————————→ [Force or extent of the claim] **Qualifier** —————————→ [What is to be proved] **Claim**

The scab "threatens . . . and at the best, . . . diminishes [the life of his . . . brother laborer]." [3]

Violent responses to scabs are justified. [4]

[Supports or authenticates the claim]
Warrant
Violence in response to aggression is justified. [4]

[Supports warrant]
Backing

[Allows for exceptions]
Rebuttal

[Additional Claims]
1. Society is still on the basis of tooth and nail. [3]
2. The scab cannot help his actions. [6, 7]
3. Scabs are less valuable workers. [7]

THE SCAB

Walter Block

One of the most universally shared attitudes is that the scab is a 1
wretched character. He is unscrupulous and sneakily in league with the "boss." Together, scab and boss plot to deprive union workers of their rights, and of the jobs that are legitimately theirs. Scabs are hired to force union workers to accept lower wages. When it becomes known that scabs are also used to beat up union workers and pickets, the case is virtually complete—the scab is the greatest enemy of the worker.

These are the facts that are taught in many of our centers of learn- 2
ing, to be challenged only at the risk of one's reputation as a scholar. Nevertheless, this flummery must be refuted.

The first point to establish is that a job is not a thing which can be 3
owned by a worker—or by any one else. A job is the manifestation of a *trade* between a worker and an employer. The worker trades his labor for the money of the employer, at some mutually agreeable rate of exchange. So when we speak of "my job," we are only talking figuratively.

Although we are in the habit of using such phrases as "my job," 4
"my customer," and "my tailor," we do not presume ownership in *any* of these instances. Take first the case of "my customer." If this phrase were taken literally, it would denote that the merchant has an ownership right over the "custom" of the people who habitually buy from him. He would *own* the customer's patronage and he would, therefore, have a right to object if "his" customer patronized another merchant.

The sword cuts both ways. Let us take the case of "my tailor." If we were to take this phrase literally, we would have to say that the tailor may not shut down his shop, relocate, or declare himself bankrupt, without the permission of the customers. He is "their" tailor.

In both these cases, of course, it is clear that the possessive pronoun is not meant to imply literal possession. Clearly, neither buyer or seller has the right to insist upon the permanence of a business relationship, unless of course, a long-term contract has been agreed upon by both parties. Then, and only then, would the merchant and the customer have the right to object if either party ended the relationship without the consent of the other.

Now let us consider "my job." What is the worker implying when he objects to the scab taking "his" job away? The worker is arguing as though he *owned* the job. He is, in other words, assuming that service, after a certain period of time, obligates the employer to the employee as strictly as if they had agreed to a contract. But in fact, the employer has never obligated himself contractually.

One wonders how the workers would react if the principle upon which their anti-scab feeling is based were adopted by the employer. How would they feel if employers assumed the right to *forbid* long-term workers from leaving their employment? What if he accused another employer who dared to hire "his" worker of being a scab! Yet the situation is entirely symmetrical.

Clearly, there is something wrong with an argument which asserts that once people *voluntarily* agree to trade, they are thereafter *compelled to continue* to trade. By what shift in logic is a voluntary relationship converted into a strictly involuntary relationship? Hiring an individual does not imply slave-holding rights over that person, nor does having worked for an employer give one the *right to a job*. It should be evident that the worker never "owns" the job, that it is not "his" job. The scab, therefore, is guilty of no irregularity when he takes the job which the worker formerly held.

The issue of violence between workers and scabs is a separate issue. The initiation of violence is condemnable, and when scabs initiate violence, they deserve our censure. But the initiation of violence is not their defining characteristic. When they engage in it, they do so as individuals, not as scabs *qua* scabs. Milkmen, after all, sometimes go berserk and commit aggression against non-aggressors. No one would take this as proof that the delivery of milk is an intrinsically evil enterprise. In like manner, the use of illegitimate violence on the part of scabs does not render the enterprise of scabbing illegitimate.

In recent times, the muddled and inconsistent thinking about scabs has become increasingly evident. Liberals, traditionally most vociferous in denouncing scabs, have of late shown signs of confusion on this issue. They have come to realize that in virtually all cases the scabs are poorer

than the workers they seek to replace. And liberals have almost always championed the poor worker. Also, the specter of racism has been raised. In many cases, Black scabs have been pitted against white (unionized) workers, Mexican workers against Mexican-American workers, Japanese workers against higher paid American workers.

The Ocean Hill-Brownsville decentralization school board clash in Brooklyn, New York, is a dramatic case in point. Under the local school

12

board system, Rhody McCoy, the Black school board administrator, fired several white teachers for alleged racist behavior toward their young Black pupils. In response, the white dominated United Federation of Teachers Union struck the entire New York City educational system, including Ocean Hill-Brownsville. If the Black Ocean Hill-Brownsville school district was to continue to function, unit administrator McCoy would have to find replacements for the striking white teachers. He did, and they were, naturally, scabs. Hence, the quandary faced by the liberals: on the one hand, they were unalterably opposed to scabs, but on the other hand, they were unalterably opposed to the racism of the United Federation of Teachers. Clearly, there was more heat than light in their attitudes.

Scabs obviously have been unjustly maligned. Employment does 13 not give the employee any proprietary privileges closed to workers who wish to compete for the same job. Scabbing and free competition are opposite sides of the same coin.

Questions for Analysis

Logic
1. In your own words, briefly fill in Block's warrant (expressed in paragraphs 3–8) for his claim.
2. On what basis does Block distinguish individual responsibility in paragraph 10?
3. On what basis does Block find confused the "Liberal" thinking he recounts?

Character
1. What about his character does Block seek to establish in paragraph 2?
2. What evidence does Block present to show that he is an objective and fair-minded reasoner on the issue?
3. What ethical appeal is made by the great attention Block gives to explaining his definitions of literal and figurative economic possession?

Emotion
1. What emotional appeal to his audience does Block make by his list of many negative terms in paragraph 1 that he uses to describe the figure he defends for the rest of the essay?
2. Describe the emotional appeal Block makes with his rhetorical question in paragraph 8.
3. To what emotions does Block appeal in paragraph 12 when he claims his opponents demonstrate "more heat than light"?

FREEDOM VS. AUTHORITY

James J. Kilpatrick

In the context of a public school classroom, is "scab" an inherently disruptive word? A recent case in Oregon throws some light on a recurring issue of free speech. 1

The facts are not in dispute. Three years ago the school teachers in McMinnville, Ore., went on strike. Among those who hit the bricks on Feb. 8 were Dale Depweg, who teaches English, and Harry Chandler, whose assignment was special education. The school district hired replacement teachers for them and others. 2

On Feb. 9, young Ethan Depweg and David Chandler went to their classes at McMinnville High School. They had a number of stickers and buttons on their sweaters. Two of the buttons read, "I'm not listening, scab!" and "Do scabs bleed?" Vice Principal Carole Whitehead asked the youths to remove them. When they refused, she suspended them for willful disobedience. 3

The boys returned on the next school day. Each of them wore a button that read "Scabs," with a diagonal line drawn through it, and a sticker that read, "Scab, we will never forget." Again they were told to remove the "scab" buttons. This time they complied. Then they brought suit in federal court for violation of their First Amendment rights of free speech. 4

A LOSS AND A WIN

District Judge Owen Panner dismissed the action out of hand, but now the students have won a round. Two months ago the U.S. Circuit Court for the 9th Circuit reinstated the case and remanded it for further proceedings. 5

Who was right? The protesting students? Or Vice Principal Whitehead? 6

My own vote goes with the boys, but the case is a close one. It is well settled that students are not stripped of their constitutional rights when they pass through a schoolhouse door. Their rights go with them. It is equally well settled that school administrators have nearly plenary authority to enforce discipline. 7

The McMinnville case appears to be controlled by what is known as the Tinker case. This arose in Des Moines, Iowa, in 1965, right at the peak of the Vietnam War. Four children of a local Methodist minister appeared at their schools wearing black armbands to signify their mourning for American soldiers lost in action. 8

All of them were sent home and suspended from school. They went   9
to court, and in 1969 the U.S. Supreme Court voted 7–2 that the children
were in the right. Justice Abe Fortas, writing for the majority, held that
the armbands constituted a "silent, passive expression of opinion, unac-
companied by any disorder or disturbance."

NOT REASON ENOUGH

True, said Fortas, the school principals in Des Moines feared the   10
armbands would be disruptive, but "in our system, undifferentiated fear
or apprehension of disturbance is not enough to overcome the right to
freedom of expression."

In language that might apply to the Oregon case, Fortas held that   11
school authorities must show "something more than a mere desire to
avoid the discomfort and unpleasantness that always accompany an unpopular viewpoint." Student speech may be suppressed only "to avoid
material and substantial interference with schoolwork or discipline."

In the McMinnville case, J. Clifford Wallace, chief judge of the 9th   12
Circuit, noted that the "scab" buttons at McMinnville High had pro-
voked no disturbance, but the record was incomplete. On remand, the
school district may attempt to show that *scab* is such an inherently provocative and insulting word that school officials reasonably foresaw a risk
of substantial disruption in a classroom.

Such a risk is part of the tension between freedom and authority. I   13
am sympathetic to the problems faced by high school principals—they
have a tough life. Even so, right up to the point of actual disturbance, I
believe we have to protect a boy's right, when his dad's on strike, to wear
a button saying "Scab!"

Questions for Analysis

Logic

1. Do you think that Kilpatrick's organization strengthens his appeal to
   reason? For example, what effect is created by suspending his own
   view until paragraph 7? Would his case tend to be strengthened or
   weakened by beginning with the particular [3] rather than the general
   issue [1]?
2. Explain the reasoning of Justice Fortas on the "passive" expression of
   opinion [9]. Does Kilpatrick claim that this precedent exactly applies
   in the instance he presents? Explain.
3. Explain the logic of the view that Kilpatrick opposes in paragraph 12,
   that *scab* is "an inherently provocative and insulting word." On what
   basis does Kilpatrick attempt to refute the logic of this view?

Character
1. How does the author attempt to establish a sense of character that includes fair-mindedness?
2. How does the author attempt to establish a sense of character that includes competence in legal and constitutional matters?
3. In what ways does the author attempt to establish a sense of character that includes sympathy and compassion?

Emotion
1. In your view, what emotions were expressed by the badges worn by the boys? Explain your reasoning.
2. In your view, what emotions in their immediate audience—the replacement teachers—were appealed to by the badges? Do you think the word *discomfort* in paragraph 11 is enough to say here?
3. In your view, what emotions are appealed to in the *reader*?

EXERCISES: STRIKERS AND SCABS

Intertextual Questions
1. Discuss the writers' views on the issue of individual freedom and responsibility. How great a part does the issue play in each argument? Which author seems to you most convincing in this regard?
2. Each writer pays much attention to issues of definition. Compare the techniques of definition employed in the essays.
3. Compare the writers' views on the issue of the violence associated with the topic. Which writer's views most nearly correspond to your own? Explain.

Suggestions for Writing
1. Basing your analysis on all three appeals—to logic, character, and emotion—write an essay that criticizes one essay from the point of view of the other.
2. Focusing on Block's example of the "Brownsville" case, write an essay that expresses your views on the issues involved.
3. Write an essay that argues for your own views on the issue of "scab" labor.

Whose Business Is Sex Education?

THE FIRST STEP IN IMPROVING SEX EDUCATION: REMOVE THE HELLFIRE

Fred M. Hechinger

"Analysis of sex education in Sweden, Holland, France, Great 1 Britain and Canada shows us lagging far behind," Zella Luria, a psychology professor at Tufts University, wrote in "Independent School" magazine.

"In America, hellfire is still close to sexuality and thus shapes our 2 education and services. Who pays the price? Our children do," Professor Luria wrote in his article, "The Adolescent Years and Sexuality."

Lately, America has been trying to catch up. Sex education in public 3 schools has grown dramatically in the last five years, in part driven by the fear of AIDS. More than 40 states require or encourage some sex education, and at least 6 out of 10 American teen-agers now receive it before high school graduation.

But the issue is still plagued by poorly informed teachers, lack of 4 effective teaching materials and many teachers' fear of opposition from parents, school administrators and some religious leaders when "safe sex," abortion and homosexuality are discussed. Hellfire reaction persists.

The state education authorities are more interested in provid- 5 ing information about AIDS and other sexually transmitted diseases than about prevention of unwanted pregnancies, concluded a report by the Alan Guttmacher Institute, a nonprofit research and education organization.

The report, "Risk and Responsibility: Teaching Sex Education 6 in America's Schools Today," says that many teachers consider even the stepped-up attention to sex education "too little and too late." They call for such instruction to begin not later than the seventh grade, and preferably even sooner. They estimate that at least a quarter of 10th graders are already sexually active.

Opposition to sex education is felt or perceived by many teachers, 7 even though national polls show that more than 85 percent of American adults favor such instruction, up from 69 percent in 1965.

Continuing reluctance to let schools deal with the issue of un- 8 wanted pregnancies appears to stem from the controversial nature of birth control and abortion. Yet, more than a million teen-agers become pregnant each year, most unintentionally. About 416,000 have abortions, 472,000 give birth and the rest miscarry.

Contrary to the assertion of some opponents of sex education that 9 it encourages intercourse and promiscuity, most sex education instructors stress the moral and pregnancy-preventing appeal of abstinence.

They also discuss the consequences of sexual activity; the responsi- 10 bility of males in helping to prevent unintended pregnancies; the practical and psychological problems created by teen-age pregnancy; the demands of parenthood, and the false message sent by the media, particularly television, in showing "sex without consequences." Most teachers also urge students to resist peer pressure to have sexual intercourse.

Still, to ignore reality by skirting birth control and abortion cripples 11 sex education, advocates say.

Pregnancy is not the only matter of concern. Each year, a quarter 12 of the sexually active women between 15 and 19 years old seek treatment for a sexually transmitted disease.

Even where sex education is offered, the time spent on it may be 13 insufficient. The Guttmacher report found that typically fewer than 12 hours of instruction are devoted to it in the seventh grade, and not much more in the 12th grade.

Other obstacles remain. "Changing students' attitudes is the hardest 14 part," a health teacher in New York told researchers. "They believe, 'It can't happen to me.'"

A teacher in North Carolina added, "Students have a lot of personal 15 knowledge about sex—most of which is inaccurate."

Teachers' knowledge is often inaccurate, too. While the birth con- 16 trol pill is the most widely used contraceptive among teen-agers, the Guttmacher report found that three-quarters of the teachers believed that the pill should be given occasional "rests," which, the institute says, "medical evidence shows are not needed and may expose the user to an unnecessary risk to become pregnant."

Fortunately for American teen-agers and the nation's health, more 17 parents and communities are beginning to learn how to shed old taboos and deal rationally with new realities.

Questions for Analysis

Character

1. How would you characterize the tone of voice Hechinger adopts? Enthusiastic? Somber? Outraged? Describe what you hear as clearly as you can. What does the tone the author takes on the issue suggest about his character?
2. In what ways does the author characterize opposing viewpoints? What qualities of character does this aspect of his argument suggest?
3. Where and how does the author attempt to link his views to those of publicly acknowledged authorities?

Emotion

1. To what emotions does the author appeal in his use of movement terms such as *lagging* [1] and *catch up* [3]?
2. What emotions are appealed to by the author's use of the terms *hellfire* [4] and *taboo* [17]?
3. The author characterizes some people as "opposing" and others as "discussing" the "issue." What differences are suggested by the use of these terms and to what emotions does each appeal?

Logic

1. Where and in what ways does the author shift between reporting views and arguing his own?
2. How does the order in which the two publications are mentioned affect the argument? What advantages to that order do you imagine the author saw?
3. The author sees sex education as an attempt "to deal rationally with new realities." [17] In what ways does he suggest that opponents of sex education are irrational?

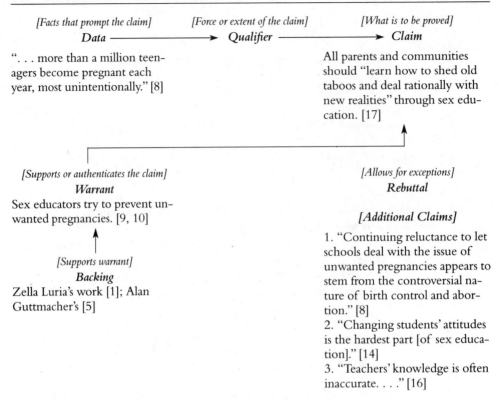

[Facts that prompt the claim] Data	→	[Force or extent of the claim] Qualifier	→	[What is to be proved] Claim

[Facts that prompt the claim]
Data ⟶

". . . more than a million teenagers become pregnant each year, most unintentionally." [8]

[Force or extent of the claim]
Qualifier ⟶

[What is to be proved]
Claim

All parents and communities should "learn how to shed old taboos and deal rationally with new realities" through sex education. [17]

[Supports or authenticates the claim]
Warrant

Sex educators try to prevent unwanted pregnancies. [9, 10]

[Supports warrant]
Backing

Zella Luria's work [1]; Alan Guttmacher's [5]

[Allows for exceptions]
Rebuttal

[Additional Claims]

1. "Continuing reluctance to let schools deal with the issue of unwanted pregnancies appears to stem from the controversial nature of birth control and abortion." [8]
2. "Changing students' attitudes is the hardest part [of sex education]." [14]
3. "Teachers' knowledge is often inaccurate. . . ." [16]

CONDOMS IN SCHOOLS: THE RIGHT LESSON

Paul Epstein

Does the distribution of condoms, as has been proposed for New York City's schools, encourage and condone sexual promiscuity? A growing body of research and the experience of AIDS educators suggests just the opposite: Condom availability, combined with AIDS education, can delay and discourage casual sexual activity.

Researchers at the Johns Hopkins Medical School conducted an AIDS education program in Baltimore that included condom distribution in a high school. They found an increased number of students choosing to abstain from sex, and a significant delay in the onset of first sexual activity among the students.

Other studies in progress are finding similar results. At a recent hearing in Cambridge, an AIDS counselor testified that since the distribution of condoms began in his program for runaway youth, clients report having fewer sexual partners. He also reported that the youngsters discussed the risks of AIDS more frequently, revealing their deepening concern. My own interviews with adolescents and college students suggest that the presence of condoms makes them more wary of casual sex, more conscious of the epidemic and more serious about their own risk.

The Centers for Disease Control consistently reports that teenagers are at high risk of AIDS transmission; the growing number of young HIV positive persons substantiates this. Recent high school surveys demonstrate that more than 80 percent of students have full knowledge of the means of AIDS transmission, but only one-quarter to one-third are actually practicing safer sex.   4

If responsible adults and officials don't take the initiative in protecting students from the risks of unsafe sex, the students will take the lead. In 1989, a class of Cambridge High School students trained as peer educators began distributing condoms to fellow students. After a series of well-publicized hearings (in themselves an education for the community), the Cambridge School Committee ruled that condoms could be distributed through the Teen Clinic at the school.   5

Subsequently, the Cambridge City Council enacted an ordinance requiring most public establishments to provide condom vending machines along with AIDS education brochures. The Massachusetts Department of Public Health has now taken a leading role, with public advertisements and condom distribution. It's too early to have data to judge results; such experiments should be taking place all over the country.   6

Some oppose distributing condoms in the schools because, they say, it will mislead students into believing there is such a thing as "safe sex." Are condoms reliable? The March 1989 Consumer Reports found that only 1 in 165 condoms breaks during vaginal intercourse; 1 in 105 during anal intercourse. Other surveys have reported higher breakage rates and they should not be dismissed: A thorough review is needed by federal health authorities, followed by a strict regulatory process.   7

Latex condoms, which account for 95 percent of the commercially available condoms, do however provide a true barrier to the AIDS virus. When used properly and combined with a lubricant containing Nooxynol 9, they significantly reduce viral transmission. Additionally, condoms provide protection against other sexually transmitted diseases. While a small risk of transmission remains for the individual, condoms are our most effective "vaccine" to date to interrupt the spread of AIDS in our population.   8

And as a deterrent, their omnipresence will be a "red flag," a constant warning of the health threat we all face. Public health research has demonstrated that people, especially those with low self-esteem, resist being told to change their behavior. If however, a health benefit (for example, vaccinations) is widely available, people will utilize it in spite of holding on to their traditional attitudes.   9

Condom distribution programs in high schools contribute signifi-   *10*
cantly to AIDS education and behavioral change. Certainly health and
educational institutions should lead the way in helping to create a new
culture of responsible relationships, and thus reduce the transmission of
AIDS.

Questions for Analysis

Logic
1. Epstein links AIDS and "responsible relationships" throughout the
   essay. Explain what seems to you to be the reasoning that connects the
   two issues.
2. Epstein cites one completed study that included condom distribution
   in high schools (paragraph 2). Does the assertion of the first sentence
   of his last paragraph seem to you to be based on that study or on a
   logical conclusion? Explain.
3. Explain the reasoning by which Epstein responds to opposing views
   in paragraph 7.

Character
1. Epstein reveals in the course of his essay that he has himself conducted
   some research. What aspect of his character does this suggest to you?
   Does it make any difference to your sense of that aspect that the
   research he mentions has not been completed or published? Explain.
2. Describe the ways in which Epstein attempts to establish a sense of
   his character that includes fair-mindedness in response to opposing
   views. Point to particular examples.
3. What attempts does Epstein make to establish himself as a compassionate person? Point to some particular examples.

Emotion
1. Describe the emotional appeals the author makes in discussing the
   example of "runaway youth" in paragraph 3.
2. Describe the emotional appeals the author makes in discussing the
   example of students who "take the lead" in paragraph 5.
3. What emotional appeal is made by describing condoms as "our most
   effective 'vaccine'" in paragraph 8?

EDUCATORS DECLARE WAR ON
TRADITIONAL VALUES

Thomas Sowell

An all too familiar scenario unfolded in San Francisco recently.   *1*

A so-called "sex education" program in the city schools invited 2
outside speakers to address the students. These speakers got very graphic
about their own far-out sex lives—to a class of sixth-graders. Visiting
parents were shocked and outraged.

The presence of the parents was the only thing that was different 3
about this scene. All across the country, "sex education" is a bait-and-
switch ploy. Schools claim to be offering biological and medical information in such programs, but in reality they spend most of their time
trying to replace the values, traditions, and inhibitions the children receive from their homes with radically different views from advocates of
the "sexual revolution."

Those parents who happen to learn about what is really going on 4
are often astounded. But the schools treat this as merely a tactical problem
to be dealt with by public relations. As far as the zealots behind "sex
education" are concerned, they are the anointed and parents are the
benighted.

That is why such zealots feel no need to level with parents or the 5
public in the first place. This attitude is not peculiar to San Francisco or
to sex education. Whether students are being brainwashed politically,
socially, or psychologically, the anointed feel no need to treat the benighted as anything more than an obstacle to progress.

A Minnesota mother, for example, ran afoul of the know-it-all 6
attitudes of the anointed in "school-based clinics." Her teen-age daughter had a falling out with her boyfriend and said, "I might as well be
dead." That set in motion a chain of events that reveals much about the
attitudes in our schools.

The boyfriend, like other students, had been taught to take any 7
suggestion of suicide seriously and to report it. Therefore, he phoned the
girl's mother to express his concern.

"I talked to my daughter," the mother said, and "everything was 8
fine." Who has ever known a teenager who did not make some extrava-
gant statement at some time or other?

But the boyfriend also reported the possibility of suicide to the 9
school officials. The school nurse then phoned the mother—and refused
to back off when the mother said that the situation was under control.

Over the mother's objections and behind the mother's back, the girl 10
was sent to a counselor. The school busybodies now managed to convince the girl that (1) she was suicidal and that (2) her mother didn't really
care about her—and that they did.

Driving a wedge between parent and child is almost an automatic 11
reflex with many of the busybodies in the education establishment. When
the mother complained to the counselor about the high-handed way
things had been done, she found the counselor "smirky," as she put it.

The anointed had won another one against the benighted. 12

These were just skirmishes in a much larger war over who is to   13
make what decisions about the raising of children. At one time, there
was no question that families had the right to decide what values their
children were to have, and parents had the right to make a whole spectrum of decisions about how best to deal with the inevitable problems
of childhood and adolescence.

Today, the public schools carry on unrelenting guerilla warfare   14
against the traditional values of the society and against the very role of
families in making decisions about their own children.

Increasingly, so-called "experts" decide at what age and in what   15
manner children are to be introduced to sexual material. The anointed
also decide at what age and in what manner children are to be introduced
to the subject of death—including visits to morgues and funeral homes,
lectures by advocates of euthanasia, and classroom exercises in which
children are conditioned to look at death in the way currently in fashion
among the avant-garde.

The particular merits and demerits of these programs are not the   16
issue. The real issue is who has the right to make such decisions in the
first place.

That is what the whole battle about "families" and "values" is all   17
about. Schools are just one of the battlefields in this undeclared war.
Politicians who have allied themselves with the self-anointed elite have
no choice but to camouflage what they are doing and to confuse the
issues as much as possible.

One of the ways of confusing the issue is to loudly proclaim their   18
support of government programs to "help" the family. That is, they see
the family as a recipient of federal largesse, not as an autonomous deci-
sion-maker for its children, or as a self-contained unit of privacy.

Baring internal family secrets in public for political pulses—as Gov-   19
ernor Bill Clinton did at the recent Democratic convention—is the an-
tithesis of preserving the traditional role of the family.

Families need respect for their own autonomy, integrity, and pri-   20
vacy, and to lose that in exchange for government handouts—to become
guinea pigs feeding at the federal trough—is truly to lose a birthright for
a mess of pottage.

Questions for Analysis

Logic

1. What does Sowell seem to see as connecting his argument about sex
   education in particular to other specific issues like suicide prevention
   programs and discussions of the meaning of death in school?
2. What exactly does Sowell see as wrong in the arguments of his opponents? Does he see them, for example, as illogical? Overly emotional?

3. In what ways does Sowell see his opponents as confusing the issue of sex education?

Character
1. How would you characterize the tone of voice Sowell adopts? Enthusiastic? Somber? Outraged? Describe what you hear as clearly as you can. What does the tone the author takes on the issue suggest about his character?
2. In what ways does the author characterize opposing viewpoints? What qualities of character does this aspect of his argument suggest?
3. Why do you think that Sowell does not attempt to link his views to those of publicly acknowledged authorities?

Emotion
1. To what emotions does Sowell appeal by the use of metaphors like "bait-and-switch" [3] and "guinea pigs feeding at the federal trough" [20]?
2. To what emotions does Sowell appeal by the use of terms like *zealots* [4], *busybodies* [11], and *anointed* [6]?
3. To what emotions does Sowell appeal by putting some of his characterizations of his opponents and their terms in quotation marks? Look, for example, at "so-called 'experts'" [15] and "help" [18].

EXERCISES: WHOSE BUSINESS IS SEX EDUCATION?

Intertextual Questions
1. What are the major differences among the authors' views of the proper role of parents and communities?
2. Both Hechinger and Sowell use terms of religion like *anointed* and *hellfire*. Compare the uses they make of religious metaphors in their arguments.
3. All the writers blend reporting with argumentation. Compare the ways in which they do so.

Suggestions for Writing
1. Write an essay that argues for your own views on the issue of sex education in the schools.
2. Write an essay that argues for your own views on how much control parents should have over the school curriculum on all nonacademic matters. Be sure to define what you consider to be the differences between academic and nonacademic matters.
3. Write an essay that analyzes the ways in which each writer attempts to refute his imagined opponents.

THE GREAT PERSON-HOLE COVER DEBATE
A Modest Proposal for Anyone Who Thinks the Word "He" Is Just Plain Easier . . .

Lindsy Van Gelder

I wasn't looking for trouble. What I was looking for, actually, was a little tourist information to help me plan a camping trip to New England.

But there it was, on the first page of the 1979 edition of the State of Vermont *Digest of Fish and Game Laws and Regulations:* a special message of welcome from one Edward F. Kehoe, commissioner of the Vermont Fish and Game Department, to the reader and would-be camper, i.e., me.

This person (i.e., me) is called "the sportsman."

"We have no 'sportswomen, sportspersons, sportsboys, or sportsgirls,'" Commissioner Kehoe hastened to explain, obviously anticipating that some of us sportsfeminists might feel a bit overlooked. "But," he added, "we are pleased to report that we do have many great sportsmen who are women, as well as young people of both sexes."

It's just that the Fish and Game Department is trying to keep things "simple and forthright" and to respect "long-standing tradition." And anyway, we really ought to be flattered, "sportsman" being "a meaningful title being earned by a special kind of dedicated man, woman, or young person, as opposed to just any hunter, fisherman, or trapper."

I have heard this particular line of reasoning before. In fact, I've heard it so often that I've come to think of it as The Great Person-Hole Cover Debate, since gender-neutral manholes are invariably brought into the argument as evidence of the lengths to which humorless, Newspeak-spouting feminists will go to destroy their mother tongue.

Consternation about woman-handling the language comes from all sides. Sexual conservatives who see the feminist movement as a unisex plot and who long for the good olde days of *vive la différence,* when men

1

2

3

4

5

6

7

were men and women were women, nonetheless do not rally behind the notion that the term "mankind" excludes women.

But most of the people who choke on expressions like "spokesper-   8
son" aren't right-wing misogynists, and this is what troubles me. Like the undoubtedly well-meaning folks at the Vermont Fish and Game Department, they tend to reassure you right up front that they're only trying to keep things "simple" and to follow "tradition," and that some of their best men are women, anyway.

Usually they wind up warning you, with great sincerity, that you're   9
jeopardizing the worthy cause of women's rights by focusing on "trivial" side issues. I would like to know how anything that gets people so defensive and resistant can possibly be called "trivial," whatever else it might be.

The English language is alive and constantly changing. Progress—   10
both scientific and social—is reflected in our language, or should be.

Not too long ago, there was a product called "flesh-colored" Band-   11
Aids. The flesh in question was colored Caucasian. Once the civil rights movement pointed out the racism inherent in the name, it was dropped. I cannot imagine reading a thoughtful, well-intentioned company policy statement explaining that while the Band-Aids would continue to be called "flesh-colored" for old time's sake, black and brown people would now be considered honorary whites and were perfectly welcome to use them.

Most sensitive people manage to describe our national religious   12
traditions as "Judeo-Christian," even though it takes a few seconds longer to say than "Christian." So why is it such a hardship to say "he or she" instead of "he"?

I have a modest proposal for anyone who maintains that "he" is just   13
plain easier: since "he" has been the style for several centuries now—and since it really includes everybody anyway, right—it seems only fair to give "she" a turn. Instead of having to ponder over the intricacies of, say, "Congressman" versus "Congressperson" versus "Representative," we can simplify things by calling them all "Congresswoman."

Other clarifications will follow: "a woman's home is her castle" . . .   14
"a giant step for all womankind" . . . "all women are created equal" . . . "Fisherwoman's Wharf." . . .

And don't be upset by the business letter that begins "Dear Madam,"   15
fellas. It means you, too.

Questions for Analysis

Logic

1. In the context of the essay as a whole, explain Van Gelder's reasoning about "what troubles" her [8].
2. Explain in your own words the ways in which the author uses the analogy provided by Band-Aids in paragraph 11 as an element in her appeal to reason.

3. The author makes an ironic "modest proposal" in paragraph 13 and following—she says one thing and means another. Explain what her reasoning really means here.

Character
1. The author implicitly disclaims wishing to sound like a fanatic on the topic. Describe some of the ways her style attempts to create a sense of character that is rational and reasonable.
2. Does the author create a sense of her character that seems to include fair-mindedness toward her opponents? Explain and exemplify your answer.
3. In paragraph 12 the author makes an appeal to the character of her reader. Describe this appeal and explain how it is created.

Emotion
1. Describe the emotional appeal made by the language of Commissioner Kehoe quoted in the beginning of the essay and explain how the appeal is created by him.
2. The topic is an emotion-laden one. Describe and explain some of the ways in which the author attempts in her arguments to temper the intense emotions that the topic might evoke in readers of any persuasion.
3. What particular emotions are appealed to in her audience by the author's "modest proposal" at the end of the essay? Explain the methods by which the author makes her appeal.

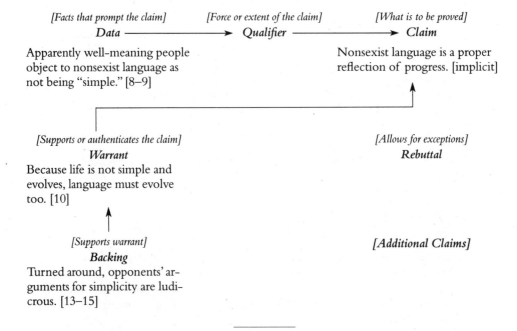

[Facts that prompt the claim]	*[Force or extent of the claim]*	*[What is to be proved]*
Data ⟶	*Qualifier* ⟶	*Claim*
Apparently well-meaning people object to nonsexist language as not being "simple." [8–9]		Nonsexist language is a proper reflection of progress. [implicit]
[Supports or authenticates the claim]		*[Allows for exceptions]*
Warrant		*Rebuttal*
Because life is not simple and evolves, language must evolve too. [10]		
[Supports warrant]		*[Additional Claims]*
Backing		
Turned around, opponents' arguments for simplicity are ludicrous. [13–15]		

THE HAND THAT ROCKS THE HELM

Richard Mitchell

> Writing about sailing, I had always used the word "helmsman" to de-
> scribe the person who steers a boat. Finally seeing the light with my
> ninth book, I decided it was time to admit women can steer too, and
> changed the traditional, exclusive word to "helmsperson," or "steerer."
> Every alteration, I felt, was doubling the size of my potential readership.

We never miss the comics page of the Sunday *New York Times,* and 1
it was there that we came across the Great Moral Awakening of one John
Rousmaniere, from whose letter to the editor the passage above is taken.
What a great moment in his inner life it must have been when it suddenly
dawned on him, not only that women actually *can* steer, but even that his
oblique admission of that hitherto unsuspected power, cleverly encoded
in "helmsperson," would increase sales of his ninth book on sailing.

We can hear the excited phone calls now: Hello, Madge, it's Flo. 2
Listen, you've just got to rush right out and buy this great new book, *Yet
Another Book on Sailing,* by John Rousmaniere! You won't believe this,
but he actually says, well, not right out, but just as good as, that women
can *steer.* Steer boats! I'm not kidding. Yes, women! I'd lend you my copy,
but I think that every woman should have her own, don't you? I mean,
after all, it's time we took a stand!

But it is only *en passant* that Rousmaniere makes his astonishing 3
discovery. He steers his course toward the undoing of an earlier letter
writer who complained that he found ugliness and awkwardness in enlightened words like "helmsperson." Ha! To that feeble whimper, Rousmaniere exclaims, in what must have been a sprightly riposte that
somehow got garbled by a subeditor, "Yet given a choice between the
risk of a little phonetic barbarism and the fact of a language that in a few
simple nouns and pronouns minimizes (if not oppresses) about half our
fellow human beings, who can choose?"

Who indeed? Not we. (Or maybe yes we, depending on what that 4
question might mean.) We do not care to be counted among the un-
countable who have minimized (if not oppressed) all female human beings ever born in the whole history of our species by falsely accusing
them of the inability to steer a boat. And here and now, in print for all to
see, we'd like to take a stand and join in the Great Affirmation, perhaps
even doubling our readership thereby, by saying, "Women can steer a
boat!"

However, while we would *like* to do that, if only for the sake of 5
doubling our readership, we won't. We can't. We are ruled, and choose

to be ruled, by the motto that we quote not often enough, the words of Ben Jonson: "Neither can his mind be thought to be in tune, whose words do jarre; nor his Reason in frame, whose sentence is preposterous." That sentence is preposterous. It is neither true nor false; it is simply without meaning, which must also be said of "Men can steer a boat."

Of making sense, there is one way. Preposterousness knows no [6] limits. Its every appearance must be sniffed out anew, and the ability to smell the preposterous is alone worthy of the name of literacy. Anything less is illiteracy, at best the reception of communication, the recognition of the words. Nevertheless, preposterousness is most likely to appear in certain contexts, and one of those is what is called, and probably being taught in some school at this very moment, Social Thinking.

How sweet its sound, how kind and humanistic. But Social Think- [7] ing is in fact, both in and out of schools, a great inculcator of irreversible illiteracy, for it depends largely, and in the schools entirely, we would guess, on the recitation of seemingly amiable propositions of the sort that could not be tested even if the educationists wanted to test them, which they don't.

Consider the Social Thinking of Rousmaniere. One day, he claims, [8] he "sees the light," and finds it "time to admit," as though he had obsti- nately denied it in the past, that "women can steer too." Wow. It is the sort of statement that seems at first, and here is the great snare of Social Thinking, too obviously true to be worth saying, and certainly indisput- able. But around here we think enough of women to suspect that some Madge might find it neither.

Oh really? she might say to Flo. Well, that's nice of him to say, but, [9] to tell the truth, Flo, I *can't* steer a boat. I know. I tried it for a while, and we kept luffing. You should have heard the kids. I'm sure I could learn, but why bother? And in fact, I'm not the least bit offended when some purely hypothetical steerer of some equally hypothetical boat is called a "helmsman." As long as this fellow isn't talking about me, why should I care? But you know, I think that maybe I do care a little when he does talk about me and gets it wrong. After all, I am included in "women," and I think this guy has lots of brass to shoot off his mouth about what I can and what I can't do, which is, in any case, none of his damned business. So how about you, Flo? Can you steer a boat?

Language is not a person who can think and will and do, any more [10] than "women" is a person who can think and will and do. It is preposter- ous to imply the presence of mind, will, and action in "women," or in "men," or in Eskimos or football players. It is just as preposterous to imply those powers in language. Pronouns do not minimize persons. Words do not oppress persons. Only persons can minimize or oppress, or praise or condemn, or lie or speak the truth. Such acts are possible only to individ- uals in whom there is, whether governed or not, the power to choose.

No sane person will find offense in the word "helmsman," whose   *11*
equivalent was regularly used by plenty of Viking women who knew
how to steer a boat. In the history of our species, no man before Rousmaniere has said "helmsman" in order to suggest that women can't steer
boats. Nor did any woman imagine such absurdity.

If we can, and do, imagine such absurdity, it is because we are far   *12*
more superstitious than our ancestors, which is to say that we are Social
Thinkers. We imagine the possibility of agency in nonpersonal nonbeings,
which is a step or two down from imagining agency in the spirits of the
trees and rivers. Where a miscreant might once have had the good sense
to blame his misbehavior on the Devil, a supposed person with a will and
intentions, he now passes the buck to Society, a nothing, a word, in which
neither will nor intention is possible. We are deprived where there is no
depriver, oppressed where there is no oppressor, and affronted where
there is no one who gives a damn whether or not we can steer a boat.

No one who knows any history at all can deny that many women   *13*
have been subject to men and treated like property or dependent children, or even domestic animals, for most of recorded history on most of
the face of the Earth. Shall we now treat them like simpletons, to be
cajoled with puny offerings of words like "helmsperson" and "herstory"?
Are they imbeciles, that we can con them into buying our books, and
anything else we want to sell them, by changing a word here and there?
Are they so dim of mind that we must make allowance for the fact that
the poor things do indeed suppose that the word "helmsman" is a slur
devised by men in order to remind them of their inadequacies? Can we
buy them off with a few he/she's?

In "helmsman" there is no contempt, for there is no contemner. In   *14*
"helmsperson" there is condescension, and a holier-than-thou conde-
scender. If that is what "women" want, well, maybe the Patriarchs did
know something after all.

Questions for Analysis

Logic

1. In your own words describe Rousmaniere's reasoning as recounted by
   Mitchell in paragraphs 1, 2, and 3. In the context of the essay as a
   whole, briefly explain what Mitchell finds wrong with the reasoning
   he recounts.
2. Much of Mitchell's reasoning employs irony—he says one thing and
   means another. Pick an example and explain what the author really
   means by what he says.
3. In your own words briefly summarize Mitchell's reasoning concerning
   the proposition that not language but only individuals can "think and
   will and do" [10].

Character

1. Describe and explain some of the ways in which Mitchell attempts to establish a sense of his character as one that is not prejudiced against women.
2. What aspects of his character does Mitchell attempt to establish through his discussion of "preposterousness" versus "literacy" beginning in paragraph 6? Exemplify and explain.
3. What aspects of his character does the author attempt to establish by his glances at historical matters in the course of the essay? Pick an example and explain its operation as an appeal to character.

Emotion

1. The topic is obviously one that evokes strong emotions in the author. Pick the moment where you feel he expresses his emotions most strongly. Describe the emotions, explain how they are created through language, and tell to what emotions in the reader they seem designed to appeal.
2. Describe and explain the emotional appeal Mitchell makes through his use of the term *sniffed* in paragraph 7.
3. Describe and explain the emotional appeal Mitchell makes through his discussion of superstition in paragraph 12.

THE WORD POLICE

Michiko Kakutani

This month's inaugural festivities, with their celebration, in Maya Angelou's words, of "humankind"—"the Asian, the Hispanic, the Jew/ The African, the Native American, the Sioux,/ The Catholic, the Muslim, the French, the Greek/ The Irish, the Rabbi, the Priest, the Sheik,/ The Gay, the Straight, the Preacher,/ The privileged, the homeless, the Teacher"—constituted a kind of official embrace of multiculturalism and a new politics of inclusion. [1]

The mood of political correctness, however, has already made firm inroads into popular culture. Washington boasts a store called Politically Correct that sells pro-whale, anti-meat, ban-the-bomb T-shirts, bumper stickers and buttons, as well as a local cable television show called "Politically Correct Cooking" that features interviews in the kitchen with representatives from groups like People for the Ethical Treatment of Animals. [2]

The Coppertone suntan lotion people are planning to give their longtime cover girl, Little Miss (Ms?) Coppertone, a male equivalent, [3]

Little Mr. Coppertone. And even Superman (Superperson?) is rumored to be returning this spring, reincarnated as four ethnically diverse clones: an African-American, an Asian, a Caucasian and a Latino.

Nowhere is this P.C. mood more striking than in the increasingly noisy debate over language that has moved from university campuses to the country at large—a development that both underscores Americans' puritanical zeal for reform and their unwavering faith in the talismanic power of words. 4

Certainly no decent person can quarrel with the underlying impulse behind political correctness: a vision of a more just, inclusive society in which racism, sexism and prejudice of all sorts have been erased. But the methods and fervor of the self-appointed language police can lead to a rigid orthodoxy—and unintentional self-parody—opening the movement to the scorn of conservative opponents and the mockery of cartoonists and late-night television hosts. 5

It's hard to imagine women earning points for political correctness by saying "ovarimony" instead of "testimony"—as one participant at the recent Modern Language Association convention was overheard to suggest. It's equally hard to imagine people wanting to flaunt their lack of prejudice by giving up such words and phrases as "bull market," "kaiser roll," "Lazy Susan," and "charley horse." 6

Several books on bias-free language have already appeared, and the 1991 edition of the Random House Webster's College Dictionary boasts an appendix titled "Avoiding Sexist Language." The dictionary also includes such linguistic mutations as "womyn" (women, "used as an alternative spelling to avoid the suggestion of sexism perceived in the sequence m-e-n") and "waitron" (a gender-blind term for waiter or waitress). 7

Many of these dictionaries and guides not only warn the reader against offensive racial and sexual slurs, but also try to establish and enforce a whole new set of usage rules. Take, for instance, "The Bias-Free Word Finder, a Dictionary of Nondiscriminatory Language" by Rosalie Maggio (Beacon Press)—a volume often indistinguishable, in its meticulous solemnity, from the tongue-in-cheek "Official Politically Correct Dictionary and Handbook" put out last year by Henry Beard and Christopher Cerf (Villard Books). Ms. Maggio's book supplies the reader intent on using kinder, gentler language with writing guidelines as well as a detailed listing of more than 5,000 "biased words and phrases." 8

Whom are these guidelines for? Somehow one has a tough time picturing them replacing "Fowler's Modern English Usage" in the classroom, or being adopted by the average man (sorry, individual) in the street. 9

The "pseudogeneric 'he,'" we learn from Ms. Maggio, is to be avoided like the plague, as is the use of the word "man" to refer to 10 humanity. "Fellow," "king," "lord" and "master" are bad because they're "male-oriented words," and "king," "lord" and "master" are especially bad because they're also "hierarchical, dominator society terms." The politically correct lion becomes the "monarch of the jungle," new-age children play "someone on the top of the heap," and the "Mona Lisa" goes down in history as Leonardo's "acme of perfection."

As for the word "black," Ms. Maggio says it should be excised from terms with a negative spin: she recommends substituting words like "mouse" for "black eye," "ostracize" for "blackball," "payola" for "blackmail" and "outcast" for "black sheep." Clearly, some of these substitutions work better than others: somehow the "sinister humor" of Kurt Vonnegut or "Saturday Night Live" doesn't quite make it; nor does the "denouncing" of the Hollywood 10.   *11*

For the dedicated user of politically correct language, all these rules   *12* can make for some messy moral dilemmas. Whereas "battered wife" is a gender-biased term, the gender-free term "battered spouse," Ms. Maggio notes, incorrectly implies "that men and women are equally battered."

On one hand, say Francine Wattman Frank and Paula A. Treichler   *13* in their book "Language, Gender, and Professional Writing" (Modern Language Association), "he or she" is an appropriate construction for talking about an individual (like a jockey, say) who belongs to a profession that's predominantly male—it's a way of emphasizing "that such occupations are not barred to women or that women's concerns need to be kept in mind." On the other hand, they add, using masculine pronouns rhetorically can underscore ongoing male dominance in those fields, implying the need for change.

And what about the speech codes adopted by some universities in   *14* recent years? Although they were designed to prohibit students from uttering sexist and racist slurs, they would extend, by logic, to blacks who want to use the word "nigger" to strip the term of its racist connotations, or homosexuals who want to use the word "queer" to reclaim it from bigots.

In her book, Ms. Maggio recommends applying bias-free usage   *15* retroactively: she suggests paraphrasing politically incorrect quotations, or replacing "the sexist words or phrases with ellipsis dots and/or bracketed substitutes," or using "sic" "to show that the sexist words come from the original quotation and to call attention to the fact that they are incorrect."

Which leads the skeptical reader of "The Bias-Free Word Finder"   *16* to wonder whether "All the King's Men" should be retitled "All the Ruler's People"; "Pet Semetary," "Animal Companion Graves"; "Birdman of Alcatraz," "Birdperson of Alcatraz," and "The Iceman Cometh," "The Ice Route Driver Cometh"?

Will making such changes remove the prejudice in people's minds?   *17*

Should we really spend time trying to come up with non-male-based alternatives to "Midas touch," "Achilles' heel," and "Montezuma's revenge"? Will tossing out Santa Claus—whom Ms. Maggio accuses of reinforcing "the cultural male-as-norm system"—in favor of Belfana, his Italian female alter ego, truly help banish sexism? Can the avoidance of "violent expressions and metaphors" like "kill two birds with one stone," "sock it to 'em" or "kick an idea around" actually promote a more harmonious world?

The point isn't that the excesses of the word police are comical. 18 The point is that their intolerance (in the name of tolerance) has disturbing implications. In the first place, getting upset by phrases like "bullish on America" or "the City of Brotherly Love" tends to distract attention from the real problems of prejudice and injustice that exist in society at large, turning them into mere questions of semantics. Indeed, the emphasis currently put on politically correct usage has uncanny parallels with the academic movement of deconstruction—a method of textual analysis that focuses on language and linguistic pyrotechnics—which has become firmly established on university campuses.

In both cases, attention is focused on surfaces, on words and meta- 19 phors; in both cases, signs and symbols are accorded more importance than content. Hence, the attempt by some radical advocates to remove "The Adventures of Huckleberry Finn" from curriculums on the grounds that Twain's use of the word "nigger" makes the book a racist text—never mind the fact that this American classic (written in 1884) depicts the spiritual kinship achieved between a white boy and a runaway slave, never mind the fact that the "nigger" Jim emerges as the novel's most honorable, decent character.

Ironically enough, the P.C. movement's obsession with language is 20 accompanied by a strange Orwellian willingness to warp the meaning of words by placing them under a high-powered ideological lens. For instance, the "Dictionary of Cautionary Words and Phrases"—a pamphlet issued by the University of Missouri's Multicultural Management Program to help turn "today's journalists into tomorrow's multicultural newsroom managers"—warns that using the word "articulate" to describe members of a minority group can suggest the opposite, "that 'those people' are not considered well educated, articulate and the like."

The pamphlet patronizes minority groups, by cautioning the reader 21 against using the words "lazy" and "burly" to describe any member of such groups; and it issues a similar warning against using words like "gorgeous" and "petite" to describe women.

As euphemism proliferates with the rise of political correctness, 22 there is a spread of the sort of sloppy, abstract language that Orwell said is "designed to make lies sound truthful and murder respectable, and to give an appearance of solidity to pure wind." "Fat" becomes "big boned" or "differently sized"; "stupid" becomes "exceptional"; "stoned" becomes "chemically inconvenienced."

Wait a minute here! Aren't such phrases eerily reminiscent of the euphemisms coined by the Government during Vietnam and Watergate? Remember how the military used to speak of "pacification," or how President Richard M. Nixon's press secretary, Ronald L. Ziegler, tried to get away with calling a lie an "inoperative statement"? *23*

Calling the homeless "the underhoused" doesn't give them a place to live; calling the poor "the economically marginalized" doesn't help them pay the bills. Rather, by playing down their plight, such language might even make it easier to shrug off the seriousness of their situation. *24*

Instead of allowing free discussion and debate to occur, many gung-ho advocates of politically correct language seem to think that simple suppression of a word or concept will magically make the problem disappear. In the "Bias-Free Word Finder," Ms. Maggio entreats the reader not to perpetuate the negative stereotype of Eve. "Be extremely cautious in referring to the biblical Eve," she writes; "this story has profoundly contributed to negative attitudes toward women throughout history, largely because of misogynistic and patriarchal interpretations that labeled her evil, inferior, and seductive." *25*

The story of Bluebeard, the rake (whoops!—the libertine) who killed his seven wives, she says, is also to be avoided, as is the biblical story of Jezebel. Of Jesus Christ, Ms. Maggio writes: "There have been few individuals in history as completely androgynous as Christ, and it does his message a disservice to overinsist on his maleness." She doesn't give the reader any hints on how this might be accomplished; presumably, one is supposed to avoid describing him as the Son of God. *26*

Of course the P.C. police aren't the only ones who want to proscribe what people should say or give them guidelines for how they may use an idea; Jesse Helms and his supporters are up to exactly the same thing when they propose to patrol the boundaries of the permissible in art. In each case, the would-be censor aspires to suppress what he or she finds distasteful—all, of course, in the name of the public good. *27*

In the case of the politically correct, the prohibition of certain words, phrases and ideas is advanced in the cause of building a brave new world free of racism and hate, but this vision of harmony clashes with the very ideals of diversity and inclusion that the multicultural movement holds dear, and it's purchased at the cost of freedom of expression and freedom of speech. *28*

In fact, the utopian world envisioned by the language police would be bought at the expense of the ideals of individualism and democracy articulated in the "The [sic] Gettysburg Address": "Fourscore and seven years ago our fathers brought forth on this continent a new nation, con- *29* ceived in liberty and dedicated to the proposition that all men are created equal."

Of course, the P.C. police have already found Lincoln's words 30 hopelessly "phallocentric." No doubt they would rewrite the passage: "Fourscore and seven years ago our foremothers and forefathers brought forth on this continent a new nation, formulated with liberty, and dedicated to the proposition that all humankind is created equal."

Questions for Analysis

Logic
1. The essay begins and ends with important national addresses. How does this organization seem designed to support the author's argument as a whole?
2. Pick a specific example of recommended changes in language that Kakutani finds unreasonable. Explain the reasoning of her opponents as she recounts it and her reasons for thinking that reasoning fallacious.
3. Explain the reasoning that leads the author to claim that "the utopian world envisioned by the language police would be bought at the expense of the ideals of individualism and democracy articulated in the Gettysburg Address." [29]

Character
1. Where do you find Kakutani attempting to establish a sense of her character that includes a thorough inquiry into the facts of the issue? Pick an example and explain its operation as an appeal to character by referring to specific uses of language.
2. Where do you find the author attempting to establish a sense of her character that includes high-minded ideals? Pick an example and explain its operation as an appeal to character by referring to specific uses of language.
3. Where do you find the author attempting to establish a sense of the character of her opponents? Pick an example and explain its operation by referring to specific uses of language.

Emotion
1. Describe the ways in which the author's title makes an appeal to emotions in her audience.
2. Find a moment where the author discusses a particular example of bias-free language. Explain both the emotional appeal that the author sees her opponents as making and the emotional appeal that she herself makes.
3. Describe the emotional appeal of the end of the essay. Have earlier moments attempted to prepare for and enhance its operation? Exemplify and explain.

EXERCISES: SEXIST LANGUAGE

Intertextual Questions

1. Both Kakutani and Mitchell seem to disagree with Van Gelder's arguments. Do you think they would disagree for the same reasons? Where and how do you think they do or do not agree with one another?

2. The essays vary in length. Do you think any of them would be strengthened or weakened by being of a different length? Pick an example and explain your reasoning.

3. In your view which writer makes the strongest appeal to reason? To emotion? To character? In a sentence or two explain your answer in each case.

Suggestions for Writing

1. Pick an example of a verbal usage recommended by one of the writers and write a brief essay explaining why you do or do not find the recommendation convincing.

2. Pick an example of a verbal usage objected to by one of the writers and write a brief essay explaining why you do or do not find the objection convincing.

3. Pick an example of your own that involves verbal usage that might have been used by one of the writers and argue for its appropriateness or inappropriateness from your own point of view.

Language and Race:
The Color of Words

THAT WORD "BLACK"

Langston Hughes

"This evening," said Simple, "I feel like talking about the word *black*." 1

"Nobody's stopping you, so go ahead. But what you really ought 2
to have is a soap-box out on the corner of 126th and Lenox where the
rest of the orators hang out."

"They expresses some good ideas on that corner," said Simple, "but 3
for my ideas I do not need a crowd. Now, as I were saying, the word
black, white folks have done used that word to mean something bad so
often until now when the N.A.A.C.P. asks for civil rights for the black
man, they think they must be bad. Looking back into history, I reckon it
all started with a *black* cat meaning bad luck. Don't let one cross your
path!

"Next, somebody got up a *black-list* on which you get if you don't 4
vote right. Then when lodges come into being, the folks they didn't want
in them got *black-balled*. If you kept a skeleton in your closet, you might
get *black-mailed*. And everything bad was *black*. When it came down to
the unlucky ball on the pool table, the eight-rock, they made it the *black*
ball. So no wonder there ain't no equal rights for the *black* man."

"All you say is true about the odium attached to the word *black,*" I 5
said. "You've even forgotten a few. For example, during the war if you
bought something under the table, illegally, they said you were trading
on the *black* market. In Chicago, if you're a gangster, the *Black Hand-
Society* may take you for a ride. And certainly if you don't behave yourself, your family will say you're a *black* sheep. Then if your mama burns a
black candle to change the family luck, they call it *black* magic."

"My mama never did believe in voodoo so she did not burn no 6
black candles," said Simple.

"If she had, that would have been a *black* mark against her." 7

"Stop talking about my mama. What I want to know is, where do 8
white folks get off calling everything bad *black*? If it is a dark night, they
say it's *black* as hell. If you are mean and evil, they say you got a *black*
heart. I would like to change all that around and say that the people who
Jim Crow me have got a *white* heart. People who sell dope to children
have got a *white* mark against them. And all the white gamblers who were
behind the basketball fix are the *white* sheep of the sports world. God
knows there was few, if any, Negroes selling stuff on the black market
during the war, so why didn't they call it the *white* market? No, they got
to take me and my color and turn it into everything *bad*. According to
white folks, black is bad.

"Wait till my day comes! In my language, bad will be *white*. Black- 9
mail will be *white* mail. Black cats will be good luck, and *white* cats will
be bad. If a *white* cat crosses your path, look out! I will take the black ball
for the cue ball and let the *white* ball be the unlucky eight-rock. And on
my blacklist—which will be a *white* list then—I will put everybody who
ever Jim Crowed me from Rankin to Hitler, Talmadge to Malan, South
Carolina to South Africa.

"I am black. When I look in the mirror, I see myself, daddy-o, but 10
I am not ashamed. God made me. He did not make us no badder than
the rest of the folks. The earth is black and all kinds of good things
comes out of the earth. Trees and flowers and fruit and sweet potatoes
and corn and all that keeps mens alive comes right up out of the earth—
good old black earth. Coal is black and it warms your house and cooks
your food. The night is black, which has a moon, and a million stars, and
is beautiful. Sleep is black which gives you rest, so you wake up feeling
good. I am black. I feel very good this evening.

"What is wrong with black?" 11

Questions for Analysis

Logic

1. Describe the ways in which Hughes's appeal to reason is affected by
   the dialogue form of his organization.
2. Does Simple's view of the origin of negative connotations in the
   example of "black cat" affect the logic of his argument? Explain.
3. In what ways, in your view, does the humor of the piece support or
   detract from its appeal to reason?

Character

1. What qualities of the author's character are created by his ability to
   use both "Black English" and "Standard English"?
2. What qualities of Simple's character that are useful for the author does
   the use of "Black English" create?

3. What positive and negative qualities of character are suggested by Hughes's name for the character Simple?

Emotion
1. What emotions in the audience are appealed to by the dismissive tone of the remarks made in paragraph 2? How might you imagine Hughes using this appeal to strengthen Simple's case in the argument as a whole?
2. Do the emotional appeals differ between the negative uses of "black" that are listed and the positive examples? Explain.
3. What emotions are appealed to in paragraph 10? How would you contrast Simple's tone of voice in that paragraph to his tone earlier in the essay?

PINK AND BROWN PEOPLE

Thomas Sowell

A man who says we should really "tell it like it is" refers to whites and blacks as "pink people" and "brown people." These jarring phrases are of course more accurate, but that may be why they are jarring. Race is not an area especially noted for accuracy—or for rationality or candor. More often it is an area of symbolism, stereotype, and euphemism. The plain truth sounds off-key and even suspicious. Gross exaggerations like *white* and *black* are more like the kind of polarization we are used to. Racial classifications have always been a problem, but in the United States such attempts at neat pigeonholing become a farce, in view of the facts of history.

Less than a fourth of the "black" population of the United States is of unmixed African ancestry. And a noted social historian estimates that tens of millions of whites have at least one black ancestor somewhere in generations past. Even in the old South, where "one drop of Negro blood" was supposed to make you socially black, the actual laws required some stated fraction of black ancestry, to avoid "embarrassing" some of the "best" white families.

What all this boils down to is a wide spectrum of racial mixtures with an arbitrary dividing line and boldly contrasting labels applied to people on either side of the line. The human desire for classification is not going to be defeated by any biological facts. Those who cannot swallow pseudobiology can turn to pseudohistory as the basis for classification. Unique cultural characteristics are now supposed to neatly divide the population.

In this more modern version, the ghetto today is a unique social   *4*
phenomenon—a unique problem calling for a unique solution. Many
of those who talk this way just happen to have this solution with them
and will make it available for a suitable combination of money and
power.

Ghettos today certainly differ from white middle-class neighbor-   *5*
hoods. But past ghettos always differed from past middle-class neighborhoods, even when both were white. Indeed, the very word *ghetto* came
historically from a white minority community of people, classified by
the fact that they held religious services one day earlier than others.
People will classify on any basis. With today's recreation-oriented week-
ends, religious classifications are often based on what service you *would
have* attended.

American ghettos have always had crime, violence, overcrowding,   *6*
filth, drunkenness, bad school teaching, and worse learning. Nor are
blacks historically unique even in the degree of these things. Crime and
violence were much worse in the nineteenth-century slums, which were
almost all white. The murder rate in Boston in the middle of the nineteenth century was about three times what it was in the middle of the
twentieth century. All the black riots of the 1960s put together did not
kill half as many people as were killed in one white riot in 1863.

The meaning of the term *race riot* has been watered down in recent   *7*
times to include general hell raising (and posing for television) in the hell-
raisers' own neighborhood. In the nineteenth century it was much uglier.
Thousands of members of one "race" invaded the neighborhood of
another "race"—both, typically, European—to maim, murder, and burn.
Today's disorders are not in the same league, whether measured in blood
or buildings.

Squalor, dirt, disease? Historically, blacks are neither first nor last in   *8*
any of these categories. There were far more immigrants packed into the
slums (per room or per square mile) than is the case with blacks today—
not to mention the ten thousand to thirty thousand children with no
home at all in nineteenth-century New York. They slept under bridges,
huddled against buildings or wherever they could find some semblance
of shelter from the elements.

Even in the area where many people get most emotional—educa-   *9*
tional and I.Q. test results—blacks are doing nothing that various European minorities did not do before them. As of about 1920, any number
of European ethnic groups had I.Q.'s the same as or lower than the I.Q.'s
of blacks today. As recently as the 1940s, there were schools on the Lower
East Side of New York with academic performances lower than those of
schools in Harlem.

Much of the paranoia that we talk ourselves into about race (and   *10*
other things) is a result of provincialism about our own time as compared

to other periods of history. Violence, poverty, and destroyed lives should never be accepted. But there is little chance of solving any problem unless we see it for what it is, not what it appears to be in the framework of reckless rhetoric.

Questions for Analysis

Logic

1. According to Sowell, what is the reasoning of the views he opposes, those that on the subject of race do not "tell it like it is"?
2. According to Sowell, what is the logical difficulty presented by what he calls an "arbitrary dividing line" within "a wide spectrum of racial mixtures"?
3. Explain Sowell's reasoning on the topic of IQ tests. Is his particular reasoning here representative of his reasoning in general in the essay? Explain.

Character

1. What does Sowell do in the course of the essay to establish his character as *not* characterized by historical "provincialism"? Point to some examples.
2. What does the variety of sentence structure in the essay contribute to your sense of the author's character?
3. What appeal to character is made by the author's frequent use of quotation marks around common words?

Emotion

1. Explain the differing emotional appeals of the terms *Black and White* and *Pink and Brown*. Do you agree with Sowell that the second pair sounds "jarring"? Explain.
2. What points does Sowell make about the current use of the term *race riot* in paragraph 7?
3. What emotions does Sowell appeal to when he deprecates emotional responses in the last two paragraphs?

HOW IT FEELS TO BE COLORED ME

Zora Neale Hurston

I am colored but I offer nothing in the way of extenuating circum- 1
stances except the fact that I am the only Negro in the United States whose grandfather on the mother's side was *not* an Indian chief.

I remember the very day that I became colored. Up to my thir- 2
teenth year I lived in the little Negro town of Eatonville, Florida. It is
exclusively a colored town. The only white people I knew passed through
the town going to or coming from Orlando. The native whites rode dusty
horses, the Northern tourists chugged down the sandy village road in
automobiles. The town knew the Southerners and never stopped cane
chewing when they passed. But the Northerners were something else
again. They were peered at cautiously from behind curtains by the timid.
The more venturesome would come out on the porch to watch them go
past and got just as much pleasure out of the tourists as the tourists got
out of the village.

The front porch might seem a daring place for the rest of the town, 3
but it was a gallery seat to me. My favorite place was atop the gate-post.
Proscenium box for a born first-nighter. Not only did I enjoy the show,
but I didn't mind the actors knowing that I liked it. I usually spoke to
them in passing. I'd wave at them and when they returned my salute, I
would say something like this: "Howdy-do-well-I-thank-you-where-
you-goin'?" Usually the automobile or the horse paused at this, and after
a queer exchange of compliments, I would probably "go a piece of the
way" with them, as we say in farthest Florida. If one of my family
happened to come to the front in time to see me, of course negotiations
would be rudely broken off. But even so, it is clear that I was the first
"welcome-to-our-state" Floridian, and I hope the Miami Chamber of
Commerce will please take notice.

During this period, white people differed from colored to me only 4
in that they rode through town and never lived there. They liked to hear
me "speak pieces" and sing and wanted to see me dance the parse-me-la,
and gave me generously of their small silver for doing these things, which
seemed strange to me for I wanted to do them so much that I needed
bribing to stop. Only they didn't know it. The colored people gave no
dimes. They deplored any joyful tendencies in me, but I was their Zora
nevertheless. I belonged to them, to the nearby hotels, to the county—
everybody's Zora.

But changes came in the family when I was thirteen, and I was sent 5
to school in Jacksonville. I left Eatonville, the town of the oleanders, as
Zora. When I disembarked from the river-boat at Jacksonville, she was
no more. It seemed that I had suffered a sea change. I was not Zora of
Orange County any more, I was now a little colored girl. I found it out
in certain ways. In my heart as well as in the mirror, I became a fast
brown—warranted not to rub nor run.

But I am not tragically colored. There is no great sorrow dammed 6
up in my soul, nor lurking behind my eyes. I do not mind at all. I do not
belong to the sobbing school of Negrohood who hold that nature some-

how has given them a lowdown dirty deal and whose feelings are all hurt about it. Even in the helter-skelter skirmish that is my life, I have seen that the world is to the strong regardless of a little pigmentation more or less. No, I do not weep at the world—I am too busy sharpening my oyster knife.

Someone is always at my elbow reminding me that I am the grand-   7
daughter of slaves. It fails to register depression with me. Slavery is sixty years in the past. The operation was successful and the patient is doing well, thank you. The terrible struggle that made me an American out of a potential slave said "On the line!" The Reconstruction said "Get set!"; and the generation before said "Go!" I am off to a flying start and I must not halt in the stretch to look behind and weep. Slavery is the price I paid for civilization, and the choice was not with me. It is a bully adventure and worth all that I have paid through my ancestors for it. No one on earth ever had a greater chance for glory. The world to be won and nothing to be lost. It is thrilling to think—to know that for any act of mine, I shall get twice as much praise or twice as much blame. It is quite exciting to hold the center of the national stage, with the spectators not knowing whether to laugh or to weep.

The position of my white neighbor is much more difficult. No   8
brown specter pulls up a chair beside me when I sit down to eat. No dark ghost thrusts its leg against mine in bed. The game of keeping what one has is never so exciting as the game of getting.

I do not always feel colored. Even now I often achieve the uncon-   9
scious Zora of Eatonville before the Hegira. I feel most colored when I am thrown against a sharp white background.

For instance at Barnard. "Beside the waters of the Hudson" I feel   10
my race. Among the thousand white persons, I am a dark rock surged upon, overswept by a creamy sea. I am surged upon and overswept, but through it all, I remain myself. When covered by the waters, I am; and the ebb but reveals me again.

Sometimes it is the other way around. A white person is set down   11
in our midst, but the contrast is just as sharp for me. For instance, when I sit in the drafty basement that is The New World Cabaret with a white person, my color comes. We enter chatting about any little nothing that we have in common and are seated by the jazz waiters. In the abrupt way that jazz orchestras have, this one plunges into a number. It loses no time in circumlocutions, but gets right down to business. It constricts the thorax and splits the heart with its tempo and narcotic harmonies. This orchestra grows rambunctious, rears on its hind legs and attacks the tonal veil with primitive fury, rending it, clawing it until it breaks through to the jungle beyond. I follow those heathen—follow them exultingly. I dance wildly inside myself; I yell within, I whoop; I shake my assegai

above my head, I hurl it true to the mark *yeeeeoowww!* I am in the jungle and living in the jungle way. My face is painted red and yellow and my body is painted blue. My pulse is throbbing like a war drum. I want to slaughter something—give pain, give death to what, I do not know. But the piece ends. The men of the orchestra wipe their lips and rest their fingers. I creep back slowly to the veneer we call civilization with the last tone and find the white friend sitting motionless in his seat, smoking calmly.

"Good music they have here," he remarks, drumming the table with his fingertips.　　12

Music! The great blobs of purple and red emotion have not touched him. He has only heard what I felt. He is far away and I see him but dimly across the ocean and the continent that have fallen between us. He is so pale with his whiteness then and I am *so* colored.　　13

At certain times I have no race, I am *me*. When I set my hat at a certain angle and saunter down Seventh Avenue, Harlem City, feeling as snooty as the lions in front of the Forty-Second Street Library, for instance. So far as my feelings are concerned, Peggy Hopkins Joyce on the Boule Mich with her gorgeous raiment, stately carriage, knees knocking together in a most aristocratic manner, has nothing on me. The cosmic Zora emerges. I belong to no race nor time. I am the eternal feminine with its string of beads.　　14

I have no separate feeling about being an American citizen and colored. I am merely a fragment of the Great Soul that surges within the boundaries. My country, right or wrong.　　15

Sometimes, I feel discriminated against, but it does not make me angry. It merely astonishes me. How *can* any deny themselves the pleasure of my company! It's beyond me.　　16

But in the main, I feel like a brown bag of miscellany propped against a wall. Against a wall in company with other bags, white, red and yellow. Pour out the contents, and there is discovered a jumble of small things priceless and worthless. A first-water diamond, an empty spool, bits of broken glass, lengths of string, a key to a door long since crumbled away, a rusty knife-blade, old shoes saved for a road that never was and never will be, a nail bent under the weight of things too heavy for any nail, a dried flower or two, still a little fragrant. In your hand is the brown bag. On the ground before you is the jumble it held—so much like the jumble in the bags, could they be emptied, that all might be dumped in a single heap and the bags refilled without altering the content of any greatly. A bit of colored glass more or less would not matter. Perhaps that is how the Great Stuffer of Bags filled them in the first place—who knows?　　17

Questions for Analysis

Logic

1. Explain Hurston's reasoning as a girl when she describes herself as feeling like a spectator in a theater in paragraph 3.
2. Explain the reasoning of the "actors" as Hurston gives us to understand it in the same paragraphs.
3. Explain Hurston's reasoning on the theme of multiple identities. What distinctions does she make beyond the general ones of "public and private"?

Character

1. Describe the tone of voice Hurston creates in her essay. How is it created? Point to some particular uses of language. What role does the sense of character that her tone creates play in her argument as a whole?
2. What different senses of her character at different moments in her life does the author create? Pick two moments and compare them.
3. At the end of paragraph 6 Hurston plays on a line from Shakespeare: "Why then the world's mine oyster." What sense of her character does her joke create here?

Emotion

1. In paragraph 6 Hurston says, "But I am not tragically colored." What emotions do characterize her life as it is expressed in her essay?
2. To what emotions in her audience do the same words appeal? Explain how they do so.
3. Describe the emotions expressed by the author in paragraph 11, and explain the ways in which her uses of language work to create your sense of them.

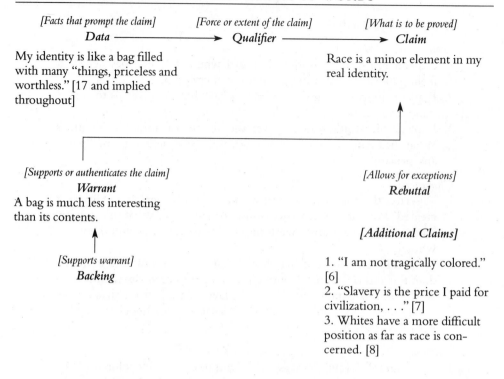

[Facts that prompt the claim]
Data ⟶

[Force or extent of the claim]
Qualifier ⟶

[What is to be proved]
Claim

My identity is like a bag filled with many "things, priceless and worthless." [17 and implied throughout]

Race is a minor element in my real identity.

[Supports or authenticates the claim]
Warrant

A bag is much less interesting than its contents.

[Allows for exceptions]
Rebuttal

[Supports warrant]
Backing

[Additional Claims]

1. "I am not tragically colored." [6]
2. "Slavery is the price I paid for civilization, . . ." [7]
3. Whites have a more difficult position as far as race is concerned. [8]

EXERCISES: LANGUAGE AND RACE

Intertextual Questions

1. The essays in this unit were written at different times. What part does this historical fact play in your reading of the writers' arguments? Explain your answer.
2. What part does history play within the argument of each writer? Pick some specific examples in explaining your answer.
3. Describe the ways in which each writer rebels against rigidities of classification.

Suggestions for Writing

1. In your view, which writer argues most effectively in all the modes of appeal—logic, character, and emotion? Write an essay in which you argue for your choice by pointing out specific virtues.
2. In your opinion, which writer argues least effectively on the whole? Write an essay that explains why you think so, with specific examples.
3. *Negro, Colored, Black, African-American*—what are the different implications of these different words for the same "race"? Write an essay in which you describe the connotations of the terms as you understand them.

What Books Should Students Read?

PREFACE TO *THE GREAT CONVERSATION*

Robert M. Hutchins

Until lately the West has regarded it as self-evident that the road to   1
education lay through great books. No man was educated unless he was
acquainted with the masterpieces of his tradition. There never was very
much doubt in anybody's mind about which the masterpieces were. They
were the books that had endured and that the common voice of mankind
called the finest creations, in writing, of the Western mind.

In the course of history, from epoch to epoch, new books have   2
been written that have won their place in the list. Books once thought
entitled to belong to it have been superseded; and this process of change
will continue as long as men can think and write. It is the task of every
generation to reassess the tradition in which it lives, to discard what it
cannot use, and to bring into context with the distant and intermediate
past the most recent contributions to the Great Conversation. This set of
books is the result of an attempt to reappraise and re-embody the tradition of the West for our generation.

The Editors do not believe that any of the social and political   3
changes that have taken place in the last fifty years, or any that now seem
imminent, have invalidated or can invalidate the tradition or make it
irrelevant for modern men. On the contrary, they are convinced that the
West needs to recapture and re-emphasize and bring to bear upon its
present problems the wisdom that lies in the works of its greatest thinkers
and in the discussion that they have carried on.

This set of books is offered in no antiquarian spirit. We have not   4
seen our task as that of taking tourists on a visit to ancient ruins or to the
quaint productions of primitive peoples. We have not thought of providing our readers with hours of relaxation or with an escape from the
dreadful cares that are the lot of every man in the second half of the
twentieth century after Christ. We are as concerned as anybody else at

the headlong plunge into the abyss that Western civilization seems to be taking. We believe that the voices that may recall the West to sanity are those which have taken part in the Great Conversation. We want them to be heard again—not because we want to go back to antiquity, or the Middle Ages, or the Renaissance, or the Eighteenth Century. We are quite aware that we do not live in any time but the present, and, distressing as the present is, we would not care to live in any other time if we could. We want the voices of the Great Conversation to be heard again because we think they may help us to learn to live better now.

We believe that in the passage of time the neglect of these books 5
in the twentieth century will be regarded as an aberration, and not, as it is sometimes called today, a sign of progress. We think that progress, and progress in education in particular, depends on the incorporation of the ideas and images included in this set in the daily lives of all of us, from childhood through old age. In this view the disappearance of great books from education and from the reading of adults constitutes a calamity. In this view education in the West has been steadily deteriorating; the rising generation has been deprived of its birthright; the mess of pottage it has received in exchange has not been nutritious; adults have come to lead lives comparatively rich in material comforts and very poor in moral, intellectual, and spiritual tone.

We do not think that these books will solve all our problems. We 6
do not think that they are the only books worth reading. We think that these books shed some light on all our basic problems, and that it is folly to do without any light we can get. We think that these books show the origins of many of our most serious difficulties. We think that the spirit they represent and the habit of mind they teach are more necessary today than ever before. We think that the reader who does his best to understand these books will find himself led to read and helped to understand other books. We think that reading and understanding great books will give him a standard by which to judge all other books.

We believe that the reduction of the citizen to an object of propa- 7
ganda, private and public, is one of the greatest dangers to democracy. A prevalent notion is that the great mass of the people cannot understand and cannot form an independent judgment upon any matter; they cannot be educated, in the sense of developing their intellectual powers, but they can be bamboozled. The reiteration of slogans, the distortion of the news, the great storm of propaganda that beats upon the citizen twenty-four hours a day all his life long mean either that democracy must fall a prey to the loudest and most persistent propagandists or that the people must save themselves by strengthening their minds so that they can appraise the issues for themselves.

Great books alone will not do the trick; for the people must have 8
the information on which to base a judgment as well as the ability to

make one. In order to understand inflation, for example, and to have an intelligent opinion as to what can be done about it, the economic facts in a given country at a given time have to be available. Great books cannot help us there. But they can help us to that grasp of history, politics, morals, and economics and to that habit of mind which are needed to form a valid judgment on the issue. Great books may even help us to know what information we should demand. If we knew what information to demand we might have a better chance of getting it.

Though we do not recommend great books as a panacea for our ills, we must admit that we have an exceedingly high opinion of them as an educational instrument. We think of them as the best educational instrument for young people and adults today. By this we do not mean that this particular set is the last word that can be said on the subject. We may have made errors of selection. We hope that this collection may some day be revised in the light of the criticism it will receive. But the idea that liberal education is the education that everybody ought to have, and that the best way to a liberal education in the West is through the greatest works the West has produced, is still, in our view, the best educational idea there is.

9

Questions for Analysis

Logic

1. Many of Hutchins's arguments have to do with refuting objections to the selections recommended by the series of books his essay introduces. Pick an example of this activity and explain the reasoning of his refutation.
2. Hutchins implies that his key term, *greatness,* is not defined as an eternal quality that is necessarily part of the nature of a book in itself. Explain the author's reasoning on the topics of "change" [2] and "progress" [5] in the selection of great books.
3. Explain the author's reasoning on the difference between a great book and one that only embodies "propaganda" [7].

Character

1. "Greatness" is a lofty subject. Exemplify and explain the ways in which you think the author's style does or does not suggest qualities of character that would make him a proper judge of greatness in writing. Do you think, for example, that he adopts a suitably lofty point of view?
2. In your view does the author seem to suggest a character that includes prejudice against other traditions than those of the West? Explain your answer with examples.

3. To what qualities of the imagined reader's character does the author appeal? Analyze an example of an appeal to the reader's character and explain its operation by referring to particular uses of language.

Emotion

1. What emotions in the reader are appealed to by the claim in the first paragraph, that until recently the main point the author argues has been "self-evident"?
2. Describe and explain the emotional appeal made by the author on the issue of "sanity" in paragraph 4.
3. The author does not hesitate to make judgments of value. To what emotions in his reader does this quality appeal? Explain your answer, using particular examples.

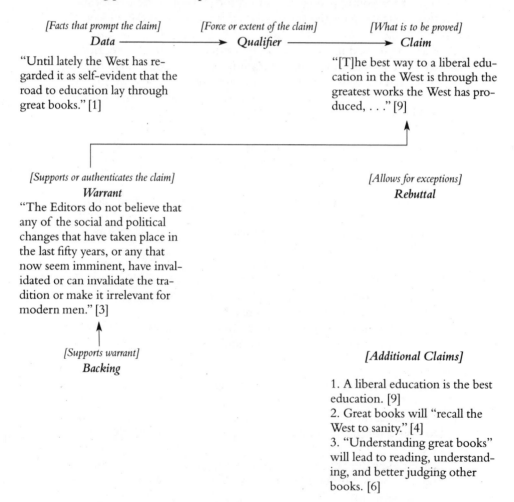

[Facts that prompt the claim]
Data —————→

[Force or extent of the claim]
Qualifier —————→

[What is to be proved]
Claim

"Until lately the West has regarded it as self-evident that the road to education lay through great books." [1]

"[T]he best way to a liberal education in the West is through the greatest works the West has produced, . . ." [9]

[Supports or authenticates the claim]
Warrant

"The Editors do not believe that any of the social and political changes that have taken place in the last fifty years, or any that now seem imminent, have invalidated or can invalidate the tradition or make it irrelevant for modern men." [3]

[Allows for exceptions]
Rebuttal

[Supports warrant]
Backing

[Additional Claims]

1. A liberal education is the best education. [9]
2. Great books will "recall the West to sanity." [4]
3. "Understanding great books" will lead to reading, understanding, and better judging other books. [6]

ON READING TRASH

Bob Swift

If you want kids to become omnivorous readers, let them read 1
trash. That's my philosophy, and I speak from experience.

I don't disagree with The National Endowment for the Humanities, 2
which says every high school graduate should have read 30 great works
of literature, including the Bible, Plato, Shakespeare, Hawthorne, the
Declaration of Independence, "Catcher in the Rye," "Crime and Punishment" and "Moby Dick."

It's a fine list. Kids should read them all, and more. But they'll be 3
better readers if they start off on trash. Trash? What I mean is what some
might call "popular" fiction. My theory is, if you get kids interested in
reading books—no matter what sort—they will eventually go on to the
grander literature all by themselves.

In the third grade I read my first novel, a mystic adventure set in 4
India. I still recall the sheer excitement at discovering how much fun
reading could be.

When we moved within walking distance of the public library a 5
whole new world opened. In the library I found that wonder of wonders,
the series. What a thrill, to find a favorite author had written a dozen or
more other titles.

I read a series about frontiersmen, learning about Indian tribes, beef 6
jerky and tepees. A Civil War series alternated young heroes from the
Blue and the Gray, and I learned about Grant and Lee and the Rock of
Chickamauga.

One summer, in Grandpa Barrow's attic, I discovered the Mother 7
Lode, scores of dusty books detailing the adventures of Tom Swift, The
Rover Boys, The Submarine Boys, The Motorcycle Boys and Bomba the
Jungle Boy. It didn't matter that some were written in 1919; any book
you haven't read is brand new.

Another summer I discovered Edgar Rice Burroughs. I swung 8
through jungles with Tarzan, fought green Martians with John Carter,
explored Pellucidar at the Earth's core, flew through the steamy air of
Venus with Carson Napier. Then I came across Sax Rohmer and, for
book after book, prowled opium dens with Nayland Smith, in pursuit of
the insidious Fu Manchu.

In the seventh grade, I ran across Booth Tarkington's hilarious Pen- 9
rod books and read them over and over.

My cousin went off to war in 1942 and gave me his pulp magazines. 10
I became hooked on Doc Savage, The Shadow, G8 and His Battle Aces,
The Spider, Amazing Stories. My folks wisely did not object to them as

trash. I began to look in second-hand book shops for past issues, and found a Blue Book Magazine, with an adventure story by Talbot Mundy. It led me back to the library, for more of Mundy's Far East thrillers. From Mundy, my path led to A. Conan Doyle's "The Lost World," Rudyard Kipling's "Kim," Jules Verne, H. G. Wells and Jack London.

Before long I was whaling with Herman Melville, affixing scarlet   *11* letters with Hawthorne and descending into the maelstrom with Poe. In due course came Hemingway, Dos Passos, "Hamlet," "The Odyssey," "The Iliad," "Crime and Punishment." I had discovered "real" literature by following the trail of popular fiction.

When our kids were small, we read aloud to them from Doctor   *12* Dolittle and Winnie the Pooh. Soon they learned to read, and favored the "Frog and Toad" and "Freddie the Pig" series.

When the old Doc Savage and Conan the Barbarian pulps were   *13* reissued as paperbacks, I brought them home. The kids devoured them, sometimes hiding them behind textbooks at school, just as I had. They read my old Tarzan and Penrod books along with Nancy Drew and The Black Stallion.

Now they're big kids. Each kid's room is lined with bookshelves,   *14* on which are stacked, in an eclectic mix, Doc Savage, Plato, Louis L'Amour westerns, Thomas Mann, Gothic romances, Agatha Christie, Sartre, Edgar Allen Poe, science-fiction, Saul Bellow, Shakespeare, Pogo, Greek tragedies, Hemingway, Kipling, Tarzan, Zen and the Art of Motorcycle Maintenance, F. Scott Fitzgerald, Bomba the Jungle Boy, Nietzsche, the Iliad, Dr. Dolittle, Joseph Conrad, Fu Manchu, Hawthorne, Penrod, Dostoevsky, Ray Bradbury, Herman Melville, Fitzgerald, Conan the Barbarian . . . more. Some great literature, some trash, but all good reading.

Questions for Analysis

Logic
1. In your view, is Swift's whole appeal to reason essentially contained in his first paragraph? If you think so, explain what the rest of the essay contributes to his appeal to reason within the categories of Toulmin's model of logic. For example, does the rest of the essay expand on the data? The claim? The warrant? The backing? If you don't think all the logical parts of the argument are essentially contained in the first paragraph, show where they are exemplified in the rest of the essay.
2. By what means does the author organize his essay? Explain how in your view the organization does or does not support the author's major point.

3. Explain some of the criteria by which the author creates throughout the essay a sense of the "eclectic mix" mentioned in his last paragraph.

Character

1. How would you characterize the general tone of voice Swift employs in the essay? Dignified? Chatty? Boasting? Describe what you hear in more than a word or two and explain the qualities of character that the author's tone seems designed to express.
2. What sense of character is created for you by the author's mentioning different family members throughout the essay?
3. What sense of character is created for you by the self-proclaimed eclecticism of the many lists of books that the author gives throughout the essay?

Emotion

1. What emotions are evoked in general by the use of the term *trash* to describe many of the books the author mentions? Do you see any advantages for the author's use of that term rather than *popular fiction* [3]?
2. To what emotions in his audience does the author appeal when he says that "any book you haven't read is brand new" [7]?
3. To what emotions does the author appeal by his account of his children's reading habits? In what ways does the account advance his argument?

WHOSE CANON IS IT ANYWAY?
IT'S NOT JUST ANGLO-SAXON

Henry Louis Gates, Jr.

I recently asked the dean of a prestigious liberal arts college if his school would ever have, as Berkeley has, a 70 percent nonwhite enrollment. "Never," he replied. "That would completely alter our identity as a center of the liberal arts." 1

The assumption that there is a deep connection between the shape of a college's curriculum and the ethnic composition of its students reflects a disquieting trend in education. Political representation has been confused with the "representation" of various ethnic identities in the curriculum. 2

The cultural right wing, threatened by demographic changes and the ensuing demands for curricular change, has retreated to intellectual 3 protectionism, arguing for a great and inviolable "Western tradition," which contains the seeds, fruit and flowers of the very best thought or uttered in history. (Typically, Mortimer Adler has ventured that blacks "wrote no good books.") Meanwhile, the cultural left demands changes to accord with population shifts in gender and ethnicity. Both are wrongheaded.

I am just as concerned that so many of my colleagues feel that the   4
rationale for a diverse curriculum depends on the latest Census Bureau report as I am that those opposed see pluralism as forestalling the possibilities of a communal "American" identity. To them, the study of our diverse cultures must lead to "tribalism" and "fragmentation."

The cultural diversity movement arose partly because of the frag-   5
mentation of society by ethnicity, class and gender. To make it the culprit for this fragmentation is to mistake effect for cause. A curriculum that reflects the achievement of the world's great cultures, not merely the West's, is not "politicized"; rather it situates the West as one of a community of civilizations. After all, culture is always a conversation among different voices.

To insist that we "master our own culture" before learning others—   6
as Arthur Schlessinger Jr. has proposed—only defers the vexed question: What gets to count as "our" culture? What has passed as "common culture" has been an Anglo-American regional culture, masking itself as universal. Significantly different cultures sought refuge underground.

Writing in 1903, W.E.B. Du Bois expressed his dream of a high   7
culture that would transcend the color line: "I sit with Shakespeare and he winces not." But the dream was not open to all. "Is this the life you grudge us," he concluded, "O knightly America?" For him, the humanities were a conduit into a republic of letters enabling escape from racism and ethnic chauvinism. Yet no one played a more crucial role than he in excavating the long buried heritage of Africans and African-Americans.

The fact of one's ethnicity, for any American of color, is never   8
neutral: One's public treatment, and public behavior, are shaped in large part by one's perceived ethnic identity just as by one's gender. To demand that Americans shock their cultural heritages and homogenize themselves into a "universal" WASP culture is to dream of an America in cultural white face, and that just won't do.

So it's only when we're free to explore the complexities of our   9
hyphenated culture that we can discover what a genuinely common American culture might actually look like.

Is multiculturalism un-American? Herman Melville didn't think so.   10
As he wrote: "We are not a narrow tribe, no . . . We are not a nation, so

much as a world." We're all ethnics; the challenge of transcending ethnic chauvinism is one we all face.

We've entrusted our schools with the fashioning and refashioning of a democratic policy. That's why schooling has always been a matter of political judgment. But in a nation that has theorized itself as plural from its inception, schools have a very special task.

Our society won't survive without the values of tolerance, and cultural tolerance comes to nothing without cultural understanding. The challenge facing America will be the shaping of a truly common public culture, one responsive to the long-silenced cultures of color. If we relinquish the ideal of America as a plural nation, we've abandoned the very experiment America represents. And that is too great a price to pay.

Questions for Analysis

Logic
1. The word *canon* in the author's title refers to the books that a given culture considers its most valuable literary works. According to Gates, what is the reasoning of the "cultural right wing," and what arguments does he bring to refute that reasoning?
2. According to Gates, what is the reasoning of the cultural left wing, and what arguments does he bring to refute that reasoning?
3. Explain Gates's own reasoning on the meaning of the key term *tolerance.*

Character
1. What qualities of Gates's character are suggested by the anecdote with which he begins the essay?
2. What qualities of character in the author are suggested for you by the ways in which he responds to opposing viewpoints? Explain your answer using particular examples.
3. In what ways does the author seek to align his views with those of publicly acknowledged authorities? Explain your answer by using particular examples.

Emotion
1. The author refers to the "West," and to "Anglo-Saxon," and "Anglo-American" culture. What are the emotional appeals of each term? What is the emotional effect of using them interchangeably?
2. What is the emotional appeal created by the use of the term *white face* in paragraph 8?
3. To what emotions in his audience does the author appeal in paragraph 12 when he says that "society won't survive without the values of tolerance"?

EXERCISES: WHAT BOOKS SHOULD STUDENTS READ?

Intertextual Questions

1. Compare the ways in which each author takes into account the factor of historical change in his essay.
2. Both Hutchins and Gates use the metaphor of conversation to describe literary culture. Compare the ways in which each author understands and uses the implications of conversation in his argument.
3. Both Hutchins and Gates see the proper selection of books as a way of solving problems. Compare the ways in which each author understands the criteria for choosing books as a matter of problems and solutions.

Suggestions for Writing

1. Write an essay on the ways in which each author uses evidence as a means of supporting his claims for the ideas about books that he advances.
2. Literature is often said to combine delight and instruction. Write an essay in which you analyze the ways in which each author addresses the issues suggested by this dual definition.
3. Each writer imagines literature in some way as a "heritage." Write an essay that analyzes the ways in which this metaphor is used implicitly or explicitly to create appeals to emotion. Who or what, for example, would *literally* be the one to give you an inheritance? What implications would there be for you in your receiving an inheritance? For refusing to accept one? For not caring to know whether it exists or not? Compare these implications to the simple act of refusing to read or not caring to know about a book that someone else recommends.

Legalizing Drugs

THE FREEDOM TO DESTROY YOURSELF

Walter E. Williams

"Men never do evil so cheerfully and thoroughly as when they do   *1*
it with religious conviction," said Blaise Pascal, the seventeenth-century
French philosopher. Such a statement can be readily applied to some of
the laws in the United States. A good example are the laws against the
sale and possession of heroin. Our society has decided that heroin consumption is not good for the individual. On this I personally agree. But
the question is whether we should outlaw those things which most of us
agree are not good for the individual.

I would estimate the production cost of an amount of heroin that   *2*
would meet the daily needs of a heavy addict to be about $5 at most. But
because heroin is illegal, the "street" price is many times more. I've heard
reports that heavy addicts must pay $200 a day for their fix. The high
price reflects the reality that heroin has to be produced surreptitiously,
that there are many middlemen, and that there are many payoffs to officials that have to be made.

Heroin addicts tend not to be highly productive members of our   *3*
society, so where will they get the money to support this habit? From
armed robberies, assaults, and burglaries. The National Association of
Retail Druggists estimates, for example, that there were 30,000 armed
robberies and after-hours break-ins at U.S. pharmacies in 1979. More
than four hundred druggists, drugstore employees, or customers who just
happened to be in the wrong place at the wrong time were killed by the
criminals—most of whom were after drugs. In addition, the addicts don't
hesitate going to elementary, junior, and senior high school campuses to
addict others in order to pay for their habit.

In other words, the fact that society outlaws heroin because it thinks   *4*
that individuals should not destroy themselves does not stop individuals

from destroying themselves. These laws actually make people who are hell-bent on destroying their own lives destroy others in the process. What, may we ask, is the moral justification for this? Rather than compliment a police officer who cracks a drug ring, what people need to do is buy more locks and travel less at night.

Cracking a drug ring reduces the amount of heroin available. This 5 means that heroin prices will rise. In turn, this means that addicts will have to mug and victimize more people in order to support their habit.

Societies, through the ages, have not been able to rid themselves of 6 prostitution, alcohol, and drugs. They have only been able to make these areas of economic activity profitable for criminals. Isn't it about time we allow individuals to destroy themselves without the requirement that they destroy innocent bystanders in the process?

Questions for Analysis

Logic
1. Explain in your own words Williams's logic for claiming that higher drug prices lead to higher crime.
2. Explain in your own words Williams's distinction between what is good for an individual and what is good for society as a whole.
3. Would you agree that the implied warrant for Williams's main claim is to the effect that "the lesser of two evils is the better?" Explain.

Character
1. Which of the following sets of phrases best describes the personality that Williams's style implies: (a) blunt, straight-talking? (b) elegant, circumspect? Point to some examples to demonstrate your view.
2. What does the quotation from Pascal that begins the essay add to our sense of Williams? Would it have been just as effective in what it achieves, had it ended the piece? Explain.
3. Williams is an economist with a Ph.D. Does this knowledge change your sense of his character created by his style alone?

Emotion
1. In paragraph 3 Williams points to "elementary, junior, and senior high school campuses" as sites for drug recruiting. Describe the emotional appeal made by this example.
2. Explain the paradox of the policeman at the end of paragraph 4. What emotions are appealed to here? What other paradoxes does Williams employ in the essay?
3. Does the word *yourself* in the title take on a richer meaning after you have read the essay as a whole? What emotions seem appealed to by the use of this word in the title?

WE ALREADY KNOW THE FOLLY OF DECRIMINALIZED DRUGS

Elizabeth Gessner

To the Editor:

It seems to me that the spate of pro-legalization articles that have appeared recently in the *Times* are founded on a misconception, namely that drug use has not already been decriminalized. Drug use underwent a de facto decriminalization in America some twenty years ago. From the Hollywood celebrity publicly snorting coke at a party to the teenager smoking marijuana in front of his high school, Americans have ceased to worry about criminal penalties for drug use. It is the failure of decriminalization that we are living with now. *1*

Prohibitions against drug use are not founded in some abstract and hypocritical morality, as is often implied. Advocates of legalization seem curiously unable to distinguish gradations in human behavior. The argument that it is impermissible to outlaw drugs because people are legally "addicted" to coffee or aspirin is the ludicrous extension of a feeble train of thought. Teenagers are not prostituting themselves in Times Square to buy another bottle of aspirin, nor are men and women destroying their families for the sake of another cup of coffee. It is not merely the sale and distribution of drugs that is destroying lives. It is the effects of the drugs themselves and the things that people do under their influence that are the real hazards to the lives and happiness of millions of our citizens. *2*

I suggest we try actually enforcing penalties for drug use and see if that has any effect before we give up and turn our society into a drug bazaar. Or possibly we should simply admit what A. M. Rosenthal perceptively argued in his column of September 26, that the lives currently being destroyed by drugs are not lives most Americans consider important. Mr. Rosenthal's analogy of drug use to slavery was a particularly apt one. Slavery was defended by many citizens as being an economic necessity, while abolitionists were ridiculed as moralizing meddlers or naive idealists. *3*

However, even if charity and morality do not compel us to abolish this new form of slavery, prudence should, for we must remember that throughout history the well-off have never succeeded in finding a refuge remote enough to protect them from the results of the injustices they have inflicted upon the poor. Our society is creating a class of slaves who have been stripped by drugs of pity, hope, love, kindness, and even fear, and I think that their retribution will eventually fall on all of us. *4*
—*Elizabeth Gessner*

Questions for Analysis

Logic
1. The phrase "de facto" in paragraph 1 means "in fact—if not in name." How does the phrase affect Gessner's claim, and what does it require of an opponent who would refute that view?
2. Besides de facto decriminalization, what other issues of definition does Gessner's essay raise?
3. In paragraph 2, does Gessner seem to you to present a clear cause and effect relation between drugs and teen-age prostitution? Explain your answer.

Character
1. Gessner says in paragraph 2 that "prohibitions against drug use are not founded in some abstract and hypocritical morality." Does the morality of her own appeal here seem solidly founded? Find evidence from her style (from her tone of voice, for example) that suggests Gessner's moral attitudes and briefly describe them.
2. Where and in what ways does the appeal of Gessner's character operate to join her personal views to more public authorities?
3. Where does Gessner seem to locate her own social position in the social structure imagined in the last paragraph? Give evidence for your answer.

Emotion
1. What emotional appeal does the author make with the example of the "Hollywood celebrity" in paragraph 1?
2. Analyze the emotional appeal made by Gessner's use of the word *curiously* in the third sentence of paragraph 2. What would be changed in her tone of voice and in the reaction she invites in her audience to that tone, were the word omitted?
3. Explain how the emotional appeal made by the analogy to slavery operates in paragraph 4. What is the audience invited to feel and why?

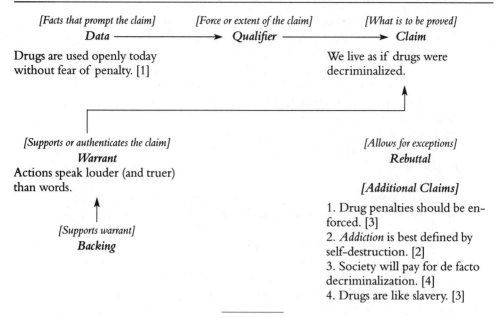

[*Facts that prompt the claim*]
Data ⟶ [*Force or extent of the claim*] **Qualifier** ⟶ [*What is to be proved*] **Claim**

Drugs are used openly today without fear of penalty. [1]

We live as if drugs were decriminalized.

[*Supports or authenticates the claim*]
Warrant
Actions speak louder (and truer) than words.

[*Allows for exceptions*]
Rebuttal

[*Additional Claims*]

[*Supports warrant*]
Backing

1. Drug penalties should be enforced. [3]
2. *Addiction* is best defined by self-destruction. [2]
3. Society will pay for de facto decriminalization. [4]
4. Drugs are like slavery. [3]

END THE WAR ON DRUGS

Joanne Jacobs

President Clinton has inherited two costly, nasty and never-ending wars from George Bush. I don't know what he should do about the war against Saddam Hussein, but I think he should end the war on drugs. 1

Bush drew a line in the snow, so to speak, and fought hard to make the hawkish supply-side strategies work. Drug war spending quadrupled, to nearly $13 billion a year for the federal effort alone, and Bush put 70 percent of the money into interdiction and enforcement. 2

The prison population doubled in the past 10 years, in large part due to more hawkish enforcement and long mandatory sentences for drug offenses. 3

"In California, the number of persons sent to prison for drug offenses tripled between 1980 and 1985, and tripled again in the following five years, rising from less than 1,000 to more than 10,000 over the decade," reports the Rand Research Review. No wonder the state is broke. 4

The result of this multibillion-dollar war: Less occasional drug use, as much or more hard-core abuse. By one measure—emergency-room admissions for cocaine and heroin overdoses—things are considerably worse. 5

Meanwhile, the murder rate has gone up in step with the drug-war budget. This is not a coincidence, observes Peter Reuter, a Rand drug- 6 policy analyst. "Frequent harassment of street drug sellers increases the incentives to use violence to maintain market share."

Furthermore, our civil liberties have suffered collateral damage, as all Americans—but especially minorities—are subjected to drug tests, warrantless searches and long-distance snooping. 7

On the campaign trail, Clinton promised a "national crusade" that will spend more on treatment and prevention. He also pledged to provide federal funds for local police to suppress drugs. 8

A crusade is better than a war, but not much. Clinton's wording still implies a one-shot campaign leading to total victory, or perhaps total redemption. 9

The president has an opportunity for leadership toward some of that change we've been hearing about: He can recast drug policy as a public-health issue. 10

After all, Clinton's half-brother is one of those drug criminals we've heard so much about. He served 15 months in federal prison for selling cocaine in 1984. Clinton participated in family therapy to aid his brother's treatment for addiction. He knows Roger Clinton Jr.'s criminal substance abuse is closely related to Roger Clinton Sr.'s legal substance abuse. 11

Perhaps Clinton guesses that if his brother had come from a poorer family—with no family friends to provide a job and no money to pay for therapy—his drug conviction would have ended his chances to find honest work or live a drug-free life. 12

The president of the Arkansas Senate was criticized this week for commuting two sentences while serving as acting governor: One was a murderer's life sentence; the other was a 50-year prison term for transporting cocaine. The drug carrier had served five years, and would not have been eligible for parole for another 18 years. 13

The foot-soldiers in the drug war are ready to change. Police chiefs and cops, probation officers, judges and prosecutors know that what they've been doing doesn't do any good. Most now advocate the pragmatic approach called "harm minimization." (Some favor decriminalization, but that much change isn't going to happen.) 14

What can Clinton do? 15

Stop promising a "drug free" America, and drop the military rhetoric. Announce that drug abuse will be treated like alcohol abuse, a serious public-health problem causing harm to innocent victims as well as to abusers. 16

Cut the drug czar's bloated office—which in the past has been filled with political hacks—and transfer it to Health and Human Services. 17

Fund treatment programs with a record of success and rehabilitation programs for prisoners. Currently, there are enough federally funded treatment slots for fewer than one out of three serious drug abusers. 18

Don't put more money into prevention programs without evidence 19 of effectiveness. Kids don't need more anti-drug education. What they need is education to prepare for a future in which they'll have better choices than using or selling drugs.

(My sixth-grader just attended a school assembly featuring a guy   20 who demonstrated jumping rope and ventriloquism—including the singing of "Hava Nagila" for "our Jewish-American friends"—and led students in hope-not-dope and self-esteem chants. She threatened to start using drugs if forced to listen to one more anti-drug spiel.)

Fund those cops on the beat to make neighborhoods safer for de-   21 cent people. Sure, patrolling mean streets is not a federal responsibility, but as long as we're going to ignore that, make sure the money goes for community policing, not task forces and SWAT teams.

The money can come from eliminating the Drug Enforcement   22 Administration. We've got the FBI; we don't need multiple agencies tripping over each other.

Take every dollar spent trying to interdict drug supplies and use it   23 to pay for education, job training and drug treatment for inner-city kids.

Eliminate mandatory sentences that put first-time drug offenders   24 behind bars for years longer than murderers and rapists, and fill jails with petty drug users. Some states are forced to release violent criminals early in order to make room for nonviolent drug offenders serving no-parole sentences.

Use the billions saved by reducing sentences to pay for locking up   25 violent criminals, for in-prison drug programs, for probation officers and for boarding schools (boot camps, if you prefer) for kids who get in trouble.

Finally, stop confiscating property unless there's proof it was bought   26 with criminal proceeds. In some cases, cars, boats and homes have been seized without a criminal conviction, or with no evidence against the owner. This is the sort of arbitrary government power the Constitution is supposed to protect Americans against. The Supreme Court just agreed to hear a test case.

President Clinton is the first president to have smoked marijuana,   27 even if he didn't inhale. I'd guess that almost all the Friends of Bill, and half his Cabinet, were drug criminals once.

U.S. drug policy casts millions of Americans as the enemy on   28 whom war must be waged. It's time for a change.

Questions for Analysis

Logic

1. How does her briefly alluding to the war with Iraq in the first paragraph support Jacobs's argument for reimagining the solution to the drug problem?

2. Explain in your own words the logic of Jacobs's point about President Clinton's half brother [11–12].
3. Explain in your own words the logic of the author's daughter's joke [20] and the kind of support it affords Jacobs's argument.

Character
1. What sense of the author's character is created in paragraph 1 by her claiming not to know what to do about the war with Iraq?
2. What sense of the author's character is created by her use of the anecdote concerning her sixth-grade daughter [20]?
3. How does her putting the issue of wrongful compensation of property last in her list of recommendations [26] affect your sense of the author's character?

Emotion
1. What does the author imply is the emotional appeal of imagining drug policy as a war? Why do you think she wishes to "drop the military rhetoric?"
2. In context, what is the emotional appeal of the story about the author's daughter [20]?
3. What is the emotional appeal involved in ending the essay with the sentence "It's time for a change?"

EXERCISES: LEGALIZING DRUGS

Intertextual Questions
1. Both Gessner and Williams evoke history as a support in their final paragraphs. Compare the ways in which a view of history fits into each writer's argument. Is either view the same as that of Jacobs? Explain.
2. Describe briefly what you imagine Williams might reply to Gessner's claim in paragraph 3 that most Americans do not consider the lives destroyed by drugs to be important. What would Jacobs say?
3. Gessner appeals explicitly to charity and morality in her last paragraph. How do you imagine Williams might reply? Jacobs?

Suggestions for Writing
1. Pick what you consider to be the strongest point made by each writer. Then, write a short essay in which you compare the strengths of each position.
2. Write a letter to the editor that you imagine Williams might write in reply to Gessner's letter or to Jacobs's essay.
3. What is your own view on the decriminalization of drugs? Using any of the material or arguments suggested by the two writers on the issue, write an essay arguing your position.

Gun Control: Common Sense or Nonsense?

KILLING OUR FUTURE

Sarah Brady

As America enters the next decade, it does so with an appalling 1
legacy of gun violence. The 1980s were tragic years that saw nearly a
quarter of a million Americans die from handguns—four times as many
as were killed in the Viet Nam War. We began the decade by witnessing
yet another President, Ronald Reagan, become a victim of a would-be
assassin's bullet. That day my husband Jim, his press secretary, also became
a statistic in America's handgun war.

Gun violence is an epidemic in this country. In too many cities, the 2
news each night reports another death by a gun. As dealers push out in
search of new addicts, Smalltown, U.S.A., is introduced to the mindless
gun violence fostered by the drug trade.

And we are killing our future. Every day a child in this country 3
loses his or her life to a handgun. Hundreds more are permanently injured, often because a careless adult left within easy reach a loaded handgun purchased for self-defense.

Despite the carnage, America stands poised to face an even greater 4
escalation of bloodshed. The growing popularity of military-style assault
weapons could turn our streets into combat zones. Assault weapons, designed solely to mow down human beings, are turning up at an alarming
rate in the hands of those most prone to violence—drug dealers, gang
members, hate groups and the mentally ill.

The Stockton, Calif., massacre of little children was a warning to 5
our policymakers. But Congress lacked the courage to do anything. During the year of inaction on Capitol Hill, we have seen too many other
tragedies brought about by assault weapons. In Louisville an ex-employee
of a printing plant went on a shooting spree with a Chinese-made semiautomatic version of the AK-47, gunning down 21 people, killing eight

and himself. Two Colorado women were murdered and several others injured by a junkie using a stolen MAC-11 semiautomatic pistol. And Congress votes itself a pay raise.

The National Rifle Association, meanwhile, breathes a sigh of re-   6
lief, gratified that your attention is now elsewhere. The only cooling-off period the N.R.A. favors is a postponement of legislative action. It counts on public anger to fade before such outrage can be directed at legislators. The N.R.A. runs feel-good ads saying guns are not the problem and there is nothing we can do to prevent criminals from getting guns. In fact, it has said that guns in the wrong hands are the "price we pay for freedom." I guess I'm just not willing to hand the next John Hinckley a deadly handgun. Neither is the nation's law-enforcement community, the men and women who put their lives on the line for the rest of us every day.

Two pieces of federal legislation can make a difference right now.   7
First, we must require a national waiting period before the purchase of a handgun, to allow for a criminal-records check. Police know that waiting periods work. In the 20 years that New Jersey has required a background check, authorities have stopped more than 10,000 convicted felons from purchasing handguns.

We must also stop the sale and domestic production of semiauto-   8
matic assault weapons. These killing machines clearly have no legitimate sporting purpose, as President Bush recognized when he permanently banned their importation.

These public-safety measures are supported by the vast majority of   9
Americans—including gun owners. In fact, these measures are so sensible that I never realized the campaign to pass them into law would be such an uphill battle. But it can be done.

Jim Brady knows the importance of a waiting period. He knows   10
the living hell of a gunshot wound. Jim and I are not afraid to take on the N.R.A. leaders, and we will fight them everywhere we can. As Jim said in his congressional testimony, "I don't question the rights of responsible gun owners. That's not the issue. The issue is whether the John Hinckleys of the world should be able to walk into gun stores and purchase handguns instantly. Are you willing and ready to cast a vote for a commonsense public-safety bill endorsed by experts—law enforcement?"

Are we as a nation going to accept America's bloodshed, or are we   11
ready to stand up and do what is right? When are we going to say "Enough"? We can change the direction in which America is headed. We can prevent the 1990s from being bloodier than the past ten years. If each of you picks up a pen and writes to your Senators and Representative tonight, you would be surprised at how quickly we could collect the votes we need to win the war for a safer America.

Let us enter a new decade committed to finding solutions to the   *12*
problem of gun violence. Let your legislators know that voting with the
gun lobby—and against public safety—is no longer acceptable. Let us
send a signal to lawmakers that we demand action, not excuses.

Questions for Analysis

Logic
1. Brady organizes her essay by reference to history. In what ways does
   this method support the logic of her argument?
2. According to Brady, what is the logic of the counterarguments made
   by the NRA?
3. Do you think that the author makes her major claim in paragraphs 10
   or 11 or elsewhere? Explain your answer.

Character
1. Where and how does Brady establish herself as informed and knowledgeable on the issue?
2. Where and how does Brady establish herself as benevolent and well-
   meaning?
3. Where and how does Brady seek to avoid the accusation of zealotry
   and fanaticism?

Emotion
1. Describe some of the ways in which Brady appeals to the audience's
   sympathy.
2. Describe some of the ways in which Brady appeals to the audience's
   sense of outrage.
3. How does Brady move between personal emotional appeals and those
   she makes as a citizen? Explain with examples.

GUN CONTROL AND SHEEP FOR THE SLAUGHTER

Mark D. McLean

Two outrages took place at Luby's Cafeteria in Killeen, Texas, in   *1*
October. George Hennard's murder of 23 people garnered all the publicity. But the fact that a madman could crash his truck through a cafeteria
window, climb out and methodically kill one-fifth of the patrons over a

10-minute period without any of the 100 or so law-abiding private citizens having the means to resist is an outrage as well.

It is likely a number of those patrons owned firearms. Some may have been carrying firearms in their vehicles, as allowed by Texas law. But Texas law, and that of many other states, allows only sworn law enforcement officers to carry concealed weapons on their persons. Texas law *does* allow one to carry an unconcealed handgun. But try exercising this "right to bear arms" in a shopping mall or on a city street without some recognizable law enforcement or security guard uniform. *2*

The first recorded examples of weapons control are found in the Old Testament. The Judge Deborah remarks in her victory song, "Neither shield nor spear was seen among forty thousand in Israel" (Judges 5:8). 1 Samuel 13:19–22 records that the Philistines would not allow the Israelites to have any blacksmiths "lest the Hebrews make a sword or spear" (1 Samuel 13:19). As a result, on the day of the Israelites' battle with the Philistines, none of the 600 men with Saul and his son Jonathan were armed with swords or spears. Only Saul and Jonathan had weapons. *3*

The purpose of weapons control has not changed over the centuries. Its goal is to control any segment of the governed population seen as dangerous to the "public safety." Governments have always found it easier to impose the "will of the people" upon the people if the people are unarmed. The question that needs to be faced with as little emotional baggage as possible is "who in the U.S. constitutes the population we need to control with gun-control laws?" *4*

In spite of the great psychological and physical harm done to individuals and our society as a whole by violent criminals, no matter what weapon they use, violent criminals still represent a small percentage of our total population. Approximately 3% of the American population committed violent crimes in 1990. The issue is how best to control that violent minority. Given our limited resources of both law enforcement personnel and finances, how can we best use them to lessen the criminal abuse of weapons? *5*

Well-crafted legislation allowing qualified private American citizens to carry a concealed weapon for the defense of their own lives or the lives of others in a legitimate act of law enforcement would have made Hennard's attack unlikely; at the very least, it would have made it impossible for him to kill so many people. *6*

It is no coincidence that the same criteria that make one ineligible to own any firearm are those that make one ineligible to vote—conviction on a felony charge, certification as mentally incompetent, or being an alien. By what criteria have congressional supporters of more restrictive gun legislation judged their constituents incompetent to own and bear firearms safely and legally in defense of themselves and their communities from the violent criminal minority? *7*

The homicide rate in Florida fell after the permit to carry laws were   *8*
eased. The same is true of a similar easing of carry laws adopted in
Oregon in 1989.

Ask yourself: Do I believe myself mentally and morally competent   *9*
to own and bear arms, including a concealed handgun, safely and legally
in accordance with all local, state and federal regulations? Then contact
your elected officials and ask them if they believe they and their constituents are mentally and morally competent to do the same.

If they don't have faith in their own mental and moral competence,   *10*
do you want them to be your representatives in government? Ask those
who don't believe you and their other constituents are competent to own
and bear arms what you have done to warrant such a verdict against your
ability to function as a competent citizen. Where does this radical lack of
faith in the character of the American public come from?

How easy will it be for the next madman to find a group of people   *11*
to slaughter with nearly 100% assurance that none of them will be able
to resist his onslaught? That will depend on the type of gun control
legislation we embrace between now and then.

Questions for Analysis

Logic

1. What seems to be the reasoning behind McLean's dismissal of the
   utility of carrying an unconcealed handgun in Texas?
2. Which "segment" of the population is it, according to McLean, the
   "goal" of gun control to control? In what ways might he hope that
   his logical argument would be supported by his analogy to the control
   of the Israelites by the Philistines?
3. Suppose the author had organized his essay by putting his last paragraph third. In your view would the force of the essay's reasoning be
   increased or diminished? Explain.

Character

1. What qualities of his ethos are suggested by McLean's familiarity with
   relevant statistics?
2. What qualities of character are suggested by the quotations from the
   Bible that McLean makes?
3. What qualities of character are suggested by the ways in which Mc-
   Lean directly addresses his audience at the end of his essay?

Emotion

1. What emotions in his audience does McLean appeal to by his use of
   statistics?
2. What emotions in his audience does McLean appeal to by his quotations from the Bible?

3. What emotions does McLean appeal to by directly addressing his audience at the end of his essay?

BITING THE BULLETS

Gerald Nachman

After a seventeen-year study, my sub-subcommittee on gun control   *1*
has come up with a compromise solution: bullet control.

By banning the large-scale sale of bullets, gun owners may keep   *2*
their weapons, the average person (or squirrel) will be safe and criminals
won't have to go around empty-handed.

It will, of course, still be possible to get conked over the head with   *3*
a gun butt, but this is just a first step. The agreement should satisfy
everyone except perhaps the hard-to-please National Bullet Association
and its 728 members.

The ban on bullets will work this way: Starting in 1984, all car-   *4*
tridges fired by "Saturday-night specials" will be illegal—however, so as
not to annoy the powerful pro-ammo lobby and collectors of antique
bullets, all other ammunition will still be readily available.

By 1990, all bullets fired by "Sunday-through-Tuesday-night spe-   *5*
cials" will be outlawed (except in woodsy states).

Bullet control is designed to mollify the rifle groups whose favorite   *6*
slogan is "Guns don't kill people—people kill people." When the committee looked into this, it found that, in actual (target) practice, bullets
kill people.

The committee also discovered that, to inflict any real damage, the   *7*
bullet should be inside a gun. To test this, several marksmen tried to pick
off a moving target by *throwing* bullets at it. Results showed that the
bullets merely ricocheted off the man and he escaped with only a few
nicks.

When the same test was tried using bullets fired from a gun, how-   *8*
ever, the fellow died (presumably from the bullets). The committee concluded that guns and bullets can be hazardous to your health when "used
in connection with each other," as our report phrases it. To be on the safe
side, though, the committee temporarily recommends a twenty-minute
"cooling off" period for people purchasing bullets.

As it now stands, any nut can walk into a gun shop and buy enough   *9*
lead to wipe out a small town. Until the new law goes into effect, a ruling
will require "all nuts to be registered and forced to cool their heels for
half an hour."

Another popular riflemen's slogan—"When guns are outlawed,   10
only outlaws will have guns"—is true enough, the committee agreed,
but many outlaws who testified before the committee said they're willing
to give bullet control a try.

"Look," said one gangster, "we hate to be unreasonable about this,   11
but we'd look pretty dumb wandering around the streets without a gun.
We can be every bit as terrifying with an empty .38 and then at least we
won't be booked for carrying a loaded weapon."

Sub-subcommittee members foresee a day when Congress may pass   12
a measure banning guns with handles and, eventually, triggers. Gradually,
the entire gun will be phased out of existence, a part at a time. Remarks
one congressman, "There's no reason to rush into this gun-control thing
helter-skelter."

Questions for Analysis

Logic
1. A *synecdoche* is a figure of speech wherein a part may stand for the
   whole, such as *hands* for sailors in "all hands on deck," or *head* in
   "fifteen head of cattle." Is *guns* in the NRA slogan "Guns don't kill
   people—people kill people" meant literally or figuratively?
2. How does Nachman understand the slogan or pretend to understand it?
3. Nachman also makes fun of a "cooling-off period." How might his
   argument run on this issue, were he to elaborate on it?

Character
1. One difficulty with any humorous argument is to distinguish the author's pretended position from his or her implied real position. What
   are some qualities of the pretended ethical appeals Nachman makes?
   For example, with regard to high intelligence, what is implied by the
   experiment implied by thrown bullets for both his real and his implied
   position?
2. Explain and exemplify some other ways in which the essay creates
   your sense of the author's real intelligence.
3. Some humor can be biting, bitter, and cruel; Nachman's seems more
   lighthearted and witty. What evidence works to create this sense?

Emotion
1. What emotional implications does the word *compromise* usually carry
   for you? What seems to be Nachman's strategy for using the word in
   paragraph 1?
2. What emotional implications do the ideas of testing and experimentation usually carry for you? What seems to be Nachman's strategy
   with regard to testing in paragraphs 6–8?

3. To what emotional response does Nachman's general tone of mock-earnestness seem to appeal? To what response does it really appeal?

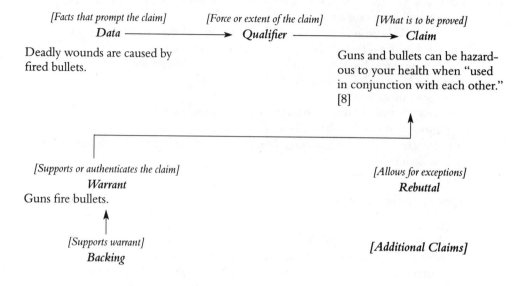

[Facts that prompt the claim]
Data ——————→

[Force or extent of the claim]
Qualifier ——————→

[What is to be proved]
Claim

Deadly wounds are caused by fired bullets.

Guns and bullets can be hazardous to your health when "used in conjunction with each other." [8]

[Supports or authenticates the claim]
Warrant
Guns fire bullets.

[Allows for exceptions]
Rebuttal

[Supports warrant]
Backing

[Additional Claims]

EXERCISES: GUN CONTROL

Intertextual Questions

1. Both McLean and Brady rely heavily on emotional appeals. How do they differ, and how do they agree in their uses of the images of slaughter?
2. With which of the other two writers do you imagine Nachman most clearly to agree in his serious position? Explain your answer.
3. All three writers employ irony. Point to some differences and similarities among them with regard to the use of this technique.

Suggestions for Writing

1. Write a letter as if from McLean to Nachman in which you express what you think McLean's response might be.
2. Write an analysis of the essay by the serious writer whose arguments you consider weakest and explain your position.
3. Write an essay that expresses your own views on the issue of gun control, being sure in some way to take account of the arguments considered here.

Should English Be the Language of America?

IN SUPPORT OF OUR COMMON LANGUAGE . . .

U.S. English

ENGLISH, OUR COMMON BOND

Throughout its history, the United States has been enriched by the cultural contributions of immigrants from many traditions, but blessed with one common language that has united a diverse nation and fostered harmony among its people. 1

As much by accident as by design, that language is English. Given our country's history of immigration and the geography of immigrant settlements, it might have been Dutch, or Spanish, or German; or it might have been two languages, as is the case in Canada, our neighbor to the north. 2

But English prevailed, and it has served us well. Its eloquence shines in our Declaration of Independence and in our Constitution. It is the living carrier of our democratic ideals. 3

English is a world language which we share with many other nations. It is the most popular medium of international communication. 4

THE SPREAD OF LANGUAGE SEGREGATION

The United States has been spared the bitter conflicts that plague so many countries whose citizens do not share a common tongue. Historic forces made English the language of all Americans, though nothing in our laws designated it the official language of the nation. 5

But now English is under attack, and we must take affirmative steps to guarantee that it continues to be our common heritage. Failure to do 6 so may well lead to institutionalized language segregation and a gradual loss of national unity.

The erosion of English and the rise of other languages in public   7
life have several causes:

- Some spokesmen for ethnic groups reject the "melting pot" ideal; they label assimilation a betrayal of their native cultures and demand government funding to maintain separate ethnic institutions.
- Well-intentioned but unproven theories have led to extensive government-funded bilingual education programs, ranging from preschool through college.
- New civil-rights assertions have yielded bilingual and multilingual ballots, voting instructions, election site counselors, and government-funded voter registration campaigns aimed solely at speakers of foreign languages.
- Record immigration, concentrated in fewer language groups, is reinforcing language segregation and retarding language assimilation.
- The availability of foreign language electronic media, with a full range of news and entertainment, is a new disincentive to the learning of English.

U.S. ENGLISH: A TIMELY PUBLIC RESPONSE

In 1981, Senator S. I. Hayakawa, himself an immigrant and distin-   8
guished scholar of semantics, proposed a constitutional amendment designating English as the official language of the United States. Senator Hayakawa helped found U.S. ENGLISH in 1983 to organize and support a citizens' movement to maintain our common linguistic heritage.

U.S. ENGLISH is committed to promoting the use of English in   9
the political, economic, and intellectual life of the nation. It operates squarely within the American political mainstream and rejects all manifestations of cultural or linguistic chauvinism.

OUR GUIDING PRINCIPLES

Our goal is to maintain the blessing of a common language—   10
English—for the people of the United States.

These principles guide us: 11

- In a pluralistic nation such as ours, government should foster the similarities that unite us rather than the differences that separate us.
- The nation's public schools have a special responsibility to help students who don't speak English to learn the language as quickly as possible.

- Quality teaching of English should be part of every student's curriculum, at every academic level.
- The study of foreign languages should be strongly encouraged, both as an academic discipline and for practical, economic, and foreign-policy considerations.
- *All* candidates for U.S. citizenship should be required to demonstrate the ability to understand, speak, read, and write simple English, and demonstrate basic understanding of our system of government.
- The rights of individuals and groups to use other languages and to establish *privately funded* institutions for the maintenance of diverse languages and cultures must be respected in a pluralistic society.

OUR ACTION PROGRAM

U.S. ENGLISH actively works to reverse the spread of foreign   12
language usage in the nation's official life. Our program calls for:

- Adoption of a constitutional amendment to establish English as the official language of the United States.
- Repeal of laws mandating multilingual ballots and voting materials.
- Restriction of government funding for bilingual education to short-term transitional programs only.
- Universal enforcement of the English language and civics requirement for naturalization.
- Expansion of opportunities for learning English.

Toward these ends, U.S. ENGLISH serves as a national center for   13
consultation and cooperation on ways to defend English as the sole official language of the United States. It directs its efforts to leading a public discussion on the best language policies for our multiethnic society; educating opinion leaders on the long-term implications of language segregation; encouraging research on improved methods of teaching English; and promoting effective programs of English language instruction.

WE NEED YOUR HELP

U.S. ENGLISH welcomes to membership all who are concerned   14
about the prospect of entrenched language segregation and the possibility of losing our strongest national bond.

We hope that you will join us and defend our common language   15
against misguided policies that threaten our national unity.

Questions for Analysis

Logic

1. Where in the essay do you find an attempt to meet the counterarguments of opponents? Can you think of objections that have not been met?

2. Explain in your own words the logic of the claim in paragraph 6 that failure to defend English will lead to "language segregation."

3. In what ways does the document seek to avoid the objection that it is prejudiced? What reasons are mentioned that might seek to counter this charge?

Character

1. "In Support of Our Common Language . . ." was modified or approved by more than one author. Do you see any evidence of multiple authorship in any aspect of the document's style? Explain with examples.

2. What does the phrase "as much by accident as by design" in paragraph 2 contribute to the sense of character U.S. English projects? What motivations or rationales might be anticipated and rejected by the implications of the phrase?

3. What contribution does paragraph 4 make to the sense of character projected? What values and assumptions seem to underlie the statement? How does it expand the meaning of *our* in the section's title?

Emotion

1. What emotions are appealed to by the examples given in paragraph 3? Can you point to evidence for the same emotional appeal elsewhere in the document?

2. What emotional response seems invited by the example of Senator Hayakawa in paragraph 8?

3. The word *serve* appears in paragraphs 3 and 12. What are the emotional implications of the word, and what does it invite the audience to feel in each case? Does it act differently in each case? Explain your answer.

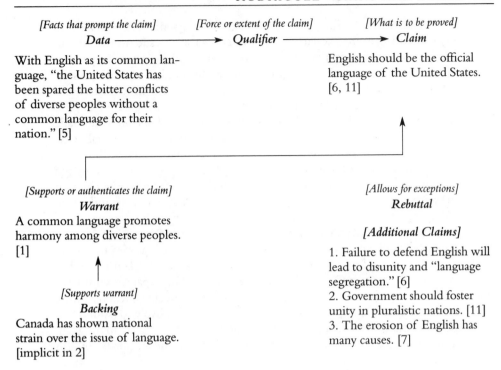

[Facts that prompt the claim]
Data ————————→ [Force or extent of the claim] **Qualifier** ————————→ [What is to be proved] **Claim**

With English as its common language, "the United States has been spared the bitter conflicts of diverse peoples without a common language for their nation." [5]

English should be the official language of the United States. [6, 11]

[Supports or authenticates the claim]
Warrant
A common language promotes harmony among diverse peoples. [1]

[Supports warrant]
Backing
Canada has shown national strain over the issue of language. [implicit in 2]

[Allows for exceptions]
Rebuttal

[Additional Claims]
1. Failure to defend English will lead to disunity and "language segregation." [6]
2. Government should foster unity in pluralistic nations. [11]
3. The erosion of English has many causes. [7]

GAINS AND LOSSES

Richard Rodriguez

My *mother*! My *father*! After English became my primary language, I no longer knew what words to use in addressing my parents. The old Spanish words (those tender accents of sound) I had used earlier—*mamá* and *papá*—I couldn't use anymore. They would have been too painful reminders of how much had changed in my life. On the other hand, the words I heard neighborhood kids call *their* parents seemed equally unsatisfactory. *Mother* and *Father; Ma, Papa, Pa, Dad, Pop* (how I hated the all-American sound of that last word especially)—all these terms I felt were unsuitable, not really terms of address for *my* parents. As a result, I never used them at home. Whenever I'd speak to my parents, I would try to get their attention with eye contact alone. In public conversations, I'd refer to 'my parents' or 'my mother and father.'

My mother and father, for their part, responded differently, as their children spoke to them less. She grew restless, seemed troubled and anxious at the scarcity of words exchanged in the house. It was she who would question me about my day when I came home from school. She smiled at small talk. She pried at the edges of my sentences to get me to say something more. (What?) She'd join conversations she overheard, but her intrusions often stopped her children's talking. By contrast, my father seemed reconciled to the new quiet. Though his English improved some-what, he retired into silence. At dinner he spoke very little. One night his children and even his wife helplessly giggled at his garbled English pronunciation of the Catholic Grace before Meals. Thereafter he made his wife recite the prayer at the start of each meal, even on formal occa-sions, when there were guests in the house. Hers became the public voice of the family. On official business, it was she, not my father, one would usually hear on the phone or in stores, talking to strangers. His children grew so accustomed to his silence that, years later, they would speak routinely of his shyness. (My mother would often try to explain: Both his parents died when he was eight. He was raised by an uncle who treated him like little more than a menial servant. He was never encour-aged to speak. He grew up alone. A man of few words.) But my father was not shy, I realized, when I'd watch him speaking Spanish with rela-tives. Using Spanish, he was quickly effusive. Especially when talking with other men, his voice would spark, flicker, flare alive with sounds. In Spanish, he expressed ideas and feelings he rarely revealed in English. With firm Spanish sounds, he conveyed confidence and authority English would never allow him.

The silence at home, however, was finally more than a literal silence. *3* Fewer words passed between parent and child, but more profound was the silence that resulted from my inattention to sounds. At about the time I no longer bothered to listen with care to the sounds of English in public, I grew careless about listening to the sounds family members made when they spoke. Most of the time I heard someone speaking at home and didn't distinguish his sounds from the words people uttered in public. I didn't even pay much attention to my parents' accented and ungrammatical speech. At least not at home. Only when I was with them in public would I grow alert to their accents. Though, even then, their sounds caused me less and less concern. For I was increasingly confident of my own public identity.

I would have been happier about my public success had I not some- *4* times recalled what it had been like earlier, when my family had conveyed its intimacy through a set of conveniently private sounds. Sometimes in public, hearing a stranger, I'd hark back to my past. A Mexican farm-worker approached me downtown to ask directions to somewhere. '¿Hijito . . . ?' he said. And his voice summoned deep longing. Another time, standing beside my mother in the visiting room of a Carmelite convent, before the dense screen which rendered the nuns shadowy fig-ures, I heard several Spanish-speaking nuns—their busy, singsong over-lapping voices—assure us that yes, yes, we were remembered, all our family was remembered in their prayers. (Their voices echoed faraway family sounds.) Another day, a dark-faced old woman—her hand light on my shoulder—steadied herself against me as she boarded a bus. She murmured something I couldn't quite comprehend. Her Spanish voice came near, like the face of a never-before-seen relative in the instant before I was kissed. Her voice, like so many of the Spanish voices I'd hear in public, recalled the golden age of my youth. Hearing Spanish then, I continued to be a careful, if sad, listener to sounds. Hearing a Spanish-speaking family walking behind me, I turned to look. I smiled for an instant, before my glance found the Hispanic-looking faces of strangers in the crowd going by.

Questions for Analysis

Logic
1. Make a list of the stated or implied reasons that English was a loss for Rodriguez in his private life.
2. Make a list of the stated or implied reasons that English was a gain for Rodriguez in his public life.
3. In your own words summarize the author's reasoning on the difference between literal and figurative silence.

Character
1. Does Rodriguez project a sense of character that seems fair-minded? Analyze some examples that support your answer.
2. Does Rodriguez project a sense of character that seems intelligent and reasonable? Analyze some examples.
3. Does the character suggested by the style of the essay seem to be founded on moral and ethical principles? Analyze the evidence that leads you to your response.

Emotion
1. In the narrative of the reactions of his family, compare the emotions Rodriguez suggests that he himself felt with those he seems to invite his audience to feel.

HOW NOT TO GET THE INFIDEL TO TALK THE KING'S TALK

Ishmael Reed

"How will we eradicate Black English?" Dick Cavett, public television's resident Anglo-lover, asked a group of linguists and John Simon. [1]

"You'd have to eradicate the black people," a linguist answered. Chilling thought, considering that there are historical precedents for people being exterminated because they didn't speak and write the way others thought they should.

When his arguments failed to convince the linguists of the exis- 2 tence of a "standard English," guest John Simon said that blacks should speak "'standard English' in order to get ahead," or as William Prashker wrote in the *New York Times* magazine section, "Black culture doesn't mean zip" when you're trying to impress "the man downtown." The Man downtown.

Of course, neither Prashker nor Simon and Cavett could ex- 3 plain the successes of Gerald Ford, or of New York City's Mayor Ed Koch, who confuses "each other" with "one another." Nor did they explain the triumphs of Dwight Eisenhower, who introduced the word "finalize" and whose press conference transcripts do not obey the rules of grammar.

Nelson Rockefeller, the late governor of New York, was a wealthy 4 man, yet this man thought that the word "horrendous" was a word of praise. Really. The former President of the United States says "fahm" for what we call "farm." I was appalled to learn, in *The Brethren,* that Chief Justice Burger's decisions are so illiterate that the law clerk has to correct them so that they won't embarrass the Court.

If people who make these errors are "idiots," as Simon says, then 5 many of our elected officials, industrialists, and writers are idiots: *As I Lay Dying.*

Did the powerful people who "rule" America—all white males 6 according to the April 16, 1979, issue of *U.S. News and World Report*— "get ahead" by speaking like characters in a Henry James novel? Did oilmen? Did Teamster presidents? I doubt it.

You not gone make me give up Black English. When you ask me 7 to give up my Black English you askin me to give up my soul. But for reasons of commerce, transportation-hassleless mobility in everyday life, I will talk to 411 in a language both the operator and I can understand. I will answer the highway patrolman who stops me, for having a broken rear light, in words he and I both know. The highway patrolman, who grew up on Elvis Presley, might speak Black English at home, because Black English has influenced not only blacks but whites too.

So when trying to get the infidel to talk so that the British Tea 8 Company can keep an eye on the infidel, the missionaries should be aware that appeals to "getting ahead" will be seen through by the millions of Black English followers both overt and covert. The phantom legions.

Don't blame the mass defections from "standard English" on them; 9 their rulers were the first to surrender.

The ironies don't end there. During an appearance before the 10

English-Speaking Union in San Francisco, John Simon spoke of repri-
manding a young woman for saying "between Bill and I" instead of "Bill
and me." He went on to say he didn't have the "foggiest notion who Bill
or the woman speaking or the woman behind the counter *were*." As
reporter Charles Haas pointed out in the December 17, 1979, issue of
New West magazine, Simon should have said "was."

Questions for Analysis

Logic
1. What are the logical parallels of cause and effect that Reed implies
   between British rule of the American Colonies and standard English
   on the one hand and the Boston Tea Party and Black English on the
   other?
2. What are Reed's stated and implied reasons for wanting to keep Black
   English?
3. What are Reed's stated and implied reasons for wanting to keep a
   command of standard English?

Character
1. What does Reed's sentence structure, as exemplified in paragraph 3,
   contribute to our sense of his character? What does the relation between the sentences contribute to the structure of the paragraph and
   a further sense of Reed's character?
2. Reed could have pointed out the error mentioned in paragraph 10
   himself or could have referred to a general grammar book. What does
   his having given credit to Charles Haas contribute to our sense of his
   character?
3. What does Reed's use of Black English in paragraph 7 contribute to
   our sense of his character? How is that style affected by the stylistic
   context of the rest of the essay?

Emotion
1. What emotions does Reed's use of Black English in paragraph 7 tend
   to evoke in his audience? If Reed were to imagine that audience as
   composed of speakers of both standard English and Black English,
   what emotions might be expected of each group?
2. What emotions does Reed invite by his emphasis on the word *eradicate*
   in paragraph 1? Are those emotions like the ones invited by his emphasis on *man/Man* in paragraph 2? Explain.
3. Do you understand the joke made by calling Dick Cavett an "Anglo-
   lover" in paragraph 1? If you do not, note carefully the differences it
   makes in your emotional relation to the paragraph when the joke is
   explained.

EXERCISES: SHOULD ENGLISH BE THE LANGUAGE OF AMERICA?

Intertextual Questions

1. Do the three essays in this section all seem to operate on a common understanding of the definition of "standard English"? Exemplify and explain your answer.
2. The three essays may be seen as not directly opposing one another's positions. Pick examples of areas that overlap and explain some similarities in the positions taken.
3. What differences among the three essays are there in any area they all address? Exemplify and explain.

Suggestions for Writing

1. Write a letter as though it were written by either Rodriguez or Reed to U. S. English, and explain the degree of support and/or opposition that you think the writer would express to the principles of the organization.
2. Write a letter from U. S. English to either Reed or Rodriguez that responds to the letter suggested in suggestion 1.
3. Write a short essay that argues for your own position on whether "standard English" should be a national goal.

Single Essays on Controversial Topics

All the earlier issues have been represented by multiple points of view and accompanied by extensive analytic apparatus. The idea of the following section is for you to practice the skills you have acquired by asking your own questions about the ways the authors argue through logic, character, and emotion and forming (if necessary) your own alternative opinions to those represented here. The range of topics includes many of those currently most controversial, and you will no doubt already have formed opinions on many of them. But whether you agree or disagree with the stance taken by these writers, you should be prepared both to analyze the ways in which their arguments operate and to respond to those arguments with supporting or opposing arguments of your own.

This section provides material for you to use in expanding and honing your analysis and argumentative writing skills without the help (or interference) of the editorial apparatus provided in the previous section. The selections have been made with the idea of giving one of the most controversial positions taken on controversial issues, so that you will have plenty of room to dissent, modify, or support the author's point of view. Remember to pay attention to all sides of the rhetorical triangle whether in analyzing or responding to the essays with essays of your own.

LEGALIZE GAY MARRIAGE

Craig R. Dean

In November 1990, my lover, Patrick Gill, and I were denied a   *1*
marriage license because we are gay. In a memorandum explaining the
District's decision, the clerk of the court wrote that "the sections of the
District of Columbia code governing marriage do not authorize marriage between persons of the same sex." By refusing to give us the same
legal recognition that is given to heterosexual couples, the District has
degraded our relationship as well as that of every other gay and lesbian
couple.

At one time, interracial couples were not allowed to marry. Gays   *2*
and lesbians are still denied this basic civil right in the U.S.—and around
the world. Can you imagine the outcry if any other minority group was
denied the right to legally marry today?

Marriage is more than a piece of paper. It gives societal recognition   *3*
and legal protection to a relationship. It confers numerous benefits to
spouses; in the District alone, there are more than 100 automatic mar-
riage-based rights. In every state in the nation, married couples have the
right to be on each other's health, disability, life insurance and pension
plans. Married couples receive special tax exemptions, deductions and
refunds. Spouses may automatically inherit property and have rights of
survivorship that avoid inheritance tax. Though unmarried couples—
both gay and heterosexual—are entitled to some of these rights, they are
by no means guaranteed.

For married couples, the spouse is legally the next of kin in case of   *4*
death, medical emergency or mental incapacity. In stark contrast, the
family is generally the next of kin for same-sex couples. In the shadow
of AIDS, the denial of marriage rights can be even more ominous.

In November, Patrick and I filed suit against the District alleging   *5*
two-fold discrimination. First, the District violated its gender-neutral
marriage law: nowhere does its legal code state that a marriage must
consist of a man and a woman or that a married couple may not be of
the same sex.

Second, the District violated its own Human Rights Act, the   *6*
strongest in the nation. According to the act, which was enacted in 1977,
"every individual shall have an equal opportunity to participate in the
economic, cultural and intellectual life of the District and to have an
equal opportunity to participate in all aspects of life."

The law is clearly on our side. In fact, cases interpreting the act   *7*
have held that the "eradication of sexual orientation discrimination is a
compelling governmental interest." Moreover, in 1987 the District Court

of Appeals elevated anti-gay bias to the same level as racial and gender discrimination.

Some argue that gay marriage is too radical for society. We disagree. *8* According to a 1989 study by the American Bar Association, eight to 10 million children are currently being reared in three million gay households. Therefore, approximately 6 percent of the U.S. population is made up of gay and lesbian families with children. Why should these families be denied the protection granted to other families?

Allowing gay marriage would strengthen society by increasing tol- *9* erance. It is paradoxical that mainstream America perceives gays and lesbians as unable to maintain long-term relationships while at the same time denying them the very institutions that stabilize such relationships.

Twenty-five years ago, one-third of the U.S. did not allow inter- *10* racial marriage. It took a 1967 Supreme Court decision, in Loving v. Virginia, a case similar to ours, to strike down these discriminatory prohibitions and redefine family and marriage. Then, as now, those who argued against granting civil rights spoke of morality, social tensions and protection of family values. But, now, as then, the real issue is justice vs. oppression.

GOVERNMENT IS THE PROBLEM

Walter E. Williams

Which is more important, eyeglasses, books or schools? It's hard to *1* tell. If you need eyeglasses, and don't have them, what good are books and schools? Eyeglasses and books are important for education, and we're doing well without much government control, doing so well that it never crossed your mind. Schools are completely controlled by government, and we have all sorts of customer dissatisfaction. Could there be a relationship between the level of government involvement and customer satisfaction?

Which is more important—marriage or work? Did you say mar- *2* riage? If that's so, how come we have anti-discriminatory and equal-opportunity laws when it comes to work but not when it comes to marriage. Take me. Thirty-two years ago, when interviewing prospective spouses, I engaged in open discrimination. No interviews were offered to Oriental, Hispanic or white women, and men of any race. Moreover, there was no consideration of women given to intemperate drinking habits, foul language and criminal behavior. I'm sure my interview procedure violated all Equal Employment Opportunity Commission (EEOC) regulations for negotiating contracts, not to mention the

Americans with Disabilities Act. Probably most men and women engage in similar grossly discriminatory behavior. But no sweat. Anybody who wants to be married tends to get married, even those that many consider undesirable. How is this happy outcome possible without government regulation?

How about Language? Language is mankind's most important tool. 3 Who discovered language? Who governs its use, deciding which words become part of the language and which get discarded from ordinary use? Nobody. Our language just evolved over time, adjusting itself to human uses, conditions and tastes; there were no government rules and dictates. Unlike the arrogant French, we anglicize anybody's word and make it a part of our vocabulary. That's one of the reasons why English is the world's most efficient language (efficiency measured as the number of bits of information conveyed per character).

All of these are examples of Williams' law: On balance, the less 4 government is involved in something, the fewer the problems, the greater the level of satisfaction and the cheaper the cost.

Imagine that the decision of what kind of eyeglasses and books 5 were to be produced, and delivered to whom at what time, was determined by Congress or state legislators. The resultant cruelty is unthinkable. Those who wanted paperback books would be in political conflict with those who wanted hardback. Similarly, those who wanted plastic lenses would be fighting those who wanted glass. It would resemble the fights between those who want prayers, the teaching of creationism and no sex education in school, and those who take the opposite view. Government allocation of resources always enhances the potential for human conflict.

Government Control, such as the attempt to establish an official lan- 6 guage, frequently leads to conflict, including wars and civil unrest, as we've seen in Quebec, Belgium, South Africa, Nigeria and other places. As our government creates bilingual legislation, we are seeing language become a focal point for conflict such as the ugly, racist-tainted "English Only" political campaigns in several states. The best state of affairs is to have no language laws at all.

Finally, there's the animal rights people. I'm wondering how they 7 got the right to speak for animals and protect them from cruelty: Did the animals vote them in? Who's to say that animals don't like cruelty anyway? After all, cruelty seems to be a way of life among animals. When's the last time you saw cats and rats, lions and zebras, or birds and worms respect each other's rights? Only humans don't treat animals like animals.

WHAT IS THE TRUTH ABOUT GLOBAL WARMING?

Robert James Bidinotto

In the summer of 1988, one of the century's worst heat waves gripped the East Coast and had Midwest farmers wondering if the Dust Bowl had returned. On June 23, at a Senate hearing on global climate change, James Hansen, a respected atmospheric scientist and director of NASA's Goddard Institute for Space Studies, gave alarming testimony. "The earth is warmer in 1988 than at any time in the history of instrumental measurements," he said. "The greenhouse effect is changing our climate now."

Hansen's remarks touched off a firestorm of publicity. A major news magazine speculated that the Great Plains would be depopulated. On NBC's "Today" show, biologist Paul Ehrlich warned that melting polar ice could raise sea levels and inundate coastal cities, swamping much of Florida, Washington, D.C., and the Los Angeles basin. And in his recent book, *Global Warming,* Stephen Schneider of the National Center for Atmospheric Research imagined New York overcome by a killer heat wave, a baseball double-header in Chicago called because of a thick black haze created by huge forest fires in Canada, and Long Island devastated by a hurricane—all spawned by the "greenhouse effect."

In Paris last July, the leaders of seven industrial democracies, including President Bush and British Prime Minister Margaret Thatcher, called for common efforts to limit emissions of carbon dioxide and other "greenhouse gases." To accomplish this, many environmentalists have proposed draconian regulations—and huge new taxes—that could significantly affect the way we live. Warns Environmental Protection Agency head William Reilly: "To slow down the global heating process, the scale of economic and societal intervention will be enormous."

The stakes are high: the public could be asked to decide between environmental catastrophe and enormous costs. But do we really have to make this choice? Many scientists believe the danger is real, but others are much less certain. What is the evidence? Here is what we know:

WHAT IS THE GREENHOUSE EFFECT?

When sunlight warms the earth, certain gases in the lower atmosphere, acting like the glass in a greenhouse, trap some of the heat as it radiates back into space. These greenhouse gases, primarily water vapor and including carbon dioxide, methane and man-made chlorofluorocarbons, warm our planet, making life possible.

If they were more abundant, greenhouse gases might trap too much heat. Venus, for example, has 60,000 times more carbon dioxide in its atmosphere than Earth, and its temperature averages above 800 degrees Fahrenheit. But if greenhouse gases were less plentiful or entirely absent, temperatures on Earth would average below freezing. 6

Because concentrations of greenhouse gases have been steadily rising, many scientists are concerned about global warming. Researchers at the Goddard Institute and at the University of East Anglia in England foresee a doubling of greenhouse gas concentrations during the next century, which might raise average global temperatures as much as nine degrees Fahrenheit. 7

WHAT IS CAUSING THE BUILDUP?

Nature accounts for most of the greenhouse gases in the atmosphere. For example, carbon dioxide (CO_2), the most plentiful trace gas, is released by volcanoes, oceans, decaying plants and even by our breathing. But much of the *buildup* is man-made. 8

CO_2 is given off when we burn wood or such fossil fuels as coal and oil. In fact, the amount in the atmosphere has grown more than 25 percent since the Industrial Revolution began around 200 years ago— over 11 percent since 1958 alone. 9

Methane, the next most abundant greenhouse gas, is released when organic matter decomposes in swamps, rice paddies, livestock yards— even in the guts of termites and cud-chewing animals. The amount is growing about one percent per year, partly because of increased cattle raising and use of natural gas. 10

Chlorofluorocarbons (CFCs), a third culprit, escape from refrigerators, air conditioners, plastic foam, solvents and spray cans. The amount in the atmosphere is tiny compared with CO_2, but CFCs are thousands of times more potent in absorbing heat and have also been implicated in the "ozone hole." 11

WHAT DOES THE OZONE HOLE HAVE TO DO WITH THE GREENHOUSE EFFECT?

For all practical purposes, nothing. Ozone, a naturally occurring form of oxygen, is of concern for another reason. In the upper atmosphere it helps shield us from ultraviolet sunlight, which can cause skin cancer. In 1985, scientists confirmed a temporary thinning in the ozone layer over Antarctica, leading to a new concern: if ozone thinning spreads to populated areas, it could cause an increase in the disease. 12

The ozone hole appears only from September to November, and *13* only over the Antarctic region, and then it repairs itself when atmospheric conditions change a few weeks later. It also fluctuates; in 1988, there was little ozone thinning.

Ozone is constantly created and destroyed by nature. Volcanoes, for *14* example, can release immense quantities of chlorine, some of which may get into the stratosphere and destroy ozone molecules.

But the most popular theory to explain the appearance of the *15* ozone hole is that man-made chlorofluorocarbons release chlorine atoms in the upper atmosphere.

Despite thinning of upper atmospheric ozone over Antarctica, no *16* increase in surface ultraviolet radiation outside of that area is expected. John E. Frederick, an atmospheric scientist who chaired a United Nations Environment Program panel on trends in atmospheric ozone, has dismissed fears of a skin-cancer epidemic as science fiction. "You would experience a much greater increase in biologically damaging ultraviolet radiation if you moved from New York City to Atlanta than you would with the ozone depletion that we estimate will occur over the next 30 years," he says.

WILL DESTRUCTION OF FORESTS WORSEN THE GREENHOUSE EFFECT?

When trees and plants grow, they remove CO_2 from the air. When *17* they are burned or decay, they release stored CO_2 back into the atmosphere. In nations such as Brazil, thousands of square miles of tropical rain forests are being cleared and burned, leading many to be concerned about further CO_2 buildup.

Worldwide, millions of acres are planted with seedling trees each *18* year, however; and new studies reveal that there has been no reliable data about the impact of forest destruction on global warming. Research by Daniel Botkin and Lloyd Simpson at the University of California at Santa Barbara and by Sandra Brown at the University of Illinois at Urbana shows that the carbon content of forests had been vastly overestimated, suggesting that deforestation is not as great a source of CO_2 as was once thought.

CAN WE BE CERTAIN THAT GLOBAL WARMING WILL OCCUR?

Virtually all scientists agree that if greenhouse gases increase and all *19* other factors remain the same, the earth will warm up. But "the crucial issue," explains Prof. S. Fred Singer, an atmospheric scientist at the Washington Institute for Values in Public Policy, "is to what extent other factors remain the same." Climatic forces interact in poorly understood ways, and some may counteract warming.

At any given time, for example, clouds cover 60 percent of the planet, trapping heat radiating from its surface, but also reflecting sunlight back into space. So, if the oceans heat up and produce more clouds through evaporation, the increased cover might act as a natural thermostat and keep the planet from heating up. After factoring more detailed cloud simulations into its computer models, the British Meteorological Office recently showed that current global-warming projections could be cut in half.

20

Oceans have a major effect upon climate, but scientists have only begun to understand how. Investigators at the National Center for Atmospheric Research attributed the North American drought in the summer of 1988 primarily to temperature changes in the tropical Pacific involving a current called El Niño—not to the greenhouse effect. And when ocean currents were included in recent computerized climate simulations, the Antarctic Ocean didn't warm—diminishing the likelihood that part of its ice sheet will break up and add to coastal flooding.

21

How heat travels through the atmosphere and back into space is another big question mark for the global-warming theory. So is the sunspot cycle, as well as the effect of atmospheric pollution and volcanic particles that can reflect sunlight back into space. Such factors throw predictions about global warming into doubt.

22

SO WHAT IS THE BOTTOM LINE? HAS THE EARTH BEGUN TO HEAT UP?

Two widely reported statistics *seem* to present a powerful case for global warming. Some temperature records show about one degree Fahrenheit of warming over the past century, a period that has also seen a noticeable increase in greenhouse gases. And the six warmest years globally since record keeping began 100 years ago have all been in the 1980s.

23

As for the past decade, the increased warmth in three of its hottest years—1983, 1987 and 1988—is almost certainly associated with El Niño events in the Pacific.

24

Paradoxically, the historical records of temperature change do not jibe with the greenhouse theory. Between 1880 and 1940, temperatures appeared to rise. Yet between 1940 and 1965, a period of much heavier fossil-fuel use and deforestation, temperatures dropped, which seems inconsistent with the greenhouse effect. And a comprehensive study of past global ocean records by researchers from Britain and M.I.T. revealed no significant rising temperature trends between 1856 and 1986. Concludes Richard Lindzen of M.I.T.'s department of Earth, Atmospheric and Planetary Sciences, "The data as we have it does not support a warming."

25

Taking everything into account, few climatologists are willing to   *26*
attribute any seeming warming to the greenhouse effect. Last May,
61 scientists participating in a greenhouse workshop in Amherst, Mass.,
declared that "such an attribution cannot now be made with any degree
of confidence."

IS THERE ANY OTHER EVIDENCE OF GLOBAL WARMING?

Atmospheric researchers use complex computer programs called   *27*
General Circulation Models (GCMs) to plot climate change. But a computer is no more reliable than its input, and poorly understood oceanic,
atmospheric and continental processes are only crudely represented even
in the best GCMs.

Computer calculations do not even accurately predict the past: they   *28*
fail to match historical greenhouse-gas concentrations to expected temperatures. Because of these uncertainties, Stephen Schneider says in
Global Warming, it is "an even bet that the GCMs have overestimated
future warming by a factor of two."

In time, the computer models will undoubtedly improve. For now,   *29*
the lack of evidence and reliable tools leaves proponents of global warming with little but theory.

SHOULD WE DO ANYTHING TO OFFSET THE POSSIBLE WARMING UP OF THE GLOBE?

Fossil fuels now provide 90 percent of the world's energy. Some   *30*
environmentalists have advocated huge tax increases to discourage use of
coal and other fossil fuels. Some have suggested a gasoline tax. There are
also proposals that the government subsidize solar, windmill and geother-
mal power; that some foreign debts be swapped for protecting forests;
and that worldwide population growth be slowed.

The buildup of greenhouse gases is cause for scientific study, but   *31*
not for panic. Yet the facts sometimes get lost in the hysteria. Stephen
Schneider confesses to an ethical dilemma. He admits the many uncertainties about global warming. Nevertheless, to gain public support
through media coverage, he explains that sometimes scientists "have to
offer up scary scenarios, make simplified, dramatic statements, and make
little mention of any doubts we might have." Each scientist, he says, must
decide the "right balance" between "being effective and being honest. I
hope that means being both."

The temptation to bend fears for political ends is also ever present.   *32*
"We've got to ride the global-warming issue," Sen. Timothy Wirth (D.,

Colo.) explained to a reporter. "Even if the theory is wrong, we will be doing the right thing in terms of economic and environmental policy."

But many scientists are troubled when inconclusive evidence is used   33
for political advocacy. "The greenhouse warming has become a 'happening,'" says Richard Lindzen. To call for action, he adds, "has become a litmus test of morality."

We still know far too little to be stampeded into rash, expensive   34
proposals. Before we take such steps, says Patrick J. Michaels, an associate professor of environmental sciences at the University of Virginia, "the science should be much less murky than it is now."

Further research and climatic monitoring are certainly warranted.   35
If the "greenhouse signal" then emerges from the data, we can decide on the most prudent course of action.

WOMEN, SEX AND RAPE
Have Some Feminists Exaggerated the Problem?

Cathy Young

The vast majority of Americans, women or men, undoubtedly take   1
a positive view of changes the women's movement has brought about in attitudes toward rape. It is now widely accepted that a woman does not have to be a paragon of chastity to prove she has been raped; that her sexual history should not be put on trial; that even if she has been having drinks with a man or invited him in, he has no right to force sex on her. These advances, however, may be undermined by the efforts of some feminists to so enlarge the concept of rape as to demonize men, patronize women and offend the common sense of the majority of both sexes.

A recent example of this extremism was provided by the panel   2
discussion on an ABC News special, "Men, Sex and Rape." Men and women in the audience as well as the panel were seated separately, implicitly reinforcing the message that *every man is a potential rapist.*

Five of the six women panelists, among them legal scholar Cathe-   3
rine MacKinnon and "Backlash" author Susan Faludi, backed the view that rape, far from being a pathology, reflects the norm in male-female relations in our society. As proof, MacKinnon asserted that 47 percent of all American women have been sexually assaulted and 25 percent raped. When a male panelist questioned these numbers, she retorted, "That means you don't believe women. It's not cooked, it's interviews with women by people who believed them when they said it."

But not all researchers on the topic do believe their female respon-   4
dents. University of Arizona psychologist Mary Koss, whose studies in

the field are among the most frequently cited, herself wrote in a 1988 article that of those women whom the researchers classified as victims of rape by nonromantic acquaintances, only 27 percent considered themselves rape victims. In situations involving dating partners, only 18 percent of the researcher-classified victims thought they had been raped. (In surveys that directly ask women about forced intercourse, fewer than 10 percent report such experiences.)

Do these feminists believe women, or do they believe that women 5 need expert guidance to know when they've been raped?

The reason for this startling "credibility gap" becomes clear when 6 one looks at how the concept of rape has been broadened by the radical feminists. In their redefinition, physical force or threat of injury are no longer required.

In a recent volume of the Journal of Social Issues, for example, 7 University of Kansas Professor Charlene Muehlenhard and three co-authors cite the finding that "the most common method men used to have sexual intercourse with unwilling women was ignoring their refusals *without using physical force* [emphasis mine]. . . . The prevalence of rape found in these studies would have been much lower if the definition had required physical force."

A couple is necking, and at some point she says, "Please don't," and 8 perhaps pulls back a little; he keeps trying and she eventually goes along rather than push him away or repeat her refusal more forcefully. Is this rape? Yes, say the hardliners: She does not resist because of fear. Even if the man does not threaten her, his size and muscle implicitly do.

But many people, myself included, will find it hard to believe that 9 most women are afraid their dates will beat them up if they resist. Indeed, many who are attacked by strangers and have far stronger reasons to fear injury still fight back or scream.

Women have sex after initial reluctance for a number of reasons, 10 and fear of being beaten up by their dates is rarely reported as one of them. Some may be ambivalent or confused; they may believe that they shouldn't want sex, and feel less guilty if they are "overpowered." Sometimes both the man and the woman are drunk, which adds to the confusion and miscommunication. Some women may change their mind, perhaps because they get sexually excited by the man's attentions. Others may be genuinely unwilling but concerned about displeasing the man or hurting his feelings. As one student, prodded by a campus presentation on date rape to conclude that she was a victim, explained to a journalist, "I thought, 'Well, he's my friend . . . whatever happens, it's not going to be that bad' . . . no big deal."

Is it unfortunate that many women are brought up to be so anxious 11 not to offend, to be liked? Yes. But the answer should be to encourage assertiveness, not make excuses for doormat behavior.

The redefinition of rape also includes "psychological coercion" 12
such as "continual arguments." Muehlenhard and her co-authors suggest
that if lack of resistance cannot be regarded as consent when a women is
threatened with being shot, it might be no different if she is threatened
with being dumped. The old "If you loved me, you'd do it" line becomes
a felony.

To the cutting-edge anti-date-rape activists, even a "no" is no 13
longer necessary for a finding of coercion; the absence of an explicit
"yes" will suffice. In the January/February issue of Ms., a scene of clearly
consensual (but wordless) rough sex from "Basic Instinct" is described as
one in which "a woman experiences date rape and then kisses the perp."

All these definitional shenanigans might be funny if they didn't 14
have serious practical consequences. Young men on college campuses are
now being told in rape prevention workshops (mandatory for male freshmen at some schools) that they may have raped some of their seemingly
willing sexual partners; and young women are being encouraged to ab-
dicate responsibility for their sexual behavior by labeling unsatisfactory
experiences as coercive. Harvard's Date Rape Task Force recently issued
a report recommending that university policy define rape as "any act of
sexual intercourse that occurs without the expressed consent of the person," as well as sex with someone impaired by "intake of alcohol or
drugs."

Of course, in the enterprise of redefining rape, there is no reason 15
to stop at requiring verbal agreement. If a woman's failure to object to
unwanted sex can be attributed to intimidation, so can explicit consent.
Inevitably, on the outer limits, this patronizing line of thinking reaches
the conclusion that in our oppressive society, *there can be no consensual sex.*
Even if a woman thinks she wants it, that's only because her desire has
been "constructed" by the patriarchy.

People have a right to the wackiest of ideas, but it is disturbing that 16
some proponents of this theory are being treated as mainstream feminists.
MacKinnon, who has emerged as a leading spokeswoman on sexual harassment and rape, has written such things as: "The similarity between
the patterns, rhythms, roles and emotions, not to mention acts, which
make up rape on one hand and intercourse on the other . . . makes
it difficult to sustain the customary distinctions between violence and
sex. . . . The issue is less whether there was force and more whether
consent is a meaningful concept." When she appears on television or is
quoted in the press, this (one would think) very relevant aspect of her
beliefs is tactfully omitted.

So anxious are they to extend the concept of rape, these crusaders 17
become almost annoyed when discussions focus too much on violent
attacks by strangers or near-strangers. They want to hammer in the point
that the greatest danger to women comes from male friends, lovers, hus-

bands. (University of Washington professor Marilyn Friedman has compared Rhett Butler sweeping up Scarlett O'Hara and carrying her upstairs to mass murderer Richard Speck.) They insist that rape at knifepoint in a parking lot is not different from an ambiguous encounter in which a woman is pushed further sexually than she wanted to go, and further, that women have no responsibility whatsoever to avert situations of the latter sort.

On the ABC panel, Naomi Wolf (author of "The Beauty Myth") 18 complained that "in this culture we tend to trivialize the harm that rape does to women." But if anything, much of the effort to broaden the definition of rape trivializes the horror of real sexual violence (by strangers or acquaintances).

The same program included footage of a treatment program for 19 jailed sexual offenders, who were made to listen to a recording of a woman calling 911 just as a rapist breaks into her house. The terrified woman gasps, "He's here! He's here!" before her voice dissolves into screams and whimpers. One would have to be utterly removed from the real world to insist this is comparable to the experience of a woman who yields because she's tired of pushing away her date's roving hands.

A friend of mine, although acknowledging that some feminist rhet- 20 oric is excessive, believes that expanding the definition of rape to include noncoercive experiences is useful because it sensitizes the society to the pain that sexual pressure and manipulation often cause. But pressure and manipulation are not a one-way street; women can apply them too. Besides, the law is not there to ensure we have trauma-free relationships.

Trying to relabel insensitive behavior as illegal can only backfire: 21 When a cad is accused of being a rapist, the unfairness of the charges may make him an object of sympathy, leading people to overlook his moral flaws.

While I, personally, do not think that "no-maybe-yes" games are 22 the stuff of romance, or that the vanishing of feminine coyness would be a great loss, to replace those rituals with new ones based on suspiciousness, calculation and consent forms in triplicate would hardly be a gain.

LET'S MOW DOWN ASTROTURF

Tim Keane

For sports fans, the year 1967 meant the debut of artificial turf to 1 pro sports with the opening of the Houston Astrodome. To most fans, it was an unwelcome change from the traditional grass fields of old to a field of plastic grass on top of concrete slabs. This monstrosity, commonly referred to as "astroturf," remains with us today, expanding from baseball parks into football fields. As many sports purists will tell you, both sports will be better off when the owners and league officials decide to outlaw astroturf wherever possible.

The arenas and domes built in the late 60's and 70's used astroturf for economic reasons, mainly that it was easier to maintain than grass and easier to dry off after rain storms. But today, improvements in drainage techniques for rain allow grass to be drained just as easily as artificial turf. And any owner's complaints about the expense of having to mow the grass daily seem ridiculous in light of the outrageous salaries they pay to players.

One of the biggest drawbacks of the astroturf and domed fields is the overall feeling of artificiality in these stadiums. They have been built with large walls and fences, with seats further back and higher up from the actual field than in the old grass ballparks. Many stadiums, such as Veterans in Philadelphia and Three Rivers in Pittsburgh, have lost that feeling of intimacy that was so important to both baseball and football in years past. Even the players' clean uniforms seem ridiculous after a long day's battle. The huge success of Baltimore's Camden Yards field in 1992 and its throwback atmosphere of the 1930's or 40's signifies the fans' desire for the old-time stadiums.

But the most damaging aspect of turf in every sense is the high rate of injuries suffered by players on this surface. Because there are only a few inches of padding between the turf and the concrete below, the surface wreaks havoc on the knees and elbows, especially those of football players. N.Y. Giants fans know this all too well, having lost standout tight end Mark Bavaro to crippling knee injuries after a brief but sensational 6-year career. Because of his extraordinary strength and balance, Bavaro was rarely knocked backwards when tackled, but usually fell forward onto the turf, knees first. Unfortunately for Bavaro, his home field used astroturf, guaranteeing more than half his season was played on the surface. The tragedy of Bavaro and dozens of players like him is that their professional careers are being terminated not by better athletes or their own limitations, but by the surface they play on.

Artificial surface also distorts the play of the game itself, most notably in baseball. The ball bounces faster off the turf than it does on grass, creating a different style of game and strategy for the fielders. It also creates two different styles of players, those who can run on turf and those who can't. Vince Coleman of the New York Mets is one such player. He began his career with the St. Louis Cardinals as an excellent fielder and base stealer on the St. Louis turf. But his transition to the grass of Shea Stadium has shown he is nowhere near the player he used to be now that he is on grass. Unfortunately for the Mets, this also means a huge loss in their million dollar investment in him. Such situations highlight that after 100 years of baseball tradition on grass, turf has come along and changed not only the quality of players but the game itself.

There are a few exceptions where turf should be allowed to be *6* used. In Seattle, where rain is the prevalent weather condition, it would be impossible to play baseball most of the summer. And in Minnesota, where harsh winters make it hard to even see the field through the falling snow, a dome also makes sense. But it is ridiculous to have domes in sunshine belt areas like Atlanta, Dallas, New Orleans and Houston, or just plain turf in Cincinnati and Kansas City, whose weather is no worse than that of New York or Boston. In short, because turf is unsettling to fans, can ruin players' careers, and changes the sports themselves, owners and league officials should wake up and lift the curse of astroturf from sports fans' lives.

THE COLOR-ONLY CROWD AND THEIR PASTEL-COLORED WHORES

Joan Ivan

A prostitute is someone who turns something usually regarded *1* as personal and emotionally precious into a public commodity with a monetary price. One of the more curious—and despicable—currently available transformations results in the Pastel Whore. This denizen from somewhere over the off-color rainbow generally offers no trouble to anyone who leaves him or her alone to conduct business. Also like other whores, the Pastels make a diseased mockery of what they market and sell, colorized versions of black and white films, which are as far from real color movies as astroturf is from grass.

Despite his notoriety as one of the more pricey Pastel Whores, Ted *2* Turner has no choice but to continue working. Turner sees himself as a businessman who lacks options, for his colorized versions of films sell more copies (by roughly thirty percent) than their black and white counterparts.

Yet the role of the customer in each of these cases cannot be over- *3* looked. Sexual salespersons would find themselves out of work if they suddenly found themselves without patrons. Thus, the johns who frequent prostitutes should be recognized as a primary source of this scourge. Similarly, Ted Turner is not to be faulted for his actions, but his johns, those of the Color-Only crowd, should suffer similar scorn.

The Color-Only crowd is a group of johns who share a common *4* dysfunctional ailment and sink to gutter level in trying to cure it. In this case, the Color-Onlyists find themselves unable to watch a black and white film without some adverse effects (what these effects are, however, is rarely articulated). So they go where their fix is for sale by Pastel-Colored Whores.

The chief complaint among Color-Onlyists is that black and white films are boring. What constitutes a boring film is hardly the subject for an argument, since the criteria are so subjective. However, let us assume for the moment that a diehard Color-Onlyist would *love* a certain black and white film, if he or she simply sat down to watch it. The real reason for the Color-Onlyist's animadversion to such films is not so much because of how black and white films *look*, but what black and white films *suggest*.

Throughout their school careers, even during college and graduate school, many Color-Onlyists were subjected to teachers who forced them to read and write and think about old stuff. When Miss Slipknot told them to read *The Last of the Mohicans*—a bad old book as opposed to a good old book—many students hated the experience so vehemently that they came to associate their loathing of Cooper's novel to other old things, good ones, such as *Beowulf, Hamlet, Moby-Dick*, and *The Scarlet Letter*. "Old" became an emotional synonym for "boring," "classic" became a synonym for "unbearably boring," and this never changed.

So it is with movies. The once-bitter student now has the option of watching a film in black and white, but refuses. Why? Because, when used in the making of a film, the colors black and white have come to signify something *old*. And an old movie—especially a *classic* movie—*has* to be as boring as an old book.

What the sexual johns and Color-Onlyists receive is the quick gratification of a desire which was once thought to be one requiring some kind of maturity to achieve. Ideally, sexual intercourse is an act in which two people display their degree of love for each other as well as celebrate the mental and emotional labor their love requires to sustain. Sex with a prostitute, however, removes all of this work and provides gratification—albeit of a physical nature only—quickly and easily.

Watching a film is an act in which two people—the viewer and the director—exchange ideas and emotions; while every moviegoer may not be acutely aware of this process, it nonetheless happens at every screening the world over. Like sex, the act of watching a film is one based on a routine of give-and-take. And again like sex, watching certain films—in this case, black and white ones—requires a certain type of maturity, specifically, the maturity to realize that not all old things are boring and that perhaps a film's color—or lack of it—somehow contributes to the total experience of watching it. Pastel Whores, like the prostitutes mentioned above, eradicate the need for this type of maturity and remove the Color-Onlyist's fear that this film may require some give on their part and that this classic may require them to temporarily suspend their belief that all old things are dull. Patronizing a Pastel Whore provides the Color-Onlyist with instant gratification.

As a wife learning of her husband's infidelities carried out in a house of ill repute is more angry with her husband than the whore whom he has patronized, opponents of colorization should focus their enmity on the Color-Only crowd rather than the Pastel Whores. For it is the Color-Onlyist, with his need for instant and unearned gratification, that perpetuates this socially transmitted disease.

WRESTLING WITH MYSELF

George Felton

It's Saturday morning, 11 a.m., right after the cartoons: time for "The NWA Main Event." As I watch the ringside announcer set up today's card, a wrestler—huge, topless and sweating, wearing leather chaps and a cowboy hat, carrying a lariat with a cowbell on it—bursts into frame, grabs the announcer by his lapels, and, chunks of tobacco spraying out of his mouth, begins to emote: "Well lookee here, this is just what eats in my craw. . . . I don't care if you're the president or the chief of police, it don't matter. I'm gonna do what I wanna do," and what he mostly wants to do is wrassle somebody good for once—enough nobodies in the ring, enough wimps running the schedule. As quickly as he spills into camera, he veers out, having delivered exactly the 20-second sound bite required. Our announcer blithely sends us to commercial, and another Saturday's wrestling hour has begun. I feel better already.

I soon find out this cowboy's name is Stan Hanson, he's from Border, Texas, and lately he's been getting disqualified in all his matches for trying to kill his opponents and then "hogtying" them with his lariat. We get to watch a recent match in which he kicks some poor guy's stomach furiously with his pointed-toe cowboy boots and drop-slams his elbow into his neck and, after getting him down, hits him over the head with the cowbell, and first whips, then strangles him with his lariat. It's great stuff, with the bell ringing madly and the referee waving his arms, but Stan's already yanked the guy outside the ring onto the apron and he's still on top, trying to kill him.

Why do I love this? Why am I crazy about Stan Hanson, who's old and fat and a man the announcer warns us "ought to be in a straitjacket and chains"? Because he personifies the great redemption of pro wrestling, the way it delivers me from civilization and its discontents. Not only is Stan Hanson mad as hell and not taking it anymore, but he's doing it all for me—getting himself disqualified so that I won't run the risk myself, but inviting me to grab one end of the rope and pull. He is my own id—the hairy beast itself—given a Texas identity and a push from behind, propelled out there into the "squared circle" where I can get a good look at it: sweat-soaked, mean, kicking at the slats, looking for an exposed neck. My heart leaps up, my cup runneth over.

Obviously I can't tell my friends about too much of this. If I even mention pro wrestling, they just stare at me and change the subject. They think I'm kidding. I am not supposed to like pro wrestling—its demographics are too downscale, its Dumb Show too transparent. They complain that it's fake and it's silly, which to me are two of its great charms. If it were real, like boxing, it'd be too painful to watch, too sad. I like knowing it's choreographed: The staged mayhem lets me know someone has studied me and will toss out just the meat the dark, reptilian centers of my brain require to stay fed and stay put. Sadomasochism? Homoeroticism? I am treated to the spectacle of Ric "The Nature Boy" Flair, astride the corner ropes and his opponent. His fist may be in the air, triumphant, but his groin is in the other guy's face, and he keeps it there. For once the ringside announcers are speechless as we all stare, transfixed, at this clearest of symbolic postures. Consciously I am squirming, but my reptilian center feels the sun on its back.

Racism? Ethnocentrism? Am I unsettled about Japanese hegemony? No problem. There is, in the World Wrestling Federation, a tag-team of scowling, unnervingly business-oriented Japanese toughs—the Orient Express, managed by Mr. Fuji—who invite me to hate them, and of course I do. Their failure is my success, and I don't even have to leave the living room. Two oversized, red-trunked Boris types used to parade around the ring under a red flag and insist, to our booing, on singing the Russian national anthem before wrestling. Since the Cold War has become passe, I notice that an upcoming match pits the Russians *against each other,* and that, as my newspaper tells me, is not passe. I hear groans of delight from below, as this reprise of Cain and Abel croons its libidinal tune.

I mean where else can I take my id out for a walk, how else to let it smell the sweaty air, root its nose through the wet leaves? Cartoons? No amount of Wile E. Coyote spring-loaded bounces, no pancakings of Roger Rabbit, none of the whimsical annihilations of Cartoonville can approximate the satisfactions of a real boot in a real belly, a man's head twisted up in the ropes, the merry surfeit of flying drop kicks, suplexes, sleeper holds and heart punches, all landed somewhere near real bodies. Pro sports? I get more, not less, neurotic rooting for my teams—my neck muscles ache, my stomach burns with coffee, after enduring a four-hour

Cleveland Browns playoff loss on TV. The Indians? Don't even get me started. The violence of movies like "RoboCop 2" and "Total Recall"? Needlessly complicated by story line.

No, give it to me straight. Wrestling may be a hybrid genre—the   7 epic poem meets Marvel Comics via the soap opera—but its themes, with their medieval tone, could hardly be simpler: warrior kings doing battle after battle to see who is worthy, women pushed almost to the very edges of the landscape, Beowulf's heroic ideal expressed in the language of an afterschool brawl: "I wanna do what I wanna do. You gonna try to stop me?"

I also appreciate the pop-culture novelty of pro wrestling, its en-   8 dearing way of creating, a little smudged and thick-fingered, but with a great earnest smile ("Here, look at this!") new betes noires for our consumption. One of the newest is something called Big Van Vader, a guy in a total upper torso headgear that looks like Star Wars Meets a Mayan Temple. He carries a stake topped with a skull and can shoot steam out of ventricles on his shoulders, but it looks like all he can do to keep from toppling over. He's horrifying and silly all at once, an atavistic nightdream wearing a "Kick Me" sign.

Such low-rent Show Biz, this admixture of the asylum and the   9 circus, is central to wrestling's double-tracked pleasure. Its emotional reductio ad absurdum taps my anger like a release valve, but its silliness allows me to feel superior to it as I watch. I can be dumb and intelligent, angry and amused, on all fours yet ironically detached, all at the same moment. It's a very satisfying mix, especially since my life between Saturdays is such an exercise in self-control, modesty and late 20th century Angst. To my students I am the helpful Mr. Felton. To my chairman I'm the responsible Mr. Felton. To virtually everybody and everything else I'm the confused, conflicted Mr. F. My violence amounts to giving people the finger, usually in traffic. When I swear I mutter. To insults I quickly add the disclaimer, "just kidding," a move I learned from watching David Letterman temper his nastiness. I never yell at people, threaten them, twist my heel into their ears, batter their heads into ring posts, or catch them flush with folding chairs. I don't wear robes and crowns and have bosomy women carry them around for me, either. In short, I never reduce my life to the satisfying oversimplification I think it deserves.

I'm a wimp. Just the sort of guy Cactus Jack or old Stan himself   10 would love to sink his elbows into, a sentiment with which I couldn't agree more. And that brings us to the deepest appeal of pro wrestling: It invites me to imagine the annihilation of my own civilized self. When Ric Flair jabs his finger into the camera and menaces his next opponent with, "I guarantee you one thing—Junkyard Dog or no Junkyard Dog, you're going to the hospital," when another of the Four Horsemen growls, "I'm gonna take you apart on national television," the real thrill is that they're coming for me. And when Stan offers me one end of the rope, we both know just whose neck we're pulling on. Ah, redemption.

SEXUAL HARASSMENT: CRYING WOLF IN ALBANY

Sheryl E. Reich

A New York State Assemblywoman, Earlene Hill, says she was harassed by male colleagues in the Assembly. Her claims were reported last week in the press, accompanied by announcements of sensitivity training in the Assembly and "isn't-it-terribles" all around. But if the label "sexual harassment" is accepted for the actions described by Ms. Hill, it trivializes a very serious matter. 1

These were the three incidents that undid Ms. Hill: An assembly-man misspoke during a speech, using the word "sex" instead of "six." To cover himself, he joked, "when I see Earlene, I think of sex." The second involved Ms. Hill's request that an assemblyman move his legs so she could get to her assigned seat. He refused, telling her she had to climb over him. Ms. Hill says a third assemblyman threatened to toss her out a window if she declined to have sex with him. 2

These acts are not really sexual harassment. All three were suppos-edly perpetrated by people with no power over Ms. Hill. The men were not in a position to deprive her of anything to which she was entitled, nor did they threaten to do so. 3

Unless stupid comments become so frequent and widespread that a woman cannot do her job, they are nothing more than insensitive re-marks. For the most part, they are bad "come-on" lines. The normal price for bad come-on lines is failure. If bad enough, the price may be social ostracism by one's higher-minded colleagues. But such behavior is not recognized by the law as a violation of any protected right, nor should it be. 4

If women want to be in the legislature, the courtroom and the boardroom, they had better get used to treatment that varies from behav-ior idealized in 19th century parlor novels. Women who want to be treated only like ladies are not going to do well when wrestling with serious issues. 5

In 15 years of practicing law, I have had to resolve problems with many difficult people—from judges to chief executive officers to jailers. I would expect my clients to question my ability to handle their problems 6 capably if I couldn't deal with a guy who won't move his legs so I could get by.

One appropriate response to the fellow who said he thought of sex *7* when he saw Assemblywoman Hill might have been, "That's funny, that's the last thing I think of when I see you." The second incident is even easier. High heels are a horrible thing to have been perpetrated on women—bad for the back, feet and Achilles' tendons. But because they concentrate tremendous weight in the tiny heel, they work marvelously well for getting people to move over; anyone groping for that last-minute seat at a movie knows that.

The threatened defenestration of Ms. Hill is obviously more seri- *8* ous. If the threat was real, or if she perceived it as real, it comes under the definition of attempted rape, and she should have reported it to the police. Ms. Hill did not do so. And since she didn't submit to the alleged demand and wasn't tossed out the window, it sounds like yet another bad come-on line; clearly she understood it as such. A suggestion that the assemblyman himself jump out the window may have been apropos.

Loutish men say stupid things, to each other and to anyone who is *9* around. Presumably, most men and women who do not act like jerks set the tone in an institution. But if that does not happen, we can't dwell on every indiscretion: there are too many important things to deal with.

Ms. Hill said she hoped that by making a public disclosure, "I have *10* helped others." But it is no help to women to popularize the notion that sexual harassment exists whenever someone is rude. Indeed, it harms women who attempt to bring real sexual harassment complaints in a world numbed by nonsensical claims like these.

THERE ARE REASONS TO CONTROL IMMIGRATION

Samuel Francis

For all the sweaty ink spilled over the anti-immigration riots in *1* Germany, I have yet to read of any "compassion for the rage" or any discussion of the "root causes" of the violence. Much of what's written about the ongoing unpleasantness has to do with the dark imagery of Hitler, and some even rehearse their animosity against Germans as a group. Where is the cooing and fluttering that we heard last spring when Los Angeles went up in smoke?

When the City of the Angels blew wide open, Rodney King was *2* dragged from obscurity to whine about the need to "just get along." HUD Secretary Jack Kemp was trotted out to explain, once more, about "enterprise zones." And for weeks afterward, politicians and press gabbled about how awful life was, is and always has been for minority "youths" upset by "neglect" and "racism." The contrast between the public reception of the L.A. riots and that of the attacks on immigrants in Germany could not have been starker.

In Germany, neo-Nazis in the course of the last year have killed 3 about a third of the people the L.A. rioters polished off in one weekend. There are now open proposals in German political circles to outlaw the anti-immigrant organizations. But no one suggests outlawing the Crips and the Bloods in L.A., though it's clear they planned and instigated no small part of the rioting there. In Germany, Chancellor Helmut Kohl publicly calls the neo-Nazis "right-wing rabble," but where is the national leader in this country who labels the liberators of Los Angeles the rabble they are?

For all the denials, the fact is that the socio-babble the left uses and 4 inflicts on us in talking about non-white urban violence works to legitimize rioting. This is why no one talks about "root causes" of neo-Nazism or even refers to their months-long rampages as "rage." "Rage," you see, is OK, but what the Nazis practice is not rage but "hatred."

Code words and propaganda aside, however, there really are "root 5 causes" of the neo-Nazi violence against immigrants, asylum-seekers and people who just look different, though expounding what those causes are in no way legitimizes what some of the more vicious anti-immigrant forces are up to. The root causes are mainly three.

First, Germany is having a pretty rough time assimilating even the 6 former East Germans who are now bound to the reunified country. Unemployment is staggering, housing is in short supply and chances for growth in the future are grim.

Second, in addition to having to assimilate Germans from the east, 7 the country takes in some 60,000 non-German asylumseekers a month, and ethnic Germans have to wonder why the newcomers are there at all, much less why they get benefits from the government.

Germany isn't the only European nation to see a revival of racial 8 violence in response to immigration. But there are many good reasons to control immigration more than these countries do, and you don't have to be a Brown Shirt to endorse them.

Yet those reasons seem to be more than the watery conservatism 9 and wilted leftism that remain on German mental and political shelves can imagine. Unless Germans come up with some new conceptual categories that capture the cultural and ethnic realities that underlie real nationhood without delivering the nation to tyranny in the process, they're likely to see a lot more images of Hitler in their future.

GAMBLING WITH OUR NATIONAL CHARACTER

George F. Will

If life is, as a poet said, a sum of habits disturbed by a few thoughts, 1
we should think clearly about those habits we deliberately develop. Consider the rapid spread of legal gambling.

Until 1989, just two states, Nevada and New Jersey, had casino 2
gambling. Then such gambling returned to Deadwood, S.D., where in
1876 Wild Bill Hickok was shot in the back while holding a poker hand.
Since then 11 more states have legalized some casinos. Staid Minnesota
today has more than New Jersey.

Lotteries helped to finance Jamestown, the Continental Army, 3
Dartmouth, Harvard, Princeton and many public works. Today 32 states
and the District of Columbia have government-run lotteries which in
1991 siphoned up $17 billion. Forty-seven states participate in some form
of gambling.

Fifty-two Indian tribes in 17 states (so far), exploiting a Supreme 4
Court ruling that states do not have regulatory powers over tribes, are
operating casinos and bingo operations grossing $6 billion annually. States
cannot tax Indian casinos, but can profit from them. For example, a
Connecticut tribe—whose casino, a three-hour drive from New York
City, soon will employ 10,000—has struck a bargain with their state: The
tribe will give a projected $100 million annually to Connecticut as long
as not even a single slot machine is legalized off the reservation. Around
the nation some cities are contemplating ceding parcels of land to Indians
as "reservations" where gambling would be legal and the cities would get
a cut.

In Tunica County, Miss., America's fourth-poorest county in the 5
1990 census, unemployment has been halved, largely because of a riverboat casino. (Four other states also have riverboat casinos.) It may net the
county $2 million annually, a sum about the size of the county's current
budget.

Five states operate keno and two others are flirting with it. Mary- 6
land hopes to raise $100 million this year from keno gambling. Maryland
keno is a high-speed video lottery offering bets every five minutes on
monitors in 1,800 bars and other places. Supporters of this say to critics:
If you object to this windfall from the behavior of consenting adults,
what taxes do you propose to use to compel a similar sum from reluctant
citizens?

In 1991 gross revenues from legal gambling nationwide were $26.7 7
billion, more than five times the box office of the domestic movie indus-

try. States received only 2.4 percent of their revenues from lotteries, but this sum—$7.5 billion—net was not trivial.

Are there social costs from all this? Lots, beginning with the ruin- 8 ous—to health, work and families—excesses of compulsive gamblers. These are people susceptible, perhaps for psychological or even physiological reasons, to what the American Psychiatric Association calls "a disorder of impulse control."

Now, classifying such destructive behavior as a "disease" can be a 9 tactic for attaining access to government and insurance money, and can further attenuate the notion of individual responsibility. And calling a behavior "addictive" is problematic. But research suggests that some compulsive gamblers are peculiarly prone to a "high," like a drug user's, from abnormally elevated levels of endorphins in the blood when they are excited by gambling. For such people, gambling truly is "suicide without death."

Furthermore, state-sponsored and advertised and hyped lotteries are 10 exploitative. Per capita sales of lottery tickets are higher in poor inner-city neighborhoods than in suburbs, and the disparity is even larger when lottery spending is compared as a percentage of household income.

Michael Berberich, writing in Notre Dame magazine, recalls with 11 appropriate disgust an Illinois lottery billboard in a Chicago ghetto: "This could be your ticket out." Thus does government peddle a spurious but tantalizing hope to people particularly vulnerable to delusive promises.

Gambling can be a benign entertainment, but it can become, for 12 individuals and perhaps for a society, a way of attempting to evade the stern fact that (as Henry James said) "life is effort, unremittingly repeated." Gambling inflames the lust for wealth without work, weakening a perishable American belief—that the moral worth of a person is gauged not by how much money he makes but by how he makes his money.

By institutionalizing a few highly publicized bonanzas, government 13 foments, for its benefit, mass irrationality. It also deepens "the fatalism of the multitude," the belief that life's benefits are allocated randomly.

Joseph Epstein, the essayist, notes that "to have come to America 14 in the first place was to take a serious gamble. To advance with the country's frontier was another gamble." Nowadays, when life for most Americans is without routine risk, gambling may be a way of infusing life with stimulating uncertainty.

But by now, with a deepening dependency of individuals and gov- 15 ernments on gambling, we are gambling with our national character, forgetting that character is destiny.

A Minicasebook on
the Homeless

This section provides you with material on which to base a longer argument in greater depth about one of today's most controversial and important issues. The material here varies widely in length, level, source of publication, and point of view. The essays range from op-ed pieces to investigative reporting and academic analysis; they include satirical cartoons and an in-depth profile and interview of a homeless person. The two academic essays on the topic are given complete with footnotes in professional form.

You can use the information alone or in conjunction with further research of the sort described in the "Guide to Finding and Using Information" at the end of the book. Good luck in your project!

WHO ARE THE HOMELESS?

Scott Shuger

For anyone living in a city, the dilemma unfolds dozens of times a day: There he is, between me and my immediate goal—The Man With The Styrofoam Cup, asking me a simple question: "Spare some change?" That question lights off others of my own that go unspoken: "What does this guy do with the money?" "How much does he make a day?" "Doesn't begging like this make him feel awful?" "Why doesn't it make him feel awful enough to stop and get a job?" "How did he get in this fix?" "Is he really in a fix, or is he taking me for a sucker?" "Why should I give to this guy rather than the other beggars on the block?" "Or do they think I can give to them all?"

"Spare some change?" comes up because I am in a limited way 2
accessible to The Man With The Styrofoam Cup. My questions come up
because he is in a radical way inaccessible to me. To most of us, the
homeless are a visible mystery. Perhaps some of the most hardened
among us would prefer them to be invisible. But the rest of us would
prefer them to be less of a mystery. We want to help, yes, but we want
our efforts to go where they will make a difference. For that to happen,
we have to know what we're up against.

HYPE FOR THE HOLIDAYS

Although there have been some harder-edged stories on the home- 3
less, the main message the media delivers about them is that despite their
predicament, they're just like us. In a news special, Tom Brokaw stated
that the homeless are "people you know." Robert Hayes, director of the
National Coalition for the Homeless, told *The New York Times* that when
he is contacted by television news programs or congressional committees
looking at homelessness, "they always want white, middle-class people to
interview." A recent study that examined the national print and broadcast
coverage given the homeless between November 1986 and February
1989 discovered that a quarter of the homeless people featured in stories
were children. That was equal to the number of those identified as unemployed and three times the number identified as substance abusers.
Only 4 percent of the stories attributed the plight of the homeless to
their personal problems.

A recent publication of the Better Business Bureau reported, 4
"Many of those living in shelters or on the street are no different from
those with a place to live. . . . Being on the street is often something out
of their control." In a *New York Times* op-ed piece, Rep. Charles Schumer
wrote that "the slightest misstep or misfortune—a temporary layoff, a
large medical bill, a divorce—could send [a low-income] family onto the
streets. Indeed that's exactly what's been happening." The concrete examples of the homeless Schumer cited are a working mother of eight
whose eldest is an honor student, and a 63-year-old woman forced to
retire from her job as a waitress because of arthritis. In another *Times* op-
ed piece entitled "The Homeless: Victims of Prejudice," two Ivy League
law students said that the homeless people they met during a summer of
intern work included a Broadway playwright, a highly decorated World
War II veteran, and an ex-professional basketball player. Not to mention
"pregnant women who lost the race to stay one step ahead of the housing
marshal, students trying to study in noisy shelters, and average families
working diligently to save enough money for an apartment."

Jonathan Kozol, in his book on homeless families, *Rachel and Her* 5
Children, features: a couple who, after their house burns down, lose their

five children to foster homes and are reduced to panhandling; a 35-year-old woman, a college graduate who worked for many years before medical complications wiped out her savings, forced her to lose her home, ended her marriage, made her give up her kids, and left her sleeping on the beach; and a teacher, who when the heater in her building failed, was "in a matter of weeks . . . reduced from working woman and householder to a client of the welfare system." To the question "Why are they without homes?" Kozol responds, "Unreflective answers might retreat to explanations with which readers are familiar: 'family breakdown,' 'drugs,' 'culture of poverty,' 'teen pregnancies,' 'the underclass,' etc. While these are precipitating factors for some people, they are not the cause of homelessness. *The cause of homelessness is lack of housing.*" (Italics in the original.)

Last December, the Salvation Army came out with a special TV commercial to boost its Christmas campaign for the homeless in New York City: *On the sidewalk in front of a wrought-iron fence, framed by a shopping bag on one side and a suitcase on the other, there's a mother and her child together in a sleeping bag, their white skins reflecting the street lights. As a man carrying a briefcase walks by, the child sits up; you can see her long blonde hair now. The mother kisses the girl and pulls her back down, hugging and patting her as they drift back to sleep.* "Home for the Holidays," the ad's caption says. 6

Honor students and playwrights, college graduates sleeping on the beach, mothers and daughters sleeping in the park—this is what I can read about or see on TV. But this is not what I see in Washington. Where in all this is the Man With The Styrofoam Cup? 7

Although real homeless people are all around me every day, I've been vulnerable to the more idealized representations of the press because my approach to street people has been typical of the white middle class: Usually, I stare straight ahead and walk on by, my head full of those skeptical questions. Sometimes, something—an excess of change, a particularly good day, or just a weariness of skepticism—would make me stop and give some money. But no matter what, there was one thing I would never, ever, do: Talk to these people. Recently, however, I decided to break that nervous middle class habit. I resolved to talk to the homeless, to ask them some of the questions I had been keeping to myself in all the years of walking right by. 8

NIGHTS OF WINE AND POSES

I first put my new approach into effect one night last winter. On the stretch of Connecticut Avenue just above Dupont Circle, it was cold and rainy, and the panhandlers were huddled in bunches near the entrances of the restaurants on the block. With most of the dinner crowd already gone, the best pickings were over for the day. That left only pedestrians like me. 9

Two men come up to me, styrofoam cups in hand: "Spare some   *10* change?" Both men are unsteady on their feet and hard to understand, with 100-proof breath. I make a donation and learn that the tall black man is named Mike and the short one is K.C. I ask them how long they've been on the streets, and they tell me six months. They've both had jobs in construction. Mike says he used to work as a bartender until he lost his job because of his drinking. When I ask where they stay at night, Mike says that the owner of an art gallery across the street lets them sleep in the lobby of the building. Mike says they get to bathe every two days at a shelter in Alexandria.

"What do you do with the money you get?" I ask. Mike gives me a   *11* thumb-to-the-lip bottle motion. Then he shrugs his shoulders in embarrassment. "I got to go to a program. An in-patient program so I cain't get out so I cain't mess up. I got to clean my act up."

Mike is very polite, calling me "sir" frequently and saying "excuse   *12* me" to every passerby. K.C. is a little closer to the edge of his personal envelope tonight. When a couple turns into the restaurant behind us, he snaps at them, "If you don't eat all your food, bring a doggy bag for us."

Some surveys say that an inordinate number of the District's home-   *13* less are veterans. So I ask, "Were either of you guys in the service?" "I was on the Ho Chi Minh Trail," replies Mike. "I was over there in Korea," says K.C. "Quit telling the man lies," scolds Mike. I ask K.C. where and when. "I'm trying to 'member man. I'm shell-blocked," he says. "I ain't no dummy. Now hold it. All I know is I was in the 101 Screaming Eagles Fort Campbell Kentucky. Basic Training Fort Dix. But where I was, I can't remember. I got shell-blocked. I've been shot up and all that shit, but I'm still alive."

Before I can pursue this, a completely drunk or stoned black   *14* woman comes over. She's in her late twenties, I'd guess. Her head is covered by a tight bandana and her eyes are only slits. Without saying anything, she greets Mike with a French kiss that lasts about ten seconds. Then she spends at least that long sticking her tongue in his ear. Even so, she's hanging on to Mike as much for navigation as for affection. "Sandra, this is him," Mike says, pointing towards me.

"I'm Chocolate," says Sandra. "That's Memphis and that's um,   *15* Black." Mike shrugs his shoulders in embarrassment again. Just then, a younger guy, more drugged than drunk, charges toward us. This guy is really revved up on something. He starts shouting at me from 25 feet away. He's in his late teens, early twenties, with a fighter's build and a bull neck. "That's my girlfren'—what you all doing to her?" He pushes the other three behind him and gets in my face. "Who do you see on this corner first? What's wrong? You gonna help us out?"

As I start to leave, Mike offers his hand. His handshake is solid. I   *16* bet the rest of him was too, several thousand drinks ago. "Give me your address," demands Sandra. "Can I go home with you tonight?" It was somewhere between pitiful and sexual. "I don't want no shelter. I want to go to your house. I want to sleep in a bed, a real righteous bed."

A block away I cross paths with two guys standing out of the rain under the overhang of a closed lunch stand. Both in their twenties, one white, the other black. It quickly becomes apparent that all they have in common is this dry spot of sidewalk. The white guy, who tells me his name is Wayne, asks me for some change, telling me he got laid off from a construction job. The black guy, without introducing himself, quickly tries to take over. "Hey, I'm in a situation too. I'm a starving artist, and nobody's giving me nothing. I don't have a job. But I'm a millionaire, I know that inside. That my art is worth money, OK? But I know I'm gonna make it. All I got to do is go to New York. I've been trying for four years to get back there. I just need enough money to go to New York. The only thing I need is like 150 bucks."

I ask him if he ever tries finding work in the want ads. "Everybody keeps saying that, man! The paper is to get you to buy it or look at it. They're still making money off you! Hey, see all these stores out here? Every one of them got a loan to get what they've got. Well, I need a loan. If I had a loan for about $10,000, I'd be a multimillionaire, man, because my art is fuckin' baaad. That's the only way I'm gonna make it— if I get a fuckin' loan."

Wayne hasn't said a word during this rap. But when the starving artist, now pretty agitated, nervously walks to the corner to search out better possibilities than me, Wayne rolls his eyes and says to me out of the corner of his mouth, "It don't take nobody no four years to get back to New York, I'm sorry." Wayne is not wildly drunk, but now that I'm standing close to him I can tell he's pretty numbed up. Wayne is one of the truly unsheltered homeless. In good weather he sleeps in the park just opposite the Q street Metro exit. In bad weather he sleeps under the portico of an attorney's office or in a nearby building that's under construction. He has shoulder-length light-blond hair coming down from under his ball cap, a moustache, and the beginnings of a beard. About four years ago, he came to this area from Texas with his family. Then his mother died and his father started a housepainting company in Virginia. Wayne used to work there. I ask him why he quit. This was, after all, the decision that finally put him on the street. I figure there had to be a pretty dramatic reason. All Wayne comes up with is this: "I just couldn't deal with it, too many Spanish workers—they can't speak English because most of them are illegal immigrants—and being the boss's son."

The artist comes back. "Can you give me a buck or 50 cents, man, so I can get on the subway?" he asks me. As I give him two quarters, I notice that he's wearing a Burberry scarf. After he leaves, Wayne says, "I

17

18

19

20

don't like him. He's a con artist. I'm watching right now to see if he gets on the subway." He doesn't.

Wayne turns his attention back to me. "I used to be in trouble all   21
the time until I got my head cleared. Put it this way," he chuckles, "I got a few tatoos from prison." Wayne says his conviction for knifing a guy in a Texas bar fight is a problem when he's looking for work. "That's why I go for jobs that are under the table."

HOPE FOR SOME HOMELESS

In my travels around Washington, I rarely see homeless women on   22
the street. But there are places outdoors where they congregate. One such spot is a steep stretch of Belmont Street in the northwest quadrant of the city. Walking north on 14th Street and turning onto Belmont any evening at around 5:30, you will gradually become aware of a pilgrim-age—first just a few shadows moving through the uneven light, but even-tually a line of them making the daily trek up to the top of the hill. Most of the shadows are families, virtually all black, living in temporary hous-ing for the homeless. There are very few men, either by themselves or attached to a family group. I fall in step with the shadow families, curious to see what could have this drawing power.

At the top of the hill is the one-time Pitts Hotel, a ramshackle   23
building now operated as a shelter for homeless families. Parked out front under the archway is a gleaming yellow Rolls Royce, District license plate 347. A man standing next to it tells me that it belongs to the building's owner, Cornelius Pitts. [For more on Pitts, see "How the Homeless Bought a Rolls for Cornelius Pitts," Marianne Szegedy-Maszak, July/August 1987.] The people file by it without taking much notice. The building has room for only 50 or so families, but every day the District's Department of Human Services deposits four additional busloads of shelter residents—mostly families—at the foot of the hill so that they can get a cooked meal.

Watching the women come and go on Belmont, you can't avoid   24
the feeling that they are fighting some powerful obstacles in addition to the lack of a permanent place to live. Many seem tired and cranky, snapping at their children and cuffing them for transgressions that are hard to see in this light. "I'm not here because I'm all drugged up," says a plump woman with four kids in tow, hurrying down the hill to make the last bus. "I work as a nurse's assistant at D.C. General, and the truth is"—her voice lowers—"I had to leave where I was living because my friend was beating on me."

Despite these dark overtones, the longer I watch and listen, the   25
more I become aware of the many hopeful signs on Belmont Street. As

a group, these women seem fairly straight. Straight enough for Tom Brokaw. They stand in stark contrast to street hustlers like K.C. or the artist. Although the meals and the pick-up buses run on such a tight schedule that most of the women are in too much of a hurry to talk to me, those who do tell me that they are working, leaving their kids with babysitters during the day. A gregarious teenage mother of an 11-month-old tells me her biggest complaint: these daily crosstown voyages for food have left her baby with a persistent cold. A soft-spoken woman with three kids tells me that she has just gotten herself on a list downtown for housing placement; she hopes that in a few more weeks the city will be able to locate a place for her. Most of the women are dressed neatly, and some of the kids are in adorable get-ups: Bows in hair and party shoes for the girls, superhero jackets and team ballcaps for the boys. Obviously, many of these people are using their meager means for the right things; given more sustenance, most of them would only do more of the same. Yes, for the Belmont families, it seems that housing *would* be a big part of the answer.

HEARTBREAK HOTEL

At Mt. Carmel House, a homeless women's shelter in Washington's Chinatown, you can meet the people the Belmont Street women are trying not to become. Ann, for instance—a sad-eyed 41-year-old black woman who has come to this women's shelter straight from a stint at the detox unit at D.C. General. Ann discovered she couldn't handle alcohol after many years of what she calls "trial and error." Before booze derailed her life, she was a data clerk at the Veterans' Administration. But now she's lost her job, and her 18-year-old daughter lives with Ann's mother. 26

Or there's Marsha, a black woman in her twenties whose five years on cocaine and one year of living on the streets have somehow left her eyeballs and her teeth the same yellow color. This time last year, she was pawning anything she could get her hands on and working as a prostitute to raise drug money. A high-school dropout who was sexually abused by her father, Marsha has a daughter by a man she used to live with; she no longer has any contact with him and the authorities have taken the child away. Last November, Marsha got shot in the head by "some crackhead going around in the streets shooting for the hell of it. I should have gone to the doctor right away," she says. "But I wouldn't go to the doctor until I'd done all my cocaine first." 27

Celeste Valente, who's been a social worker at Mt. Carmel House for eight years, says that the shelter's 40-odd resident population now includes more younger women than it used to. There's been a decrease in the mentally ill clientele (now 30 percent of the population, down from 80 percent a few years ago) and an increase in drug addicts (almost 28 all those in the shelter who are not mentally ill are substance abusers). Valente guesses that "more than 80 percent of the women who come here have been raped or were the victims of incest."

Another woman living at Mt. Carmel is Virginia, who's spent the *29* last year in shelters—four in all. She's white, in her forties, with "done" hair, pink lipstick, and rouged cheeks. Her handbag says "Maui" on it. She could easily pass for a suburbanite down here doing volunteer work. In fact, she now volunteers a couple of nights a week at a nearby dinner program. "When I was working," Virginia remembers, "I gave about $1,500 of my United Way funds to the House of Ruth [another women's shelter in Washington]. And when I became homeless, that's the first place I went." Virginia's father was career Army. She was born in Austria. She has a literature degree from Georgetown. "I had the life," she says.

Here it seems I've come across a person worthy of Jonathan Kozol, *30* the Salvation Army, and all the other "it could happen to anyone" theorists. But there's a difference they might not like. Virginia's an alcoholic. And she spent a long time in what she describes as a "sick" relationship with a sexually abusive man. After she was laid off from her job managing an engineering office, she stayed in her apartment, watched TV, and drank for eight months. "I drank copious amounts of beer," she tells me, "three six-packs to a case a day."

KARMIC CROSSED WIRES

During the eighties, Lafayette Park, just across Pennsylvania Avenue *31* from the White House, became a campground for homeless squatters. Indeed, some people have lived there for most of the decade, conducting what they call a "peace vigil." The vigil is often on the itinerary of school classes visiting from out of town. The peace squatters have positioned themselves along the south edge of the park, where their placards about Hiroshima and nuclear freeze face the president's front door. Sixties-like, they give themselves new names like "Sunrise." One vigiler I talk to, who's lived here for three years, used to work as an art restorer before joining the scene he describes as a "karmic crossfire." He doesn't want to live anywhere else. He supports himself by performing three nights a week in a "folk rock" band. The rest of the time he's out in the park, sometimes sleeping in his jury-rigged plastic shelter, sometimes cooking up a stew, or greeting pedestrians with lines like, "Peace, brother. Thanks for smiling"—whether the guy is smiling or not.

But some of the homeless in Lafayette Park are conducting more *32* private vigils. Take the man on the park bench, hands on knees, open bottle of beer at his feet, just staring intensely at the White House. With the green of his poncho and the way his eyes are bulging, he looks like a frog on a lily pad. "I'm here to talk to George," he tells me. When he sees my fatigue pants, he goes to Red Alert, "Are you Marine Corps, FBI, Secret Service? Are you wearing a tape recorder?" I reassure him. He's so close to jumping out of his skin that I worry about what would happen if he were to notice the two men in uniform on the White House roof. "Yeah, George is a good man," the guy on the bench says, continuing to stare straight ahead. "I don't have nothing against him. He's a naval aviator and all that. When he went out to San Francisco after that earthquake, I talked to him." I asked the man if he flew out there to do that. "Nope," he says, never taking his eyes off his quarry, "talked to him by Telstar."

The Telstar man has plenty of company in Washington. Near my 33 office for instance, there is the tall, helmeted man who keeps a guardpost at the corner of Q and Connecticut. When you get close to him, you can see that he's wearing a flannel West German army uniform. He's sort of handsome and he has that straight-from-the-diaphragm voice and ramrod posture so valued in drill instructors. His long reddish brown hair runs in a thin, tight braid down his back. Tucked in his helmet and pointing straight up are three toothbrushes, looking like periscopes.

When I ask him his name, he replies, "General. U.S. General. None 34 of that Noriega thing for me." I notice that he's wearing a Top Gun squadron patch; he tells me where he got it: "The Surgeon General distributed it to the field artillery and ballistics command and the dominions of trade. Top Gun. Miramar California. I took the training out there about eight weeks ago. It was about the failure to inform people at the White House. And to maintain gun standards, computer standards, or surgical standards."

When I ask General what he's doing at this corner, he tells me, 35 "This is the field marshal air combat warning post here for the businesses and the banks. This post is the way that the military has become involved about the levering of the topmost business developments." What's he watching out for? The answer comes back instantly: "The Turks." As to how long he'll be in this assignment, General guesses about 40 years. "It should improve sometime in the nineties as far as the Motorola business is concerned. Eventually I will tend towards Walkman business. How the General maintains his districting or vector businesses is highly dependent upon Walkman skills."

General does not know he's homeless. When I ask him where he 36 goes at night and in bad weather, he tells me that he confers with the president. He readily distinguishes himself from panhandlers, whom he dismisses as "people who have no ownership interests or no mortgage or paper interests." However, in a way, he does have his own version of "Spare some change?" As I'm leaving, he says to me, "You should bring me a banknote so that the interests you represent can be represented here."

THE GRATE SOCIETY

Under an overpass in Foggy Bottom just east of the Potomac and just north of the exclusive Watergate apartment complex are some steam grates that have long served as a thermal oasis for the homeless. The night I walk by is chilly, so the grates are pretty full. When I approach, several of the men there ask me for change. The hot air rushing out of this hole in the ground produces a loud hum you have to shout over. The steam itself provides a two-part sensation: first your face gets hit by a pleasant rush of warmth, then your nose gets hit by the stench of stale booze. Booze that's soaked through clothes, that's soaked through skin, that's soaked through lives. 37

There are nine or ten men at the grate this night. It's an interracial group. Some are huddled at the edges, some just racked out across it. The two men who asked me for money talk to me a lot, but some of the others never even look in my direction. 38

One man tells me he's been out here for two years, another says eight. The liveliest talker is a young black guy named Tony. In his mid-twenties, he's handsome and, in an alcoholic sort of way, articulate. Tony points to a woman coming our way. "Here comes my girlfriend. That's why I'm out here, because of her." A black woman weaves towards us. She's really drunk. She plops down sullenly at the edge of the grate, no use for anybody. "I met her in July when I came out the Navy," Tony says, unaccountably thrilled to see her. 39

Tony says he's not really homeless because he can stay with his aunt at 14th and Euclid. But it's real late and he's still out here drinking. 40

Tony says he was in the Navy for eight years. "Aviation. Backseater in F-14s. I was a second lieutenant. I worked in the Indian Ocean on the *Nimitz*. Just got out in July. I'm going back. I'm in the reserves." There's a pause. "I was supposed to been back—I'm not going to lie to you. I'm AWOL. When I came out of high school and went to the Navy, I started out as an NCO—a noncommissioned officer. I was an NCO all the way. I went to school in Annapolis. When I go back, they may drop me down to like E-4. After I get out of the brig. I see Navy cars go by here every day. They're MPs, man, I know they lookin' for me. 41

"I want to re-up for maybe four more years. And then come back and get me a job at one of these airports as an aviator or air traffic controller. But it's gonna be a while for me now because last Saturday night, some girl stabbed me in my chest. And all I got is one lung now." As he's telling me this, Tony's unbuttoning his shirt. He shows me a Band-Aid just under his clavicle. It's not a very elaborate dressing, and I don't 42 see any signs of actual injury. "I just got out of the hospital. And today two guys tried to jump on me." Tony shows me his punching hand. The knuckles on it are very swollen. "So it's gonna be a while—maybe another two months—until I go back."

Tony says the Navy sent him here on shore leave to bury his grandmother. "That's when I met Karen," he tells me, nodding toward the poor woman who just joined us. "Took a liking to her. And she turned my head around." He says Karen used to drive trucks in the Army, that she was in Vietnam. He says she's 38. She looks 58. Tony reaches between his knees into the red plastic milk crate he's sitting on and pulls out a white plastic flask. Gin, he tells me. A pint a day. Pointing at the others, he explains, "They drink that hard stuff." *43*

Tony's story was fascinating, but it wasn't true. You can't start out in the service as an NCO, and "second lieutenant" is not a rank in the Navy. *44*

The old man at my feet, whom Tony introduces as Jimmy, "the granddaddy of the grates," mumbles at me. In the slurred words of a lifelong drunk he tells me that he's worked as a tow-truck driver at an Amoco station for 18 years. But, he says, "See those," pointing at some of Georgetown's poshest apartments, "I don't make enough money to rent no apartment for $250 a month. So I stay here." Jimmy's incredibly dirty. He never looks up at me. His attention is riveted on a little pack of picture cards he keeps riffling through. They're not baseball cards, although they're that size. Because they're predominantly pink, I assume they're pornographic. When Jimmy hands me one, I see they're not. They're pictures of food. The card in my hand is "Shrimp with Greens." *45*

The closest thing to an American monument to homelessness is the shelter run by the Community for Creative Non-Violence (CCNV) in the former Federal City College building at the intersection of 2nd and D in downtown Washington. This is the building that the federal government agreed to lease to homeless advocate Mitch Snyder in 1984 after Snyder led a 51-day fast. Housing 1,400 homeless—1,265 men and 135 women—it's the largest shelter in the country, perhaps in the world. CCNV's literature calls it "a national model." *46*

Since its inception, the CCNV shelter has received over $13 million in combined federal and D.C. appropriations, and another $500,000 in corporate donations. I wanted to get an idea of what that money is buying. To do that, I decided to take my idea of talking to the homeless one step further by going to the shelter and asking for help. *47*

SHELTER SKELTER

I showed up at CCNV late on a Saturday afternoon in January, dressed in my worst clothes and having not washed or shaved for days. In front of the building, Saturday night is already well underway. Thirty or *48* so men are standing on the porch and along the sidewalk, talking loudly and taking regular pulls from the brown paper bags they all seem to have. One of the louder guys is a gapped-toothed man in a purple parka. He's shouting out at anybody walking by and going through a loud review of the lunch he had at some soup kitchen: "Uhhhh-uhhhh, barbecue chicken! I'm telling you, they got *down*. . . ."

When they're not drinking and cursing, the men spend a lot of time spitting. The sidewalk is phlegm-spotted. It's hard to find a dry spot on the steps to sit on. Almost as soon as I do, I attract the attention of a disastrously drunk man who until then had been working full-time trying to keep from impacting the sidewalk. He's lurching about furiously, like a man on the deck of a storm-blown ship. He finally makes it over next to me. Even sitting down, he's weaving. He mumbles something to me I can't make out. The second time, I catch it: "Do you have five cents?" When I say I don't, he repeats the question. Then he mumbles something else, "What's in the bag?" For authenticity, I have a paper bag with me. The drunk grabs my arm and tries to pull me towards him. "What's in the bag?" "Nothing for you," I tell him, moving away. This catches Purple Parka's attention. From his perch, he looks down at me and barks. "Talk to the man like that and I'll bust yo' ass on the sidewalk." [49]

When a woman comes to the front of the building with some stuff to donate, Purple Parka comes down and swarms all over her, putting his arm around her and trying to take her through a door where she doesn't want to go. "Be sociable," another man tells him. "You not on the staff." Parka snaps back, "I ain't yo' nigger." When a girl with a pretty hairstyle walks by, he shouts at her, "I want your hair!" She replies, "You gonna buy me some more?" [50]

I move down to the wooden benches near one corner of the building. From here, I can see something that I couldn't before. Behind a van across the street, two guys are fighting. They must be pretty drunk; the pace doesn't let up a bit even when one guy slams the other's head into the van. [51]

There's a constant stream of men coming in and out of the building. A beer can in a paper sack is practically part of the uniform. A few weeks before tonight, *Newsweek* ran a picture of the area where I'm sitting now. In the shot, the CCNV building and grounds looked spic-and-span. The three guys now on the bench to my right, sharing a joint, weren't there. And neither were the two women and one guy on the sidewalk right in front of me, passing a reefer between them. A young black guy dressed in the immaculate fashion of followers of Muslim leader Louis Farrakhan—black suit, bow tie, highly polished shoes—comes over to the trio. I expect him to tell them to put the joint out. But instead he takes off his Walkman and lends it to one of the women. She closes her eyes and sways to the music, continuing to take her tokes. A [52] guy yells down to the group from the balcony, "You know she be horny when she smokes that shit!"

So far, out of the hundred or so people I've seen at CCNV, I'm the only white. That's why I notice when three white guys come out of the building. They're walking down the ramp when a tall man with one of those Eraserhead hairdos that's high and flat on top and shaved bald all around the sides suddenly comes up in their faces and edges them towards the wall. He says something to them and then they sheepishly continue on their way. Eraserhead has now joined Purple Parka out front as one of CCNV's unofficial greeters. He's got a pocket square tucked into his sports jacket, and is wearing a fancy-looking watch and four rings. *53*

I go inside to find out what prospects there are for getting put up for the night. I'm told that the shelter is full until Tuesday, but that a van will eventually come to take me to one of the city's emergency shelters. I decide to wait in the lobby. Over the next couple of hours there I see a lot. *54*

Residents continue to stream in and out of the building. (There is no sign-in or sign-out. The building is open most of the time. Between midnight and 4 a.m. the front door is opened for five minutes every half hour.) About a third of the people I see are carrying Walkman sets. At least half are carrying beer or liquor. The stuff's usually in a paper bag, but several people, Eraserhead among them, are carrying beer in plastic cups. Later, a CCNV spokesman named Lawrence Lyles tells me that CCNV policy is that "we allow people to have beer and hard stuff, but not illegal drugs. As long as they maintain themselves. This is the residents' house. If you were home, you'd drink a little beer, wouldn't you?" But more than a few of the residents are not maintaining themselves. Drunks—weaving, falling-down drunks—are a common sight in the lobby. Some of them get up the steps only because they are carried up. Only once does a staff member ask anybody what he's carrying in. And when the resident laughs off the question, the staff member doesn't pursue it. What I see supports what an experienced city social worker tells me later: "There are drugs in CCNV. The place is out of control." *55*

Conversation here tends to be animated, often hostile. "If all you needed to live was a teaspoon of water," one man snaps at another, "I wouldn't give it to you." Another man explains in a loud voice why he wants a stiletto. "Because if I miss you one way, I'll cut you coming back." "Look," says one laughing guy to his friend, pointing to a bearded, wasted white man whose eyes are set on infinite, "Charlie Manson is on parole." *56*

A handsome man with longish gray-black hair comes down to get his mail. He's carrying two books, the first I've seen here. He's neatly dressed in a completely coordinated Army camouflage uniform. In this scene, he looks as solid as a rock. He's walking towards me as he finishes *57* his letter. "They say they will give me money if I go to a psychiatrist," he tells me, his face lit up now by a scary smile. "But I will stay here instead!"

Even in this chaos, there are some touches fit for a public service announcement. An older black man asks a feeble-looking white man about how he's mending since he got hit by a car. He listens patiently as the man shows him his injuries and explains what medical appointments he has set up in the days ahead. A lady gives a man in a wheelchair a spin he clearly enjoys. *58*

At about 8 p.m., one of the staff members very politely informs the few of us who've been waiting for transportation that there will be no van run tonight. He quickly goes on to tell us that there's room at one of the city's newest emergency shelters. And it's within walking distance, over at the Department of Employment Services just around the corner. *59*

On my way there, I fall in with two other guys, Tom and James, headed for the same place. They are both refreshingly clean-cut and substance-free. We all shake hands and quickly hit it off. The DES shelter is actually in the employees' parking garage underneath the building. It's well heated, and the nice lady volunteer who checks us in issues us like-new Army cots and a tuna sandwich apiece. There are about 50 people already on cots when we arrive—the place is full. The three of us help each other set up our cots. Tom takes a shower and brings some cups and water back from the bathroom to make up some Kool-Aid he's brought with him. He shares it with James and me and gives us each a cookie, too. The shelter atmosphere is pretty much like that of a barracks; there's plenty of "smokin' and jokin'" but the drunks are mostly down for the count. The roving armed guard probably helps. *60*

The three of us talk among ourselves. Tom's a white guy with a bushy moustache. He just got out of jail—during a routine traffic stop the day before, he got arrested on an old warrant for driving without a license. He made bail, but he's from Virginia, and without a license or car (it got impounded), and low on money, he has no way to get back. And he has no place to stay here. His court date is next month, and he figures he will get some jail because, as he puts it, "this isn't the first time." *61*

James is black and works in the kitchen at the Marriott in Crystal City. He's wearing an Army jacket, from his days as a parachute rigger in the Airborne. This is his first day on the streets. He had been living with his girlfriend, but they had a fight. James works on the side as a party DJ. At one of these parties, a girl gave him her phone number to give to a friend of his, but James's girlfriend discovered it in his jacket and went nuts, throwing James out of the house and all of his stuff down the stairs. I ask James if there isn't a family member he can stay with until this boils over. "I tried staying with my mother," he answers, "but she had too many restrictions—she won't give me a key, she won't let me in past 11 at night, and there's no TV downstairs. I'm a party animal." *62*

Lying back on my cot, I spend a long time staring at the garage   *63*
ceiling, trying to figure out James's logic. Why would somebody clean
and employed choose this—and tomorrow night maybe something much
worse—over coming in at 11 to a house with only one TV? Would
"people you know" do that?

CONSPICUOUS DYSFUNCTION

The Depression taught most Americans that there are plenty of   *64*
ways to become poor that aren't one's fault. By now this is a lesson well
learned. Perhaps too well-learned. Americans tend to believe that homelessness is exclusively a social problem, a system failure. This idea goes
hand-in-hand with the traditional liberal notion that the solution to the
problem is simply the provision of housing and jobs. While there is
something to this, it's not *the* solution—as I found out for myself there's
too much else going on with the homeless.

Allowing for the possibility of some overlap, here's how I would   *65*
roughly classify the homeless people I met: At least three-quarters were
(current or recovering) substance abusers, three-quarters were unattached
men, and about a third seemed to some degree mentally ill. But there is
another important factor I observed in about half of the homeless people
I talked to—one that takes a little explaining. I call it the "X-factor"
because I'm not having much luck figuring it out.*

Ronald Reagan once came in for a lot of well-deserved criticism   *66*
for saying that anybody who is homeless is so only because he chooses
to be. That's a ridiculous notion. Sleeping in the park in the winter, being chronically sick and disoriented—nobody chooses *that*. But just the
same, people like the New York artist, Wayne from Texas, and James are
carrying something around in their heads that's separating them from
opportunities and propelling them towards ruin. The artist has his inco-
herent put-down of the classifieds, Wayne has his equally confused contempt for the work at his father's business, and James has his odd standards
about acceptable living conditions. Here are some other examples of the
X-factor I came across in talking to the homeless:

- One of the beggars I frequently see is a 24-year-old black guy
  who goes by the street name "Quickness." He can usually be
  found around Dupont Circle either zoned out or trying to be. He

*It's interesting to compare my description of the homeless population based on my own
experience with what you can find in print elsewhere. Most respected policy studies and
surveys are now saying that about a third of the homeless are mentally ill, a third are
substance abusers, and a third are "other." That is, they find less substance abuse than I
did, about the same amount of mental illness, and tend to leave the rest of the population
an undifferentiated mystery while I think some of that remainder is in the grip of X-
factor thinking.

tells me that he originally came to Washington to sell PCP, but he got caught and spent three years in jail. He's been on the streets for the seven months since he got out. When I ask him what he wants out of life, he tells me "money." His parents are back in Florida, and they know he's up here, but he won't go back to them and he won't even tell them he's homeless. Quickness prefers staying in the streets to that.

- A fiftyish man whom I often see late at night begging near my office, an articulate man who appears sane and drug- and alcohol-free, tells me that he served in submarines in the Navy and then worked at the Nuclear Regulatory Commission. He says that he lost his job at the NRC because of differences with his bosses. Later, he landed a job stuffing envelopes for a political organization, but he quit because he didn't agree with the material he was mailing and went back to the streets, where he makes about $2 an hour (it turns out that's the typical figure for a Washington beggar).

- A young woman I met who splits her begging between Dupont Circle and Georgetown tells me that she recently failed the Civil Service exam. I ask her if she has tried to get into a job training program. "I feel that I don't have the time for that. I just want something right now. Something I can just walk into and get right then and there."

All of these people fail the Bill Shade test. Bill is the only single   67
male homeless person I met who I am convinced is actively trying every day to become unhomeless. Bill was working in construction when he got burned out of his apartment. Most of what Bill collects from begging he turns over to the woman who takes care of his daughter. Once I was talking to Bill when I noticed the Help Wanted sign behind his head. He read my mind: "I already went in there, but they want a girl to work behind the counter." So instead he sweeps the sidewalk in front of the shop. He works odd jobs whenever he can. He cleans up around the bank where he sleeps. He puts quarters in expired parking meters to save people he doesn't know from paying the $15 ticket. He's hoping to get the funds together to move back to Baltimore with his daughter. If reading this story makes you feel like helping a single homeless person directly, call me or write me about Bill Shade.

I'm finding it hard to articulate the troublesome mental baggage   68
that hampers the New York artist or Quickness say, but not Bill Shade. It's not, contra the Reagan camp, mere laziness—these people work much harder every day than most just to keep from freezing to death. It's something more like a twisted sense of pride—a sense of personal specialness tweaked so ridiculously high that anything—even sleeping out-

side and begging for food—is viewed as better than forms of compromise that you and I would readily accept, like fitting in at work, getting a job out of the newspaper, or coming home at 11. For all I can tell, some of this odd thinking is the extreme rationalization so common in alcoholics and substance abusers, and some is a sign of a treatable organic thought disorder, like mild schizophrenia. But I'm also convinced that some of the homeless I met who evinced the X-factor were neither mentally ill nor addicts. What do we make of them?

If you've raised children in the seventies and eighties, then you   69
know how the emphasis on rampant instant gratification and conspicuous consumption of such television fare as "Dallas," "Lifestyles of the Rich & Famous," and "L.A. Law" can distort your children's desires and expectations. Sometimes being "tough"—emphasizing setting goals and working hard to achieve them, etc.—brings kids around on this. But many parents have experienced the bewilderment that comes when that doesn't work. How do we reach Johnny? How do we bring him down to earth so that he can make a good life for himself? Parents can use up a decade or more wrestling with such questions, often without arriving at an answer. Well, maybe the bewilderment I feel in the face of the foregoing examples is similar, with a similar cause. But about two or three times more extreme. It seems that some of the homeless have just soaked up way too much of our culture's obsession with "too much, too soon."

There can be all the low-cost housing in the world, and an un-   70
treated paranoid won't set foot in it, and an untreated schizophrenic might burn it down. (Dr. E. Fuller Torrey, a psychiatrist who is an expert on the homeless mentally ill, told me that he has encountered both outcomes.) And a drug addict will spend the rent money on crack. So homelessness is in large measure a mental health problem and a drug problem that defies the conventional liberal answers of housing and jobs. But notice this about the X-factor homeless: They aren't likely to be people for whom jobs and housing alone would be the answer, either. Once a man decides to eat only caviar, he will turn down bread as fervently as an ordinary man turns down poison. If low cost housing were made available to the New York artist (and for all I know, it already has been), but there was no $10,000 loan, how would he pay the rent? If he were offered a nonglamorous job to make the rent, would he take it?

There certainly seem to be homeless people who are nearly like you   71
and me, save for some intervening bad breaks. Many of the women on Belmont Street appear to fit that bill, as does Bill Shade. So for people like these, fixing the bad break—making jobs and housing available—*is* what's called for. But media depictions to the contrary, there are more homeless people—the untreated mentally ill, the addicted, and those with the X-factor—*who are not like us.* As a result, if they are ever to realize secure and steady lives, they will require different kinds of help.

Traditional liberals don't want to admit such differences—and that's wrong—because they want us to help all the homeless—that's right. Neoconservatives admit the differences (right) because they don't want to help them all (wrong). The correct position is to admit the differences among the homeless while strenuously working to help them all. If conservatives need to care more, liberals need to *see* more. It's a cruel joke to pretend that an untreated mentally ill person is better off in the streets than he would be if he were compelled somehow to take medication, or to pretend that Quickness would hold down a job with the same tenacity as Bill Shade. To make real progress in the fight against homelessness, we must first be honest about who the homeless are. 72

VIRGINIA'S TRAP

Peter Marin

Several years ago in New Orleans, I met a young African-American woman, Virginia,* who at the age of twenty-one was on her own in the world with two small children. She had just gotten out of a shelter after being homeless for a year, and over the coming twelve months she and her boys would become homeless several times again. Even when they had somewhere to stay, Virginia was so close to the edge, so precariously situated, that it took only the slightest mishap or misstep to send her back onto the street. 1

Michael Harrington once wrote that we should not talk about "poverty," but about poverties. He meant that there are so many ways of being poor that no single description or analysis can apply to them all. Virginia's situation shows that the same thing is true of homelessness. There are in actuality a variety of homelessnesses, each one different from the others in terms of causes, particulars, and solutions. Furthermore, the kind Virginia endures—a recurrent homelessness so much a part of the cycle of poverty that it becomes a predictable part of people's lives—gets much less attention than it deserves. 2

Too often, most of us think of homelessness as the result of a long downward slide (as with alcoholics, for example), or else of a catastrophic event—serious illness, mental collapse, the sudden loss of a job or a home. In both cases, it seems like a sudden and forced exile, almost a falling off the earth, something that places people beyond our ordinary social or economic orders and into another reality altogether. 3

But Virginia's kind of homelessness is quite prevalent around us, and very poor people learn, unfortunately, to take it almost for granted. 4

*The names of the people in this story have been changed.

It's a part of our society, part of the poverty that shadows many lives and carries people in and out of homelessness, from low-paying jobs to unemployment to shelters to the street to welfare to low-paying jobs and eventually, again and again, to unemployment and the street.

Race is an important factor in this kind of homelessness, and somewhere between 40 and 50 percent of the homeless population (more, in large cities) is now African American. Virginia is a young single mother without job skills, prospects, or a mate, and many of the families now on our streets or on welfare are headed by women in similar circumstances. So, in a number of ways, her story is a representative one.

I first met Virginia when I was asked to speak in New Orleans at a conference of city planners and administrators concerned about the homeless issue. I asked a local advocate for the homeless to suggest a couple of people who could come to the conference and talk about their lives. One of them turned out to be Virginia, who was then in a short-term church-run program for homeless mothers and was therefore living in an apartment for three months.

One legacy of black-white relations in the South is that there is always some guardedness and masking that goes on. And though my sense of Virginia is limited by what she *let* me see, I liked her from the start. She was tall and slim with a soft face and high cheekbones and her hair cut boyishly short. There was both gentleness and directness in her manner, and a kind of shy diffidence, and she seemed to draw her voice—and her whole being, as well—inward with her breath as she spoke, so that you felt yourself leaning forward, straining to hear, even when you could make her words out clearly.

The audience at the conference liked her, too, when she described her life without self-pity or complaint. Fact followed fact; she didn't editorialize, but, as she went on speaking, becoming more sure of herself, describing what it was like in shelters or walking the streets all day with her children, the people listening were moved by her sorrowful self-possession, perhaps more than they might have been by something more shrill or consciously dramatic.

When the conference ended, Virginia and I kept in touch. Sometimes when she was in financial difficulty, she'd call and I'd wire money. I'd been well paid for my lecture, and I decided to send her whatever she needed until the fee was gone. Month after month, I followed, long-distance, the twists and turns of her fortune. Then, last summer, I went back to New Orleans to learn and write about women who were homeless or on welfare, and had a chance to see, close up, Virginia's struggle to get by.

The economic aspects of that struggle were immediately evident. Virginia's welfare payments were $190 per month—that's what the state of Louisiana gives to a woman with two children. With one child, you get $138. With three, you get $234. For every additional child, your check increases by an average of $38. Clearly, the total is never enough to lift you out of the worst kind of poverty.

Measure Virginia's payment against her expenses. When the church   11
program ended, she stayed on in her apartment, which cost her $150 a month. Her utilities came to $100. A telephone, which was a necessity both to look for work and to keep in touch with the world, cost another $30 or so, at minimum. Food stamps provided her with food, but, even so, her basic expenses totaled $280 a month; she was $90 behind *before* spending a penny on clothing, toys, or transportation.

Of course, Virginia looked for work. But all she could find were   12
part-time, split-shift jobs at fast-food outlets for minimum wage. Employers in New Orleans prefer such arrangements, because they keep the cost of benefits low and avoid overtime wages entirely. Say that Virginia worked twenty hours a week for $3.35 an hour. That's $60 a week in take-home pay. But she would have to pay someone to watch her kids, and when you deduct that and throw in the cost of transportation—$10 a week—there wouldn't be much left at all.

Moreover, this income would not be allowed as a supplement to   13
welfare, because, under federal law, any money you make must be reported to the welfare office so that the same amount can be deducted from your next monthly check. That means that for every dollar you make you lose a dollar; you're left, always, in the same sorry predicament. And if you don't report your earnings—as Virginia sometimes did not— then you are, according to the law, committing fraud.

What happened to Virginia was predictable and inevitable. She fell   14
further and further behind on her bills. First the telephone was disconnected; then her utilities were cut off. Finally she stopped paying the rent altogether and was evicted. Homeless again, she took the children to the shelter she'd been in before entering the church program. For several months, she kept looking for work but found nothing. And then she chose the only option left open to her and did what almost everyone on welfare in New Orleans ends up doing: she put her name down on the waiting list for an apartment in the city's "projects" and took the first one that became available.

There are about a dozen projects scattered throughout New Or-   15
leans—huge federally funded developments that were built in the 1930s and 1940s and are now administered by the city. Official estimates put the number of people in the projects at anywhere from 40,000 to 60,000, almost all of them black and most on welfare. But homeless-advocates estimate that, when you add in illegal residents and doubled-up families, the total is even higher, perhaps as much as a quarter of the city's African-American population of 330,000.

Old picture postcards of the projects show neat lawns and tidy two-   16 and three-story brick buildings surrounded by trees, street lamps, and wrought-iron benches. These days they're dusty, run-down wastelands, largely ignored by the city government that manages them. In some projects, a third of the apartments have been gutted and abandoned; drugs and guns abound; violence is commonplace, and at night you often hear gunfire. When Virginia lived in the projects, she kept her windows boarded up and wouldn't let her children play outside. "Minute I'd let them out," she said, "I'd hear shootin' and they come runnin' inside. I always told them to git down low and don't be scared."

For those who live in the projects, it's the meanest kind of life. The only reason for moving in is economic, and once you're there it isn't easy to get out. Again, the numbers reveal why: Rents are geared to income, and an apartment like Virginia's, utilities included, costs $60 a month. Figure again $30 for a phone, and assume that food stamps provide food. That leaves approximately $25 a week for all other expenses—more than you'd have living outside the projects. And if you teach yourself to need little and expect nothing, you can last there forever, though impoverished and in constant danger.

But Virginia didn't last. She missed a couple of welfare appointments and her checks stopped arriving. She fell behind in her rent and was evicted again. Homeless once more, she went to stay with an older woman friend, whose one-bedroom apartment was paid for by a lover. Virginia and her boys slept on a fold-out couch in the living room and got all of their meals, in return for which Virginia signed over her now-restored welfare checks to her friend. She was, she told me later, a virtual prisoner. But even that didn't last. The boyfriend grew tired of her presence, and her friend told her to leave.

When Virginia was growing up in New Orleans—to hear her and others tell it—the city was more prosperous, neighborly, orderly, and livable than it is now. The black neighborhoods were thriving, whites had not yet fled the city for the suburbs, and inexpensive housing and decent jobs were easier to come by.

Virginia had three sisters and two brothers, a mother who took good care of them, and a father who drank a bit too much but worked steadily on the docks as a foreman. He had managed to buy a small house, and their life was stable and ordinary. But when Virginia was seven, her mother died. Her father's drinking increased. Her two older sisters and a brother moved out, and at eleven she was left in the house with a younger brother and sister. "My daddy was gone all the time," she says. "We was in the house by ourselfs many a night. Sometimes he came home and sometimes not. We never knew where he was, 'cause he didn' want us knowin' his business."

Then, Virginia's father was shot and wounded in a bar by a jealous woman. He lost his job on the docks, and the house was sold at auction.

Virginia and the other two children moved in with an older sister, who sent Virginia to a Catholic day school. Their father disappeared on the streets of the city, and Virginia's oldest brother became her surrogate father—until he was shot five times and killed in a barroom brawl.

Virginia managed to graduate from high school, but in her senior   22
year she fell in love with a boy and was soon pregnant. She had the baby, stayed on with her sister, met another man, and got pregnant again. Neither of the men could take care of her or wanted to marry her. Both went off, but Virginia showed no anger when talking about them: "I don't bear them no grudge in my mind."

Of the first one, she said: "He tried. He wanted to be a man. But   23
he couldn't find no job or nothin'. He got discouraged and got hisself in trouble. I think he was misled to wrongness."

Of the second: "He never had no chance. He grew up in the   24
projects not carin' about things. That was his lifestyle. Now he got another baby by a woman younger than me."

When I asked about birth control, she said: "See, when you're just   25
startin' out, you don't know what you do now. I was only nineteen and a good girl, and my sister—she kept that stuff quiet."

When Virginia had her second child, her sister told her she couldn't   26
take care of her anymore; it cost too much, there was too little space. So Virginia went to a Salvation Army shelter and, after several months, into the church program she was in when I met her.

There's nothing unusual in this story—at least not in terms of what   27
I heard in New Orleans. Most of the stories I heard had many of the same elements as Virginia's: early or adolescent pregnancies; men drifting in and out; little preparation for work or the world; little family support; and, perhaps most importantly, personal tragedies that had destroyed an orderly world or deprived people of the sustenance they needed.

For instance, there was Lobelia, a thirty-five-year-old woman in the   28
projects who had had eight children by six different men. She was tough and outwardly cheerful, and had been twice hooked on drugs but was clean when I met her and trying hard to replace crack with Christ. She had a twenty-inch scar on her thigh from a recent fight with a neighbor over a man, and she wouldn't, she told me, let any male visitor into the house unless he brought whiskey, food, or money. "I ain't no whore," she said.

I didn't quite know what to make of her until she told me one day   29
that her father, whose favorite she was, died when she was thirteen. "I went so wild with grief," she said, "there wasn't no controlling me. My mama had the doctor declare me crazy and they put me away for a year." When she got out, she immediately started having sex and children, and soon her mother would have nothing to do with her. So she went

from one relative to the next until, homeless and on welfare, she moved to the projects.

Mixed in with economic troubles, there are always these other dif- 30 ficulties—sorrows of the heart and grievances of the soul—that isolate men and women and take away their ability to maintain order in their lives. Is that a surprise? In perhaps the best book ever written about the near-homeless poor, *People of the Abyss*, Jack London speculated that, in a competitive and individualized economic system, those who fail soonest are those without the energy and will, as well as the means, to survive. What I'm suggesting here is that those at the bottom are neither the weakest nor the worst but often those with the least sense of human connectedness or the strongest sense of betrayal: the wounded, the abandoned, the excluded, the abused—all those who cannot on their own and without the help of others discover how to fit into the world or even a reason for trying. I remember once asking Virginia what she most wanted in the world, expecting her to say something about safety or money or a job or a man. Instead she said, in a voice so soft I had to bend to hear, "I want my momma to be livin'."

There's something else worthy of attention in Virginia's story, par- 31 ticularly because you hear it so often from women in trouble. All of the women I spoke with in New Orleans have been forced to care for their children without help from men, and almost all have had two or some-times three sets of children by different men, all of them outside of marriage. Most women had their first children in their middle or late teens, often with men they say they loved. Birth control isn't much talked about or used; abortion hasn't much appeal; and since most of the men involved are without money, jobs, skills, or prospects, going on welfare is, for most of these women, the only possible choice. And since family aid goes only to households without men, welfare regulations have destroyed or nullified the cultural sanctions that keep men and women together.

Once on welfare, women are almost like hostages: bored and iso- 32 lated from the larger world, with little hope of changing their lives. They become stationary targets for disenfranchised men for whom sex is an anodyne and a consolation and a way of proving one's worth or simply that one *exists*. Out of boredom and the human need for attention and pleasure, more children are born. In the South, especially among poor, black people, children are valued in a way that makes abortion virtually unthinkable.

I talked to a woman who was in her late twenties, Tanya, a second- 33 generation project dweller. She had had three children by two different men friends and was still nursing one of them. Now she was pregnant again. The father was a man she hardly knew and didn't like; she had slept with him while drunk and without precautions, believing, falsely, that she couldn't conceive as long as she kept suckling her infant. "It wasn't quite rape," she said. "But it was, almost. I just lay there, not ready, not caring, feeling nothing. But I didn't bother to say no." Still, she could not bring herself to have an abortion. She had intended to get one, but, after her doctor let her listen to the fetal heartbeat with a stethoscope, she "couldn't do nothing. It was like my own heart I heard." She sat there, musing, and asked me: "Would someone like you like me if I had an abortion? Do you think God would like me?"

It's easy to see the children as echoes of the large families from   34
which these beleaguered women come, and they provide at least some sense of connection to the past and to a larger world, some sense of purpose, and someone to love, in lives that might otherwise be too empty and crimped to bear.

Tanya's two older children—a boy of ten, a girl of eight—told me   35
that between them they had two "daddies" and considered one of Tanya's long-term boyfriends a third. They felt that all of their daddies' other children by other women were their brothers and sisters—eight in all, they said, toting it up on their fingers. And the mothers of those children were in many cases surrogate aunts, and the children of those women by still *other* men were, they thought, their cousins, all part of a network extending outward or expanding by the collapse and formation of sexual relationships and the birth of new babies.

It is true, of course, that, within this network, relationships are not   36
always determined by biology. Tanya's son, for instance, told me he felt closer to his sister's natural father than to his own. They went fishing and spent part of the summer together. The sister, in turn, spent much of her time with her brother's daddy's new girlfriend, whom she was, she said, growing to love.

When I asked the kids if they would rather have had one perma-   37
nent father there all the time, they wistfully nodded yes. But nonetheless, these families *work*. They aren't just a breakdown of "normal" family life, but a variation—a system of kinship and connection, which acts as a buffer against loneliness and isolation, creating a meaningful, social world. Viewed one way, they seem evidence of a culture in decline or trouble; but in another sense, they are continuing and extending a culture, keep-ing it alive.

Among the critical elements at work in lives like Virginia's and   38
Tanya's are culture and racism. I link them together because they are not easily separated in the South. Everywhere, you see poor black men and women clinging to certain aspects of traditional black culture: large fam-ilies, language, music. But because these people are surrounded by a still-racist society, you cannot tell precisely what they would leave or keep if they were free to choose. In general, the overriding sense in the projects

is of people caught between the remnants of African-American traditions and the demands of the "mainstream" American order that they're expected to join in order to survive. The problems of "assimilation," of mediating between a cultural past and an economic future, seem as painful for many African Americans as they do for Native Americans.

For decades now, African-American intellectuals have argued that *39* entry into mainstream American life, whether voluntary or forced, has involved terrible losses for black people in terms of culture, community, and identity. Though nobody in the projects articulated that problem to me in precise terms, it was nonetheless at work wherever I looked. Yet even in the midst of despair and individual tragedy, many of the traditions of black culture have remained sufficiently intact to exert a hold on people and partially sustain them. There's a whole world alive in the projects about which outsiders understand very little. Though this world cannot be entered, you can sense and hear it from a distance, from the outside. It's there in the dialogue, a patois so private that when spoken fast it sounds like a foreign language. It's there in the music, in the systems of kinship, in the perceptions of time and space, in the assignment of values, in the attitudes toward pleasure, work, leisure, family, and friendship. It's there in the still-astonishing capacity for generosity, sweetness, and sacrifice; in the tenacity in the face of suffering; in the passion for relationships rather than competition; and in a system of meaning that somehow raises life itself—its complexities, joys, and griefs—to a crowning position unchallenged by personal success or material accumulation.

This is the surviving culture of the rural South that I'm trying to *40* describe. Obviously, it is a culture in disarray, and many cling to it because they have little choice. But if others hold tight to it, willingly, is that so surprising? Look around. There's something so joyless and pained about the individualized sink-or-swim economy we expect people to enter, something so empty of community and vitality—it is not difficult to understand why some are reluctant to enter it, or to trade away the little they have for the little it offers in return.

All of this is part of Virginia's story, in the background of the more *41* obvious issues of wages and rents. At the point last summer when I was visiting her, Virginia was on the verge of returning to the streets. She was about to leave her friend's apartment, with absolutely nowhere to go.

Had I not been there, she might have become homeless again. But *42* she had one welfare check in hand and asked me for a loan of $200. With the total, she said, she'd be able to move into an apartment of her own. I tried to tell her that, even if she got a place, she'd be unable to keep up the rent payments and would be out on the street in two months and we both would have wasted our money. "I don't care," she said. "I ain't going back to the shelter. And I got a feeling this time that somethin' good is gonna happen."

One Sunday, with newspaper in hand, we went hunting for apart-   *43*
ments. Virginia wanted to get as far away from the projects as possible, so
we drove out to an area on the city's edge. Over the last three decades,
developers had moved into what had been rural territory to build apartment complexes for an anticipated invasion of baby boomers, which
never materialized. The rents are low and there are still open spaces and
stands of trees and, at twilight, a whole host of country smells, though it
is only twenty minutes by bus—"a straight shot," in Virginia's words—to
downtown New Orleans.

We only had to look at two places before Virginia found what she   *44*
wanted: a rather dingy one-bedroom apartment in a colonial-style complex with a dirty pool, a laundry room, and both black and white tenants.
The ad in the paper mentioned something about moving in for $199,
but Virginia talked to the manager alone, and when she emerged she
had handed over all of her money—$400—for the first month's rent
plus what he had mysteriously told her were "one-time unrefundable
charges."

The apartment was on the first floor, out on the edge of the com-   *45*
plex, where all the black tenants lived. The living room had a glass door,
which slid open to a swampy common that had once been a lawn. The
whole place smelled of the mildew and mold growing on the wall a
couple of feet above the damp shag carpet. But Virginia loved it. It was
the nicest place she'd lived in, she said, "since my daddy's house." The
manager, who had overcharged her, took a liking to her, and dragged out
of storage an old box spring and two torn high-backed velvet chairs and
a lopsided table. Said Virginia, "It's my own, my first real home."

And then, to my surprise, and right before I left New Orleans,   *46*
something good *did* happen. Virginia had a friend who worked at a
downtown hotel, and for more than a year had called the hotel every few
weeks to see if a job was available. Three days after she moved into the
apartment, she called again and they told her that someone had quit and
that, if she came in to be interviewed, they would put her to work.

Within a week, she had a steady job and had found someone to   *47*
watch her kids free of charge. It was a good job, as such jobs go. The
hotel was old and locally owned and the owners treated their employees
in a familial way. The pay was close to five dollars an hour, and there
were scheduled raises and a health plan and below-cost hot lunches in the
cafeteria. It was clear, Virginia told me, that, if you did your work and
showed up on time and didn't mess up, you could stay there a lifetime.
"You're gonna have to show me," she said excitedly, "how to open a bank
account and *save*. I never done it before."

But there was a hitch. The hours and pay weren't steady. In the   *48*
winter, when the hotel was full, you might work seven hours a day, six
days a week—forty-two hours in all. But in the summer, when the flow

of tourists slowed, you might work only three or four days a week, and five or six hours a day.

During the busy season, Virginia could clear $175 a week for rent, *49* food, clothing, toys, etc.—enough to get by and perhaps save a bit. But during the off-season, her take-home pay would be lower than her expenses. She could get some food stamps, as long as she reapplied for them every time her income dipped. But what about other expenses? She'd no doubt fall behind, just as before; then the phone would be cut off, the lights would go, there would be a monthly struggle to come up with the rent—and, sooner or later, she'd be homeless again.

I can't help worrying that that's exactly what has happened to Vir- *50* ginia. When I talked to her several months ago, work had slowed and she was having terrible problems. And recently, I tried to track her down but failed. The phone at her apartment had been disconnected. At the hotel, they told me that Virginia didn't work there anymore, and they didn't know where she'd gone.

WHAT WE REALLY KNOW ABOUT THE HOMELESS

Randall K. Filer

Most Americans would like to believe that rationality underlies *1* public policy. Given the seriousness of homelessness, we might suppose that policy decisions are based on an understanding of the issues.

But this is not so, as a colleague, Marjorie Honig, and I found in *2* surveying the research on homelessness in the U.S. Many assertions have gained credibility merely through repetition, while basic issues regarding the causes of homelessness have rarely been addressed.

What do we know, then, about homelessness in America? *3*

We have only a ballpark estimate of the number of people currently *4* living in public places or shelters (including hotels). In 1984 the Department of Housing and Urban Development estimated a homeless population of about 350,000, a figure confirmed by several other studies. In every city with an actual count, this count was equal to or less than the HUD estimate for that city.

These numbers fall far short of the three million to four million *5* claimed by advocacy groups, which often expand the definition to include those they call the "hidden homeless"—that is, those who do not have their own dwellings (including people sharing housing with friends and relatives). One group of congressmen has defined the homeless as including everyone on a waiting list for any federally assisted housing program. Such definitions are so imprecise that they have little relevance for homeless policy and have not found wide acceptance. Estimating the current number of homeless requires combining the HUD figure for 1984 with an assumption about growth rates since then, something we know little about.

Although many believe homelessness has been increasing in recent years, there is little evidence to support this assertion. We know that more people are sleeping in shelters. The number of shelters, however, has increased rapidly. Thus we may be observing an increase in the total homeless population, or a constant population may be more likely to sleep in shelters. Reliable estimates of growth are available for only one city, Nashville. Researchers at Vanderbilt University have counted the homeless there every six months for the past several years and found no increase in homelessness. Replication of earlier counts elsewhere is needed to determine what has happened in larger cities.

The number living in the streets or in shelters may mean less than it appears. Many homeless (particularly families) enter shelters directly from sharing housing with friends and relatives. The importance of focusing on this group is to remind us that the scope of the problem is ambiguous. Some of the poor who currently make other housing arrangements may become homeless in the future. Furthermore, the more generous the programs for the homeless are, the greater this number will be as people respond to the incentives created.

We do not know how the behavior of the potential homeless will differ if either the economy or public policies change, since we know little about the alternative arrangements of the near homeless—including the conditions in which they are living. We also do not know how many of those now in shelters would be thrown into the streets, as opposed to being taken in by their families and friends, if there were no shelters. Ultimately, the homeless problem is difficult to distinguish from the problem of the very poor in general.

We know a great deal about who is homeless. The bulk (between 60% and 80%) are single men. Most suffer from one or more pathologies, especially mental illness and substance abuse. The widely cited figure that a third of the homeless are mentally ill is roughly the percentage who claim prior treatment in a mental hospital. This is undoubtedly a lower bound on the extent of mental illness among the homeless. Our knowledge of the current mental health of the homeless is hampered by the wide range of definitions used and the fact that few studies involved professional diagnoses. Those that did use such diagnoses show rates of mental illness substantially greater than one-third.

Perhaps the best data come from a 1989 study of adult homeless people (most of whom were single) in Baltimore conducted by clinicians from Johns Hopkins University. In this study, 42% of the men and 49%

of the women were found to suffer from "major mental illness (including schizophrenia and dementia)." An additional 30% of the men and 46% of the women suffered from other mental illness, such as phobias and anxiety disorders.

We also know that substance abuse is common. Many published estimates of its extent are low because they include only people institutionalized for treatment and deal only with those in shelters, many of which explicitly exclude the intoxicated. Once again, the rare studies with actual diagnoses provide the best data. In Baltimore, 75% of the men and 38% of the women were found to be substance abusers. Contrary to popular impression, alcohol remains the drug of choice among the homeless. The Baltimore study is typical of many others, with 53% of the men abusing just alcohol, 7% abusing other drugs only, and 15% addicted to both alcohol and another drug. 11

Although the common perception is that mental illness and substance abuse cause homelessness, homelessness itself may also contribute to mental illness and substance abuse. The same applies to crime. Homeless men have more convictions than other low-income men. We do not know, however, whether this is because some men have characteristics that make them more likely to commit crimes and to become homeless, whether a criminal record makes it harder to get and hold a job (increasing the probability of homelessness), or whether homelessness itself makes men more likely to commit crimes. 12

Homeless families are very different. They are almost exclusively headed by women. Most enter homelessness directly from shared housing, but very few have lived recently with either a husband or boyfriend. Most are eligible for public assistance, but only a minority receive benefits. Criminal records are more common in the general low-income population but do not approach levels among homeless single men. Heads of homeless families are, however, more likely than very poor mothers with homes to have had traumatic childhoods, including being abused and living in foster homes. 13

Our understanding about who the homeless are is much better than our knowledge about what causes homelessness. Despite the implication of the word "homeless," we know almost nothing about the connection between homelessness and housing markets. There is no reliable evidence that homelessness is more extensive in cities with tight housing markets. The assertions that homelessness is linked to rent control or low vacancy rates are intuitions with little empirical support. We do not know the role that changes in housing markets (including the replacement of public housing programs with housing vouchers, stricter building and zoning codes, and the explicit policies designed to reduce the number of single room occupancy hotels) have played in creating homelessness. 14

Although few of the homeless currently work, we know little about *15* their work histories. Neither do we know if their nonparticipation is because of lack of interest or inability to find work. If the latter, we do not know if the season is lack of skills or personal characteristics that make it hard for some to adapt to an increasingly structured labor market with fewer day-labor jobs. We also do not know whether these problems are mitigated by tight labor markets and whether, therefore, homelessness would decline if macroeconomic policies became more stimulatory.

Although many homeless individuals and most homeless families *16* are eligible for public assistance, these programs have not enabled them to avoid homelessness. We do not know if this is because benefit levels are inadequate, or if severely dysfunctional people do not take advantage of available programs.

Issues of causality are complicated by the fact that many factors are *17* interrelated. We cannot yet disentangle these to discover the most cost-effective points for policy intervention. For example, whether mental illness or substance abuse renders an individual incapable of working depends on the nature of the illness and the structure of the available jobs. People with functional problems may be unable to cope with a tight housing market or slack labor market but might, in other circumstances, earn enough to purchase shelter.

When facing a crisis the impulse to adopt policies quietly rather *18* than wait for the slow pace of research to help design these policies is understandable. But in a time of budgetary stringency, every dollar must count. Although we should not wait for a full understanding of the causes of and cures for homelessness before we begin to act, it is imperative that we begin to ask the right questions before we waste resources on ineffectual solutions.

BROTHER, DON'T SPARE A DIME

L. Christopher Awalt

Homeless people are everywhere—on the street, in public build- *1* ings, on the evening news and at the corner parking lot. You can hardly step out of your house these days without meeting some haggard character who asks you for a cigarette or begs for "a little change." The homeless are not just constant symbols of wasted lives and failed social programs—they have become a danger to public safety.

What's the root of the homeless problem? Everyone seems to have *2* a scapegoat: advocates of the homeless blame government policy; politicians blame the legal system; the courts blame the bureaucratic infrastructure; the Democrats blame the Republicans; the Republicans, the Democrats. The public blames the economy, drugs, the "poverty cycle" and "the breakdown of society." With all this finger-pointing, the group most responsible for the homeless being the way they are receives the least blame. That group is the homeless themselves.

How can I say this? For the past two years I have worked with the homeless, volunteering at the Salvation Army and at a soup kitchen in Austin, Texas. I have led a weekly chapel service, served food, listened, counseled, given time and money and shared in their struggles. I have seen their response to troubles, and though I'd rather report otherwise, many of them seem to have chosen the lifestyles they lead. They are unwilling to do the things necessary to overcome their circumstances. They must bear the greater part of the blame for their manifold troubles.

Let me qualify what I just said. Not everyone who finds himself out of a job and in the street is there because he wants to be. Some are victims of tragic circumstances. I met many dignified, capable people during my time working with Austin's homeless: the single father strug- gling to earn his high-school equivalency and to be a role model for his children; the woman who fled a good job in another city to escape an abusive husband; the well-educated young man who had his world turned upside down by divorce and a layoff. These people deserve every effort to help them back on their feet.

But they're not the real problem. They are usually off the streets and resuming normal lives within a period of weeks or months. Even while "down on their luck," they are responsible citizens, working in the shelters and applying for jobs. They are homeless, true, but only tempo- rarily, because they are eager to reorganize their lives.

For every person temporarily homeless, though, there are many who are chronically so. Whether because of mental illness, alcoholism, poor education, drug addiction or simple laziness, these homeless are content to remain as they are. In many cases they choose the streets. They enjoy the freedom and consider begging a minor inconvenience. They know they can always get a job for a day or two for food, cigarettes and alcohol. The sophisticated among them have learned to use the system for what it's worth and figure that a trip through the welfare line is less trouble than a steady job. In a society that has mastered dodging respon- sibility, these homeless prefer a life of no responsibility at all.

Waste of Time: One person I worked with is a good example. He is an older man who has been on the streets for about 10 years. The story of his decline from respectability to alcoholism sounded believable and I wanted to help. After buying him toiletries and giving him clothes, I drove him one night to a Veterans Administration hospital, an hour and a half away, and put him into a detoxification program. I wrote him monthly to check on his progress and attempted to line up a job for him when he got out. Four months into his program, he was thinking and speaking clearly and talking about plans he wanted to make. At five months, he expressed concern over the life he was about to lead. During the sixth month, I called and was told that he had checked himself out and returned home. A month later I found him drunk again, back on the streets.

Was "society" to blame for this man? Hardly. It had provided free 8 medical care, counseling and honest effort. Was it the fault of the economy? No. This man never gave the economy a chance to solve his problems. The only person who can be blamed for his failure to get off the streets is the man himself. To argue otherwise is a waste of time and compassion.

Those who disagree will claim that my experience is merely anec- 9 dotal and that one case does not a policy make. Please don't take my word for it. The next time you see someone advertising that he'll work for food, take him up on it. Offer him a hard day's work for an honest wage, and see if he accepts. If he does, tell him you'll pay weekly, so that he will have to work for an entire week before he sees any money. If he still accepts, offer a permanent job, with taxes withheld and the whole shebang. If he accepts again, hire him. You'll have a fine employee and society will have one less homeless person. My guess is that you won't find many takers. The truly homeless won't stay around past the second question.

So what are the solutions? I will not pretend to give ultimate an- 10 swers. But whatever policy we decide upon must include some notion of self-reliance and individual responsibility. Simply giving over our parks, our airports and our streets to those who cannot and will not take care of themselves is nothing but a retreat from the problem and allows the public property that we designate for their "use" to fall into disarray. Education, drug and alcohol rehabilitation, treatment for the mentally ill and job training programs are all worthwhile projects, but without requiring some effort and accountability on the part of the homeless for whom these programs are implemented, all these efforts do is break the taxpayer. Unless the homeless are willing to help themselves, there is nothing anyone else can do. Not you. Not the government. Not anyone.

"I'D LIKE TO GIVE HIM SOMETHING...BUT I NEVER CARRY CASH."

TURNING A BLIND EYE TO THE HOMELESS

Jerome D. Simpson

They have no address, get no mail, have no phone, rarely have *1*
transportation, and have no access to showers, bathrooms or laundry
facilities. And they have to find something to eat and a place to sleep. At
REST, an Oklahoma City day center for the homeless where I work, the
two most requested items are disposable diapers and sanitary napkins.
Such is the daily struggle faced by the homeless, whose numbers in the
U.S. are growing.

Although no one has produced an exhaustive demographic study, *2*
we do know a few general characteristics about America's homeless.
Probably about one of three men is a veteran. About 5 percent are elderly.
Children are the fastest-growing segment of the homeless population;
some 1 to 3 million teenagers wander our streets searching for a safe place
to spend the night (though many of these are runaways and technically
not homeless). A number of the homeless are mentally ill, but exact
figures are not available.

Why is this problem much worse in the U.S., one of the world's *3*
wealthiest countries, than in Europe or Japan? Many Americans seem to
have no difficulty accepting the fact that in the great cities of Africa, Asia
and South America, economic factors have driven many people to the
streets where they live and beg for food. But when it comes to their own
country, Americans often blame the homeless themselves.

The total number of homeless people in the U.S. during a year's *4*
time has not been established to the satisfaction of most providers of
services to the homeless. Recently the waters were muddied further by
two federal agencies: the Census Bureau and the Interagency Council on
the Homeless.

At the Region VI Conference on the Homeless (held in Arlington, *5*
Texas, last spring) service providers from Louisiana, Arkansas, Texas,
Oklahoma, New Mexico and Arizona were stunned when representatives of the federal government casually described homeless people as
alcoholics, drug addicts, mentally ill, in poor health (due, they hinted, to
cigarette smoking) or social misfits of one type or another. More astonishing, officials asserted that money could not help alleviate homelessness.
The most breathtaking proposal came from the director of the Interagency, who recommended that shelters become self-supporting and quit
relying on government funding.

The government representatives sat stony-faced when a represen- *6*
tative from the Texas delegation read aloud a statement that the commit-

tee had adopted the night before expressing concern that the 1990 census data on the homeless would be misapplied. "We fear these numbers, which were never meant to be exhaustive, will be taken by the media as well as local, state and federal agencies to be the total 1990 count of all homeless persons." It further pointed out that "the census figures show but one lone unsheltered homeless person on the streets of Little Rock." The speaker then asked that other delegations stand in a show of solidarity. Almost everyone responded.

A Census Bureau press release reported that the bureau counted 178,828 persons in emergency shelters for the homeless and 49,700 persons visible at street locations. But it also disclaimed the numbers, claiming that the count "was not intended to, and did not, produce a count of the 'homeless' population of the country." Attached to the one-page press release was a three-and-a-half page "fact sheet" that attempted to explain the methods of the count.

These methods make one wonder why the Census Bureau released its figures at all. First, the bureau conducted the count only on the evening of March 20 and the early morning of March 21. People who live in homes with addresses were more thoroughly visited. Second, the bureau had requested approximately 39,000 local jurisdictions to supply lists of shelters, streets and public locations that the homeless frequent. Less than half—14,200—replied. Among the information the bureau did receive, in some instances "descriptions of the locations were imprecise or incorrect [and] in other instances, local jurisdictions identified locations where homeless persons could be found during the day but not at night." It further confesses that counts "probably do not include persons who were well hidden, moving from one location to another, or in shelters or street locations other than those identified by local governments, local sources, or from national lists of shelters used by the bureau." The count also missed, the bureau concedes, those "living in cars, dumpsters, rooftops, and other nontraditional housing structures." The bureau also acknowledges that the count was influenced by local conditions, the availability of shelters and "other factors."

The federal representatives at the conference seemed to represent the Bush administration's apparent attitude toward homelessness: that it is a chronic problem, not an acute one, and therefore does not need help from the federal government. The administration seems to think that neither the economy nor federal policies have contributed to homelessness. This is consistent with President Bush's remarks on child poverty: "The root cause [is] parents' behavior, not government policy."

Estimates I consider reliable, such as those made in 1987 by the Urban Institute of Washington, D.C., suggest that about 600,000 Americans are homeless at any one time and perhaps as many as a million in any one year. Homelessness is increasing and will continue to increase if the federal government does not intervene. Some 8.5 million Americans are unemployed and without benefits, and for many homelessness is only a few months away.

The country has lost approximately 1.2 million low-income hous- 11 ing units since 1980. The federal government's funding commitment to provide housing assistance for new low-income housing declined 82 percent between 1980 and 1988. The government should reaffirm its commitment to provide decent housing for all its people, a right once confirmed by Congress. That, and an effort to increase job opportunities and job training, are vital.

The government could take other piecemeal steps using programs 12 now in place until it can organize for the larger agenda. The Veterans Administration is in a unique situation to bring immediate relief to many. VA centers should increase their outreach to homeless veterans and cooperate more with existing homeless centers and shelters. The VA should provide job counseling services in the larger shelters and hire more people to assist veterans suffering mental illness or substance-abuse problems. Certainly the VA should assist veterans with their medical and legal problems.

The number of homeless women and families has tripled since 13 1984. Why not provide housing assistance for families or women with children through existing programs such as Aid for Dependent Children or Supplemental Security Income? To have women and children living in shelters is more than a disgrace; it is an indictment of our entire society.

Finally, the federal government should provide significant financial 14 help to homeless centers and shelters much in the way it assists schools and other agencies. Some claim that this endeavor would perpetuate the problem. But funding now provided by churches, individuals and foundations is unstable, and represents a burden, particularly for churches, the traditional refuge of the poor.

Centers for the homeless face an almost unending train of needs. 15 (A Denver center recently announced that it would use a lottery from now on to determine which families it will accept.) REST, which aims to help its guests establish a stable life, offers a job-placement service. Every morning it is swamped with applicants. When the counselors do obtain interviews for the job seekers, they often must also help them get haircuts, showers (over 100 showers are taken daily at REST, which has a daily population of about 300), a change of clothes, transportation to the interview and then to the work site. (REST furnishes lunches to the new workers until their first paycheck. Each morning from 20 to 25 people stop by REST to pick up a sack lunch—a poignant sight in this land of plenty.)

The 1990 annual report of the Interagency Council on the Home- 16 less illustrates the federal government's blame-the-victim mentality. It noted that "as the numbers of homeless persons grew in the early 1980s, a general reduction in the number of persons arrested for vagrancy and related offenses (which previously kept most homeless persons out of sight) helped make the homeless more visible." Indeed, we can no longer pretend not to see the homeless. We must demand the government's aid and commitment to meet their needs.

FAMILY HOMELESSNESS: A SYSTEMIC PROBLEM

Kay Young McChesney

In the 1980s, for the first time since the Great Depression, a significant number of families are living in shelters or on the streets in the United States. Families—mothers and children, couples and children—make up at least a third of the total number of homeless, and are the fastest growing segment of the homeless population, according to a U.S. Conference of Mayors survey of 29 cities (Waxman & Reyes, 1987). [1]

Why are significant numbers of families homeless now? In answering that question, this paper argues that families are homeless for structural rather than individual reasons. It then discusses the implications of the structural argument for three policy approaches to family homelessness currently in widespread use. Finally, it recommends alternative programs and policies that would have the desired effect of reducing the total number of families that are homeless. [2]

THE LOW-INCOME HOUSING RATIO

The rapid increase in homelessness in the 1980s is the result of a shift in the low-income housing ratio—the balance between the number of households living in poverty and the amount of affordable low-income housing available (cf. Clay, 1987; Dolbeare, 1986, 1988; Gilderbloom & Appelbaum, 1988; Hopper & Hamberg, 1986; McChesney, 1987; Wright & Lam, 1987). [3]

The welfare of American families improved steadily for over 20 years after World War II. After the War on Poverty began in 1964, the family poverty rate fell rapidly, reaching its lowest point, 10.8%, in 1969. While times got harder after 1973, with high unemployment rates and high inflation rates, in 1979 the number of families living in poverty still stood at 12.6% (U.S. Bureau of the Census, 1989, p. 9). [4]

However, under the influence of severe back-to-back recessions [5]

(1980, 1981–1982), and the Reagan administration's cuts in eligibility and benefit levels for Aid to Families with Dependent Children (AFDC), the economic situation of families worsened significantly. By 1983, the family poverty rate reached its highest level in 21 years, 17.9%. Between 1979 and 1983, more than 1.7 million families with children under 18 fell below the poverty line—an increase of 44% (U.S. Bureau of the Census, 1989, p. 9).

Faced with recession, regressive tax policies, and cuts in benefits, the poorest families lost the most. Danziger and Gottschalk (1985) found that over the period of 1973–1984, the mean income of the poorest 20% of families dropped by 34%, while that of the next poorest fifth fell by 20%. In addition, between 1980 and 1984, the average tax burden for the poorest fifth of the U.S. population rose 24%, while cash welfare benefits declined 17% and food stamp benefits fell 14% (Hopper & Hamberg, 1986). 6

Thus, by 1983 there were significantly more poor families who could afford only low-cost housing than there had been only a few years before. Homelessness among families on a national scale was inevitable, unless the supply of affordable low-cost housing increased rapidly to meet the needs of large numbers of newly poor households. Instead, the total number of affordable housing units decreased. 7

Hopper and Hamberg (1986) detail the sequence of events leading to the decline. In response to high interest rates and the 1980/1981–1982 recessions, the number of housing starts fell below the number needed for newly formed households, creating a housing shortage. As the shortage in supply increased, housing costs rose in response to high demand. In a condition of shortage, higher income families had to "buy down" or "rent down," filling up housing that lower income families might previously have occupied. Gentrification increased as middle-income families that could no longer afford to buy homes in the suburbs rehabilitated inner-city houses or bought rental units that had been upgraded into co-ops or condos. By 1983 the National Housing Conference (1984) estimated that only half of "typical" households that would have bought homes in previous years could afford to purchase a midpriced house. An estimated four million households that in previous years would have bought homes spilled over into the rental unit market. Vacancy rates fell to 5% nationally and as low as 3.7% in the Northeast and 4.4% in the West, well below the number needed to accommodate normal turnover (Hopper & Hamberg, 1986). Housing costs rose faster than family income. During the 1973–1983 decade, median rent rose 137%, from $133 to $315, while median family income rose only 79%, from $7200 to $12,900 (U.S. Bureau of the Census, 1983, cited in Hartman, 1986). As always, the poorest families were the hardest hit. Hartman (1986) found 8 that by 1983, for renters with an annual income under $3000, the median rent-income ratio—the proportion of a family's income spent for rent—exceeded 60%.

At the same time that the low-income housing shortage was be- *9*
coming acute, the Reagan administration introduced a new housing policy: "We're getting out of the housing business. Period" [Housing and Urban Development (HUD) deputy secretary, cited in Hartman, 1986]. HUD appropriations for subsidized housing programs fell from a high of $32.3 billion in fiscal year 1978 during the Carter administration, to $9.8 billion in fiscal year 1988 under Reagan, a decrease of more than 80% in constant dollars. In addition, for those families already in federally subsidized housing, HUD increased the amount a low-income family paid for rent from 25% of adjusted household income to 30% (Leonard, Dolbeare, & Lazere, 1989).

By 1983, the excess of poor families over available low-income *10*
housing was apparent nationally, as homeless families began seeking shelter across the country. Subsequently, although the economy improved after 1983, the shortage of affordable housing has continued. By 1985, the most recent year for which data from the American Housing Survey (AHS) are available, there were 11.6 million low-income renter households (income less than $10,000 per year) in comparison to 7.9 million affordable low-cost housing units (rent less than $250 per month), for a shortfall of at least 3.7 million units (Leonard et al., 1989, p. 7).

However, this ratio understates the actual shortage of low-cost *11*
housing. Using the same AHS data, Leonard et al. (1989, p. xiii) found that of all the units renting for $250 or less in 1985, 800,000 were vacant, and nearly a third of the occupied low-rent units were occupied by renters who were not low-income households (leaving roughly 4.7 million low-rent units for 11.6 million low-income households). Thus, their data suggest that nationally there were nearly two and a half times as many low-income households as there were available low-income housing units. As a result, the median poor renter household spent 65% of its income on housing, and 85% of poor renter households paid more for their housing than the amount considered affordable under federal standards (Leonard et al., 1989, p. x).

Since 1985, poverty rates have declined slightly, but they remain *12*
high—16.2% for all families with children under age 18 as of 1987, the most recent year for which poverty data are available (U.S. Bureau of the Census, 1989, p. 9). Comparable data from the 1987 AHS are not yet available. However, unless current policies change, the decline in the number of low-cost housing units is expected to continue. The General Accounting Office estimates that as many as 900,000 (out of a total of 1,928,000) units of federally subsidized low-income housing could be lost to low- and moderate-income use by 1995 as long-term lease restric-

tions expire; some of the 1.3 million units of public housing may be lost as well (Clay, 1987, p. 11).

In addition, substantial portions of the unsubsidized low-income   13
housing stock are expected to be lost to affordability due to the 1986 tax law overhaul (Apgar, Brown, Doud, & Schink, 1985; Clay, 1987). The old tax law included a number of tax shelters that indirectly subsidized the cost of investing in rental housing, and these provisions were elimi-nated in the new 1986 tax law. Consequently, rents on existing units are expected to rise between 15% and 30% to compensate for the loss of favorable tax provisions. The construction of new rental housing is also expected to decline sharply under the 1986 tax provisions, causing the shortage of total units to grow, and putting further pressure on rents (Clay, 1987, p. 27).

Thus, if the U.S. continues its present course, while the total num-   14
ber of poor households is expected to remain high, the total number of affordable housing units available to poor households is expected to con-tinue to decline. The implications of a continuing shortage of affordable housing for families are severe. In a Los Angeles study of homeless fami-lies, we interviewed mothers with infants as young as 2 weeks old who were forced to live on the street, because there was no room at the shelter (McChesney, 1987). In other words, what these dry, abstract numbers mean is that unless policies change, increasingly large numbers of chil-dren and their mothers and fathers will continue to live on the streets in the United States for the foreseeable future.

POLICY APPROACHES TO
FAMILY HOMELESSNESS

Let us assume that public policy for family homelessness has one   15
overall goal: to decrease the total number of families who are homeless. At the aggregate level, the cause of family homelessness is clear: When the number of poor households exceeds the number of low-income housing units, a shortage of low-income housing exists. When that hap-pens, households do two things. Those that can do so pay more for their housing (Gilderbloom & Appelbaum, 1988, p. 24). Those that cannot pay more double up with family or friends (Hopper & Hamberg, 1986; McChesney, 1987). The remainder, who cannot do either, become homeless.

If homelessness is the net result of the aggregate low-income hous-   16
ing ratio, then it follows that homelessness is *not* caused by individual characteristics or behaviors. Whatever the specific reasons for the low income (for example, having worked in a plant that closed, or having small children and no available child care), a person is ultimately home-less because there are not enough affordable low-income housing units

to go around. At most, personal characteristics operate as selection mechanisms.

Thus, viewing homelessness from the vantage point of the low-income housing ratio has important implications for public policy. If family homelessness is the net result of the low-income housing ratio, the only strategies that will be effective in dealing with it are those that either decrease the number of poor households competing for affordable housing or increase the number of low-income units they can afford. In other words, homelessness is like a game of musical chairs. The more people playing the game, and the fewer the chairs, the more people left standing when the music stops.   *17*

There are three major types of programs in use nationwide for assisting homeless families: emergency shelter, service delivery, and transitional living programs. Each of these three strategies can be seen as having an implied rationale for the cause of homelessness inherent within its use as a "solution" for homelessness. The following examination of the underlying logic of these arguments tests each of the three strategies against the objective—decreasing the total number of homeless families. Do they decrease the number of players (poor households) or add chairs (low-cost housing units)? If not, there will still be people left standing when the music stops.   *18*

Emergency Shelters

The first response of most communities to family homelessness is to open emergency shelters for families. The implicit rationale behind this strategy is that homelessness is due to temporary displacement, and therefore families need only emergency shelter while they look for permanent housing.   *19*

Emergency shelter is a necessity. Mothers who are fleeing domestic violence need emergency shelter. So do all families who have run out of other options and will face the street if emergency shelter is not provided. In Los Angeles, as in other jurisdictions where adequate emergency shelter is not provided, researchers can easily find and interview mothers with children who sleep in a laundry room, in the back of an open truck, or on the beach, because they cannot get into a shelter (McChesney, 1987).   *20*

However, the availability of emergency shelter provides only short-term relief if there is no permanent housing available. In four out of the five shelters in the University of Southern California Homeless Families Study, families were routinely released back to the street or, at best, to another shelter (McChesney, 1987). Newcomers to family shelters in Los Angeles were initially very grateful to have food and warmth and shelter for their children. However, at the end of their 3- or 4-week stay, when they realized that they were going to be sent back to the street and would not be placed into permanent housing, they often became   *21* justifiably bitter. Under such conditions, emergency shelters are at best a "band-aid" approach to the aggregate problem of family homelessness. While they are essential in the short run, they do nothing to either decrease family poverty or increase the number of affordable housing units. Thus, they will have no effect on the total number of households that do not have access to permanent affordable low-income housing. They will not change the number of people left standing when the music stops.

Service Delivery

A second common strategy for aiding homeless families is the delivery of services, for example, mental health services. The implication of such a strategy is that clients are homeless because, for example, they are psychiatrically disabled. Therefore, if they are assisted with their problems, they will be able to find housing on their own. 22

However, while the argument that psychiatric disability is a direct cause of family homelessness might seem like a logical hypothesis at the individual level, it does not make much sense in the aggregate. There is no evidence to suggest that the prevalence of psychiatric disability in the population is markedly higher in the 1980s than it was in the 1970s, before the increase in homelessness began; meanwhile, there is plenty of evidence that the *economic* circumstances of families changed markedly between 1979 and 1983. 23

Further, even at the individual level, while mental health services may be of assistance to some families, the mere delivery of services by itself will not solve a family's homelessness. For example, one woman in my sample whose husband was unemployed had been living with her husband and their three children in the airport for several months prior to coming to the shelter. This woman ("Alicia") clearly met the *Diagnostic Statistical Manual* (*3rd ed.*) criteria for a diagnosis of clinical depression, including suicidal ideation. She was sent for mental health care, given a prescription for antidepressants, and asked to return for follow-up. 24

From the mental health system's point of view, giving Alicia antidepressants and a follow-up appointment was a typical and reasonable response. However, by itself, it was inadequate. She had no symptoms of depression prior to becoming homeless, and she became suicidal only when it became clear that the shelter was going to discharge the family back into the streets because their 30-day stay was up. In essence, the psychiatrist in this case was put in the absurd position of recommending medication to help Alicia "adjust" to her homelessness, because there was no housing available. At that point in time Alicia did need mental health services. But she needed services *with* housing, not services *instead* of housing. Delivering mental health services to families will not decrease their poverty or increase the number of affordable housing units available 25 to them; therefore it will not decrease overall homelessness. The number of people left standing when the music stops will not change.

Likewise, delivery of social services in the absence of permanent housing is an ameliorative rather than a curative approach to homelessness. For example, a social worker may help a sheltered homeless mother get her AFDC case reopened. This is useful. However, without permanent housing, the efforts of the social worker are likely to be quickly undone. When the family leaves the shelter without a permanent address, they are very likely to lose their AFDC again. When no permanent housing is provided, most service delivery is apt to have at best only a transitory effect. That does not mean that services should not be provided. However, it must be understood that delivery of social services will not decrease the total number of homeless families. The number of people left standing when the music stops will not change. 26

There is one major exception to this rule, however—services that lead to a major increase in income. For example, in some communities there are enough total units of housing, but there is a shortage of housing affordable to the poor. Under these circumstances, services that lead to families receiving both a cash grant large enough to cover move-in costs, *and* either a permanent rent subsidy or a job with wages high enough to enable the family to pay market rates on an ongoing basis, will reduce the total number of homeless families. In the musical chairs analogy, every family that receives this type of help successfully exits the game: there is one less family left standing when the music stops. 27

Transitional Housing

On finding that, in spite of the presence of emergency shelters, mental health services, and social services, family homelessness continues to increase, some communities respond by developing transitional housing programs. There are two types of transitional housing programs. In many programs, the homeless are provided with housing for several months while being trained in "living skills" such as budgeting, shopping, and home management. The implicit hypothesis behind such a strategy is that program participants are homeless because of "defects" in their personal characteristics or behaviors that can be "fixed" by program participation. In other programs, the homeless are merely provided with temporary housing for several months while they look for permanent housing. The implication here is that, given enough time and a stable base from which to look, a family will eventually find permanent housing. 28

Again, as seen in the aggregate, these hypotheses do not make sense as an explanation for the increase in family homelessness. There is no reason to believe mothers' personal characteristics—their ability to man- 29 age money or to look for new housing, for example—have changed in the last 20 years. What has changed is the low-income housing market.

For the sake of argument, assume that graduates of transitional   30
living programs are more capable in approaching the rental housing market due to the training in living skills they have received, or because of housing search assistance. As they move into permanent affordable housing they will merely displace other poor households that would have occupied the same low-income units. At best, when seen from the view of the overall low-income housing shortage, transitional living programs provide a few additional units of low-income housing through which the poor are forced to rotate at 6-month intervals.

However, there are alternatives. For example, at ConServe, in   31
Washington, DC, the services, rather than the housing, are transitional. In this competency-based program, homeless families move directly from the shelter into permanent housing, with the assistance of a time-limited rent subsidy of $350–$400 a month. They are assigned to a case manager who works closely with them over a period of a year or more as needed. Placement in permanent housing enables families to put down roots—develop their own support networks and community ties—in a community where they expect to remain, as opposed to spending 6 months or more developing friendships and ties that will end when they leave transitional housing.

In short, the low-income housing ratio indicates that, no matter   32
how essential these three types of programs are, none of them will accomplish the goal of decreasing the total number of families that are homeless. Policymakers must understand that no matter how much money they spend on emergency shelters or stand-alone service delivery or transitional living programs, the number of homeless families will not change. None of these programs directly decrease the number of poor families or increase the number of units of housing affordable to the poor. No people have exited the game, and no chairs have been added. Although the faces may be different, the same number of people are still left standing when the music stops.

New York City provides a case in point. In the early 1980s, New   33
York City adopted an emergency shelter approach rather than a permanent housing approach to deal with the growing numbers of homeless families in the city. In 1981 the average length of stay for a family in the system was two months. In other words, the system was being used as temporary shelter. By November of 1987, New York City was sheltering 5200 families a night with an average stay of 13 months at an average cost of $1612 per month per family for hotel rooms without cooking facilities (personal communication from the Human Resources Administration, 1987). Had the city chosen to put the same level of resources

into building permanent affordable housing 10 years earlier, the severity of the low-income housing crisis in New York might have been considerably moderated. In 1987, New York City announced a $10.4 billion, 10-year program to build about 225,000 permanent units of low-income housing, suggesting that the city might finally have begun to attend to the structural roots of the problem.

THE SEARCH FOR MONEY AND LEADERSHIP

If the low-income housing ratio is the root cause of family homelessness, why is it that most communities are using only short-term stopgap measures to address the problem? In a typical city, the media, advocates, and citizens who become concerned about homeless families are more easily able to mobilize local community resources than state or national ones. Thus, communities begin to respond to family homelessness with emergency shelters and services first, both because these programs are clearly essential, and also because they can be begun by nonprofit organizations on a small scale in a piecemeal fashion at a relatively low cost. In Los Angeles, for example, shelters for homeless families are sponsored by churches, by inner-city missions and service organizations such as the Salvation Army, by women's organizations such as the Junior League, and by groups of concerned citizens who start small nonprofits in order to open a shelter—in other words by George Bush's "thousand points of light."

Unfortunately, the resulting "system" is typically an uncoordinated jerry-built patchwork of small private shelters and services providers. Services are fragmented and their quality is highly variable. In Los Angeles, one infamous shelter routinely sleeps 135 mothers and children on the floor and pews without bedding; sanitary conditions are so poor that outbreaks of hepatitis and dysentery occur frequently. Yet the shelter remains open, because there is no other place for these families to go. In Atlanta, until 1988, the only free shelters for families required that mothers and children leave by 7:00 AM carrying all their belongings with them, even though they would return to the same shelter that night. The reason was that the shelters were run by volunteers who had to leave early in the morning to go to work and could not return until after they had finished work.

Volunteers are usually long on love and short on cash. No matter how hard they try, concerned citizens and private nonprofits are usually unable to meet even the need for short-term shelter and services for homeless families in their cities, let alone the long-term needs for affordable housing and less poverty. While many private nonprofits understand that emergency shelters are not the ultimate answer to family homelessness, running a family shelter with some additional health, mental health, or social welfare services is something that they can actually do with limited resources.

While private nonprofit service delivery "systems" are most typical, in some cities local or state governments are involved in providing services for or paying for homeless families, either voluntarily or involuntarily. In New York and St. Louis, for example, considerable amounts of money are provided by the city for homeless shelters and services as a result of successful class action suits brought by Legal Aid. While no one would claim that the emergency services delivery systems in these cities are exemplary, the infusion of city resources, in addition to private non-profit resources, tends to result in additional beds and a more uniform service delivery system. However, law suits tend to concentrate on pro-vision of emergency services. No one has yet convinced a judge to rule that the city, county, state, or federal government being sued has a duty to provide permanent, affordable housing to its citizens. 37

On the other hand, in some jurisdictions, for example, Massachu-setts and San Francisco, a comprehensive coordinated plan for dealing with the short-term needs of homeless families is in operation, with some attention given to the long-term issues of poverty and permanent low-income housing. In every case, behind the comprehensive plan there was a strong political leader who had made a personal commitment to dealing with homelessness. Unfortunately, the authority and especially the funding base of even the most committed mayor or governor is limited. Strong state and local leaders need the backing of the federal government in order to accomplish the objective of eliminating family homelessness. 38

Traditionally the major impetus in both poverty policy and housing policy has come from the federal government, and with good reason. The federal government is the only level of government with both the authority and the resources to make major inroads into the problems of poverty and the shortage of low-income housing. As we have seen, two things are needed to accomplish the objective of decreasing the number of homeless families: money, and political leadership. Neither was forth-coming from the Reagan administration, and so far, the Bush administra-tion has been "kinder and gentler" only in word, not in deed. 39

The Reagan administration's major policy initiative in the areas of poverty and housing was to launch a concerted attack on the poor, one prong of which decimated the already inadequate low-income housing budget inherited from the Carter administration. Mr. Reagan's view that the homeless are "homeless by choice" was publicly stated. His adminis-tration made a systematic effort to portray homelessness as an individual problem—a problem of people who do not want to work, who are psychiatrically disabled, or who in some other way are to blame for their homelessness. (In fact, in 1988 I twice heard an assistant secretary of 40

HUD give an entire speech on homelessness without once mentioning the word "housing.") If homelessness can be made to seem a personal problem or a family problem, then it can be viewed as a local community problem—the sort of problem the federal government need not be involved in. Somehow, the Reagan administration got away with this, leaving a total vacuum in federal leadership for long-term solutions to poverty and the shortage of low-income housing. In the process, private nonprofit organizations, states, and local jurisdictions were left to try to pick up the slack.

In this political climate, advocates and congressional leaders who 41
were trying to get the federal government to address long-term issues of poverty and housing were severely handicapped. In order to get a homelessness bill through Congress, supporters had to drop comprehensive provisions designed to address the shortage of low-cost housing. Consequently, the McKinney Act, first passed in 1987 and reauthorized each year since then, emphasizes emergency assistance. While the bill includes a little money for prevention, virtually all McKinney funds go to short-term needs—emergency food, emergency shelter, and emergency services.

This short-term targeting of the limited federal funds available 42
places cities in positions that defy logic. Thus, for example, while New York City may use federal funds toward the $1600 a month average it costs to keep families in "temporary" welfare hotel rooms for 18 months, the city cannot, by law, use the same money to place the families in permanent housing. Nor can the city use the money to build or rehabilitate additional housing units.

POLICY RECOMMENDATIONS

Since the low-income housing ratio is the root cause of family 43
homelessness, then in order to accomplish the goal of decreasing the total number of homeless families, major changes in U.S. poverty policy and in U.S. housing policy need to be made.

Housing Policy Recommendations

The most clear-cut way to decrease the number of homeless fami- 44
lies is to increase the number of affordable, low-cost rental units. That suggests two goals for federal housing policy: (a) preserve existing public and private low-income housing units, and (b) add additional units to the low-income housing stock.

With regard to preservation of existing low-income housing units, 45
several recommendations can be made. First, the loss of inner-city units to urban renewal could be slowed by requiring developers to rehouse all

low-income households to be displaced on a one-for-one basis in equivalent low-income housing *before* demolition of old units. Second, during the Reagan administration, maintenance of public housing was seriously underfunded, resulting in many public housing units becoming dilapidated or abandoned. Adequate funds for ongoing maintenance, as well as for remedying the effects of past neglect, need to be appropriated by Congress in order to retain existing units of public housing. Third, as previously mentioned, the GAO reported that as many as half of 1.9 million federally subsidized low-income housing units may be converted to market-rate housing units by 1995 as their federally subsidized mortgages expire (Clay, 1987, p. 11). Incentives to induce owners to continue these units as low-income rental units are included in the 1990 Omnibus Housing Bills, HR1180/SB566, and they need to be retained by the conference committee and signed into law.

The second necessity in housing policy for families is the creation   46
of additional affordable low-income housing. Since the market economy will not, by definition, meet the demand for housing for poor families, the two remaining sources of supply are the government and private nonprofit organizations. By itself the federal government has had mixed success in its public housing ventures (Bratt, Hartman, & Meyerson, 1986). As a substitute for government housing, Clay (1987) and Gilderbloom and Appelbaum (1988) have recommended a form of public-private partnership—community-based housing. Modeled after highly successful European programs, some of which have housed families at low cost for several generations, this housing would be financed by the federal government but developed by private nonprofits. As a condition of federal financing, such housing would be held by tenant-owners in limited equity cooperatives, or by community nonprofits. In both cases, a condition of federal financing would be that the units would be held in perpetuity without right of resale for profit—thus, the units would be permanently removed from the for-profit sector. In communities with a shortage of total housing units, nonprofit developers would be encouraged to build new low-income units, while in communities where affordability rather than total housing supply is the major problem, nonprofits would be encouraged to convert existing for-profit units into nonprofit housing.

Hartman and Stone (1986) suggested that federal financing of non-   47
profit housing be in the form of direct capital grants for construction and rehabilitation costs. They showed that in the current for-profit system about two-thirds of the cost of housing comes from the cost of borrowing money—interest on construction loans and mortgages. Therefore, using capital grants rather than interest-bearing loans to finance construction and rehabilitation should cut the cost of each unit in the program to

two-thirds below market rate. This model has worked very well in Europe, and should be highly successful here as well *if* adequate funding were provided.

Perhaps the most important lesson we can learn from the affordable housing shortage of the 1980s is that a change in attitude is essential. Low-income housing is at least as important to the ecology of cities as northern spotted owls are to the ecology of Pacific Northwest forests. Whereas low-income housing units used to be considered a blight in need of removal through slum clearance, now we understand that low-income housing units need to be protected almost as if they were endangered species. Given high rates of poverty, when low-income housing units are lost, homelessness is sure to follow. 48

Poverty Policy Recommendations

In addition to increasing the number of affordable low-cost housing units, the other important way to decrease the number of homeless families is to lessen the number of families living in poverty. Work that pays more than a poverty wage is the key to decreasing family poverty. For the last 25 years the "baby boomers" have inundated the U.S. economy with an oversupply of workers (Levy, 1987). When there are more workers than there are jobs, some people—usually those with the least education and training, and/or those with perceived "handicaps" such as being women, minorities, or disabled—will be unable to find work (McChesney, in press). Under these economic conditions the United States' major antipoverty strategy has been to provide the poor with charity—welfare. (The only economic strategy that has been able to absorb all those excess workers was fighting a war.) 49

Conditions will be different in the 1990s. As we move into the first peacetime shortage of workers in the United States in this century, there will be more jobs than there are workers, especially in industries that require technical skills and education (Johnston & Packer, 1987). Consequently, we have a real opportunity to revamp the basic assumptions underlying our social welfare programs—away from income support and toward employment and training. 50

With the new shortage of workers, especially entry-level workers, the concept of AFDC as a long-term income support program could be abolished. A uniform, mandatory payroll deduction program for supporting children in single-parent families, with government providing benefits up to a standard level where absent parents' wages are inadequate (similar to the original version of the Wisconsin program), should be substituted for AFDC (Ellwood, 1988). In addition, for able-bodied parents who are ineligible for unemployment insurance, AFDC could become a full-fledged employment and training program, with income support, child care, and health benefits for trainees, and with transitional 51 assistance for parents entering the labor force. Similarly, unemployment insurance should be expanded to cover all who need it, but its emphasis should be changed to retraining and job placement, perhaps with relocation benefits to move job seekers to cities where they have found work.

If projections for the coming decade's labor force supply and skills mix are correct, the 1990s will provide an important economic window for making fundamental changes in poverty policy. If policies are changed so that child care, health care, and employment and training are provided, many single mothers will have the opportunity to leave AFDC rolls permanently and join the labor force. While many of these families would still be living under the poverty line (unless service sector wages rise), they would have an increase in disposable income and could afford to pay more for housing, thus potentially decreasing the total number of homeless families. If such a rise in disposable income among families were coupled with significant progress in increasing the number of affordable low-income housing units, there should be a clear decrease in the total number of homeless families in the United States. *52*

Conclusion

In summary, when there are many more poor households than there are affordable low-income housing units, some families will become homeless, regardless of the personal characteristics of their members. Therefore, the only way to decrease the total number of homeless families is to decrease the number of households living below the poverty line and/or increase the number of low-income housing units until they are roughly equal in number. *53*

Private nonprofits have been the major providers of assistance to homeless families in most cities. The kinds of programs that nonprofits can afford—emergency shelters, service delivery, and transitional housing—can be of great assistance to families in meeting their short-term needs. However, most of these types of programs will be ineffective in reducing the total number of homeless families because they do not decrease the poverty rate or increase the total number of low-income housing units. What is needed to decrease the number of homeless families in the United States is a fundamental change in both national poverty policy and national housing policy. *54*

References

Apgar, W. C., Brown, H. J., Doud, A. A., & Schnik, G. A. (1985). *Assessment of the likely impacts of the president's tax proposals on rental housing markets.* Cambridge, MA: Joint Center for Housing Studies of MIT and Harvard University.

Bratt, R. G., Hartman, C., & Meyerson, A. (Eds.). (1986). *Critical perspectives on housing.* Philadelphia, PA: Temple University Press.

Clay, P. L. (1987). *At risk of loss: The endangered future of low-income rental housing resources.* Washington, DC: Neighborhood Reinvestment Corporation.

Danziger, S., & Gottschalk, P. (1985). *The changing economic circumstances of children: Families losing ground* (Discussion Paper No. 801-85). Madison, WI: Institute for Research on Poverty.

Dolbeare, C. (1986). *Rental housing crisis index.* Washington, DC: National Low Income Housing Coalition.

Dolbeare, C. (1988). *The low income housing crisis and its impact on homelessness.* Paper presented at the Advisory Commission on Intergovernmental Relations policy conference on Assisting the Homeless, Washington, DC.

Ellwood, D. T. (1988). *Poor support: Poverty in the American family.* New York: Basic Books.

Gilderbloom, J. I., & Appelbaum, R. P. (1988). *Rethinking rental housing.* Philadelphia, PA: Temple University Press.

Hartman, C. (1986). *The housing part of the homelessness problem.* Paper presented at conference on Homelessness: Critical Issues for Policy and Practice, Boston.

Hartman, C., & Stone, M. E. (1986). A socialist housing alternative for the United States. In R. G. Bratt, C. Hartman, & A. Meyerson (Eds.), *Critical perspectives on housing* (pp. 484–513). Philadelphia, PA: Temple University Press.

Hopper, K., & Hamberg, J. (1986). The making of America's homeless: From skid row to new poor, 1945–1984. In R. G. Bratt, C. Hartman, & A. Meyerson (Eds.), *Critical perspectives on housing* (pp. 14–40). Philadelphia, PA: Temple University Press.

Johnston, W. B., & Packer, A. H. (1987). *Workforce 2000.* Indianapolis, IN: Hudson Institute.

Leonard, P. A., Dolbeare, C. N., & Lazere, E. B. (1989). *A place to call home: The crisis in housing for the poor.* Washington, DC: Center on Budget and Policy Priorities.

Levy, F. (1987). *Dollars and dreams: The changing American income distribution.* New York: Russell Sage Foundation.

McChesney, K. Y. (1987). *Women without: Homeless mothers and their children.* Unpublished dissertation, University of Southern California.

McChesney, K. Y. (in press). Child and youth homelessness: Causes in society and in the economy. In L. Salomon, J. Kryder-Coe, & J. Molnar (Eds.), *Homeless children and youth: An analysis.* Transaction Press.

National Housing Conference. (1984). *Housing costs in the United States.* Washington, DC: Author.

Parham, P. G. Testimony before Washington, DC, City Council Committee on Human Services. *Oversight hearing on general contracting practices within the Department of Human Services.* Washington, DC: City Council.

U.S. Bureau of the Census. (1989). *Poverty in the United States: 1987* (Current Population Reports, Series P-60, No. 163). Washington, DC: U.S. Government Printing Office.

Waxman, L. D., & Reyes, L. M. (1987). *A status report on homeless families in America's cities—a 29-city survey.* Washington, DC: U.S. Conference of Mayors.

Wright, J. D., & Lam, J. A. (1987). Homelessness and the low-income housing supply. *Social Policy, 17*, 48–53.

HOMELESSNESS AS PSYCHOLOGICAL TRAUMA
Broadening Perspectives

Lisa Goodman
Leonard Saxe
Mary Harvey

Homelessness has become a national tragedy that affects individuals and families throughout the United States, including increasing numbers of women and children (Institute of Medicine, 1988; Rossi, Wright, Fisher, & Willis, 1987; U.S. Conference of Mayors, 1986; U.S. General Accounting Office, 1988, 1989). Safe, adequate, and affordable housing is the most pressing need of homeless people. However, as the number of homeless people increases (Rossi, 1990; U.S. Conference of Mayors, 1987), it is also essential to identify and address associated mental health issues. Most recent literature on the relationship between mental health and homelessness has described attempts to identify individual characteristics that may be risk factors for homelessness (e.g., Breakey et al., 1989; Wood, Valdez, Hayashi, & Shen, 1990). In contrast, we argue that homelessness is itself a risk factor for emotional disorder (see, e.g., Dohrenwend & Dohrenwend, 1974; Institute of Medicine, 1988; Rivlin, 1986) and we propose that psychologists can play an important role in addressing the psychological consequences of homelessness, regardless of the presence or absence of prior mental health difficulties.

In this article, we use the construct of psychological trauma as a means of understanding the potential effects of homelessness on individuals and families. Psychological trauma refers to a set of responses to extraordinary, emotionally overwhelming, and personally uncontrollable life events (Figley, 1985b; Van der Kolk, 1987a). These events may be discrete and clearly bounded, such as rape, or prolonged and ongoing, such as battering or combat (see, e.g., Figley, 1985b; Van der Kolk, 1987b). A wide range of symptoms or psychological conditions have been included under the rubric of psychological trauma, many of which involve the rupture of interpersonal trust and the loss of a sense of personal control. Each of these phenomena will be discussed in more detail later in this article.

Trauma theory and research may provide a useful lens through   *3*
which to view and understand the experience of homelessness in at least
three respects. First, the event of becoming homeless—of losing one's
home, neighbors, routines, accustomed social roles, and possibly even
family members—may itself produce symptoms of psychological trauma
in some victims. Typically, the transition from being housed to being
homeless lasts days, weeks, months, or even longer. Most people living
on the street or in shelters have already spent time living with friends or
relatives and may have experienced previous episodes of homelessness
(see, e.g., Shinn, Knickman, & Weitzman, 1989, 1991; Sosin, Piliavin, &
Westerfelt, 1991). The loss of stable shelter, whether sudden or gradual,
may produce symptoms of psychological trauma. Second, among those
who are not psychologically traumatized by becoming homeless, the ongoing condition of homelessness—living in shelters with such attendant
stressors as the possible loss of safety, predictability, and control—may
undermine and finally erode coping capabilities and precipitate symptoms of psychological trauma. Third, if becoming homeless and living
in shelters fail to produce psychological trauma, homelessness may exacerbate symptoms of psychological trauma among people who have histories of victimization. For these people, homelessness may constitute a
formidable barrier to recovery.

We do not attempt to prove that homelessness causes psychological   *4*
trauma. Rather, we draw on psychological trauma theory to elucidate
preliminary empirical and anecdotal findings, to highlight the benefits of
applying psychological theory to the study of homelessness, and to offer
potentially fruitful avenues for further research. In the first section of this
article we review selected literature on psychological trauma and consider
in greater depth its relationship to homelessness. In the second section
we examine the mental health and social policy implications of viewing
homelessness as a cause of, or contributor to, psychological trauma. We
argue that mental health professionals can use their understanding of
psychological trauma to make shelters and other settings more responsive
to the needs of homeless people. We conclude that improving the conditions of shelter life could prevent the development of psychological
trauma or mitigate its most damaging symptoms.

PSYCHOLOGICAL TRAUMA AS A CONSEQUENCE OF HOMELESSNESS

The category *psychological trauma* has been used to explain a variety   *5*
of symptoms and conditions commonly found among victims of extraordinary stress (see, e.g., Figley, 1985b; Van der Kolk, 1984, 1987b).
Many of these symptoms have been grouped to form the diagnostic
entity *posttraumatic stress disorder* (PTSD) in the revised third edition of

the *Diagnostic and Statistical Manual of Mental Disorders* (*DSM-III-R*; American Psychiatric Association, 1987). This diagnosis captures the constellation of symptoms common among victims of an acute traumatic event, including persistent reexperiencing of the traumatic event through intrusive recollections, dreams, or dissociative states; a numbing of general responsiveness manifested by a restricted range of affect or a markedly diminished interest in significant activities; and persistent symptoms of increased arousal, such as irritability, angry outbursts, hypervigilance, and sleep disturbances. Other symptoms included under the more general rubric of *psychological trauma*, and common among victims of chronic or ongoing trauma, include substance abuse, self-mutilation, intolerance of intimacy, a general sense of helplessness, and a sense of isolation and existential separateness from others (Figley, 1985a; Harvey, 1991).

Individual reactions to potentially traumatic events vary widely, depending on complex interactions between person, event, and environmental factors (Harvey, 1991; Koss & Harvey, 1991; Toro et al., 1991). The nature and duration of the event or events, the age and predisposing attributes of the victim, and the reaction of the larger community each play a role in determining the nature and extent of a victim's response (Green, Wilson, & Lindy, 1985; Harvey, 1991). 6

Recently, Smith (1991) investigated the prevalence of PTSD among a sample of 300 randomly selected homeless single women and mothers in St. Louis, Missouri. Using the Diagnostic Interview Schedule (DIS; Robins, 1981; Robins & Helzer, 1984), she found that 53% of the respondents could be diagnosed as exhibiting full-blown cases of PTSD. In addition, data from clinical observations, self-reports, and empirical studies suggest that at least two commonly reported symptoms of psychological trauma—social disaffiliation and learned helplessness—are highly prevalent among homeless individuals and families. These phenomena are discussed below, first in the context of trauma theory and then in the context of homelessness. The relationship between preexisting psychological trauma and current homelessness is also explored. 7

Social Disaffiliation

A key feature of psychological trauma is the felt and real experience of social disaffiliation. Bowlby (1969, 1973) described the human need for intimate and long-lasting attachments as a biological imperative that results from long-term evolutionary development. According to this theory, feelings of safety and connection are essential for children to attain the emotional security necessary to develop self-reliance, autonomy, and self-esteem. In adulthood, relationships with others continue to provide a fundamental sense of existential meaning and self-worth. 8

Building on Bowlby's work, Van der Kolk (1987a) proposed that the essence of psychological trauma is the perceived severance of secure 9 affiliative bonds, which damages the psychological sense of trust, safety, and security. "Trauma occurs," he wrote, "when one loses the sense of having a safe place to retreat within or outside oneself to deal with frightening emotions or experiences" (p. 31). Janoff-Bulman and Frieze (1983) described the same phenomenon from a social cognition perspective. They noted that trauma victims "no longer perceive themselves as safe and secure in a benign environment" because they "have experienced a malevolent world" (p. 5).

Trauma victims' sense of being without sanctuary in a world filled   *10* with malevolent forces is often compounded by actual failures of social support networks and by the social withdrawal of those on whom the victims have relied for support. People often react to victims by rejecting them. Some people are unsympathetic because they see victims as somehow responsible for their fate (Lerner, 1970; Ryan, 1971). Others do not want to associate with victims because they perceive them as "losers" (Bard & Sangrey, 1979). Still others perceive victims as depressed and therefore unpleasant to be with (Coates, Wortman, & Abbey, 1979). These and various other reactions can confirm and amplify victims' subjective feelings of isolation and so become obstacles to recovery from psychological trauma.

Homelessness, like other traumas, may produce a psychological   *11* sense of isolation or distrust as well as the actual disruption of social bonds. Anecdotal accounts (e.g., Hirsch, 1989; Kozol, 1988) reveal how becoming homeless strips people of most of their accustomed social roles. In most cases, homeless people can no longer fulfill their obligations as workers, neighbors, friends, or caregivers (Kozol, 1988). Many shelters and transitional facilities separate husbands from wives and teenage boys from their parents (Molnar, 1989), thereby diminishing the opportunities for homeless people, particularly family members, to perform their accustomed social roles. Patterns of relating to others, developed over a lifetime, are interrupted. Homeless people can lose faith in their own ability to care for themselves and in the willingness of others to help them, and may develop an abiding sense of distrust of others.

A number of empirical studies have provided evidence that social   *12* disaffiliation, a core feature of psychological trauma, is characteristic of many homeless individuals. Some researchers have suggested that social disaffiliation often precedes homelessness. Studies conducted in three cities demonstrated that homeless respondents were nearly twice as likely never to have married than were respondents who were not homeless (Farr, Koegel, & Burnam, 1986; Fischer, Shapiro, Breakey, Anthony, & Kramer, 1986; Roth, Bean, Lust, & Seveanu 1985). In another study comparing 536 domiciled and homeless persons in Chicago, Sosin, Colson, and Grossman (1988) found that the homeless respondents were more likely to have experienced out-of-home placement as children and were more likely to have lived alone as adults than had their domiciled counterparts.

Other research evidence, particularly in the area of family home- *13* lessness, suggests that homelessness may also precipitate or exacerbate feelings of interpersonal distrust and foster social isolation. In a recent study comparing the quantity and quality of social relationships among a sample of 50 homeless mothers and 50 housed mothers receiving Aid to Families with Dependent Children (AFDC), Goodman (in press) found that the homeless women scored significantly lower on a measure of degree of trust of others as sources of help. Although the relationship between homelessness and distrust revealed in this study was correlational rather than causal, qualitative sections of respondent interviews support the idea that a large proportion of the homeless mothers felt less able to trust others because they had not been protected from homelessness by friends, relatives, and social service providers.

Further evidence comes from a comparison of two studies, each of *14* which investigated the social networks of homeless mothers at different points in the transition to homelessness. Shinn et al. (1989, 1991) found that newly homeless mothers (i.e., those making first-time requests for shelter) were actually more likely than housed mothers on AFDC to have a living mother, grandmother, or close relative and to have seen these contacts recently. In contrast, Bassuk and Rosenberg (1988) found that mothers who had been homeless for a longer period of time reported significantly fewer supports than did their housed counterparts. When asked to name up to three individuals on whom they could count in times of stress, 74% of the housed and only 26% of the homeless women were able to name three adults. A comparison of these studies reveals relatively higher levels of social isolation among mothers who have spent time in shelters than among women just entering the shelter system, suggesting that homelessness may precipitate or coincide with a rapid disintegration of social networks.

Learned Helplessness

Although Van der Kolk (1987a) emphasized the relational ruptures wrought by a traumatizing event or series of events, other researchers have stressed the sense of helplessness that often ensues from such events (e.g., Flannery, 1987; Peterson & Seligman, 1983; Walker, 1978; Wilson, Smith, & Johnson, 1985). These authors viewed the sense of helplessness as a core element of psychological trauma and used the construct of learned helplessness (e.g., Seligman, 1975) to understand the diminished sense of efficacy and self-worth that is prevalent among trauma victims (Figley & McCubbin, 1983; Walker, 1978). People are said to experience learned helplessness, a phenomenon that is often accompanied by profound depression, when they lose the belief that their own actions can influence the course of their lives (Seligman, 1975). Research indicates that learned helplessness is most likely to occur when people hold themselves personally responsible for their situations, perceive the situations as long-term, or believe that the situations are caused by global rather than specific factors (Garber & Seligman, 1980). However, it should be noted that some behaviors that appear to reflect learned helplessness may actually be adaptive responses to an environment that does not offer alternatives to continued victimization (Flannery & Harvey, 1991).

Behaviors indicative of learned helplessness may be consequences 15 of homelessness because, like other traumas, becoming homeless frequently renders people unable to control their daily lives. Homeless people, whether they live in the streets, in cars, in shelters, in welfare hotels, or in other temporary accommodations, experience daily assaults on their sense of personal control. They may depend on help from others to fulfill their most basic needs, such as eating, sleeping, keeping clean, guarding personal belongings, and caring for children. Although the poverty that precedes most homelessness (Rossi, 1990) is itself likely to engender feelings of [helplessness] and depression (e.g., Holzer et al., 1986), homelessness, by adding a new dimension of deprivation, is likely to greatly exacerbate these feelings.

Although researchers have not yet directly investigated the extent 16 of learned helplessness among homeless people, they have documented high rates of depression, a component of learned helplessness, among the homeless. For example, in Breakey et al.'s (1989) survey of homeless people in Baltimore, affective disorders were the most frequently identified *DSM-III-R* Axis I diagnoses other than substance abuse. In a study of homeless women in New York City, D'Ercole and Struening (1990) reported that on a commonly used measure of depression, their respondents obtained a mean score well above that used as a cutoff for clinical depression. These findings are not proof that homelessness leads to depression, as depression has also been shown to precede homelessness (see Breakey et al., 1989; Koegel, Burnam, & Farr, 1988). However, they are consistent with the theory that becoming homeless and living in a shelter can exacerbate a person's sense of helplessness and thus heighten the risk of depression. Anecdotal accounts provide further support. In a poignant description of homeless families in New York City shelters and hotels, Kozol (1988) recorded one mother's sense of helplessness and despair:

> There's a crucifix on the wall. I ask her: "Do you pray?" "I don't pray! Pray for what? I been prayin' all my life and I'm still here. When I came to this hotel I still believed in God. I said: 'Maybe God can help us to survive.' I lost my faith. My homes. And everything. Ain't nobody— no God, no Jesus—gonna help us in no way. God forgive me. I'm emotional . . . I'm scared to sleep. If I eat, I eat one meal a day. My

stomach won't allow me. I have ulcers. I stay in this room. I hide."
(p. 67)

Learned helplessness theory suggests that the real absence of control   *17*
in the lives of homeless people eventually can engender a generalized
passivity. The ongoing experience of helplessness may lead to an apparent unwillingness on the part of some homeless people to fight for
themselves or to utilize the often meagre services available to them. Some
may come to view their daily difficulties with apparent indifference, as if
they do not expect to move into better circumstances, whereas others
may become overly dependent on social service or mental health professionals. In either case, as the stressors inherent in being homeless persist,
feelings of helplessness and the passivity these feelings engender can become entrenched and pervasive (Flannery, 1987).

Trauma Histories among Homeless People

A growing body of literature suggests that a significant proportion   *18*
of homeless people, especially women, have histories of traumatic victimization. In an investigation of the rates of victimization experiences
among homeless women with and without children in New York City
(D'Ercole & Struening, 1990), 43% of 141 respondents reported being
raped by a family member or other adult, 74% reported being physically
abused, and 25% reported being robbed. In a study comparing homeless
and housed mothers in Boston, Bassuk and Rosenberg (1988) found that
41% of the homeless and only 5% of the housed respondents reported
physical abuse in their childhoods; 41% and 20% respectively reported
that they had been battered in at least one adult relationship. And in a
study comparing newly homeless and housed mothers in New York City,
Shinn, Knickman, and Weitzman (1989, 1991) found that 11.4% of the
shelter requesters, compared with only 6.5% of the housed mothers,
reported childhood histories of physical abuse; 9.9% and 4.2%, respectively, reported childhood sexual abuse; and 27% and 16.6%, respectively,
reported having been abused or threatened as adults.

Finally, in a recent study comparing the prevalence of histories of   *19*
physical and sexual abuse among 50 homeless mothers and 50 housed
mothers receiving AFDC in two New England cities, Goodman (1991)
found that although there were no significant differences between the
two groups on three of the four types of abuse investigated, the prevalence of abuse among both groups was extraordinarily high. Fifty-seven
percent of the total sample reported having been physically abused in
childhood, 46% reported having been sexually abused in childhood, 67%
reported adult physical abuse, and 37% reported adult sexual abuse. Indeed, 89% of the total sample had experienced some form of physical or
sexual abuse in their lifetimes.

Many homeless women may therefore bring symptoms of psycho-   20
logical trauma to their new circumstances. Some may present with clear
diagnoses of PTSD, others with histories of alcohol and substance abuse,
and still others may suffer from social disaffiliation and learned helplessness. Thus, even when becoming homeless or living under the extraordinary stress of shelter life do not produce symptoms of psychological
trauma, homeless people may nevertheless manifest such symptoms. For
these people, homelessness may exacerbate existing psychological difficulties and complicate the recovery process. The traumatic effects of
abuse and homelessness may compound each other to produce even
greater psychological damage.

TREATMENT AND POLICY IMPLICATIONS

Viewing homelessness as a psychologically traumatic experience has   21
a number of implications for psychologists and other mental health practitioners. Given that the presence and severity of psychological trauma
depends in large part on community response to victims and the overall
environment in which they function (see, e.g., Green et al., 1985), improving the psychosocial conditions of shelter life could mitigate or even
prevent the development or exacerbation of psychological trauma.

In this section, we offer some examples of services and systemic   22
interventions that might result from the application of trauma theory to
the understanding of homelessness. Several of the examples we cite are
drawn from initiatives that have been undertaken by innovative shelter
providers throughout the country (Goodman, 1989). Shelters and other
settings in which homeless individuals and families reside and function
must promote social connections among homeless people and between
homeless people and their communities. Routines must be developed
that ensure safety, offer support, encourage mastery, and preserve, enhance, or restore feelings of self-worth and efficacy. Such efforts should
be part of a comprehensive service program that includes, at minimum,
case management (to coordinate services and link them with the housing
search process), job training, child care, medical care, substance abuse
treatment, psychological and educational services for children, and transportation to needed services (Bassuk, Carman, & Weinreb, 1990).

Several caveats to this discussion should be noted. First, because re-   23
searchers have not yet addressed the processes by which homelessness affects people, and systematic studies of programs for homeless individuals
and families have not been conducted (Saxe & Goodman, 1990), the
suggestions that follow are offered tentatively, as guidelines for services
and interventions that should be tested empirically for their effectiveness.
Second, these suggestions are not aimed at homeless people who suffer
from major mental illnesses such as schizophrenia, as they are likely to

require a more specialized array of services. Third, the present discussion focuses on homeless people in emergency or transitional shelters rather than on those who live on the streets or stay with friends. Fourth, the specific effects of homelessness on children are not addressed here, although children may suffer most from the deleterious conditions of shelter life (Bassuk & Rosenberg, 1990; Bassuk, Rubin, & Lauriat, 1986; Molnar, Klein, Knitzer, & Ortiz-Torres, 1988; Rafferty & Rollins, 1989). Finally, although the following comments focus on improving shelter conditions, people who have suffered the trauma of homelessness may continue to need psychological and other supportive services even after they regain permanent housing.

Social Support

As we noted earlier, many homeless people experience actual disruption of their social bonds as well as feelings of distrust and existential separateness. Researchers have demonstrated that positive social support following a traumatic event can help victims reestablish psychological well-being by enhancing self-esteem and a sense of connection to others (e.g., Janoff-Bullman & Frieze, 1983; Van der Kolk, 1987c). Furthermore, without a support network on which to rely in times of crisis, homeless people may have more difficulty returning to permanent housing and are at higher risk for repeated episodes of homelessness. Helping homeless individuals and families reestablish their relationships and their links to the community will enable them to take full advantage of housing opportunities when these arise. [24]

As a first step, every attempt should be made to help homeless individuals and families enter shelters in their own communities. The effort and expense of travel can impede the maintenance of social ties among homeless people who are removed from their neighborhoods. Physical distance may engender a sense of psychological distance that increases the sense of isolation. Shelter providers should encourage and help homeless residents maintain social networks, thereby building on strengths rather than focusing on deficits (Bassuk, 1990). In many cases, homeless people will have stayed with relatives before becoming homeless, straining and sometimes even exhausting these ties (see, e.g., Shinn et al., 1989, 1991). Once the daily pressure of living together is lifted, social bonds often can be rejuvenated (Goodman, 1989). [25]

Service providers must also help create a sense of interdependence and community within shelters. Staff should ensure that the shelter environment is physically safe and secure, because violence, substance abuse, and other disturbances in the shelter may inhibit occupants from establishing or maintaining social connections. Further, shelter staff can facilitate formal and informal opportunities for residents to share common experiences and develop a sense of mutuality and trust. Comfortable [26] common rooms, such as kitchens or dining rooms, allow residents to congregate and talk, play games, or share housing information. Peer support groups offer more formal opportunities for building supportive relationships. As Van der Kolk (1987c) noted, "Often fellow victims provide the most effective short-term bond because the shared history of trauma can form the nucleus for retrieving a sense of communality" (p. 154). Group members can learn not only that others are trustworthy, but also that they themselves are useful to other people. These groups may be especially helpful to people with abuse histories who need a safe place in which to reveal past experiences (Browne, 1990). Groups may continue even after shelter guests move into permanent housing, thereby supplementing other attachments in the community.

Finally, shelter staff should make every effort to involve residents of   27
local communities in working with their homeless neighbors. Most shelters for homeless individuals and families are not staffed by residents of the immediate neighborhood, because community members are often fearful, distrustful, or even hostile. As a result, homeless people in shelters are stigmatized and further isolated. Some shelters have been successful in enlisting the help of local community members, especially volunteers residing in the same area in which the homeless people formerly lived (Goodman, 1989). These volunteers can help reintroduce homeless individuals into the community.

Personal Control

In addition to enhancing homeless people's sense of community,   28
interventions should be designed to reduce helplessness and increase a sense of personal control. Although some trauma researchers have addressed the importance of helping victims after their beliefs concerning their own helplessness (e.g., Hartman & Burgess, 1985), others have emphasized the need to make real changes in the posttrauma environment (e.g., Flannery, 1987). In the case of homelessness, we propose that individuals must not only be helped to develop the internal resources to cope with stressful conditions, but also must be provided with as much real control as possible in order to increase autonomy and reduce the possibility of perpetuating traumatic conditions.

For example, shelter residents should have as much of the responsibility for organizing shelter life as they are able and willing to take.   29
Within reasonable limits, residents should negotiate shelter rules among themselves. These rules might govern visiting hours, eating and sleeping times, who may visit the shelter, how and to what extent shelter residents should cooperate in performing chores (such as meal preparation and child-care tasks), and even how shelter funds should be spent. Meetings might also be held to plan upcoming events, to share housing information, or to discuss emerging shelter problems or conflicts.

To help shelter residents gain some control in the world outside the   *30*
shelter, service providers should give residents as much information as
possible about their entitlement to benefits. Shelter staff, moreover,
should collaborate with residents to develop a feasible set of goals, often
called a *service plan,* based on clients' needs and wishes and on available
resources (Bassuk, 1990). Such a plan should include a reasonable strategy for obtaining permanent housing. Kozol (1988), in his account of
homeless families in New York, described the sense of futility and despair
that homeless people experience when their goals and daily activities are
imposed by unreasonable bureaucracies. For example, they may spend
their days searching for an affordable apartment that they know does not
exist, driven by the fear that their benefits will be cut if they do not try.
Impossible requirements such as these should be eradicated and replaced
by goals generated by the clients that are consistent with available services
and resources.

Finally, to ensure that available resources actually reach the intended   *31*
clients, case management should be made available to all shelter residents
who may be vulnerable to falling through the cracks of an increasingly
complex and fragmented service delivery system. These case managers
should be ready to assume a variety of roles including "that of service
broker, counselor, ombudsman, and advocate" (Bassuk, 1990, p. 25).

CONCLUSION

Most discussions of the mental health issues associated with home-   *32*
lessness address intrapsychic and interpersonal risk factors for homelessness. The psychological effects of losing one's home and entering the
ranks of the homeless are less well understood. Given the suggestive
research evidence presented in this article and the implications of psychological trauma theory, we believe that many homeless individuals and
families may be suffering both short- and long-term psychological devastation wrought by homelessness itself. This disturbing but as yet inconclusive evidence makes a more systematic research approach imperative.
To assess accurately the unique psychological effects of homelessness,
researchers should use an ecological framework (Bronfenbrenner, 1979;
Koss & Harvey, 1991; Milburn & D'Ercole, 1991; Toro et al., 1991) that
examines individual outcomes in the context of prior psychological resources, social context (including ethnic or racial membership, family
and community support, and political climate), community response to
homeless individuals and families, and the nature of the recovery environment developed in shelters. Furthermore, for their findings to be useful
to service providers and policymakers, researchers should seek to identify
the special characteristics or resources of those who respond adaptively to

the trauma of homelessness and should examine the nature of recovery environments that seem to prevent or mitigate negative outcomes.

There is widespread agreement that services to the homeless severely mentally ill population must be comprehensive and coordinated and provide for clients' mental health, housing, and support needs (Levine & Rog, 1990). Our analysis suggests that coordinated and comprehensive services should be offered to all people who reside in emergency and transitional shelters. Further, mental health consultation from clinicians and community and social psychologists is essential in the early stages of shelter planning. Training programs should be developed to help shelter staff work effectively with homeless people with diverse needs, many of whom may be suffering from social disaffiliation, learned helplessness, and other aspects of psychological trauma. Such programs increase knowledge and enhance skills among service providers and provide support to staff, thus reducing burnout and high turnover rates (Bassuk, 1990). Involvement of mental health practitioners may lead to shelters that are better designed to empower and support those who must suffer through the indignities of being without a home.

References

American Psychiatric Association. (1987). *Diagnostic and statistical manual of mental disorders* (3rd ed. rev.). Washington DC: Author.

Bard, M., & Sangrey, D. (1979). *The crime victim's book.* New York: Basic Books.

Bassuk, E. L. (1990). General principles of family-oriented care: Working effectively with clients. In E. L. Bassuk, R. W. Carman, & L. F. Weinreb (Eds.), *Community care for homeless families: A program design manual* (pp. 25–31). Washington, DC: Interagency Council on the Homeless.

Bassuk, E. L., Carman, R. W., & Weinreb, L. F. (1990). *Community care for homeless families: A program design manual.* Washington, DC: Interagency Council on the Homeless.

Bassuk, E. L., & Rosenberg, L. (1988). Why does family homelessness occur? A case control study. *American Journal of Public Health, 78,* 1097–1101.

Bassuk, E. L., & Rosenberg, L. (1990). Psychosocial characteristics of homeless children and children with homes. *Pediatrics, 85,* 257–261.

Bassuk, E. L., Rubin, L., & Lauriat, A. (1986). Characteristics of sheltered homeless families. *American Journal of Public Health, 76,* 1097–1101.

Bowlby, J. (1969). *Attachment and loss: Vol. 1. Attachment.* New York: Basic Books.

Bowlby, J. (1973). *Attachment and loss: Vol. 2. Separation.* New York: Basic Books.

Breakey, W. R., Fischer, P. J., Kramer, M., Nestadt, G. N., Romanoski, A. J., Ross, A., Royall, R. M., & Stine, O. C. (1989). Health and mental health problems of homeless men and women in Baltimore. *Journal of the American Medical Association, 262,* 1352–1357.

Bronfenbrenner, U. (1979). *The ecology of human development: Experiments by nature and design.* Cambridge, MA: Harvard University Press.

Browne, A. (1990). Family violence and homelessness. In E. L. Bassuk, R. W. Carman, & L. F. Weinreb (Eds.), *Community care for homeless families: A program design manual* (pp. 119–128). Washington, DC: Interagency Council on the Homeless.

Coates, D., Wortman, C. B., & Abbey, A. (1979). Reactions to victims. In I. H. Frieze, D. Bar-Tal, & J. S. Carroll (Eds.), *New approaches to social problems: Applications of attribution theory* (pp. 21–52). San Francisco: Jossey-Bass.

D'Ercole, A., & Struening, E. (1990). Victimization among homeless women: Implications for service delivery. *Journal of Community Psychology, 18,* 141–152.

Dohrenwend, B. P., & Dohrenwend, B. S. (1974). *Stressful life events: Their nature and effects.* New York: Wiley.

Farr, R. P., Koegel, P., & Burnam, A. (1986). *A study of homelessness and mental illness in the Skid Row Area of Los Angeles.* Los Angeles: County Department of Mental Health.

Figley, C. R. (1985a). From victim to survivor: Social responsibility in the wake of a catastrophe. In C. R. Figley (Ed.), *Trauma and its wake: The study and treatment of post-traumatic stress disorder* (pp. 398–415). New York: Brunner-Mazel.

Figley, C. R. (Ed.). (1985b). *Trauma and its wake: The study and treatment of post-traumatic stress disorder.* New York: Brunner-Mazel.

Figley, C. R., & McCubbin, H. I. (Eds.). (1983). *Stress in the family: Volume II. Coping with catastrophe.* New York: Brunner-Mazel.

Fischer, P. J., Shapiro, S., Breakey, W. R., Anthony, J. C., & Kramer, M. (1986). Mental health and social characteristics of the homeless: A survey of mission users. *American Journal of Public Health, 76,* 519–524.

Flannery, R. (1987). From victim to survivor: A stress management approach in the treatment of learned helplessness. In B. A. Van der Kolk (Ed.), *Psychological trauma* (pp. 217–233). Washington, DC: American Psychiatric Press.

Flannery, R., & Harvey, M. (1991). Psychological trauma and learned helplessness: Seligman's paradigm reconsidered. *Psychotherapy, 28,* 374–378.

Garber, D. S., & Seligman, M. E. P. (1980). *Human helplessness.* New York: Academic Press.

Goodman, L. A. (1989). *Community of Hope.* Unpublished manuscript.

Goodman, L. A. (1991). The prevalence of abuse in the lives of homeless and housed poor mothers: A comparison study. *American Journal of Orthopsychiatry, 61,* 489–500.

Goodman, L. A. (in press). The relationship between social support and family homelessness: A comparison study of homeless and housed mothers. *Journal of Community Psychology.*

Green, B. L., Wilson, J. P., & Lindy, J. D. (1985). Conceptualizing post-traumatic stress disorder: A psycho-social framework. In C. R. Figley (Ed.), *Trauma and its wake: The study and treatment of post-traumatic stress disorder* (pp. 53–69). New York: Brunner-Mazel.

Hartman, C. R., & Burgess, A. W. (1985). Illness-related post-traumatic stress disorder: A cognitive behavioral model of intervention with heart attack victims. In C. R. Figley (Ed.), *Trauma and its wake: The study and treatment of post-traumatic stress disorder* (pp. 338–355). New York: Brunner-Mazel.

Harvey, M. R. (1991). *An ecological approach to the treatment of trauma victims.* Manuscript submitted for publication.

Hirsch, K. (1989). *Songs from the alley.* New York: Ticknor & Fields.

Holzer, C., Shea, B., Swanson, J., Leaf, P., Myers, J., George, L., Weissman, L., & Bednarski, P. (1986). The increased risk for specific psychiatric disorders among persons of low socioeconomic status. *The American Journal of Social Psychiatry, 6,* 259–271.

Institute of Medicine. (1988). *Homelessness, health, and human needs.* Washington, DC: National Academy Press.

Janoff-Bulman, R., & Frieze, I. H. (1983). A theoretical perspective for understanding reactions to victimization. *Journal of Social Issues, 39*(2), 1–17.

Koegel, P., Burnam, A., & Farr, R. K. (1988). The prevalence of specific psychiatric disorders among homeless individuals in the inner city of Los Angeles. *Archives of General Psychiatry, 45,* 1085–1092.

Koss, M. P., & Harvey, M. R. (1991). *The rape victim: Clinical and community interventions* (2nd ed.). Newbury Park, CA: Sage.

Kozol, J. (1988). *Rachel and her children: Homeless families in America.* New York: Ballantine Books.

Lerner, M. (1970). The desire for justice and reactions to victims: Social psychological studies of some antecedents and consequences. In J. Macaulay & L. Berkowitz (Eds.), *Altruism and helping behavior* (pp. 205–229). San Diego, CA: Academic Press.

Levine, I. S., & Rog, D. J. (1990). Mental health services for homeless mentally ill persons: Federal initiatives and current service trends. *American Psychologist, 45,* 963–968.

Milburn, N., & D'Ercole, A. (1991). Homeless women: Moving toward a comprehensive model. *American Psychologist, 46,* 1161–1169.

Molnar, J. (1989, August). *A developmental profile of children and families in poverty.* Paper presented at the 97th Annual Convention of the American Psychological Association, New Orleans, LA.

Molnar, J., Klein, T., Knitzer, J., & Ortiz-Torres, B. (1988). *Home is where the heart is: The crisis of homeless children and families in New York City.* New York: Bank Street College of Education. (ERIC Document Reproduction Service No. ED 304 228).

Peterson, C., & Seligman, M. E. P. (1983). Learned helplessness and victimization. *Journal of Social Issues, 2,* 103–116.

Rafferty, Y., & Rollins, N. (1989). *Learning in limbo: The educational deprivation of homeless children.* New York: Advocates for children of New York, Inc.

Rivlin, L. G. (1986, Spring). A new look at the homeless. *Social Policy,* 3–10.

Robins, L. (1981). National Institute of Mental Health Diagnostic Interview Schedule. *Archives of General Psychiatry, 38,* 381–389.

Robins, L., & Helzer, J. (1984). *PTSD section for the Diagnostic Interview Schedule.* Unpublished manuscript, Washington University, St. Louis, MO.

Rossi, P. H. (1990). The old homeless and the new homelessness in historical perspective. *American Psychologist, 45,* 954–959.

Rossi, P. H., Wright, J. D., Fisher, G. A., & Willis, G. (1987). The urban homeless: Estimating composition and size. *Science, 235,* 1336–1341.

Roth, D., Bean, J., Lust, N., & Seveanu, T. (1985). *Homelessness in Ohio: A study of people in need.* Columbus: Ohio Department of Mental Health.

Ryan, W. (1971). *Blaming the victim.* New York: Vintage Books.

Saxe, L., & Goodman, L. (1990). Research issues for homeless families. In J. P. Morrissey & D. L. Dennis (Eds.), *Homelessness and mental illness: Toward the next generation of research studies* (pp. 88–93). Washington, DC: National Institute of Mental Health.

Seligman, M. E. P. (1975). *Helplessness: On depression, development and death.* San Francisco: Freeman.

Shinn, M., Knickman, J., & Weitzman, B. (1989, August). *Social relationships and vulnerability to becoming homeless among poor families.* Paper presented at the 97th Annual Convention of the American Psychological Association, New Orleans, LA.

Shinn, M., Knickman, J. R., & Weitzman, B. C. (1991). Social relationships and vulnerability to becoming homeless among poor families. *American Psychologist, 46,* 1180–1187.

Smith, E. (1991). [Patterns of alcoholism in subsamples of the homeless]. Unpublished raw data.

Sosin, M. R., Colson, P., & Grossman, S. (1988). *Homelessness in Chicago: Poverty and pathology, social institutions and social change.* Chicago: University of Chicago School of Social Service Administration.

Sosin, M. R., Piliavin, I., & Westerfelt, H. (1991). Toward a longitudinal analysis of homelessness. *Journal of Social Issues, 46*(4), 157–174.

Toro, P. A., Trickett, E. J., Wall, D. D., & Salem, D. A. (1991). Homelessness in the United States: An ecological perspective. *American Psychologist, 46,* 1208–1218.

U.S. Conference of Mayors. (1986). *The continued growth of hunger, homelessness, and poverty in America's cities.* Washington, DC: Author.

U.S. Conference of Mayors. (1987). *Status report on homeless families in America's cities: A 29-city survey.* Washington, DC: Author.

U.S. General Accounting Office. (1988). *Homeless mentally ill: Problems and options in estimating numbers and trends.* Washington, DC: Author.

U.S. General Accounting Office. (1989). *Homelessness: Homeless and runaway youth receiving services at federally funded shelters.* Washington, DC: Author.

Van der Kolk, B. A. (Ed.). (1984). *Post-traumatic stress disorder: Psychological and biological sequelae.* Washington, DC: American Psychiatric Press.

Van der Kolk, B. A. (1987a). The psychological consequences of overwhelming life experiences. In B. A. Van der Kolk (Ed.), *Psychological trauma* (pp. 1–31). Washington, DC: American Psychiatric Press.

Van der Kolk, B. A. (Ed.). (1987b). *Psychological trauma.* Washington, DC: American Psychiatric Press.

Van der Kolk, B. A. (1987c). The role of the group in the origin and resolution of the trauma response. In B. A. Van der Kolk (Ed.), *Psychological trauma* (pp. 153–172). Washington, DC: American Psychiatric Press.

Walker, L. E. (1978). Battered women and learned helplessness. *Victimology, 2,* 525–534.

Wilson, J. P., Smith, W. K., & Johnson, S. K. (1985). A comparative analysis of PTSD among various survivor groups. In C. R. Figley (Ed.), *Trauma and its wake: The study and treatment of post-traumatic stress disorder* (pp. 142–172). New York: Brunner-Mazel.

Wood, D., Valdez, B., Hayashi, T., & Shen, A. (1990). Homeless and housed families in Los Angeles: A study comparing demographic, economic, and family function characteristics. *American Journal of Public Health, 80,* 1049–1052.

A Guide to Finding and Using Information

USING THE LIBRARY

Books vs. Periodicals

Conducting research in a college or university library may at first seem like a daunting task: The sheer number of sources available to you can appear overwhelming and intimidating. However, taking the time to learn what kinds of research materials your library provides and how to use them will ultimately lend depth as well as validity to your essays. Do not try to exhaust every source in one day, for by trying to find everything, you may end up finding nothing. Instead, keep a record of the different sources you have already used, as well as the ones you still wish to consult; this will help you keep the entire research process manageable.

When they hear the word *library,* most people naturally think first of books. Yet while books are excellent sources for all kinds of information, it is important to remember that a library contains numerous other sources, such as academic and scientific journals, magazines, newspapers, government publications, dissertation abstracts, and bibliographies. Any of these sources may prove invaluable to your research, for, while a book may provide a thorough treatment of some particular issue, articles in journals and newspapers can provide up-to-the-minute information on the same subject. This current information is especially important in the sciences and social sciences, where new experiments and research are almost constantly altering past findings and conclusions. Keep in mind that, while mastering the use of different sources may at first seem difficult, employing a variety of sources in your research papers will provide you with a wider and deeper discussion. However, it is also important to remember that the purpose of research is to expand your argument, not to replace it with a series of statistics or quotations. The sample research paper at the end of this section illustrates this point.

The Research Librarian

Nothing will be more helpful to you than the assistance of a trained research librarian. These members of the library's staff are usually located at the reference desk. Before embarking on a search, consult such a librarian to help you determine which sources will be best for you at your particular stage and level of research. Never be embarrassed about asking the reference librarians anything about the library or its workings: Their job is to assist you, and their expertise is wasted unless it is used.

LOCATING BOOKS

The Card Catalog

The card catalog is a record of all the library's books, classified alphabetically by their authors, titles, and subjects. If you know the title or author of a specific book you want, simply look for it in the corresponding card catalog. For example, if you wanted to find a copy of *Walden* by Henry David Thoreau, you could look either in the title cards under W or in the author cards under T. The card will resemble this one:

> P3541   **Thoreau, Henry David.**
> Thor   Walden. With an introduction
>   by Harold Smith. New York:
>   Random House, 1983.

The code in the upper-left corner is the book's call number, its "address" within the library. If you go to the shelf that houses books with this call number, you will be able to locate your book.

Always have a piece of scrap paper handy on which to record call numbers, and be sure to copy them completely and accurately. You may waste time looking for PZ4014 because you forgot that the proper number of your book is really PZ4114(t). The extra seconds you spend writing down call numbers could save you minutes when searching the shelves (commonly called "stacks"), and these minutes can add up to hours.

The subject catalog is slightly different from the author and title catalogs. It allows you to look up a particular subject (which can be a person, event, or issue) and find a list of books in the library that address the topic. For example, if you were researching animal rights, you would simply look under A in the subject catalog to find a number of cards with the heading "animal rights." Each card would look like an author or title card and provide you with the call number for a particular book.

Be aware that different libraries house their card catalogs in different ways. Some libraries keep the author and title cards together, but separate from the subject cards. Others keep all three catalogs separate, while still others combine all three.

If the card catalog provides no works dealing with your topic, try looking under a related topic before stopping your search. For example, if you are researching a paper in artificial intelligence, under "Artificial Intelligence" you may find a card that reads, "See Also: Computers"; you can then search under this heading. But you may find no cards at all with the heading "Artificial Intelligence," or the cards headed "computers" may not provide you with exactly the kind of books you need. In these cases you might search under "Robotics" or some other heading. In any event, always search under a variety of subject titles to be sure that you do not overlook what might be an important source. A reference book called *Library of Congress Subject Headings* can help you find the subject word you need to commence your search, if your library is organized by the Library of Congress system.

Electronic Catalogs

Many university libraries as well as many public libraries now feature electronic card catalogs, which can greatly reduce the time it takes you to search the card catalog. These catalogs work exactly like the card catalog, allowing you to search for books according to their authors, titles, or subjects. In addition, electronic catalogs can tell you if the book you want is in the library or currently on loan to another patron. If possible, try to use these catalogs first: Not only will you save time, but also these electronic catalogs are updated more often than their paper equivalents.

On-Line Catalogs and Databases

Some libraries subscribe to large databases that are used across the United States and Canada. The chief virtue of a database is that it usually provides up-to-date listings for specific articles and books concerning topics in different fields and disciplines. If you would like to search a database, your library may allow you to do so yourself, or a reference librarian may do it for you. Since on-line computer time can be expensive, your library may charge a fee for this service. Some of the more popular on-line databases are:

Bibliographical Retrieval Services (BRS)
DIALOG (a compendium of other databases)
Educational Research Information Center (ERIC)
Research Libraries Information Network (RAIN)
Online Computer Library Center (OCLC)

Remember that if you are given a book title from a database, you will then have to look it up in your library's card catalog to find out whether your library owns the book and where it is shelved.

Finding Your Books

Libraries use one of two systems to assign call numbers to books. The first is the older Dewey Decimal System, which uses numbers to classify books according to their categories:

000–099 General Works
100–199 Philosophy
200–299 Religion
300–399 Social Sciences
400–499 Language
500–599 Natural Science
600–699 Technology
700–799 Fine Arts
800–899 Literature
900–999 History and Geography

These divisions are further subdivided by groups of ten to classify works more narrowly within their broader fields. For example, 800–899 indicates literature in general, and the numbers 810–819 indicate American literature. Many public libraries still use this system to classify their books.

The Library of Congress system begins with letters to classify books within 21 general categories:

A   General Works
B   Philosophy, Psychology, and Religion
C   Auxiliary Sciences of History
D   History (General)
E,F   American History (North and South)
G   Geography, Anthropology, and Recreation
H   Social Sciences
J   Political Science and Official Documents
K   Law
L   Education
M   Music
N   Visual Arts
P   Language and Literature
Q   Science
R   Medicine
S   Agriculture
T   Technology
U   Military Science
V   Naval Science
Z   Bibliography and Library Science

Like the Dewey Decimal System, these categories are further subdivided according to more specific topics. Most university libraries now classify their books according to the Library of Congress system; however, some of those libraries still classify their older holdings by the Dewey Decimal System.

Once you have compiled your list of call numbers, you are ready to search your library's stacks. Simply go to the shelf that houses works on the subject depicted by your book's call number. For example, if your call number was PN1899.W5, you might find it on a shelf marked PN1860–2000. Larger, multifloor libraries often feature maps near elevators or staircases. Consult these to save time.

After you find your book, it is a good idea to scan its "home shelf" for other books on the same topic. Since the library uses a classification system based on subjects, books concerning the same subject will be housed together. This check will show you the range of titles the library offers on your topic. It will also provide a rough idea of the extent to which people have written about your topic; for example, the number of books on the death penalty will be considerably larger than the number of books on the death of Socrates. You also may find some titles you overlooked when searching the card catalog. Finally, if the book you seek has been slightly misplaced, you may find it near its proper position.

Recalls and Interlibrary Loans

If the book you want has been lent to another patron, many libraries allow you to recall the book and then borrow it for a designated length of time. If you want a book not owned by your library, you may acquire the book by requesting an interlibrary loan in which your library will try to borrow the book from another library and then lend it to you. Both recalls and interlibrary loans are performed by the library's staff; consult the circulation librarian for specific details.

Encyclopedias

Encyclopedias are helpful if you are looking for a general overview of a broad topic. However, you should avoid using encyclopedias in your research for just this reason: When arguing, you want to be as specific as possible, and the information contained in encyclopedias is often general and always dated with regard to current issues.

LOCATING PERIODICALS

Periodicals refers to any newspaper, magazine, or journal published on a regular basis. Most libraries subscribe to a number of periodicals, which they keep on their periodical shelves for a predetermined length of time. After this time is up, the periodicals are bound in covers (usually marked according to volume number) and housed in a different part of the library. Almost any research project must feature periodicals, because they are the primary sources for current information and opinions.

When searching for periodicals, proceed in the same manner as you would when searching for books: Keep a list handy to which you add complete citations as you research your topic, and, after compiling your initial list, search the library's periodical stacks for the articles. Ten is a practical number to use for measuring lists of citations: After finding roughly ten citations, search for the articles. Keep in mind, however, that your library may not subscribe to the particular periodicals you need; if this happens, you may want to talk to your circulation librarian about an interlibrary loan.

Using Indexes

While articles in periodicals are not listed in a library's card catalog, you can consult various indexes that function in the same general way. Most libraries keep their books and periodicals in different sections. Periodical indexes can generally be found in the periodical section, but feel free to ask your research librarian where to find a certain index or collection of periodicals.

The *Readers' Guide to Periodical Literature*

The *Readers' Guide to Periodical Literature* is the most widely consulted index to magazines. While no newspapers appear in the *Readers' Guide,* all the articles from over 100 magazines are listed every year. To use the *Readers' Guide,* simply look up your subject, which will appear alphabetically within the *Readers' Guide.* For example, if you were researching the ethics of genetic engineering, you might find the following entry:

> **Engineering, Genetic**
> Change for the Better? [scientists debate
> virtues of gen. eng.] W. Waltz. il *Scientific
> Quarterly* 11:17–22 Nov 7 '92

In simple terms this entry tells you that the article "Change for the Better?" was written by W. Waltz, is illustrated (il), and appears on pages 17 through 22 of *Scientific Quarterly,* volume 11, which is dated November 7, 1992. The bracketed passage is a summary of the article. The *Readers' Guide* features such summaries only when the title of the article does not connote in some way the subject of the article. Many other indexes use a format similar to the one employed by the *Readers' Guide;* if you are having difficulty understanding the codes of an index, instructions on how to read them usually appear in the index's preface.

The *Readers' Guide* is published monthly and then bound in one volume every year. If you are researching a controversial or current subject, begin with the most recent *Readers' Guide* available and work backward in time. When the number of articles in a year on a given issue substantially decreases, you will know that the level of controversy surrounding it has also decreased.

Social Sciences Index

The *Social Sciences Index* is very similar in format to the *Readers' Guide.* This index, however, is limited to articles about the social sciences, such as anthropology, psychology, sociology, and political science. The majority of articles listed in the *Social Science Index* are written by and addressed to scholars in various disciplines and will be found in academic journals rather than popular magazines.

Newspaper Indexes

Widely circulating newspapers such as the *New York Times* and the *Wall Street Journal* often provide their own indexes, arranged according to subject.

Infotrack and *Newsbank*

Infotrack and *Newsbank* are electronic indexes that allow you to search a large number of newspapers or periodicals for different subjects, titles, or authors in a very short time. *Infotrack* lists only newspaper articles; *Newsbank* does the same for magazines and is keyed to a corresponding collection of microfiche containing all articles in its database.

The chief benefit of these indexes is that you can search for articles on a subject without having to consult a new index for each different year. For example, if you were to search "abortion" in *Infotrack* or *Newsbank,* you would receive a list of articles on abortion published in the last few years. Another advantage of these indexes is that they are usually connected to a printer, which allows you to print out interesting citations as you see them on your computer screen, without having to write them down yourself. You then have a "ready list" of articles to locate.

One disadvantage of using *Infotract* and *Newsbank* is that their databases tend not to be as complete as those used by the editors of the *Readers' Guide.* Remember, therefore, that indexes such as *Infotrack* and the *Readers' Guide* should complement each other during your search.

Government Documents

Many university libraries are listed as United States Government Depositories. Every time any branch of the government releases a publication (such as the results of a study, the findings of a congressional committee, an analysis of information from the last census), a copy of that publication is sent to each of these libraries. Even if your library is not a government depository, it should still own the current indexes to these publications and should be able to acquire the ones you need through interlibrary loan.

Abstracts

An abstract is a short summary of the main points of a book or article. Collections of abstracts allow you to "skim" a number of articles in one sitting without having to look for the articles themselves. While you will eventually have to read a number of articles carefully, reading abstracts can save you time by helping you narrow your search to articles that pertain directly to your topic. Abstracts are very helpful to those researching a scientific issue, for they frequently summarize the findings of experiments and research. Some of the most popular collections are:

> *Biological Abstracts*
> *Book Review Digest*
> *Chemical Abstracts*
> *Historical Abstracts*
> *Physics Abstracts*
> *Women's Studies Abstracts*

Other Indexes and Sources

Your library may have a number of other indexes for different disciplines and subjects. Some of the more popular ones are:

> *Biography Index* (biographical information found in current books and periodicals)
> *Education Index* (articles pertaining to all areas of educational theory and child development)
> *Humanities Index* (articles on various topics in the humanities, such as archaeology, classics, folklore, religion, philosophy, and the arts)
> *Index Medicus* (periodical literature about medical topics)
> *MLA International Bibliography* (scholarly articles on language and literature of different countries and cultures)
> *Public Affairs Information Service* (articles concerning social and economic issues and international relations)

Finding Your Articles

Once you have compiled your list of citations, find out whether your library subscribes to the periodicals you need by consulting the library's Union List of Serials, an alphabetical listing of all your library's periodical holdings. Next look on the periodical shelves to see how long your library keeps its periodicals before binding them. If the articles you need are already bound, find out where your library keeps its bound periodicals, and locate your article there. Some periodicals may be kept on microfiche; ask your research librarian for details.

If you find an article that you think will be useful to you, make a photocopy of it. Do not summarize the articles as you find them; you might spend time summarizing an article only to find a better one after skimming several others. Be sure that you write on your photocopies the name of the publication in which you found the article, as well as the publication's volume number and the article's page numbers. This will help you when you are ready to compile your "Works Cited" list.

PUTTING YOUR RESEARCH TO USE

Taking Notes

The ability to take useful notes is a skill you will develop over time. Many beginning writers take too many notes and waste time copying one lengthy quotation after another. While all writers have different systems for taking notes, there are a few basic guidelines you should follow as you begin to develop your own:

- Be organized.
- Summarize instead of quoting.

BE ORGANIZED Even people who rarely write essays know that writers often put their notes on 3×5 index cards. The advantage of this technique is that, unlike larger pieces of paper, index cards are easy to rearrange. Arranging the information you have stored on note cards in different ways can give you a feel for the different ways your paper could be organized. To use index cards effectively, however, you must always adhere to one simple rule: *only one note or piece of information per note card.* At times you may be tempted to combine two notes on a similar idea on one card to avoid wasting space; the space you save, however, may be inconsequential compared with the inconvenience, annoyance, and confusion that may later ensue. As long as you have one note per card, you can literally "lay your cards on the table" and rearrange them in different ways; for example, what you may at first regard as a piece of evidence for your "backing," you may later decide to treat as a separate "claim."

Always keep all your note cards in the same place; when conducting research, you may find an argument that sounds similar or flatly contradictory to something you previously read. Having all your note cards with you will allow you to cross-reference arguments and facts without repeating yourself.

You probably will not use all the information on your note cards in the final draft of your essay. As your research proceeds, your focus will narrow, calling for more detailed and specialized information that you simply did not have at the start of your research. In this way, research becomes a process of discovery and not just an attempt to bolster your initial opinions.

What format your note cards take is up to you. An easy and efficient method, however, is one such as this:

(Source of note)   (Note card number)
(Note)

One final suggestion: Photocopy all bibliographic information for each source you consult and keep the photocopies in alphabetical order. This will save you the time of copying this information on separate bibliography cards, and when it comes time to write your essay's "Works Cited" section your references will already be alphabetized. (See "Documenting Sources" later in the chapter).

QUOTING VS. SUMMARIZING Because they want to be sure to "get it right," many beginning writers quote *everything,* wasting time as well as effort. A good rule of thumb when taking notes is to make one note card a "summary card" in which you write, in a sentence or two, a brief summary of the article or book you have just read. Next find one or two quotations that represent the work as a whole and copy them *exactly* on subsequent cards. (If the source is short enough to photocopy, you may want to highlight some quotations on your photocopy.) For each source, then, you will have a note card that summarizes the source, followed by a few cards that illustrate your summary. Of course, if you do find a quotation that you feel you will be able to use, copy it onto a note card.

Longer articles or books may require more note cards to summarize and more data to record. This is normal, although you should never spend too much time with a single source; summarizing each page of a long article or book may cause you to rely too heavily on that source and thereby write a lopsided argument.

A final tip for a project involving extended research: Review your notes every few days. Doing so will give you an idea of the course your research seems to be taking and the avenues you still need to explore.

When and How to Quote in Your Essay

Never include quotations in your paper simply because you feel that you "need them in an essay" or that you've "written too much without one." Quotations should be used as *evidence that supports the claim or warrant at hand.* If you are relying on a warrant with the backing of expert testimony, statistics, etc., quoting the material will strengthen your argument's ethos by showing your reader that your opinion is an informed one.

Always introduce your quotations gracefully into your text; don't just list them. A general test is to read a passage containing quotations aloud: The quoted material should "flow" into your own prose. Here are two possible ways to introduce the same quotation into an essay:

> Incorrect: Samuel Johnson also praised London. "When a man is tired of London, he is tired of life."
>
> Correct: As Samuel Johnson once remarked, "When a man is tired of London, he is tired of life" (Boswell, 231).

Notice how the second example inserts the quotation so that it reads as a natural part of the sentence. Also notice that immediately after the end quotation marks and before the punctuation mark, the writer has included a parenthetical reference indicating the author and page number of the quotation's original location. Phrases such as "once remarked," "as one expert has said," "as one critic has observed," "as one study has found," and so on, are all common ways to introduce quotations into your paper.

Above all, be sure that your paper is not a "quotation dump" in which you string together a large number of quotations—no matter how valid—without any of your own interpretations or remarks. This will indicate to your audience that you are hiding behind the opinions of others rather than using their opinions to strengthen your own argument.

Plagiarism

Plagiarism is an act of deception that occurs when you take someone else's words or ideas and pass them off as your own. However minor or inconsequential any such deception might seem to you, trying to deceive your audience violates the spirit of the objective pursuit of truth that has taken human beings out of the caves and put them on the moon. Institutions of higher learning always expect you to act as part of this great tradition, and the penalties for plagiarism are stiff, ranging from an F to expulsion.

An example of plagiarism—using the above sample quotation—would be to say, "When a man is tired of Manhattan, he is tired of life." Here is another, more detailed example:

> Original   "Anyone who knows the frantic temper of the
> Passage: present schools will understand the transvaluation of
>   values that would be effected by [the abolition of

grades]. For most of the students, the competitive grade has become the essence. The naive teacher points to the beauty and the ingenuity of the research; the shrewd student asks if he is responsible for that on the final exam."—Paul Goodman p. 34

Example of Plagiarism: If grades were abolished, our entire set of educational values would be upset. Many students see their grades as the essence of academic success; while their teachers may concern themselves only with their subject matter, the students want to know what they will need to know to pass an exam.

Although only a few exact words from the original appear in the example (*values, essence*) the exact idea is repeated without any credit to Paul Goodman. An example of quoting without plagiarizing would be:

Correctly Quoted: Paul Goodman has argued that abolishing grades would result in a "transvaluation of values" concerning education as a whole. Many students view their grades as the "essence" of education and are more concerned with what they need to know for exams rather than the "beauty and ingenuity" of their subject matters (Goodman, 34).

In general, when in doubt, provide a citation. This will save you the embarrassment of being accused of academic dishonesty.

Documenting Sources

The most obvious purpose of parenthetical references is to tell your readers the author and location of an idea or quotation in the event that they want to read more about your topic after they have finished your essay. The "Works Cited" page provides information for locating the sources themselves. Also note that this page is no longer called a "Bibliography," since that implies a list of books, and your sources may include periodicals, government documents, and so on.

The standard formats for all possible "Works Cited" entries can be found in the third edition of the *MLA Handbook for Writers of Research Papers* (New York: Modern Language Association of America, 1988). Every writer of research papers should consult this book when preparing his or her final draft. However, here are the formats for the most common types of sources:

A Book by a Single Author
Willeford, Charles. *New Hope for the Dead*. New York: Ballantine, 1985.

A Book by Two Authors
Killian, James, and Robert Cole. *Medical Ethics in America*. Boston: Globe, 1991.

A Book by More Than Two Authors
Black, Kristine, Katherine Whalen, and Amy Sadlowski. *Television and Children*. San Diego: Harcourt, 1991.

An Anthology or Compilation
Peil, Manfred, ed. *Modern Views on Classic Films*. Los Angeles: Smithdon, 1992.

A Work in an Anthology
Neary, Adam. "The Impossibility of Utopia." *Essays in Modern Political Theory*. Ed. Lenore Kingsmore. New York: Political Press, 1982.

An Unsigned Encyclopedia Article
"Coffee." *Encyclopedia Britannica*. 1992 ed.

A Signed Encyclopedia Article
Haseltine, William A. "AIDS." *Encyclopedia Americana*. 1992.

A Book by a Corporate Author
Editors, Inc. *How To Write Effective Prose*. New York: Editors, Inc., 1990.

An Introduction, Preface, Foreword, or Afterword
Sirr, Lauren. Preface. *School Certification and Its Critics*. Chicago: Copper Press, 1982.

A Multivolume Work
Moccio, Dominic, and Virginia Jones, eds. "Chandler and His Contemporaries." *The Detective Story*. Vol. 2. Philadelphia: Franklin, 1992. 3 vols.

A Translation
Salvatore Trebelli. *My Life on Stage*. Trans. Erin Cairns. New York: Musicland, 1972.

A Book in a Series
Barish, Paul. *Municipal Bonds*. Marketwise Press Essays on Finance Series 7. New York: Marketwise Press, 1991.

A Newspaper Article
Donner, Matthew. "The Plight of the Intern." *New York Times* 1 April 1990, sec. 2: 1+.

An Article from a Monthly Periodical
Genero Pinho, "Revitalizing Traditional Opera." *Opera Monthly*
Feb. 1991: 77–89.

An Unsigned Editorial
"Finally a Solution." Editorial. *Nation* 16 Dec. 1988: 12.

The APA System

The chief exception to the MLA system for documenting sources is the system used by the American Psychological Association (APA). As with the MLA, the APA requires short parenthetical references within the text of your essay which—unlike the MLA—require the date of publication. For example:

> Although many scientists claim that animal testing is unnecessary, few labs are taking steps to alter the current situation (Smith, 1992, 21).

Another difference between the MLA and APA is that the APA calls for the "Works Cited" page to be labeled "References." Furthermore, if your list of references includes more than one work written by the same author in the same year, you must cite the first work as "a," the second as "b," and so on. For example, if you used a second article written by Smith in 1992, you would cite it as (Smith, 1992b, page number). Finally, notice that first names are not provided in the APA system—only first initials—and that only the first words of titles and subtitles are capitalized. (Proper nouns are also capitalized.)

A Book by a Single Author
Anderson, N. (1992). *Modern sport psychology.* New York: Jacob-
son Press.

A Book by Two or More Authors
Bennet, M., & Juran, S. (1989). *Inventing culture.* Boston: Globe.

An Anthology or Compilation
Porpora, J. (1988). *Collected lyrics and letters.* Los Angeles: Music-
hall Press.

A Work in an Anthology
Lippman, S. (1987). Modern school law and its effects on teaching. In *First kill all the lawyers!* Chicago: Maplewood.

A Book by a Corporate Author
National Association of Anglers (1990). *The ten best bass rivers in
America: A guide.* Seattle: Nature Press.

An Introduction, Preface, Foreword, or Afterword
DePastino, A. (1983). Introduction. In R. Hastings, *A History of Radio* (i–xii). San Francisco: MediaPress.

A Translation
Segouin, J. (1976). *Selling the sunset.* (S. Moccio, Trans.) New York: Brookson.

A Book in a Series
Schultz, J. (1982). *The Elizabethan world.* (Vol. 11 of The history of thought series). New York: Edgeboro.

A Newspaper Article
Keane, V. (1990). More trouble for the troublemakers. *New York Newsday,* p. 21.

A Magazine Article
Burke, C. (1991, June). Doctors and demons. *Medical Ethics,* pp. 21–28.

Sample Research Paper

The following sample research paper illustrates MLA style and makes a cogent argument against the death penalty.

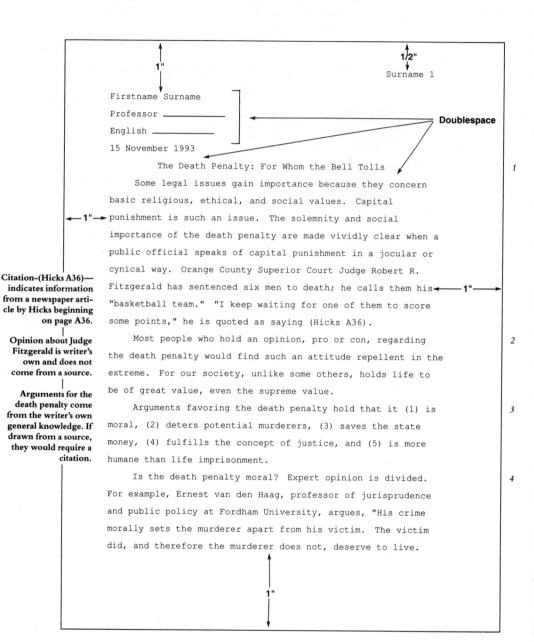

1"

1/2"

Surname 1

Firstname Surname

Professor ———————

English ———————

15 November 1993

Doublespace

The Death Penalty: For Whom the Bell Tolls

Some legal issues gain importance because they concern

basic religious, ethical, and social values. Capital

←1"→ punishment is such an issue. The solemnity and social

importance of the death penalty are made vividly clear when a

public official speaks of capital punishment in a jocular or

cynical way. Orange County Superior Court Judge Robert R.

Citation-(Hicks A36)— indicates information from a newspaper article by Hicks beginning on page A36.

Fitzgerald has sentenced six men to death; he calls them his ←——1"——→

"basketball team." "I keep waiting for one of them to score

some points," he is quoted as saying (Hicks A36).

Opinion about Judge Fitzgerald is writer's own and does not come from a source.

Most people who hold an opinion, pro or con, regarding

the death penalty would find such an attitude repellent in the

extreme. For our society, unlike some others, holds life to

be of great value, even the supreme value.

Arguments for the death penalty come from the writer's own general knowledge. If drawn from a source, they would require a citation.

Arguments favoring the death penalty hold that it (1) is

moral, (2) deters potential murderers, (3) saves the state

money, (4) fulfills the concept of justice, and (5) is more

humane than life imprisonment.

Is the death penalty moral? Expert opinion is divided.

For example, Ernest van den Haag, professor of jurisprudence

and public policy at Fordham University, argues, "His crime

morally sets the murderer apart from his victim. The victim

did, and therefore the murderer does not, deserve to live.

1"

1

2

3

4

Surname 2

His life cannot be sacred if that of his victim was" (61). However, Michael E. Endres, professor of criminal justice at Xavier University, says that capital punishment is immoral because

> the death penalty serves no rehabilitative purpose;
> it exceeds the requirements of justice and social
> unity; alternatives to it may serve the same purpose
> as well; finally, the incapacitation or special
> deterrence of a given offender is insured by
> execution, but there are other effective ways to
> inhibit reoffending. (67)

5   If it is moral to execute convicted, responsible adults, is it also moral to execute children or adults who are mentally retarded or insane? Only in 1990 did Missouri raise its age limit for capital punishment from fourteen to sixteen ("Juveniles" 1). Is a sixteen-year-old a responsible adult? If not, should an offender this young be executed? Currently, more than seventy-five death-row inmates committed their crimes before they were eighteen years old, and in the last decade at least four such offenders have been executed (Horgan 19). The United States of America joins only four other nations in executing juvenile offenders: Bangladesh, Barbados, Iran, and Iraq (Horgan 19).

6   Diminished mental capacity is a mitigating factor in capital offenses, and psychiatric evidence must be considered in all cases (Hood 63-64). However, psychiatrists who assess the defendant's mental state from the standpoint of both

Author being quoted, Michael E. Endres, is identified in the lead-in to the quotation; thus his name is omitted from the parenthetical citation at the end. The full source is found under "Endres" in "Works Cited."

Quotation more than four lines long is indented ten spaces and appears without quotation marks. Citation comes after final punctuation, separated by two spaces.

Source of information on age limits for juveniles is an anonymous newspaper article. Full information is under "Juveniles" in "Works Cited."

Both of the facts about the execution of minors come from page 19 of Horgan.

The two citations of Hood are for different kinds of information. The first is for a fact from Hood. The other is for Hood's opinion. Since both are from Hood, citations are required.

mitigation and potential for further violence are often in a double bind, for the very condition that mitigates the crime may, from another point of view, be the factor that makes the defendant a bad risk (Hood 64). Furthermore, psychiatry is more an art than a science and thus does not provide conclusive evidence for a decision regarding life or death.

Paragraph 7 states the writer's own conclusion, not that of a source.

The moral questions regarding capital punishment are open to so much controversy that it would be difficult for an informed person to take a definitive stand one way or the other on moral grounds.

7

The exact quotation is from Hood, page 167. Since Hood's name is mentioned in the lead-in to the quotation, his name is not repeated in the parenthetical citation.

Does the death penalty deter potential murderers? Roger Hood is clear on this question: "The evidence as a whole gives no positive support to the deterrent hypothesis" (167). One might argue, of course, that the mere existence of the death penalty is not a deterrent unless executions are actually carried out. Thus, as the number of executions increases, the frequency of murder should decline. However, according to

8

The citations indicate that the writer is summarizing pages 117–48 of Hood and using facts from pages 124–25 and 126 of Hood and page 17 of Horgan.

Hood (117-148), no evidence indicates that more frequent executions lead to lower homicide rates. For example, the last executions in Australia took place in the mid-1960s, but "the reported homicide rate per 100,000 of population has fallen, and the murder rate has remained constant" (Hood 124-25); in the United States, when the first execution took place after a decade-long moratorium, the homicide rate almost doubled, from 4.8 per 100,000 to 8.8 (Hood 126). Some admittedly inconclusive evidence suggests that executions may actually bring about more murders. One study, reported by

Surname 4

Horgan, indicates that in New York State between 1907 and 1963, the number of murders rose by an average of a bit more than two in the month following an execution (17).

9

Dividing murderers into two categories is useful when one considers the deterrence argument: what Adam Hugo Bedau terms "'carefully contemplated murders,' such as 'murder for hire'" (172) and so-called crimes of passion. As Bedau points out, those who carefully plan murders do so with a view of avoiding detection and punishment; hence, the threat of the death penalty plays little or no role in the decision to commit the crime. No threat would deter the killer who is carried away by uncontrollable rage or hatred.

The idea of dividing murderers into two types is the writer's own, but the quotation from Bedau provides information about one type. The citation points to a discussion on page 172 of Bedau.

10

If capital punishment is a deterrent, then painful methods of execution surely would have more effect than painless ones, yet Texas, Utah, and other states have adopted lethal injection as the method of execution--ameliorating the severity of the death penalty, supposedly for "humanitarian" reasons. On the other hand, states that use lethal gas as a means of execution do not make the agony of death by asphyxiation a matter of public knowledge. If the death penalty is a deterrent, the agonies of execution should not be reduced, as in Texas, or kept hidden from the public, as in California.

11

Since no one has been able to show that the threat of the death penalty reduces the number of murders, the argument for capital punishment on the basis of its deterrent value crumbles.

Surname 5

Does capital punishment save the state money? Robert L.   *12*
Spangenberg, an attorney who directs the Boston Legal
Assistance Project, points out that "states spend anywhere
from $1.6 million to $3.2 million to obtain and carry out a
capital sentence; states could incarcerate someone for 100
years or more for less money" (Horgan 18). Of course, even if
executing convicted murderers did cost more purely in terms of
dollars than incarcerating them, a cost/benefit analysis might
reveal that the death penalty is economically sound because it
provides social benefits such as protection from potential
murderers. However, as Bedau says,

> Since no adequate cost/benefit analysis of the death
> penalty exists, there is no way to resolve these
> questions from that standpoint at this time.
> Moreover, it can be argued that we cannot have such
> an analysis without already establishing in some way
> or other the relative value of innocent lives versus
> guilty lives. (38)

It appears, then, that economic arguments in favor of   *13*
capital punishment have no solid basis.

Does the death penalty fulfill the requirements of   *14*
justice? Immanuel Kant argued that justice demands--consists
in--complete equality; thus, if one murders, the commensurate
punishment is death. Bedau (17) quotes from The Metaphysical
Elements of Justice:

> What kind and what degree of punishment does public
> legal justice adopt as its principle? None other

The citation shows that Horgan (page 18) presents the information from Spangenberg.

Surname 6

than the principle of equality . . . , that is, the
principle of not treating one side more favorably
than the other. Accordingly, any undeserved evil
that you inflict on someone else among the people is
one that you do to yourself. . . . Only the law of
retribution . . . can determine exactly the kind and
degree of punishment. . . . All other standards
fluctuate back and forth and, because extraneous
considerations are mixed with them, they cannot be
compatible with the principle of pure and strict
legal justice. (Kant 101)

As Bedau points out, the principle of equality applies to
murderers who are intrinsically vicious and have rationally
willed to kill another. "If modern criminologists and
psychologists are correct, however," says Bedau, "most murders
are not committed by persons whose state of mind can be
described as Kant implies" (17). Even if we accept Kant's
principle of justice, we find that it is inapplicable in the
real world.

Finally, is it more humane to execute a convicted
murderer than to require him or her to spend years, or life,
in prison? It is, of course, impossible to make such a
judgment <u>for</u> the condemned. Lifers in prison do commit
suicide, and convicted murderers do ask for death rather than
life imprisonment. As Bedau says, however, it is impossible
to determine which is more severe, life in prison or death, for
there is no way to compare the two alternatives (27). We do

The writer found the quotation from Kant on page 17 of Bedau. The quotation, however, is from page 101 of Kant's book, as indicated in the parentheses at the end of the quotation. The writer knows Bedau's source because Bedau documented carefully.

Quotation marks show that the writer has used an exact quotation from Bedau's book (from page 17, as the citation indicates).

From Bedau (page 27) the writer gained the idea that it is impossible to determine whether life in prison or death is the more severe punishment; however, because Bedau's idea is paraphrased (that is, restated in the writer's own words), quotation marks are not used. However, Bedau must still be given credit.

know, however, that death makes it impossible to correct
errors in judgment. In any case, society does not base its
penalties on the preferences of the convicted.

There is, then, no agreement about the morality,   16
deterrent value, economic effectiveness, justice, or
humaneness of the death penalty--and there is always a
possibility that an innocent person will be put to death.

> In the past 18 years, at least 27 people condemned
> to death have later been found innocent by a higher
> court. Some of these reversals came about through
> sheer serendipity. The innocence of Randall Dale
> Adams, released [in 1989] after spending 12 years on
> death row in Texas for murdering a police officer,
> came to light only because a filmmaker happened to
> take an interest in the case. Others have not been
> so lucky. From 1900 to 1985, at least 23 Americans
> were executed for crimes they did not commit,
> according to a 1987 report in the Stanford Law
> Review. (Horgan 18)

The death penalty should be abolished. I believe that it   17
dehumanizes my society and hence robs me of part of my
humanity. The Declaration of Independence sets the standard:
"We hold these Truths to be self-evident, that all Men are
created equal, that they are endowed by their Creator with
certain unalienable rights, that among these are Life,
Liberty, and the Pursuit of Happiness." Individuals or the

Surname 8

state can take life only when no alternative exists, and quite
obviously alternatives to capital punishment do exist.

18

John Donne said it, and Ernest Hemingway echoed it: "Any
man's death diminishes me, because I am involved in Mankinde;
And therefore never send to know for whom the bell tolls; It
tolls for thee"--and me.

Surname 9

Works Cited

Bedau, Adam Hugo. Death Is Different: Studies in the
    Morality, Law, and Politics of Capital Punishment.
    Boston: Northeastern UP, 1987.

Donne, John. "Meditation 17." College Survey of English
    Literature, Ed. Alexander M. Witherspoon et al. Shorter
    ed., rev. New York: Harcourt, 1951. 340-41.

Endres, Michael E. "The Morality of Capital Punishment."
    Rpt. in The Death Penalty: Opposing Viewpoints. Ed.
    Bonnie Szumski, Lynn Hall, and Susan Bursell. St. Paul:
    Greenhaven Press, 1986. 62-67.

Hicks, Jerry. "O. C. Judge Decries Delay in Executing the
    'Deserving.'" Los Angeles Times 9 June 1991, Orange
    County ed.: A1+.

Hood, Roger. The Death Penalty: A World-Wide Perspective; A
    Report to the United Nations Committee on Crime
    Prevention and Control. Oxford: Oxford UP, 1989.

Horgan, John. "The Death Penalty." Scientific American July
    1990: 17-19.

Kant, Immanuel. The Metaphysical Elements of Justice. 1797.
    Trans. John Ladd. Indianapolis: Bobbs, 1965.

"Juveniles." Lifelines [National Coalition to Abolish the
    Death Penalty] April/May/June 1991: 1.

van den Haag, Ernest. The Death Penalty: A Debate. New York:
    Plenum, 1983. Excerpt rpt. in The Death Penalty:
    Opposing Viewpoints. Ed. Bonnie Szumski, Lynn Hall, and
    Susan Bursell. St. Paul: Greenhaven Press, 1986. 58-61.

GLOSSARY

ad hominem Latin for "to the man"; personal attack on an opponent instead of on the opponent's arguments

ad populum Latin for "to the people"; an argument that appeals to general sentiments or prejudices

allusion A reference to a person or fact (for example, the American Revolution) that the audience is expected to know without explanation

analogy A comparison for purposes of explanation, usually between something concrete and something abstract

appeal A traditional name for the method by which the arguer hopes to convince the reader; for example, the appeal to reason

assertion A declaration of belief

assumption Ideas or values that the writer takes as givens

audience The imagined readers of your argument

authority A reliable, expert source of support

backing The authority or evidence on which a warrant is based

begging the question An attempt to assume in advance what needs to be proved

bibliography A list of works on a subject

claim The conclusion your argument is attempting to prove

cliché An expression so worn out as to convey little meaning

connotation The associations inspired by a word; its flavor or spirit, as opposed to the strict meaning, its **denotation**

data Facts that prompt you to make your argument

deductive reasoning Reasoning from general principles to particular conclusions

denotation The literal, dictionary definition of a word

diction Word choice: "high" diction is formal, "low" diction informal

enthymeme A syllogism whose parts are not all clearly stated

ethos The qualities of character, intelligence, and morality that an arguer conveys through the manner of argument

equivocate To deliberately use ambiguous words to confuse the issue

grounds A term in Toulmin's system that is equivalent to "data"

hyperbole A statement exaggerated for effect

hypothesis A conditionally held theory to aid in exploring the meaning of what you seek to explain

inference The intuitive act of recognizing an implication

inductive reasoning The type of reasoning that proceeds from particular facts to general explanations

irony Intentionally saying one thing to convey another

logos The traditional name for the appeal to reason or logic

metaphor A comparison that illustrates meaning through figurative language, for example, "Babe Ruth was the Sultan of Swat."

non sequitur A statement that does not follow from a previous statement

paradox An apparent contradiction that contains a deeper meaning, for example, "nothing is so invisible as the obvious"

paraphrase Restating a point in your own words

pathos The traditional name for the appeal to emotion or feeling

persona The implied character created by the writer to speak for him or her; for example, at a given time a writer's persona may seem to be a joker, but the writer is a *person* whose complex identity may not be reduced to a role played at a particular time

plagiarism Using someone else's words or ideas without giving proper credit

point of view The attitude with which a writer approaches the subject

post hoc, ergo propter hoc Latin for "after this, therefore because of this"; the false assumption that, because one event happened after another, the first somehow caused the second

premise The underlying assumption from which one begins to make a point

qualifier A restriction or modification in the extent of an argued claim

refutation The process of meeting and overcoming the arguments of your opponent

rhetoric Traditionally, the art and study of persuasion; now loosely used to suggest an emphasis on manner at the expense of matter

rhetorical question A question asked figuratively, for effect, rather than literally, for information

simile Using "like" or "as" in acknowledgment that one is using figurative language: "In the world of baseball, Babe Ruth was like a giant."

syllogism A classical method of deductive reasoning in which two premises considered together lead with certainty to a conclusion

syntax Word order

thesis The central idea of an argument or essay

tone The way a writer "sounds"; the writer's attitude

Toulmin system The method of reasoned argument invented by Stephen Toulmin and emphasized in the appeals to reason analyzed in this book

transition A link between points or sections in writing

trope A name for "figure of speech"

warrant The underlying generalization (explicit or implicit) that the writer expects the reader to share and that connects the data with the claim

writing process A general term for the stages involved from prewriting through the production of a final draft

INDEX OF AUTHORS AND TITLES

ACKNOWLEDGMENTS

Page 29 "Don't Even Begin to Sacrifice Free Speech" by Joe Patrick Bean. Reprinted from the Christian Science Monitor, March 29, 1991, with the permission of the author.

Page 32 "Freedom of Hate Speech" by Richard Perry and Patricia Williams. Reprinted with permission of *Tikkun*, vol. 6, no. 4, a bi-monthly Jewish critique of politics, culture, and society. Subscriptions $31/year. Phone 800-846-8575.

Page 37 "Free Speech? Yes. Drunkenness? No." by Vartan Gregorian. Reprinted with the permission of the author.

Page 41 "Quiet Progress Toward Pay Equity" by Ruth Walker. Reprinted by permission from *The Christian Science Monitor*. © 1989 The Christian Science Publishing Society. All rights reserved.

Page 43 "Let the Marketplace Decide Pay" taken from *The Writer's Art* by James J. Kilpatrick. Copyright © 1985. Dist. by Universal Press Syndicate. Reprinted with permission. All rights reserved.

Page 46 "Why Women are Paid Less Than Men" by Lester C. Thurow. Copyright © 1981 by The New York Times Company. Reprinted by permission.

Page 50 "Curbing The Sexploitation Industry" by Tipper Gore. Copyright © 1988 by The New York Times Company. Reprinted by permission.

Page 53 "Romantic Rot" by Charlene Choy. Reprinted by permission of the author.

Page 55 "Raised on Rock-and-Roll" by Anna Quindlen. Copyright © 1987 by The New York Times Company. Reprinted by permission.

Page 59 "Most Oppose Women in Combat" by Suzanne Fields. Copyright © 1992 by Suzanne Fields, distributed by the Los Angeles Times Syndicate.

Page 65 "Arms and the Woman" by Lou Marano. Reprinted by permission of The Washington Post and the author.

Page 71 "On AIDS and Moral Duty" by Willard Gaylin. Copyright © 1987 by The New York Times Company. Reprinted by permission.

Page 81 "The Trials of Animals" by Cleveland Amory. Copyright © 1989 by The New York Times Company. Reprinted by permission.

Page 83 "A Scientist: 'I Am the Enemy'" by Ron Karpati. Reprinted by permission of the author, who is a pediatric oncologist and bone marrow transplant physician.

Page 87 "In Defense of the Animals" by Meg Greenfield. From NEWSWEEK, 4/17/89. © 1989, Newsweek, Inc. All rights reserved. Reprinted by permission.

Page 91 "Radical English" by George F. Will. © 1991, Washington Post Writers Group. Reprinted with permission.

Page 94 "Critics of Attempts to Democratize the Curriculum Are Waging a Campaign to Misrepresent the Work of Responsible Professors" by Paula Rothenberg. Reprinted by permission of the author.

Page 98 "Equal Cultures—or Equality?" by Cathy Young. Reprinted by permission of the author.

Page 103 "Let's Put Pornography Back in the Closet" by Susan Brownmiller. Reprinted by permission of the author.

Page 107 "Notes from a Free Speech Junkie" by Susan Jacoby. Reprinted by permission of Georges Borchardt, Inc. for the author. Copyright © 1973 by Susan Jacoby.

Page 110 "Nobody Ever Got Raped by a Book" by Mike Royko. Reprinted by permission: Tribune Media Services.

Page 115 "Offering Euthanasia Can Be an Act of Love" from *Dying with Dignity: Understanding Euthanasia,* by Derek Humphrey. Copyright © 1992 by Derek Humphrey. Published by arrangement with Carol Publishing Group. A Birch Lane Press Book.

Page 117 "Euthanasia is Not the Answer" by Matthew E. Conolly. Reprinted by permission of the author.

Page 122 "Must They Tinker With the Dying?" by Nancy M. Lederman. Copyright © 1993 by The New York Times Company. Reprinted by permission.

Page 125 "Take The Name—Pass It On" by Jennifer Ozersky. Reprinted by permission of the author.

Page 127 "With All Politeness, No—I'll Keep My Own Name, Thank you" by Emma Coleman. Reprinted by permission of the author.

Page 129 "The Game of the Name" by Patricia Saunders-Evans. Reprinted by permission of the author.

Page 136 "The Scab" by Walter Block from *Defending the Undefendable.* Reprinted by permission of the author.

Page 140 "Freedom vs. Authority" by James J. Kilpatrick

Page 143 "The First Step in Improving Sex Education: Remove the Hellfire" by Fred M. Hechinger. Copyright © 1989 by The New York Times Company. Reprinted by permission.

Page 146 "Condoms in Schools: The Right Lesson" by Paul Epstein. Copyright © 1991 by The New York Times Company. Reprinted by permission.

Page 148 "Educators Declare War On Traditional Values" by Thomas Sowell. Reprinted by permission of the author.

Page 152 "The Great Person-Hole Cover Debate" by Lindsy Van Gelder. Reprinted by permission of the author.

Page 155 "The Hand That Rocks the Helm" by Richard Mitchell. Reprinted by permission of the author.

Page 158 "The Word Police" by Michiko Kakutani. Copyright © 1993 by The New York Times Company. Reprinted by permission.

Page 165 "That Word 'Black'" by Langston Hughes. Reprinted by permission of Harold Obert Associates Incorporated. Copyright 1953 by Langston Hughes. Copyright renewed 1981 by George Houston Bass.

Page 167 "Pink and Brown People" by Thomas Sowell. Reprinted by permission of the author.

Page 169 "How It Feels to be Colored Me" by Zora Neale Hurston from *I Love Myself When I Am Laughing.* Reprinted by permission of the Estate of Zora Neale Hurston.

Page 175 "Preface to *The Great Conversation*" by Robert M. Hutchins. Reprinted from *Great Books of the Western World.* © 1952, 1990 Encyclopaedia Britannica, Inc.

Page 179 "On Reading Trash" by Bob Swift. Reprinted with permission of The Miami Herald.

Page 181 "Whose Canon Is It Anyway?" by Henry Louis Gates, Jr. © 1989 Henry Louis Gates, Jr. First appeared in the New York Times Book Review. Reprinted by permission of Brandt & Brandt Literary Agents, Inc.

Page 185 "The Freedom to Destroy Yourself" by Walter E. Williams. Reprinted by permission of Walter E. Williams and Creators Syndicate.

Page 189 "End the War on Drugs" by Joanne Jacobs. Reprinted by permission of Tribune Media Services.

Page 193 "Killing Our Future" by Sarah Brady. Reprinted by permission of Handgun Control.

Page 195 "Gun Control and Sheep For The Slaughter" by Mark D. McLean. Reprinted with permission of The Wall Street Journal. © 1992 Dow Jones & Company, Inc. All rights reserved.

Page 198 "Biting the Bullets" by Gerald Nachman from *Out On a Whim* by Gerald Nachman. Reprinted by permission of the author and the author's agents, Scott Meredith Literary Agency, Inc., 845 Third Avenue, New York, NY 10022.

Page 201 "In Support of Our Common Language." Reprinted by permission of U.S. English Foundation.

Page 205 "Gains and Losses" by Richard Rodriguez from *Hunger of Memory* by Richard Rodriguez. Copyright © 1982 by Richard Rodriguez. Reprinted by permission of David R. Godine, Publisher.

Page 207 "How Not to Get the Infidel to Talk the King's Talk" by Ishmael Reed. Copyright © 1982 Ishmael Reed. Reprinted by permission of the author.

Page 212 "Legalize Gay Marriage" by Craig R. Dean. Copyright © 1991 by The New York Times Company. Reprinted by permission.

Page 213 "Government Is the Problem" by Walter E. Williams. Reprinted by permission of Walter E. Williams and Creators Syndicate.

Page 215 "What Is The Truth About Global Warming?" by Robert James Bidinotto. Reprinted with permission from the February 1990 Reader's Digest. Copyright © 1990 by The Reader's Digest Assn., Inc.

Page 220 "Women, Sex and Rape" by Cathy Young. Reprinted by permission of the author.

Page 223 "Let's Mow Down Astroturf" by Tim Keane. Reprinted by permission of the author.

Page 225 "The Color-Only Crowd and Their Pastel-Colored Whores" by Joan Ivan. Reprinted by permission of the author.

Page 227 "Wrestling With Myself" by George Felton. Reprinted by permission of the author who teaches writing and copywriting at the Columbus College of Art & Design.

Page 230 "Sexual Harrassment: Crying Wolf in Albany" by Sheryl E. Reich. Copyright © 1993 by The New York Times Company. Reprinted by permission.

Page 231 "There Are Reasons to Control Immigration" by Samuel Francis. Reprinted by permission of Tribune Media Services.

Page 233 "Gambling With Our National Character" by George F. Will. Copyright © 1993, Washington Post Writers Group. Reprinted with permission.

Page 235 "Who Are the Homeless?" by Scott Shuger. Reprinted with permission from The Washington Monthly. Copyright by The Washington Monthly Company, 1611 Connecticut Avenue, NW, Washington D.C. 20009. (202) 462-0128.

Page 252 "Virginia's Trap" by Peter Marin. Reprinted by permission of the author.

Page 261 "What We Really Know About the Homeless" by Randall K. Filer. Reprinted with permission of The Wall Street Journal. © 1992 Dow Jones & Company, Inc. All rights reserved.

Page 264 "Brother, Don't Spare a Dime" by L. Christopher Awalt. Reprinted by permission of the author.

Page 267 Cartoon by permission of Sean Delonas.

Page 269 "Turning a Blind Eye to The Homeless" by Jerome D. Simpson. Copyright 1991 Christian Century Foundation. Reprinted by permission from the October 16, 1991 issue of The Christian Century.

Page 272 "Family Homelessness: A Systemic Problem" by Kay Young McChesney. *Journal of Social Issues*, Vo. 46, No. 4, pp. 191–205. Reprinted by permission of Society for the Psychological Study of Social Issues.

Page 287 "Homelessness as Psychological Trauma" by Lisa Goodman, Leonard Saxe, and Mary Harvey. Copyright © 1991 by the American Psychological Association. Reprinted by permission.